Made in Asia/America

Power Play:
Games, Politics, Culture
A series edited by
TreaAndrea M. Russworm
and Jennifer Malkowski

Duke University Press
Durham and London 2024

Why Video Games
Were Never (Really)
about Us

Made
in Asia/
America

Edited by Christopher B. Patterson
and Tara Fickle

© 2024 Duke University Press
This work is licensed under a Creative Commons Attribution-
NonCommercial-NoDerivatives 4.0 International License,
available at https://creativecommons.org/licenses/by-nc-nd/4.0/.
Printed in the United States of America on acid-free paper ∞
Project Editor: Ihsan Taylor
Designed by Aimee C. Harrison
Typeset in Untitled Serif and DT Getai Grotesk Display
by Westchester Publishing Services

Library of Congress Cataloging-in-Publication Data
Names: Patterson, Christopher B., editor. | Fickle, Tara, editor.
Title: Made in Asia/America : why video games were never (really)
about us / edited by Christopher B. Patterson and Tara Fickle.
Other titles: Power play (Duke University Press)
Description: Durham : Duke University Press, 2024. | Series:
Power play | Includes bibliographical references and index.
Identifiers: LCCN 2023033376 (print)
LCCN 2023033377 (ebook)
ISBN 9781478030263 (paperback)
ISBN 9781478026037 (hardcover)
ISBN 9781478059264 (ebook)
ISBN 9781478093961 (ebook other)
Subjects: LCSH: Asian Americans in popular culture. | Asian
Americans and mass media. | Video games—Social aspects. |
Video gamers. | Racism in popular culture. | BISAC: SOCIAL
SCIENCE / Ethnic Studies / American / Asian American & Pacific
Islander Studies | GAMES & ACTIVITIES / Video & Mobile
Classification: LCC E184.A75 M33 2024 (print) | LCC E184.A75
(ebook) | DDC 794.8/452995073—dc23/eng/20231025
LC record available at https://lccn.loc.gov/2023033376
LC ebook record available at https://lccn.loc.gov/2023033377

Cover art: Christian Kealoha Miller, still from *Neofeud 2*.
Silver Spook Games, 2024. Courtesy of the designer.

Open access support provided by the University of British
Columbia Open Access Fund for Humanities and Social Sciences
Research and the Office of the Vice-President, Research and
Innovation, the University of Oregon, and the Oregon Humanities
Center.

In loving memory of
Y-Dang Troeung (1980–2022).
You were my summoner,
my familiar, my collaborator,
my sweet-teaser. Thank you
for always playing along.
—Chris

To the players and the workers,
the spoilsports and the lurkers.
Yes, that's you.
—Tara

Contents

xi   Acknowledgments

1   Introduction
       Asia / Games \ America
       TARA FICKLE AND CHRISTOPHER B. PATTERSON

Part 1   **Gaming Orientalism**

27   **Designer Roundtable #1**
       Mixed Connections
       EMPERATRIZ UNG, PATRICK MILLER,
       MINH LE, AND MATTHEW SEIJI BURNS

35   **1 Gaming while Asian**
       EDMOND Y. CHANG

52   **2 The Asiatic and the Anti-Asian Pandemic**
       On *Paradise Killer*
       CHRISTOPHER B. PATTERSON

66   **3 Asian, Adjacent**
       Utopian Longing and Model Minority
       Mediation in *Disco Elysium*
       TAKEO RIVERA

Part 2 **Playable Bodies**

89 **Designer Roundtable #2**
Choose Your Mothership
SISI JIANG, DOMINI GEE, TOBY ĐỖ, AND NAOMI CLARK

99 **4 Playable Deniability**
Biracial Representation and the Politics
of Play in *Metal Gear Solid*
KEITA MOORE

115 **5 Designing the Global Body**
Japan's Postwar Modernity in *Death Stranding*
YASHENG SHE

132 **6 The Trophy Called "Asian Hands"**
On the Mythical Proficiency of Asian Gamers
PRABHASH RANJAN TRIPATHY

Part 3 **Localizing Empire**

149 **Designer Roundtable #3**
De-Cultural Imitation Games
JOE YIZHOU XU, LIEN B. TRAN, CHRISTIAN KEALOHA MILLER,
AND PARALUMAN (LUNA) JAVIER

159 **7 Colonial Moments in Japanese Video Games**
A Multidirectional Perspective
RACHAEL HUTCHINSON

176 **8 The Video Game Version of the Indian Subcontinent**
The Exotic and the Colonized
SOUVIK MUKHERJEE

190 **9 High-Tech Orientalism in Play**
Performing South Koreanness in Esports
GERALD VOORHEES AND MATTHEW JUNGSUK HOWARD

Part 4 **Inhabiting the Asiatic**

207 **Designer Roundtable #4**
The Crumbs of Our Representation
ROBERT YANG, DIETRICH SQUINKIFER (SQUINKY),
RACHEL LI, AND MARINA AYANO KITTAKA

217 **10** Chinese/Cheating
Procedural Racism in Battle Royale Shooters
HUAN HE

232 **11** Romancing the Night Away
Queering Animate Hierarchies in *Hatoful Boyfriend* and *Tusks*
MIYOKO CONLEY

250 **12** The Fujoshi Trophy and Ridiculously Hot Men
Otome Games and Postfeminist Sensibilities
SARAH CHRISTINA GANZON

Part 5 **Mobilizing Machines**

269 **Designer Roundtable #5**
How Do We Talk about Things That Are Happening
without Talking about Things That Are Happening?
MIKE REN YI, PAMELA PUNZALAN, MELOS HAN-TANI, AND YUXIN GAO

277 **13** Hip-Hop and Fighting Games
Locating the Blerd between New York and Japan
ANTHONY DOMINGUEZ

290 **14** "This Is What We Do"
Hong Kong Protests in *Animal Crossing: New Horizons*
HANEUL LEE

307 **Coda**
Role / Play \ Race
CHRISTOPHER B. PATTERSON AND TARA FICKLE

Contents **ix**

319 Bibliography
349 Contributors
353 Index

Acknowledgments

The art of collaboration did not come naturally for either of us. We were kids who preferred to play by ourselves; we are adults who prefer to write and read with only the company of our selves. The energy and willingness to make this collection came not from us but from the many collaborators, contributors, editors, and players who guided us along the way.

/

There are several thinkers and editors whose guidance was pivotal to this project. Thank you to Bo Ruberg, LeiLani Nishime, Lily Wong, Petrus Liu, Vernadette Vicuña Gonzalez, Joseph Jonghyun Jeon, Betsy Huang, Amanda Phillips, Soraya Murray, TreaAndrea Russworm, and Jen Malkowski. Thank you to Ed Chang, Robert Yang, Naomi Clark, Melos Han-Tani, Marina Kittaka, and Christian Kealoha Miller, whose voices appear in this book but whose roles often blended with ours as organizers and curators. Thank you to Duke University Press and Courtney Berger, who shepherded this work and gave much-needed encouragement, as well as Eric Zinner at New York University Press, who suggested the manuscript's title. Thank you to the University of British Columbia Library and Research offices, and the Oregon Humanities Center, for funding this book's Open Access initiative, so that readers around the globe could (legally) download it. Thank you to the anonymous reviewers who read it so generously from the beginning.

/

Tara would like to thank, in addition to those above, interlocutors who have sustained and supported this project in various forms since its inception: Jon Abel, Tina Chen, Se Young Kim, Keita Moore, and Brendan O'Kelly. She would also like to thank her daughter Mimi, who since her own inception has taught Tara more about play than she could have imagined.

/

Chris would like to thank his Vancouver squad: Christine Kim, Danielle Wong, Kim Bain, Mila Zuo, Ayasha Guerin, Ulrike Zöllner, David Chariandy, and all the "bubbles" who have been there for him and his family. Thank you to his family—the Guillermos, the Pattersons, and the Troeungs, especially Dion, Cameron, Chanel, Jacob, Heung, and Yok. Thank you most of all to his departed wife, Y-Dang, and their son, Kai.

/

Though it might seem redundant, we must also thank all our contributors to this book, whose generosity, patience, and works gave us desperately needed injections of hope and beauty. Many of you were our mentors, our guides, our sages. The opportunity to create a book with your names, your personalities, and your ideas has been a true gift.

/

And finally, we must thank each other, Tara and Chris. This book was made in times of great challenge for both of us. We are both the person who called the other believing our worlds were crashing, and that we would leave the project in the safe and capable hands of the other. And we are both the person who gave all we could, who took on more of the work, who patiently waited for the other to recover. From one of these people to the other: Thank you for being exactly what we needed, a collaborator and a companion.

Tara Fickle
Christopher B. Patterson

Introduction

Asia / Games \ America

In the opening sketch of *Saturday Night Live* on October 25, 2019, host and musical guest Chance the Rapper reprised his role as "Laz," a basketball reporter asked to cover unfamiliar sports: in this case, a video game tournament.[1] The sketch finds Laz baffled by the *League of Legends* esport he witnesses, having mistakenly assumed it "was going to be a basketball game with NBA legends. This is . . . not that" (figure I.1). The SNL audience, too, is meant to share Laz's disbelief not only that playing video games can be considered a sport but also that anyone would actually want to watch and report on it. Nearly breaking character and erupting into laughter, Laz quips, "I did not know this was a thing. I guess esports is what white and Asian kids have been doing while Black kids were inventing hip-hop." After being surprised by yet another unfamiliar sight—a "geeky" Asian esports player (played by Bowen Yang) relentlessly pursued by a group of admiring "e-girls"—Laz says, his face in shock, "what I just saw was so unexpected that my brain went into a Tom Hanks in *Saving Private Ryan* mode." After

I.1. Chance the Rapper as "Laz," on *Saturday Night Live*. Image courtesy of NBC.

a wakeful headshake, he then deadpans: "Lazlo Holmes, coming to you live from the upside down."

We begin with this offbeat anecdote of Black and Asian pop cultural dynamics as a means of playing with and exploring how game worlds appear to the "real world"—in particular, through the "upside-down" depiction of Asian male esports stars and the "e-girls" (a sometimes derogatory term aimed at female gamers) who desire them. During a period of escalating Cold War political tensions and ongoing racisms against Asians as robotic, geeky, economic aggressors, the game world that might see esports players as objects of heterosexual desire certainly can appear upside down (even more upside down in this case, as the actor playing the esports star, Bowen Yang, publicly identifies as gay). Whereas in a previous skit, Laz appeared baffled by the rules of hockey, where he saw "lots of white dudes on skates running into each other at full speed," here it is less the game itself that confuses Laz than the nerdiness, bizarreness, and foreignness of the culture surrounding it. Hence, Laz refuses to read the esports players' names aloud and derides the tournament as "League of Legos."

In seeing esports as an "upside-down" world, the *Saturday Night Live* sketch humorously encapsulates the tangle of social anxieties, affects, and political meanings that video games represent as a medium often represented through Asian racializations. The skit's association of "white and Asian kids" with video games and "Black kids" with "inventing hip-hop" reestablishes the "normal world" of devalued Asian masculinity (and serves as a self-referential joke, considering Chance's own hip-hop success). The skit places front and center the imagined associations of video games not only as a "white and Asian" cultural practice, but as an invention comparable to the association of "Black kids" and the invention of hip-hop, both recent global medias produced through transnational routes—in the case of video games, the transpacific flows between "Asian kids" in Asia and "white kids" in America. Figured as both "model minorities" and "forever foreigners," Asian American racializations trace the tangled flows that video games represent. Chance, a successful rapper himself, reiterates tropes about Asian Americans as "honorary whites," yet in doing so he also points to how the emergence of gaming technology and game cultures has been made possible by material and imperial routes across the transpacific, creating hybrid and transnational forms of play, community, and spectatorship. Embedded within his remark is a point about racial privilege—about which groups have better widespread access to technology, to computers, to digital literacies, and to the means necessary to play games in the first place.[2] As Mary Yu Danico and Linda Trinh Vo have shown, gaming cultures among youth often respond to a lack of acceptance in "real sports," pushing Asian American youth to foster alternative communities in PC rooms, arcades, and online forums.[3] Though Black youth have remained visible in some esports (particularly in fighting game communities), Chance's sketch-breaking line, "I guess esports is what white and Asian kids have been doing while Black kids were inventing hip-hop," still delivers an unsettling truth nested within his Black masculine bravado: that the divergent pathways of youthful play route some racialized communities into physical and traditional sports, and others into the mental and futuristic realm of esports.

If video games are the terrain on which esports is played, then the perceived merging of nerdiness with foreignness marks the culture of video games as itself a blend of Asia and America, a mixture that invokes at least three racial anxieties: (1) the economic and affective anxieties of "yellow peril," (2) the disgust and disdain for racial mixture, miscegenation, and fetish, and (3) the privilege and power of new media technology as limited to particular populations in North America, alongside the exploitation and unfreedoms of many who manufacture and program such technology in Asia (an oft-overlooked piece of the puzzle that is likewise absent in the sketch). The world of gaming thus feels upside down not merely because it turns Asian geeks into desired celebrities, but because its logics expose and thus threaten the normalized racial boundaries of Asia and America. The upside-down world

Introduction   **3**

of games displays the anxieties that have defined the Asia/America geopolitical relationship since at least the end of the nineteenth century: the fear of an America invaded by, indebted to, mixed with, and mastered by Asians, whose gamelike advantage has always been depicted through technological and gamelike prowess.

Made in Asia/America is the first edited collection to explore this upside-down world, the way its logics, flows, and intimate relations orbit the social anxieties and racializations of Asia/America. By recognizing the various ways that Asia, America, and games have been historically entangled, this collection sees games as not merely reflecting or refracting given national racializations but also offering other ways of imagining otherness; hence, games can help us understand the racial and geopolitical assumptions that are present when we talk about Asia, America, and Asian America. This collection's contributors explore the medium of games through the rich and historical transpacific intimacies that video games trace. If the connection between video games and Asia/America resembles a world that is upside down, then how might these relations invert, expose, or exceed our own racial, gendered, and national gravity?

We deliberately speak of "Asia/America" rather than "Asia and America" or "Asian America," using the solidus to signal how games slide along elements of Asia, America, and Asian America through what David Palumbo-Liu calls a "dynamic, unsettled, and inclusive movement."[4] We also strategically use the term to unsettle zero-sum logics of place—which would insist that any globally circulating product is either "Made in Asia" or "Made in America"—and to emphasize the dynamic transpacific processes whereby games are "made": as a function of labor and of "nonhuman" resource production, bearing the traces of imperial history as pursuits of intellectual creative classes, and as artifacts and conduits of ideology. We also hope to recognize how our worlds are often made through the effects of narrative, history, art, and indeed, games. While narratives *about* games can make gaming into a pathologizing practice, games themselves make games into practices of interaction and self-reflection. In writing about performance art, Dorinne Kondo argues that being conscious of "making" helps both creators and scholars understand world making (rather than worldbuilding) as acts of transformation that affect our material world. For Kondo, world making "is always collaborative, in relation with other people, abstract forces, objects, and materials that are themselves imbued with potentiality."[5] This emphasis on making rather than building has also become popular among independent game designers, who

4 Fickle and Patterson

often prefer to be called "game makers" rather than game programmers or game designers as a way to highlight the many creative roles of game making and to disrupt "the production paradigms of the larger game industry."[6] In centering how games are made and where games come from, we ultimately mean to explore how video games make and remake our communities, our selves, and our worlds.

Video Games Have Always Been Asian/American

Since the unexpected rise of Japanese arcade games like *Space Invaders* (1978), *Pac-Man* (1980), and *Donkey Kong* (1981), and the release of the Nintendo Entertainment System (which debuted in the United States in 1985), video games have been associated with Japanese media products rooted in post–World War II Japanese aesthetics. Since this time, Asia as a whole has become the manufacturing home for video game hardware, the primary site of e-waste disposal in the never-ending cycle of innovation and obsolescence, the center of game innovation and the birthplace of most game genres, and the largest reliable resource of consumers. Today, nearly half of all game players reside in Asia. South Korea remains the capital of esports, and Asian and Asian North American players are some of its best-known stars. In game development, South and East Asian employees are well represented in certain sectors of Silicon Valley (but not, as we discuss in our designer roundtables, as industry creatives) and in outsourced game production sites across Asia. And, providing the narrative grist of these material nexuses, games have been central to the racialization of Asians, as early Chinese immigrants to the United States in the late 1800s were cast as gambling addicts, and stereotypes of Asian inscrutability in characters like Charlie Chan or Fu Manchu often presumed that Asians were cold, calculating, and strategic foreign entities who saw the world itself as a game to be won.

The history of Asian/American racialization offers fundamental but contradictory discourses about Asians as simultaneously hypercompetitive and unplayful, as "cheaters" and uncreative rule-followers, offering both models and warnings of what games can do. The immediate association of Asian/ Americans with gaming cultures has bred new forms of techno-orientalism, which, as David S. Roh, Betsy Huang, and Greta A. Niu point out, involves "imagining Asia and Asians in hypo- or hypertechnological terms in cultural productions and political discourse."[7] Intertwined with these paradoxical

Introduction **5**

discourses of Asian racializations in and around games are notions of games as gateways for non-Asians to enter a "digital Asia" whose aesthetics and forms are firmly intertwined with Japanese gaming industries, thus allowing non-Asian subjects to inhabit "Asianness" as a form of virtual identity tourism.[8] Indeed, some of the most influential theoretical work in game studies hails from Asian and Asian Americanist scholarship: Lisa Nakamura on "virtual tourism," "cybertypes," and the "gamic model minority"; Wendy Chun on the (white) "console cowboy" who exercises "control" over (Asian) media, Koichi Iwabuchi on Japanese companies seeking to neutralize the "cultural odor" of their exported products (the process whereby Japanese games are rendered into both global *and* local commodities), and more.[9] In our previous books, we built off the work of these scholars to see games as a "ludo-orientalist" medium, as Tara wrote, "wherein the design, marketing, and rhetoric of games shape how Asians as well as East-West relations are imagined,"[10] and as an "Asiatic" medium, as Chris wrote, to characterize games for their "forms, spaces, and personages that many players will find similar to Asia, but that are never exclusively Asian, or are obscured from any other recognizable racial genre."[11] Following the ideas and conversations of our previous work, this collection engages in the labor, as many collections do, of recognizing and bringing together a transdisciplinary field that has thus far felt scattered and diffuse.

Given the proliferation in games of so many racial stereotypes and fantasies, *Made in Asia/America* considers whether the shift to a digital, interactive medium—the transition from "stereotypes" to "cybertypes," or "orientalism" to "techno-orientalism"[12]—has constituted a novel phenomenon or is simply further evidence of how, as Nakamura pointed out in 1995, racial thinking is easily encoded into digital media through its supposed absence.[13] As a "strategy of representational containment," orientalism clearly continues to shape the production and reception of "exotic" game settings and characters.[14] It provides the aesthetic template for combining, as Souvik Mukherjee points out in this collection, the "misty" with the "mystical," and a retrograde cast of endlessly recycled samurai, ninjas, and geisha girls alongside a handful of more "empowered" yet hypersexualized female fighters; hordes of non-player character (NPC) "natives"; and, as Takeo Rivera writes in this collection, Asian sidekicks who function as "adjacent" in ways that have long shaped Asian/Americans' perceived proximate or "honorary" relationship to whiteness.[15]

6   Fickle and Patterson

The association of the digital itself with East Asianness—what Wendy Chun dubs "high-tech orientalism"—has become such a staple of science fiction media that even when Asians are not directly represented, their racial forms remain starkly visible in settings (as in *Blade Runner*) and in Eastern spiritualist tropes (as in *Star Wars*). In video games, yellow peril stereotypes and caricatures peaceably coexist alongside model minority ones and are often present without direct representation of Asian bodies but emerge through settings, mechanics, and game logics.[16] So, too, such racializations are often disguised because they don't reference or name Asian bodies, countries, or spaces directly but, rather, reference racial difference through digital objects, aesthetic forms, and Asiatic styles. When they are explicitly present, Asian racializations are further obscured in games as they connote positive rather than negative feelings of pleasure, fun, silliness, cuteness, and masculine heroism. Yet anti-Asian racialization has often been entangled with positive feelings, what Frank Chin and Jeffrey Paul Chan in 1972 famously called "racist love,"[17] a term that Leslie Bow revisited in 2021 to explore "how the Asian American reduction to type masquerades as racial knowledge while operating as a fetishistic pleasure."[18] As Bow and many Asian American authors stress, racist love does not necessarily read as anti-Asian (and can even be voiced as "pro-Asian"), yet it still builds from and perpetuates a virulent antagonism against peoples from Asia through typing, commodifying, fetishizing, and foreignizing. Finally, familiar racialized narratives about Asians continue to circulate in discourses *about* games, including assumptions about Asian bodies' dexterity and singular affinity for gaming—what Todd Harper and Tripathy in this volume call the "myth of Asian Hands." To state that "video games have always been Asian/American" or that they are "Made in Asia/America" is not a claim to ownership but a refusal of the ways games and games discourses have obscured, erased, and distracted from the racializations that have been ever present within them.

As we discuss with the twenty Asian/American game designers in this volume's roundtables, discourses of game players and designers additionally re-present familiar racialized dynamics of Asian invisibility and hypervisibility, wherein, as Dean Chan wrote in 2009, Asian/American workers in games industries are "both hyper-visible and out of sight."[19] As has long been the case with the US census and other national data, Asian Americans are simply disregarded as statistically insignificant in most quantitative and qualitative research on video game play patterns.[20] However, the few sources

Introduction   **7**

that do take up Asian American play suggest that Asian Americans are the *most likely* to play video games, and, like Black and Latin/x groups, remain overrepresented as players, but underrepresented as designers.[21] Many of the Asian/American designers and artists in this volume speak to the way that white supremacies in the US gaming industry are evidenced through the presumed association of Asians with programming work rather than narrative or other "creative" forms of design. The designers in this collection, situated in places like Shanghai, Manila, and Hawai'i, provide insights on the multiple ways games are racialized within a range of geopolitical contexts, even as they remind us that, on a global scale, only 25 percent of the global game market is in North America, while about half remains in Asia.[22] Whether we are talking about the international or the domestic context, we agree with games scholar Adrienne Shaw that representation (in the liberal multiculturalist sense of pluralism and diversity) should not be our primary yardstick for evaluating games, as it too often flattens the complex relationships between representation and other factors that shape audience reception and player motivation.[23] Many of our designers, for example, speak to the way that the North American and European game industry has in recent years sought to appeal to the CJK (China, Japan, and Korea) player base through a very different set of racial tropes and narratives that exceed traditional US rubrics for "good" and "bad" representations.

While Asianness has been omnipresent yet obscured in the ways that games are made, innovated on, and played, it has remained nearly invisible in academic game studies discourses. Asianness in games has remained, as Rachael Hutchinson argues in this collection, the elephant in game studies conference rooms, and those who wish to discuss Asianness in games (as we've experienced in multiple venues) often find themselves the spoilsport of the game studies magic circle. As one Asian American conference attendee put it to us, "Asian fetishes are the social lubricant that has allowed game studies to flourish." The erasure of Asianness vis-à-vis eroticization, and the friction it produces, feel especially apropos for an academic field that is absorbed in ideas of pleasure and play. Similarly, if we understand games as an Asiatic media, they too position players (as well as games scholars) within an analogous position of implicit domination, sovereignty, and agency over techno-orientalized worlds. To win a game can thus follow a similar logic of understanding, analyzing, and theorizing a game: the ability to master an Asian technological space. Given that, as Tan Hoang Nguyen writes, Asian/American subjects (specifically men) are already culturally relegated to a "bottom position" in an East/West hierarchy, the positioning of North Americans as the playing subjects who desire and extract pleasure from Asiatic media reinforces the way that games, as Nguyen emphasizes of sexually explicit material more broadly, "are instrumental in shaping how we think about what is normal, natural, and possible."[24] In game studies, this naturalized—and *de*sexualized—intellectual form of subjection is evident when scholars write about games that have gone through laborious processes of translation, localization, and remarketing for North American audiences as if they are simply universal (i.e., Western) products whose historical origins and context are in need of little more than parenthetical acknowledgment, *or* when a particular game's Asia–North America relations are denied as having anything to do with colonialism, orientalism, or other structures of power.

The problem we trace in this collection is not just that the "cultural odorlessness" that Iwabuchi identified in Japanese products has been overwhelmingly successful in "deodorizing" games of their creative and manufacturing origins, but that game scholars rarely even consider Asian/American theorists of popular culture like Iwabuchi, Hiroki Azuma, Chen Kuan-hsing, or Christine Yano as relevant to their studies.[25] While this indifference is certainly not exclusive to game studies, it exercises an especially troubling form of epistemic violence in a field entrusted with studying video games, an Asiatic cultural phenomenon that has become a dominating force in reflecting transpacific geopolitics and in shaping Asian/American racializations.[26] In game studies discourses where Asianness has become nearly meaningless and Asian/American theorists irrelevant, orientalist readings of games frequently blur with the orientalism of the games themselves.[27] For the writers and designers in this collection, the forms of Asian racializations in games deserve to be seen as complex and dynamic expressions that can reveal the continuous colonial biases and violences embedded within North American and European game audiences. As Souvik Mukherjee writes in this collection, such racializations have been reproduced within specific contexts in Asia—and at times are even self-orientalized/internalized as a secondary marketing technique.

The ahistorical emptying out of Asianness in many game cultures is inextricable from the circulation of global capital in a neoliberal age. Yet the point that many of our contributors compellingly drive home is that this absence must be understood also as a racial issue, not epiphenomenal to but constitutive of such flows. As Naoko Shibusawa has argued, including histories of Asian racialization in studies of racial capitalism is crucial for

Introduction   **9**

"an understanding of US labor and immigration history, and history of US empire—particularly the master's tool of capitalist divide-and-conquer."[28] Similarly, micha cárdenas has urged scholars to "decolonize the digital by understanding the communicative capacities of digital technologies as an outcome of the settler colonial socioeconomic support structure of the United States."[29] Video games have emerged as a powerful node at this intersection between the need to revisit histories of empire in Asia and the need to decolonize the digital. In the next section, we tackle the persistent issue of empire, race, and colonialism in game studies, and subsequent attempts to combat it, by noting the looping insularity of the field in the way that video games, masked as they are as commodities made *for* us (the academic Global North "us," as well as the "US" of the United States), are ultimately made and remade through game studies as being *about* us.

Playing with Ourselves: On Game Studies

The meat of this book was written and edited during the anti-Asian rhetorics of COVID-19, when we were both engaged in virtual book tours for our previous books on video games, often presenting them together. As we felt the blunt mechanisms of yellow peril discourse through everyday invocations and on every news source, we also felt its background hum within game studies spaces, as we witnessed scholars engage with media from Asia as if they had been created solely for English-speaking, North American, majority-white audiences. Our attempts to root out these issues publicly was often met with suspicion and disregard, and the virtual chats during our book talks, on more than one occasion, became spaces of masked ridicule. Difficult as these engagements were, they also helped us in understanding the presumptions that many games studies scholars bring to what a game studies book is supposed to do: that game studies texts are ultimately *about* games and how we play them, and that games are exceptional forms of media, so that to do game studies is ultimately not to do literary studies, new media studies, critical ethnic studies, or other disciplinary modes.

The protective attitudes we faced during our book talks were rooted in game studies before video games even came along. The "founding fathers" of modern game studies, Dutch historian Johan Huizinga (1872–1945) and French sociologist Roger Caillois (1913–78), characterized games by naming their boundaries: games were playful rather than serious; had "no material interest"; and were

10   Fickle and Patterson

further divided from the social and political world through a "magic circle."[30] Similarly, Bernard Suits's foundational game studies text, *The Grasshopper* (1978), has been revisited in game studies to define "a game" by naming its negation as erotic play, so that the pleasures, passions, and desires in games could not be confused with sexual pleasures and erotic desires.[31] In the 1990s and early 2000s, game studies scholars would go even further in the enclosure of games by naming *video games* as a particularly novel and exceptional media unlike games found in poetry, parlors, stagecraft, and sports (all games that Huizinga and Caillois wrote about). In turn, scholars focusing on the social impacts of games (Lisa Nakamura, Henry Jenkins, and others) were overshadowed by an insular debate within game studies itself, known today as *the narratology/ludology debate*, which centered on the underwhelming binary question "Are video games more narrative (like books, films, television), or more ludic (like games and sports)?" However, the greatest impact of the narratology/ludology debates was not in their disagreements about what games are (narratives vs. games), or how to study them (humanities vs. social sciences), but in their implicit *agreements* about the importance of the debates itself: that deciding what video games *are* is of paramount importance, that games in themselves are exceptional either because they give "player agency" (says narratology) or because they offer virtual spaces outside politics and identity (says ludology). Seen as the founding discursive argument of game studies, the narratology/ludology debate can be characterized as a binary rivalry that calcified the insular inquiries of game studies while also obscuring this insularity through the appearance of competing sides.

In the 2010s, game studies began a second life, where its discourses turned toward a critical cultural studies mode that spotlighted difference in the field while revealing how game studies texts had featured a consistent reinscription of a default whiteness, straightness, and maleness as ideal players, characters, and creative designers.[32] Many of these thinkers' works became spotlighted during and after the #GamerGate scandals in 2014, when feminist game journalists were attacked, harassed, and doxed by self-identified gamers in response to a perceived contamination of video games by feminists and other "social justice warriors." As Soraya Murray has argued, #GamerGate was a "paradigmatic irruption" of the hidden identity politics within gaming (as the territory of men).[33] The afterlife of #GamerGate has, though, for good reason, drawn many game studies discourses further inward in attempts to understand how the toxicity of #GamerGate drew on dominant academic discourses of games as exceptional media outside the "petty politics" of identity, representation, colonialism, and feminism.[34] Our previous work has contributed to this conversation by joining other scholars in focusing on the problem(atic)s of the field, and in demonstrating the forms of ahistoricity that the field perpetuates by theorizing play as a universal and transhistorical phenomenon.[35]

At the time of writing, many anthologies and books have made fantastic headway in terms of critical cultural studies (*Gaming at the Edge*, *On Video Games*), racial and social justice (*Gaming Representation*, *Woke Gaming*), queerness (*Queer Game Studies*, *Video Games Have Always Been Queer*), and eco-criticism (*Playing Nature*). Despite these boundary-breaking texts, game studies has yet to be recognized as a theoretically generative field that can offer new frameworks for understanding trenchant and urgent issues like the carceral state, refugee migrations, settler colonial logics, or permanent war, and the study of games rarely appears in texts situated in media studies, ethnic studies, or other interdisciplinary fields.[36] Though we can partially blame this absence on the stigmatization of games as violent and adolescent objects, we also find that defensive positions and insular debates in games studies have kept the study of video games far more concerned with the game industry and gaming cultures than in understanding the incredible and often unseen impact of games across the globe.[37] The fact that the narratology/ludology debate has been so field-defining for game studies *and* that nearly all our colleagues outside game studies have never even heard of this debate should be all the impetus we need to reimagine how we study games, why we do it, and who our studies are for.

On Practice: Interaction

If game studies is a field itself defined by a medium so closely tied to Asia in its innovations, player base, and manufacturing, then any collection spotlighting these relations must not only refuse the calls toward formal, political, and geographical boundaries, but, like Kirby sucking in a bad guy, must be able to create something new with every encounter, must be able to reform and expand, must allow new forms of interaction. In curating and organizing this collection, we thus sought to answer the inescapable questions "What is a video game?" or "What is play?" not with universalizing definitions (or what Eve Sedgwick might call "strong theories") but through the insistence on an editorial practice that invites *interaction*. While terms like *collaboration* and *coalition* are usually associated with building desired outcomes (political movements, communities), we find ourselves attracted to interaction as a curatorial and editorial practice due to its ambiguity and ambivalence concerning exactly *what* we make together. Like the excitement and hesitancy we might feel when starting up a new video game, interaction as praxis can feel ambiguous and ambivalent, creative and curious, voyaging and wayward. As a form of *making* rather than *building*, interaction ventures into risk and anarchy rather than preplanned blueprints or algorithms (to use micha cárdenas's sense of algorithmic analysis as a political artistic practice).[38] Put simply, this collection takes up the challenge of no longer using games to write *about* games but to instead seek out what games *make*, to explore how game making is also world making.

Our use of interaction is inspired by video games as a form of interactive media that, according to Adrienne Shaw, can stage communal, enjoyable, and even intimate activities that also "[do] not necessitate identification."[39] Interaction is not about seeing others as political allies or as tools for a particular and timely issue (as useful and important as this is) but about feeling the responsibility of being in relation with others. In games, interaction is less about the end results and more about the (pedagogical) experience: it is the chime noise we make when we approach another player in *Journey*; it is the attack we make on a dungeon with three random teammates (any of whom could rush in early or suddenly go afk [away from keyboard]); it is getting cornered by an opponent and not knowing whether they will shoot you, spare you, squat you, or break out in dance. It is in these gamic senses of curious play that we see the interactions of our project as ultimately a crucial form of acting with and on the world. In interaction, political aims, analytic methods, and keyword definitions are not methodically controlled, but invoke unforeseeable frictions and generate new frameworks for our gathering, thereby inviting multiple publics into the world we make together. As Dorinne Kondo writes of the theater, interactivity can be world making through the copresence of "affecting and being affected by each other," though it can also lead to the uncertain outcomes of "forming temporary communities" or "exclusionary affective violence."[40] Through its ambiguity, interactivity challenges the normative approaches of identity, empathy, or deference, which risk, as the poet Solmaz Sharif eloquently puts it, "the absolute and unhindered continuance of what is."[41] Instead, interactivity risks the possibility of change: the strengthening, dismantling, and transitioning into something new.

During the four years we worked on this collection (2019–23), we sought to practice interaction in our roles as writers, editors, curators, and organizers.

Introduction   **13**

First, we wrote the call for papers in a way that refused the insular looping back to well-trodden and often orientalist theorizations of play by asking our potential contributors to explore more relational inquiries, such as:

» How do games combat facile discussions of racial and other forms of diversity, discourses that are key to justifying and sustaining forms of inequality that radiate beyond the domestic to the global, and that hence are also questions of empire?

» How do we make arguments about games that expose imperial networks and build on antiracist projects without merely demanding more representation/inclusion from game companies who have historically and continually participated in networks of empire and racialization?

» How do we see meritocratic myths of gaming as anonymous level playing fields within what C. L. R. James called the historical boundaries and lines of colonial and radical sportsmanship?[42]

» How might the lines that limn the experimental play of magic circles reframe our understanding of academic (discip)lines, cultural line(age)s, and, of course, color lines?

We have anchored these inquiries through traditions in critical race and ethnic studies that draw attention to racial difference in forms of representation as well as in the formal resemblances of race, as ludic qualities of racial form,[43] or as "Asiatic" and "virtual other."[44] Indeed, we seek to center Asia/ America in this study not by dividing race in games from the fetishizations of code, algorithm, and platform but by allowing these ideas to change our work so we can better understand formal, mechanical, and other resemblances of difference at work in games.

Second, during our feedback and editorial sessions, we challenged our contributors not to follow the conventions of an individual scholarly chapter with long essays that sought to capture a subfield for new readers. Instead, we advocated for short chapters (less than six thousand words) to allow space for a greater diversity of ideas and contexts. We then encouraged contributors to read each other's work so that chapters built on each other and also provided comparisons to better distinguish their diversity of theoretical standpoints, their positions within academia (as graduate students, and as junior, midcareer, and senior scholars), their types of game analyses, and their disciplinary conventions (almost none of them come from an Asian American studies or game studies department). We also encouraged contributors not to envision their

14   Fickle and Patterson

chapters as necessarily academic in the sense of emphasizing an argument and providing proof for it. Instead, we encouraged playful experimentation and argumentative shifts, yielding essays like Edmond Y. Chang's "Gaming while Asian" (chapter 1), a chapter that merges academic writing with auto-theory within a "choose your own adventure" interactive story. We also sought to disrupt our own positions of authority as the collection's editors by asking for feedback from our contributors for this very introduction, while this collection's coda was not even planned in the first full draft but was inspired by our readings of the chapters and particularly by roundtable 5. In a sense, our editorial efforts attempted to produce this book as interaction manifest.

Third, we sought to disrupt the insularity of game studies by inviting a diverse array of game makers into the collection who identified as Asian/North American and as marginalized (as neurodiverse, queer, transgender, or nonbinary; as Indigenous, mixed white, Latinx, and Arab; as lacking formal education; as non–Native English–speaking; and as living outside North America). We hosted five roundtables of four game makers each, and sought to understand the textured, global understandings of race depicted in many of their games. We conducted these roundtables over Zoom in the spring of 2021, during a global pandemic, when the playful space of games provided opportunities to reflect on the increasingly serious (and increasingly anti-Asian) world punctuated by unexpected moments of connection and community, in many cases facilitated by video games. When finished, we decided not to bunch these roundtables into a separate section of the book but instead to use them as framing devices to begin each section, as we hoped to break the reader out of a consistent disciplinary context by hearing the experiences of game makers whose own contexts vary widely (Tokyo, New York, Hawai'i, Hong Kong, Toronto, Shanghai, Manila, Houston). The roundtables thus operate less as guided interviews and more as spaces of interactive play, seen by Ian Bogost as a space that "guarantees neither meaningful expression nor meaningful persuasion, but it sets the stage for both."[45] By introducing each set of chapters, these roundtables blur the lines between guest and host, interviewer and interviewee, researcher and participant, game scholar and game maker (many of our contributors, like us, are both), and set the stage for our understanding of games through interactive conversations among Asian/American peoples.

Finally, we have attempted to practice deep, critical interactions by organizing and hosting an ongoing panel series at the annual Association of Asian American Studies conference (AAAS), an enriching critical ethnic studies space that has unfortunately had little concern for gaming as a medium. In 2018, we hosted the first-ever panel focused on game studies at AAAS, which featured one editor (Chris) alongside three of the contributors to this volume (Takeo Rivera, Miyoko Conley, Edmond Chang). We had a very small audience, yet those who came expressed gratitude to us for hosting such a rarely explored theme in Asian American studies. We followed this up year after year, interacting with more scholars featured in this collection (Rachael Hutchinson, Haneul Lee, Huan He, Gerald A. Voorhees, Anthony Dominguez), as well as game makers (Robert Yang, Marina Kittaka). By bringing together these scholars and game makers year after year, we were able to deepen our engagement with them and with each other, offering discussions, feedback, and collaborative plans to create a collection that can span and expand what an edited collection can do. The results were not only in this collection, but in events outside academia, such as the 2021 #StopAsianHateJam Game Jam organized on itch.io by Chris and the contributors Mike Ren Yi, Pamela Punzalan, and Melos Han Tani.

Our decision to build an anthology on the concept of Asian/American gaming was a daunting endeavor, as we hoped to avoid merely providing a synthesis of the fields of Asian American studies and game studies, but rather to reflect the multiple interests, disciplines, and publics that our contributors bring to this work. Often this meant disagreements about what games are or what they do, or what Asian Americans are or what they do. Together, these chapters don't represent a particular set of racialized bodies or an "authentic" or stable "Asian American gamer" subjectivity, or even a common set of game definitions, analytics, or play practices. Rather, the interactions that form this book reveal what Kandice Chuh might call the necessary tracing of processes of racialization, where Asia/America marks not an identity within the American empowerment empire but a historically contested and dynamic site that can offer various interactive, coalitional, and collaborative gestures.[46] By signaling an unconstrained, nonregulated form of diversity, interaction acknowledges our reliance on others not as objects of study but as contaminants that change our own views. As Anna Tsing writes, such contamination can signal not death or degradation, but a "transformation through encounter" that threatens the impulses to remain "self-contained."[47] Chandan Reddy similarly argues that analyses of race can bring a "genuine openness" to traditional methods of producing knowledge, and can refuse nationalist and institutional racial discourses through an ambiguity that is also "an effect of being contaminated."[48] We thus see interaction as a form of ambiguous contamination that can keep fields like game studies critical, animated, broad, and impactful.

Without interaction, discourses tend to become self-contained. Influenced by critical thinkers of race and empire, this book seeks not to close off lanes of identity or borders of nationality, but to leave ourselves open to encounter, to embrace the receptivity of our Asian/American positions, and to become contaminated by the intimacies, frictions, turbulences, and erotics of working through and beside difference. In other words, rather than attempt to restabilize studies of games with solid ground, this collection embraces the upside-down quirkiness of games that can overturn our everyday categories of race, nation, queerness, and Asia America itself.

Overview of Chapters

The experience we call a game is created by the interaction between different rules, but the rules themselves aren't the game, the interaction is!
—Anna Anthropy, *Rise of the Video Game Zinesters*

Our interactive approach to editing this collection has led us to understand games as contested sites where meanings of Asia and America are negotiated and produced, a view that scholars in our anthology develop from the interdisciplinary foundations of Asian American studies, Asian studies, transpacific studies, gender studies, cinema studies, and postcolonial studies. In this gamelike setup, the conventions of these fields provide the rules that stage our interactions. Each chapter not only considers games and Asia/America but also pushes at the very boundaries and definitions of both by focusing on how games reimagine otherness through examples of personal relations to games (Chang), Blerd (Black and nerd) cultures (Dominguez), the human-animal ontologies of visual novels (Conley), the biracial representations of empire (Moore), the forms of ludic protests under pandemic (Lee), and many more.

Part 1, "Gaming Orientalism," works to enhance and expand the frameworks of Asian American studies and game studies to produce new theoretical variations, focusing on forms of (techno-)orientalism (Chang), "Asiatic" queerness (Patterson), and "Model Minority Mediation" (Rivera). The section opens with an eclectic roundtable featuring Minh Le, the creator of

Introduction **17**

Counter-Strike; the games writer Matthew Seiji Burns; the fighting game champion Patrick Miller; and the indie game maker Emperatriz Ung. Our discussion asks how games, despite their lack of Asian American representation, operate as hybrid Asian/American aesthetic and mechanical products that allow Asian Americans themselves to feel at home in gaming. In the proceeding chapter, "Gaming while Asian," Edmond Chang revisits these points through a "choose your own adventure" style, welcoming the reader to game the chapter itself as a way to "inhabit the possible and imagine the impossible." Christopher B. Patterson's "The Asiatic and the Anti-Asian Pandemic: On *Paradise Killer*" considers the meanings and impacts of his previously coined term "the Asiatic" during the COVID-19 pandemic, when discourses of Asian people were becoming far more serious than playful and anti-Asian violence had risen in some contexts to seemingly unprecedented levels. The section ends with Takeo Rivera's "Asian, Adjacent: Utopian Longing and Model Minority Mediation in *Disco Elysium*," which focuses on the character Kim Kitsuragi, who, as "Asian, adjacent," does not represent a particular ethnic background but performs as a "model minority superego to a whiteness characterized principally by failure and ruin."

Part 2, "Playable Bodies," follows the first section of theoretical framing with a focus on queered experiences of bodies within video games, within game making, and in the processes of manufacture. It begins with a roundtable that features the game makers Naomi Clark (creator of *Consentacle*), Sisi Jiang (creator of *LIONKILLER*), Domini Gee (creator of *Camera Anima*), and Toby Đỗ (creator of *Grass Mud Horse*), who discuss racial representation in games from the perspective of the North American industry, noting how pernicious racist stereotypes of Asians as "below-the-line" rather than "creative" workers get exacerbated by racist presumptions of Asian American designers' perpetual foreignness and their connection to a monolithic Asian "mothership." The chapters follow this conversation by considering how bodies appear in games and games discourses as geopolitical entities. Keita Moore's chapter, "Playable Deniability: Biracial Representation and the Politics of Play in *Metal Gear Solid*," considers how the biracialism of *Metal Gear Solid*'s "Solid Snake" provides an Asian American representation that blunts critiques of global militarism by depicting Japan as a space entirely set apart "from the conflicts of the Cold War and Pax Americana." Thereafter, Yasheng She's "Designing the Global Body: Japan's Postwar Modernity in *Death Stranding*," considers the white body of Sam in the 2019 game *Death Stranding* as it moves through sublime postapocalyptic (and ostensibly American) atmospheres, as well as its "fidgety movements" that, through the Asiatic medium of this Japanese-designed game, objectifies the American white body "as a mechanical marvel." Finally, Prabhash Ranjan Tripathy's "The Trophy called 'Asian Hands': On the Mythical Proficiency of Asian Gamers" follows the discourse of "Asian hands" as it circulates within fighting game communities as "trophies, something to be possessed only via defeating," and as codifying the (white) Western player not as mere "hands" but as creative force.

Part 3, "Localizing Empire," widens the issues of the body to consider space and regional histories, exploring how games, as an entertainment media that emerged during the Cold War, were made possible by manufacturing routes that include extractive mining in Africa, processing factories in Malaysia and southern China, and innovations in Japan. The section begins with a conversation among designers who work and/or focus on "non-American" contexts: Joe Yizhou Xu in Shanghai, Paraluman (Luna) Javier in Manila, Christian Kealoha Miller in Hilo, Hawai'i, and Lien B. Tran, who develops games aimed at audiences in the Global South. The chapters that follow ask how games can be reread to reveal how empire, capitalism, and racialization operate in seemingly "odorless" or apolitical games. Rachael Hutchinson's "Colonial Moments in Japanese Video Games: A Multidirectional Perspective" insists that theories and histories of Japan are crucial to understanding games, not only because the country is a central producer/creator but also because of its "double colonial legacy" as a colonial power in Asia and as a neocolony (or a subempire) of the United States after World War II. Similarly, Souvik Mukherjee's "The Video Game Version of the Indian Subcontinent: The Exotic and the Colonized" asks how "local" South Asian games from India, Bangladesh, and Sri Lanka have responded to categories of "Global South" and "Third World" even as they have gone "largely unheeded in the global discourses on videogames." Finally, Gerald Voorhees and Matthew Jungsuk Howard's "High-Tech Orientalism in Play: Performing South Koreanness in Esports" refocuses theories of techno-orientalism from China and Japan to South Korea to explore how South Korean Asian masculinity has been reconceived as a fetishized object, one that emanates from the neoliberal masculinities of esports.

Part 4, "Inhabiting the Asiatic," responds to many of the previous sections' critiques by considering the ways players and game makers inhabit Asiatic medias to transform, parody, and queer the traditional and imperial conventions of games and dominant gaming cultures. It opens with the game

Introduction **19**

makers Robert Yang (creator of *Radiator 2*), Dietrich Squinkifer (Squinky) (creator of *Dominique Pamplemousse*), Rachel Li (creator of *Hot Pot for One*), and Marina Ayano Kittaka (cocreator of *Even the Ocean*), who reflect on games as opportunities to simulate, or alternately render "unplayable," experiences of disorientation, alienation, and marginalization, especially in regard to racial, queer, and trans elements of play. The chapters that follow continue these inquiries of proximity to and reinhabitations of Asianness. Huan He's "Chinese/Cheating: Procedural Racism in Battle Royale Shooters" traces the racial associations between video game hacking and Chineseness as "part of a longer sociohistorical legacy of Asiatic hacking." Rather than reject cheating as a form of play (or nonplay), He considers "Chinese cheating" as an analytic to understand how cheaters are figured as players unable "to be contained by the virtual borders of any specific game or genre." The next two chapters explore the genre of visual novels, which are ineluctably tethered to aesthetics of anime and are read as Japanese cultural products. Miyoko Conley's "Romancing the Night Away: Queering Animate Hierarchies in *Hatoful Boyfriend* and *Tusks*," considers English-language dating simulations as a parodic form of queer game design to "illustrate how tightly woven race, sexuality, and representations of non-humans are in determining which lives are considered more valuable." Similarly, Sarah Christina Ganzon's "The Fujoshi Trophy and Ridiculously Hot Men: Otome Games and Postfeminist Sensibilities," focuses on romantic visual novels (*otome* games) by exploring how their creators and their fandoms repurpose ("localize," "deterritorialize," or "transcreate") these games to create and contain "postfeminist sensibilities unique to the cultural contexts of their places of origin."

The final section—part 5, "Mobilizing Machines"—continues to understand the Asia/America spectrum within its implicit political and historical separations rooted in histories of militarism, tech, and artistry, and attempts to catalogue the ways that games have not only sought to understand our world, but to make new worlds. The opening roundtable brings together game makers who discuss the social and political impacts of games centered on particular geopolitical and racialized frictions, especially in local acts of protest and community-building. It features Mike Ren Yi (creator of *Yellow Face*), Melos Han-Tani (creator of *All Our Asias*), Yuxin Gao (creator of *Out for Delivery*), and Pamela Punzalan (creator of *Asian Acceptance*). Anthony Dominguez's "Hip-Hop and Fighting Games: Locating the Blerd between New York and Japan" documents the historical rise of Team Spooky, a game stream group who cultivated Blerd (Black and nerd) cultures through community

20   Fickle and Patterson

tournament gatherings of Japanese fighting games within Manhattan's Chinatown Fair Arcade. In so doing, Team Spooky highlights the synthesis of New York City's hip-hop culture, Japanese otaku culture, and the spaces of Chinatown, made possible through "the fusion of physical and digital spaces." Finally, moving from New York to Hong Kong, Haneul Lee's "'This Is What We Do': Hong Kong Protests in *Animal Crossing: New Horizons*" catalogues the use of the game *Animal Crossing: New Horizons* by Hong Kong protestors during the 2020 COVID-19 outbreak. As Hong Kong media often portrayed protestors as specters of violence, the *kawaii* styles and group settings of *Animal Crossing* allowed protestors to reinvent online space "to perform various modes of protest sheltering from real-life clashes with the Hong Kong riot police," where "antistate activities can exist unsuppressed." Our coda, "Role / Play \ Race," concludes the book by speculating on the world-making potentials of games in providing new ways of understanding race—not just race in games, but in our everyday. We thus conclude the collection by making a case for the study of games based not on the massive economic potential of the industry or the similarly boundless potential of the medium but on understanding games as an inherently political site where race, alongside other configurations of difference and power, is *made* and *remade* through play.

This collection's conception began with conversations that, like much of our previously published work, focused on the construction of identities like "Asian American" or "gamer" within a ludic logic of "games of representation" (following on the work of Pierre Bourdieu, Michel Foucault, and Mark Chiang). In our original call for papers for this collection, we asked writers to show how games could expose the way Asian American identity often names something inessential, rather than a particular authentic or stable subject. However, we soon found that this argument was already of no surprise to Asian American game studies scholars or game makers, and merely provided a reliable rule-set for our interactive engagements to produce ever-expansive ideas about how race and identity are not merely revealed by games but are made anew and push the ways we imagine ourselves. Games make such imagining possible through the affordances of their imagined magic circles—a contested term that for us describes not how games help us escape from "reality" but, rather, how games help us challenge "the real" itself as a magic circle where logics of race and space are taken for granted *as* real. Rather, the real games of race and representation, like the real games of colonization and empire-building (remember that a key stage of British and Russian empire-building in Asia was referred to as the Great Game), do not take place only

Introduction   **21**

when one is "away from keyboard"; they are embedded in all our practices of interactive play. Thus, too, can "the real" be transformed through such play practices. Games trace the social and political anxieties hidden within our play—and so allow us to understand, and work to transform, the racializations of our times.

Notes

1 *Saturday Night Live*, "E-Sports Reporter—SNL."

2 For more on sports and race, we recommend James, *Beyond a Boundary*; Guttmann, *Games and Empires*; and Uperesa, *Gridiron Capital*.

3 Danico and Vo, "'No Lattes Here.'"

4 Palumbo-Liu, *Asian/American*, 1.

5 Kondo, *Worldmaking*, 54.

6 Ruberg, *The Queer Games Avant-Garde*, 25.

7 Roh, Huang, and Niu, "Technologizing Orientalism," 2. Although only one chapter of the 2015 influential *Techno-Orientalism* anthology focused on games—Choe and Kim's influential "Never Stop Playing"—the editors recognized that techno-orientalism was especially resonant in games and other "new media" where "the Asian subject is perceived to be, simultaneously, producer (as cheapened labor), designer (as innovators), and fluent consumer (as subjects that are "one" with the apparatus)" (14).

8 See Nakamura, "Race in/for Cyberspace"; and Goto-Jones, "Playing with Being in Digital Asia."

9 Chun, *Control and Freedom*, 18; Iwabuchi, *Recentering Globalization*.

10 Fickle, *The Race Card*, 3.

11 Patterson, *Open World Empire*, 58.

12 We have chosen not to capitalize *orientalism* because the capitalization suggests a particular culture, region, nation, or state.

13 Nakamura, "Race in/for Cyberspace."

14 Roh, Huang, and Niu, "Technologizing Orientalism," 3.

15 For more on this proximity to whiteness, see Tuan, *Forever Foreigners or Honorary Whites?*

16 The yellow peril stereotype, which first emerged in the mid-nineteenth century as a response to Asian (specifically Chinese) labor immigration, characterized Asians as a menacing, consuming, hyperefficient horde. The model minority stereotype, most often associated with the post–World War II years, reworked this logic of unparalleled economic success as attributive of cultural and even genetic traits such as work ethic, meekness, frugality, an affinity for math, etc.

17 Chin and Chan, "Racist Love."

18 Bow, *Racist Love*, 7.

22 Fickle and Patterson

19 D. Chan, "Being Played."

20 Duggan, "Public Debates about Gaming and Gamers."

21 Nielsen, "How Diverse Are Video Gamers," states, "Asian-Americans are even more likely to game (81%), leading all other races and ethnicities; African-Americans are the next most likely (71%)."

22 "Video Game Industry Statistics."

23 Shaw, *Gaming at the Edge*.

24 T. H. Nguyen, *A View from the Bottom*, 3.

25 Iwabuchi defines "odorless" or *mukokuseki* as "literally meaning 'something or someone lacking any nationality,' but also implying the erasure of racial or ethnic characteristics or a context" (*Recentering Globalization*, 28).

26 K.-H. Chen's *Asia as Method*, for example, critiques Western theory for seeing Asian scholars as informers rather than theorists.

27 In their 2014 anthology, *Gaming Cultures and Place in Asia-Pacific*, Larissa Hjorth and Dean Chan emphasize that, like Asia/America, "Asia-Pacific" functions as a "geo-political and economic construct" that has the potential to carve out sufficient imaginative space, and thus "any nuanced study of Asia-Pacific game cultures has the capacity to also disrupt and serve as a critique of the residual Techno-Orientalism in many Western approaches" (1).

28 Shibusawa, "Where Is the Reciprocity?," 270.

29 cárdenas, *Poetic Operations*, 16.

30 Huizinga, *Homo Ludens*, 10. Though both Huizinga's and Caillois's texts themselves did not seem opposed to readings of games as impactful on social and political life, game studies discourses have often interpreted them as such. As Fickle writes in *The Race Card*, both Huizinga and Caillois considered the value and novelty of their work "in their assertion that play served a 'cultural' function" (114).

31 Suits, *The Grasshopper*, 42. For more on this critique of Suits, see Patterson, *Open World Empire*, 14.

32 In 2010, Adrienne Shaw criticized games studies for its lack of critical engagement and argued for a "critical cultural study of games" that compelled game scholars to adopt cultural studies modes of critical engagement and reflexivity. See Shaw, "What Is Video Game Culture?"

33 S. Murray, *On Video Games*, 39.

34 Jodi Byrd has argued that game studies has unwittingly contributed to cultural events like #GamerGate in its separations between the "domain of serious and legitimate scholars as opposed to the low theory cultural dabblers who read games as texts" ("Beast of America," 606).

35 See Fickle, *The Race Card*, chap. 4.

36 While works by McKenzie Wark, Alexander Galloway, Colin Milburn, Alenda Chang, and others have attempted to break theoretical ground well outside game studies, their (as well as our own) work on games rarely seems to circulate outside games studies discourses.

37 As Penix-Tadsen (bringing together voices of Thomas Apperley and Chakrabarti et al.) notes, much game scholarship has remained "blind to its own cultural biases," which has led to repeating "'global' histories" that "mostly omit the global south from consideration" (*Video Games and the Global South*, 9).

38 cárdenas sees "algorithmic analysis" as a way "to identify the components and operations that make up the process we are analyzing—to understand them better, where a process can be an artwork, an identity, or a moment of violence" (*Poetic Operations*, 3).

39 Shaw, *Gaming at the Edge*, 86.

40 Kondo, *Worldmaking*, 26.

41 Sharif and Naimon, "Between the Covers Solmaz Sharif Interview."

42 James, *Beyond a Boundary*.

43 See Fickle, *The Race Card*.

44 See Patterson, *Open World Empire*.

45 Bogost, *Persuasive Games*, 15.

46 Chuh, *The Difference Aesthetics Makes*, 126.

47 Tsing, *The Mushroom at the End of the World*, 8.

48 Reddy, *Freedom with Violence*, 47.

Gaming Orientalism

Part 1

Mixed Connections

Designer Roundtable #1

FEATURING:

Emperatriz Ung, a Chinese Colombian writer, game designer, and educator from the American Southwest who earned her MFA in game design from the Tisch School of the Arts. Ung has worked as a narrative designer for mobile games and has been awarded fellowships, scholarships, and residences from the Asian American Writers' Workshop, Millay Arts, the Academy of Interactive Arts & Sciences Foundation, and Kundiman.

Patrick Miller, who teaches people to play fighting games, and whose personal works include *From Masher to Master* (2014), a book that introduces fighting game fundamentals, and *Bruce Lee Is Your Roommate* (2016), a short Twine story collaboration with Irene Koh.

Minh Le, the co-creator of *Counter-Strike* (1999) who has worked on such titles as *Day of Defeat* (2003), *Rust* (2003), *Tactical Intervention* (2013), *Plan 8* (in development), and numerous mobile game projects.

Matthew Seiji Burns, who created *Eliza* (2019), a visual novel about an AI-assisted therapy tool, and wrote for Zachtronics games *EXAPUNKS* (2018), *Opus Magnum* (2017), *SHENZHEN I/O* (2016), and other titles. With Tom Bissell, he wrote *The Writer Will Do Something* (2015), a Twine game about being a writer on an AAA game (a game from a major publishing company).

Minh Le: I got into the game industry at a very young age; I started playing games when I was eight years old. My dad was really into computers—he bought the early IBM computers. I grew up in Vancouver—I came to Canada when I was two—and Vancouver is a very, I guess, it's a very multicultural city. The people that I played with were very diverse. I didn't really feel Asian because there were a lot of Asians in Vancouver, but we were all, you know, we all identified as Canadians. Even though I am an Asian developer, myself, that never really came into my mindset. I didn't see a lot of Asian developers in my early stages. These days, it's changed quite a bit.

Emperatriz Ung: Similarly, a lot of my family members were computer engineers, so there were always computers around, and I was introduced to that at an early age, and it was an escape. That was how I spent a year and a half when I dropped out of high school. When I was a teen parent, I was in high school and didn't have time or resources to afford a new PS3 or Xbox 360. What kept me connected were actually browser games, flash games. They were short, it was something I could play while my son was down for a nap. And it really opened my mind up to how things could be, but there wasn't a community at the time in New Mexico for any kind of game design or game development. Either you were an artist, or you were a programmer; anything in between, there wasn't really a space for it. It wasn't until I was doing my master's on the East Coast that I came into contact with the New York City Independent Games community, especially the Game Developers of Color Expo, and that was what encouraged me to dive in.

Matthew Seiji Burns: To be honest, I wasn't attracted to games and computers the first time I saw them. I didn't see what was cool about games until the fidelity got a little bit better. Friends of mine had Nintendos, but I wasn't engaged until I could start to see and hear these other worlds—like in *Myst* (1993), you can hear the wind blowing, and you can see these trees.

But I think like everyone else, I struggled to find a place to start because you just have ideas, and you don't really know how to make them real. So I literally just showed up at Activision and applied for a job as a tester. I started from the ground floor, as they say.

Patrick Miller: I mean, I was born in 1985. I grew up with *Ninja Turtles*, *Karate Kid*, *Power Rangers*, like hand-to-hand combat. So when I was a kid, I assumed I had learn how to fight people in case some ninjas, like roll up on you, right? Then when I played *Street Fighter* (1987), I remember thinking anyone could just fight each other, right? Suddenly, when *Street Fighter II* (1991) blew up, there were arcade cabs all over the place. I'd go down to the 7–11 on Clemente Street and play an arcade cabinet and rumble with people, and then again two blocks away in a laundromat. So to me, games were always about the collisions you could have with other people and being able to see other people around you. Oh, I see that person, six foot tall, probably about thirty years old, but they got a hell of a Zangief. And having fighting games as a medium to communicate and learn about other people has always fascinated me.

Minh Le: It's interesting that you [Patrick] mention *Street Fighter* because even though I'm into first-person shooter (FPS) games, *Street Fighter* was a global phenomenon for me as well. Growing up, I played it in the arcades, and pretty much every type of genre. But when *Doom* (1993) came out, it changed the industry and pretty much everyone I knew was playing *Doom*. I gravitated toward FPS games because of their immersion factor. It was the one genre that made me feel I could really put myself in a different world. That was my main attraction for making *Counter-Strike*. People always ask me, "Why did you make *Counter-Strike*? Do you like terrorism?" No, that's not the case at all. The reason I made *Counter-Strike* was because I was born in '77, and I grew up watching movies like *Rambo*, and all these '80s action movies, and some of the movies that really influenced me were Hong Kong action movies, like the ones with Chow Yun-Fat, like *Hard Boiled*. And I felt that style of action was similar to FPS games.

Tara Fickle: Your comments seem to highlight a central limitation of a project like this, in bringing you all together with the one similarity you all have, right, is that you're Asian. But what we're really excited to hear from you is the very nuanced ways your backgrounds come to matter or not matter in your gaming practices.

Emperatriz Ung: I was really surprised that, coming into games from the literary world, there were no Asian/American groups, really. Microsoft now has an internal group, formed less than two years ago. Whereas in literature we have organizations like the Asian American Writers Workshop, which is thirty years old now. Walking into the games industry, I saw that there wasn't the space for these groups, and people were actually kind of weird about it.

Mixed Connections **29**

Some people said they didn't feel the need to be represented. Part of me was like, well, I don't think it's exactly about representation, but about community and supporting each other.

Matthew Seiji Burns: That tracks with my experience too. I never really thought about Asian and Asian American identity when I was younger, partly because I could afford to not think about it, and I had a certain amount of privilege growing up in LA. And while working at a game company, I didn't feel like I was treated in any really different ways, maybe because there's a lot of game industry in Japan. A lot of developers are really into Japanese games and grew up playing them. And eventually they worked in the game industry and went to Japan and worked in Japan for a while. So during one of my first jobs I met someone who had just returned from Japan, who had married a Japanese woman while he was there. It came up that I was half Japanese, on my mother's side. And he just had this weird smile on his face. And he looked at me in this, you know, looking past me kind of thing. Maybe he was looking forward to his own children. I might be reading a little bit into it. But that was the moment where I first thought about being half Japanese in the game industry.

Tara Fickle: It's notable to me that both Patrick and Minh talked about the people they played games with growing up as being quite diverse. The fighting game community is one of the more diverse genres and communities.

Minh Le: Yeah, the FPS players are generally more toxic than other genres. When I played RTS (real-time strategy) games like *StarCraft* (1998), the player base was much more friendly and easier to connect with outside of gaming. But with the FPS genre, the games are way more competitive and emotional. And it skews toward a younger age as well. When I was younger, I was, admittedly, probably more toxic. I played the game to beat others, not to connect with others.

Patrick Miller: When it comes to fighting games, there have been all kinds of attempts to explain how the player community around the world grew into what it is, and especially in North America, how it became significantly more racially diverse, though still mostly dudes. In arcades, anyone can quarter up and play, right? So the barrier to entry starts out pretty low. And then you have *Street Fighter*, which launches with eight characters from around the world.

Chun Li is probably the most recognizable female video game character, and there is probably more media about her than any other female character in a video game. You have Balrog, who's this dated Mike Tyson stereotype but is also one of the first Black characters in a mainstream video game. And so for fighting games in general, there's rich opportunity for character fantasies here. And because these games were predominantly made by Japanese studios, they could get away with a shit ton of super racist character designs that do not register in a way that Americans are used to.

Matthew Seiji Burns: I remember seeing an early study about racial representation in games that concluded that Asians were overrepresented in games. They didn't say why, but, well, it's because they counted games made in Japan. But that doesn't mean Asian representation is good in games; it just means that a lot of games made in Japan happen to have Japanese characters. There's a lot of room to explore forms of Asianness that haven't even been thought of in games, though games seem very Asian friendly.

Patrick Miller: And we don't have an Angry Asian Man or some other pop-culture group to really start looking at what an Asian American video game experience or community might look like. Plus, when you look at video games at scale, North American studios are trying to make inroads into the Chinese audience. Everyone who's thinking about video game earnings in terms of billions of dollars is aiming at China, right? And so they will adopt as much as they can, whether it's art styles, character design, aesthetics, marketing. And the other thing is, if you think about it, fighting games are essentially the video game version of kung fu movies, right? And hand-to-hand combat, either in sports or in media, can create venues for resistance against white supremacy. You got Ali, you got Bruce Lee, you got all kinds of stories being told in the tradition of martial arts movies. So when, you know, a pro *Hearthstone* player rolls up and is like, hey, "Free Hong Kong," obviously, that's going to create a lot of problems for Blizzard. And that is part of this incredibly rich history of using sports to give people a soapbox to stand on.

Matthew Seiji Burns: When I was working at Microsoft, there was a whole division called "Geopolitical Review." They check every Microsoft product for any kind of potential problem across any region. So anything that could

Mixed Connections 31

be considered religious is forbidden. Anything that could be seen as taking a side in any ongoing geopolitical conflict. Anything having to do with China and Taiwan. And, I'm sure, anything having to do with China and Hong Kong now. All of those kinds of things have to be completely removed.

Chris Patterson: I do want to follow up on the topic of mixed race, as many of us here, including Tara and I, identify as mixed race. And I've always wondered if that mattered when it came to playing games and writing about games. Tara and I have both asked each other about this during interviews, and we both can't really come up with satisfactory answers. As a literary scholar or fiction writer, if I present myself as Filipino, or white, or mixed race, people have a very hard time reading me or knowing what to do with my work, whereas when I write about games, I don't feel urged to put myself in a kind of box that's instantly recognizable.

Emperatriz Ung: When I was in writing workshops and literature, being mixed race—half Latina, half Asian—I was called out early in my creative work by my peers and teachers, before I had a chance to enter any industry. And any bilingual work was automatically shut down. A peer of mine was like, I don't understand how your father is Chinese, but you have a grandmother who speaks Spanish, which is like not a critique at all, or even a comment really, but they spent a whole half page. It was development spaces like "Latinx in Gaming" that saved me. Then again, I've been on a development team once, where they knew I was mixed race and spoke Spanish and some Mandarin, and if they needed Spanish, instead of writing it themselves, I became the resident expert on totally different cultures.

Chris Patterson: In other conversations with Asian diasporic designers, we've talked about how being mixed—particularly mixed Asian—signifies a kind of bridge that makes us more useful to the industries, more trustworthy as writers and designers, and also more comfortable. For me, I rarely cared about self-representation in games until I played *Soulcalibur II* (2002), and first played as Talim, one of the first Filipina characters in a game. Suddenly, it was important to me that I was playing this character from the Philippines. But before that, I would have said representation in games didn't do much for me personally. So, too, *Eliza* is one of those games where seeing mixed-race representation became unexpectedly meaningful.

32   Designer Roundtable 1

Matthew Seiji Burns: I absolutely wanted the main character in *Eliza* to be mixed race for that reason. I just hadn't seen it very often. Prior to *Eliza*, the only game I could think of where mixed race is explicitly stated is this old PS2 game, *Ring of Red* (2001). The main character is half Japanese and half German, and throughout the game, they're using that to tease him, like, "What do you think of that, halfbreed?" And in *Assassin's Creed Liberation* (2012), there's a side story, where the character can pass in different contexts because she's mixed race. So the game uses the "stealth mechanics" of being mixed, and she can enter into different situations based on how she presents.

Patrick Miller: In my experience, most game dev teams are not operating off a strong model of creative direction. When I've seen mixed-race representation in video games, it's usually coming from fighting games, usually a part-Japanese character. Ken from *Street Fighter* is technically a quarter Japanese. Laura and Shawn Matsuda in *Street Fighter III* (1997) and *Street Fighter V* (2016) are Japanese Brazilian, and there's some fascinating diasporic stories there. Like, when I did a research fellowship in Japan, I was training Brazilian jiu jitsu with Japanese Brazilian immigrants who worked in factories. And it was super cool to see how the character design had paid some homage to the sport. But a lot of times when I see mixed-race characters, it's about being between two different national or racial borders. And it's executed without much nuance or sensitivity.

Matthew Seiji Burns: In games coming from Japan, I feel mixed race is often used in a slightly exotic, fetishistic way. In anime, you might see a girl who's half Russian or something like that, and it's used to give her blond hair. It's very much a kind of a visual typing. But a lot of this gets lost in the localization process, when products from Japan, which might have dodgy racial representations, are "fixed," and are turned into something a little bit less awful by the US branches. It happens to a lot of Japanese games, where racial representation is dialed back or made more appropriate for a global or Western audience. It reminds me a lot of food, food as imperialism, food as being an ambassador to a new culture.

Patrick Miller: If I could offer a tip for the academics reading this, if you're ever wondering why video games are the way they are, the place that I would start is economics. Because video games are expensive as hell to make. And this is a hits-driven industry. So that means the more you increase your possibility for scale, in general, the higher your risk, and so you're going to have to make the game more broadly appealing to try and minimize risk. In other words, we do not have a healthy ecosystem as other industries might. If you want to make a film that isn't meant to be a Hollywood blockbuster, you can get academic funding, you can get grants, you might be able to just shoot it on your own and shoestring it. But when you look at the prospect of trying to do interesting, personal, smaller-scale games, usually the problem you're going to run into is that the people who have the skills that you need to satisfy the vision you want are going to be too expensive to justify taking that risk.

Tara Fickle: Which is interesting, because there's the industry assumption that whiteness is the most cost-effective representation, which goes back to what Minh was saying about making players feel comfortable. Whiteness is this thing that helps you inhabit this character fantasy, right?

Minh Le: That's true. When I play games, even though I'm Vietnamese, I feel more comfortable picking a Caucasian character. And I put my mindset in that as well. That guy's cool. He does all the cool stuff. To me, he's always been the hero.

Edmond Y. Chang

Gaming while Asian

To E. Tang

1. Forebears

"I know something about labyrinths," says the narrator of Jorge Luis Borges's famous story "The Garden of Forking Paths." He continues, "I am the great-grandson of Ts'ui Pen. He was Governor of Yunnan and gave up temporal power to write a novel . . . to create a maze in which all men would lose themselves . . . His novel had no sense to it and nobody ever found his labyrinth."[1] First published in 1941 and translated from Spanish into English in 1948, the short story has become an ur-text for early digital culture, electronic literature, and game studies and continues to wend and wind its way through digital technologies that evince branching narratives, unusual temporalities, puzzles, and playfulness, qualities Espen Aarseth labels "ergodic," a text where the reader and player are "constantly reminded of inaccessible strategies and paths not taken, voices not heard. Each decision will make some parts of the text more, and others less, accessible, and what you may never know the exact results of your choices."[2] According to Mou-Lan Wong, "The Garden of Forking Paths" is an "intertextual hub," and it collects, connects, and "anticipates various interactive pop-culture narratives from printed texts to digital and cinematic media."[3] Borges's exotic mythologizing and playful inscrutability has become foundational to technocultural design, narratives, and worlds such that "The Garden"'s techno-orientalist logics have become deeply entangled, naturalized in the way we imagine, interact with, and play games.[4]

As the story unfurls, the narrator learns from a British sinologist named Stephen Albert of the truth of the narrator's ancestor and the textual, spatial, and temporal mysteries of the "Garden." The narrator describes the labyrinth, saying, "I imagined it infinite, made not only of eight-sided pavilions and of twisting paths but also of rivers, provinces and kingdoms. . . . I thought of a maze of mazes, of a sinuous, ever growing maze which would take in both past and future and would somehow involve the stars."[5] The metaphor of unending twisting and sinuous (and *sino*-ous) paths would be forever imprinted, embedded, and enacted by digital technologies and games with no purer expression than the emblematic phrase, "You are in a maze of twisty little passages," from Will Crowther's 1970s *Colossal Cave Adventure*.

This story, this mystery adventure of an unwitting Asian spy during World War I wanting to prove that "a yellow man could save [Germany's] armies" lays bare the metonymic ways Asianness is narrated and encoded into the experiences, discourses, and analyses of games;[6] the inscrutability of the story vis-à-vis the inscrutability of the labyrinth vis-à-vis the inscrutability of the narrator condenses into what Tara Fickle names "ludo-Orientalism" or the "design, marketing, and rhetoric of games shapes how Asians as well as East-West relations are imagined and where notions of foreignness and racial hierarchies get reinforced."[7] The narrator of "The Garden of Forking Paths" not only plays the games of espionage and fugitive, functioning as a literal pawn of war, he must also play the game of representation, of being multiply othered, of simultaneously being "unreal and unimportant" yet "infinitely visible and vulnerable" as an outsider, a foreigner, a racialized body.[8] It takes a Western perspective to make legible the secrets of the labyrinth and of the narrator; Albert is the one to solve Ts'ui Pen's puzzle: the book and labyrinth are one and the same even as Asianness and the game are mapped onto one another. How might this powerful "conceptual technology" construct the binaristic opposition of West versus East, US games versus non-US games, hardcore versus casual, competition versus cooperation, even as it evacuates game spaces by ostensibly rendering them neutral, level, and difference-blind?[9] How might this othering and orientalist logic be absorbed, encoded into the

36   Edmond Y. Chang

bedrock of play, game design? Better yet, how might the gates and switches of who gets included or imagined narratively, representationally, and ludically be critiqued and challenged? In other words, what might it mean to suffer, survive, even surpass the "infinite penitence and sickness of the heart" of gaming while Asian?[10]

If you want answers, go to 3.
If you want to play a game, go to 8.
If you want to get some pizza instead, go to the next section.

2. Teen Night

I met my friends for "teen night" at the local Chuck E. Cheese. For a flat fee, we got all-you-can-eat pizza, fountain soda, and, of course, never-ending tokens for Skee-Ball and video games. It was the '80s. I was in middle school, and I remember it was a big deal that they played Michael Jackson's *Thriller* video on the big screen, which MTV could only air after nine o'clock because it was too scary for children. I also remember the arcade got a new game: *Dragon's Lair*. It was the first coin-operated video game to cost fifty cents to play.

Dragon's Lair (1983) was an interactive LaserDisc video game developed by Rick Dyer and Don Bluth. The game was basically a library of animated sequences or cutscenes that followed predetermined paths. The player "controlled" the protagonist Dirk the Daring by using the joystick to select a direction or by pressing an action button whenever the game flashed a cue; reflexes and timing were more important than the player's choices given that each track was scripted. Eventually, you could figure out the right path, the right script. In a sense, it looked like a movie, it played like a movie, and at the time, it was a very big deal.

I was terrible at the game. I was not living up to my Asian arcade expectations. The game also presented a different challenge, that of identification. *Dragon's Lair*'s teaser voice-over proclaimed the game was the "fantasy adventure where you become a valiant knight, on a quest to rescue the fair princess from the clutches of an evil dragon. You control the actions of a daring adventurer. . . . Lead on, adventurer. Your quest awaits!" Even at that tender age, I knew I was never going to be Dirk the Daring, especially since I could not get past the first handful of screens. If his quest was my quest, if his adventure was my adventure, what did it mean that I could not (or did not want to) rescue the princess? Dirk was the tall, dark-haired, square-jawed,

· Gaming while Asian **37**

broad-shouldered, well-muscled fantasy hero. He was everything that I could never be not because I could not spend a fortune trying to master every jump, dodge, and action but because games—then and now—were not made for me. Since representation was not open to me, I was left with the second-class experience of identification. And if I could not identify, then I had to resign, be excluded from the fantasy.

If you decide to play a different game, go to 5.
If you go home to watch cartoons, go to 10.

3. Players

Sometime in 2016, a gaming meme circulated the highways and byways of the internet: an image in the style of motivational posters featuring a rectangular matrix of faces, of leading men from video games with the text "Video Game Protagonists: Kids Love Brown-Haired 30-Something White Males" on a black background. The disconnect between the demographics of gamers and the limited palette of playable characters is wide and telling. For instance, Dean Chan reveals, "Asian American gamers are, paradoxically, both hypervisible and out of sight," stereotyped as players of prowess or underexamined as a population.[11] With the rise of competitive video gaming and esports, Asian and Asian American players are being held up as poster children, even fetishized, becoming celebrities for their computer and console skills. These players take on and are mapped with a "ludic identity," as Christopher Patterson argues, that "reiterates techno-Orientalist racism . . . well suited for the programming and engineering labor of information technology" and thereby making "Asians appear magically fit for both e-sport success and model minority success."[12]

Meanwhile, a 2015 Nielsen study found that Asian Americans are "likely to feel video game characters are not inclusive. Almost half of these gamers believe all races aren't well represented in gaming character options, while less than a quarter think they are. On the other hand, Hispanics, African-Americans and non-Hispanic whites are much more positive about race representation."[13] In the same report, though Asian Americans are underrepresented in terms of characters, a majority are game players: "Asian-Americans are even more likely to game (81%), leading all other races and ethnicities: African-Americans are the next most likely (71%), followed by non-Hispanic whites (61%) and Hispanics (55%)."[14] What these statistics reveal is that the game of representation cannot be won by numbers alone, that inclusion in one arena often means exclusion in another while simultaneously reinforcing dominant norms, stereotypes, and roles. But there is play in this contention, potential for rupture and resistance in the paradox. As Lisa Nakamura argues, "If gamers are themselves the source of some of the most virulent racist, sexist, and homophobic messages in videogames, they are also the source of some of the most ingenious and potent campaigns against them."[15]

If you want to compete, go to 6.
If you want to collaborate, go to 10.

4. Magic Circles

The "magic circle" of play, a too-often-cited concept from philosopher Johan Huizinga's *Homo Ludens* (1938), is the idea that games are not the same as and separate from real life, from the real world. Unfortunately, the magic circle (or its more vernacular invocation, "It's just a game!") has regularly been raised like a shield or force field to deflect or ignore analysis and critique, particularly from feminist, queer, and antiracist perspectives, and to perpetuate the commonsense dictums that games are only play, just for fun, and color-, gender-, queer-, and other differences–blind.[16] Video games, gaming, and playing are neither level nor neutral. As Mia Consalvo argues, "Players never play a new game or fail to bring outside knowledge about games and gameplay into their gaming situations. The event is 'tainted' perhaps by prior knowledge. There is no innocent gaming."[17] Understanding that games are not insulated or marked off from the real world and that the magic circle is permeable, imperfectly protecting some while leaving others out in the open, makes plain that "much of the pleasure of videogames comes at the expense of women and people of colour, both literally and figuratively."[18] In fact, the very foundations of Huizinga's ludic philosophy (among others) is predicated on what Tara Fickle calls "ludo-Orientalist" understandings; the magic circle takes "all the well-worn stereotypes of the Orientalist imaginary, seemingly emptied of both racial content and national context, being redeployed instead as formal qualities of the imaginative process called play."[19] The only "innocent" players and games are those who already benefit from power, privilege, who inhabit the ideal citizen gamer subject—one that is imagined as straight, white, male, masculine, affluent, and able-bodied, and whose identities, bodies, and worlds are not so easily appropriated or consumed as exotic, ethnic, alien, or other.

The End.

5. Yellow Wizard

One arcade game I enjoyed growing up was Atari's *Gauntlet* (1985), a fantasy dungeon crawler game that allowed up to four people to play at once. It was one of the first cooperative arcade games I had ever played. Players could pick one of four characters: Thor the warrior, Thyra the Valkyrie, Questor the Elf, and Merlin the wizard. I always played the wizard, preferring fighting at range and possessing the most powerful magic. The game's narrator would exclaim, "Warrior needs food" or "Elf shot the food" or "Valkyrie is about to die." In the game, each avatar was assigned a color: red for Thor, blue for Thyra, green for Questor, and yellow for Merlin. The irony of me playing a yellow wizard as an Asian man never escaped me, nor did the negative connotations of the color: cowardice, sickness, mental illness, excess. The physically weak magic user, standing in the back, reliant on mystical powers, overlaps too neatly with the stereotypical and yellow peril characterization of Asian bodies and identities as foreign, diseased, feminized, yet simultaneously dangerous and powerful. So ingrained and internalized are these connections, intentional or inadvertent, that I misremember the game narration as marking color and character: "Yellow wizard needs food, badly!" or "Yellow wizard shot the food" or "Yellow wizard is about to die."

If you decide to play a different game, go to 8.
If you try to escape, go to 9.
If you want to hunt a yeti, go to the next section.

6. Choice

Every *Choose Your Own Adventure* book begins with the same preface: "BE-WARE and WARNING! This book is different from other books. You and YOU ALONE are in charge of what happens in this story." Popular in the '80s and published by then Bantam Books, these compact "gamebooks" offered young readers the opportunity to take on the role of the protagonist. The books' second-person format hailed the reader to make a choice every few pages that would shuffle them to another page, another part of the story, another set of choices until they reached one of the many possible endings. When hitting a dead end or an undesirable ending, "reader-players" could backtrack, climb back up the narrative decision tree and take a different path down a different set of page numbers. Of course, the rhetoric and novelty of choice would quickly lose their luster, given that while "the reader was indeed offered unprecedented interactive control by making a series of choices which determined the multiple endings he or she would reach, all the possible paths he or she could go down had been carefully chosen, designed and planned out by authors."[20] The interactive fallacy of the novels—which would be remediated into other mediums, particularly video games—promises reader and player the power to make decisions and affect outcomes, the authority of active exchange, even authorship (instead of passive consumption), even as that agency is a fantasy already constrained and contained by the top-down designs and structures of the text. This fantasy of choice belies what Eli Cook calls "a kind of neoliberal 'ground zero'" wherein *Choose Your Own Adventure* books were "one of the first important instances in which gamified notions of free, individual choice first came to shape mass culture in the United States."[21]

Of course, who is imagined and able to choose, even in a limited manner, often defaults to the cultural ideal and norm; as with video games, the imagined reader-player is young, white, straight, and male. According to R. A. Montgomery, one of the series founders and writers, "From the outset, we wanted *Choose Your Own Adventure* books to be non-gender specific. . . . It was a conscious decision."[22] However, the publisher would foil this decision by featuring cover and interior art that feature mostly boys as the protagonists. While the creators desired the books to be gender-neutral, the narratives relied on and continued other problematic definitions and tropes, particularly for adventure stories that perpetuated genre conventions that included "exotic" locales, Indigenous "savages," and non-Western culture. For example, starting in 2005, Chooseco reran and added to the *Choose Your Own Adventure* line with *The Abominable Snowman* by R. A. Montgomery as its number one volume. The prologue states, "You and your best friend Carlos have travelled to Nepal in search of the fabled Yeti or abominable snowman. Last year while the two of you were mountain climbing in South America, a guide told you about the legendary creature and you haven't stopped thinking about the Yeti since."[23] The plot of the novel begins with Carlos going missing. The reader-player must find him and the mysterious yeti. The book drips with orientalist imagery including drawings featuring pagodas, men and women with slanted eyes, Buddhas, and Bengal tigers. Down one of the narrative paths, the reader is taken to a mountain monastery where they are told, "Those who share the secret knowledge of the Yeti are pledged to reveal this knowledge only to appointed people. You, and you alone, are one of the appointed. It has been seen in the stars; it has been read in your hand."[24] The reader-player, making the right decision, then meets

Gaming while Asian   **41**

a monk who dispenses sage advice, saying, "Listen well with heart, head, and body. Listen with eyes more than ears. Heed the cry of the *Yeti*."[25] One can hear the bamboo flute and *erhu* as the words are solemnly spoken. (Chooseco's company logo is for some reason a Chinese dragon in silhouette.)

Choice becomes the mechanism through which readers (and players) inhabit different possibilities, yet too often it becomes the game mechanic of what Lisa Nakamura calls "identity tourism."[26] In the case of *The Abominable Snowman*, mostly white readers get to "appropriate an Asian racial identity without any of the risks associated with being a racial minority in real life."[27] The power and privilege to choose is not evenly distributed even, or perhaps especially, in these gamebooks and games more generally. Moreover, who is represented and designed to be able to choose continues to reveal the ludo-orientalist history and "infrastructure of gaming itself as a raced project."[28] Ironically, in the quoted scene from *The Abominable Snowman*, the narrative itself reveals that the interactive fallacy constrains even the ideal citizen reader-player as the protagonist is told that they are chosen, that they can choose, yet all of this has been destined by signs and stars. In other words, there is no choice.

> *If you think you don't have a choice, go to the next section.*
> *If you really think you do have a choice, go to 4.*
> *If you don't know what to do, go to 12.*

7. Menu

```
100 REM Character Selection
105 PRINT "Which do you want to play?"
110 PRINT
115 PRINT "(M)onk"
120 PRINT "Nin(J)a"
125 PRINT "(K)ung Fu Master"
130 PRINT "(G)eisha"
135 PRINT "(D)ragon Lady"
140 PRINT "Computer (P)rogrammer"
145 PRINT "(S)py"
150 PRINT "(E)xchange Student"
155 PRINT "(F)ortune Cookie"
160 PRINT "(Y)ellow Fever"
165 PRINT "(N)o MSG"
```

```
170 PRINT "(O)ther"
175 PRINT "Additional (C)hoices"
180 PRINT
185 INPUT "Select from above:"; BadChoice$
190 IF BadChoice$="M" THEN GOTO 8
195 IF BadChoice$="J" THEN GOTO 3
200 IF BadChoice$="K" THEN GOTO 8
205 IF BadChoice$="G" THEN GOTO 8
210 IF BadChoice$="D" THEN GOTO 3
215 IF BadChoice$="P" THEN GOTO 8
220 IF BadChoice$="S" THEN GOTO 13
225 IF BadChoice$="E" THEN GOTO 2
230 IF BadChoice$="F" THEN GOTO 12
235 IF BadChoice$="Y" THEN GOTO 5
240 IF BadChoice$="N" THEN GOTO 9
245 IF BadChoice$="O" THEN GOTO 4
250 REM Please Select Again
255 PRINT "That choice is not available to you. Please select again."
260 GOTO 100
```

8. Yellow Face

Yellow Face is a text game by Mike Ren Yi released for the web and mobile devices in 2019. According to the developer's notes, it is "an interactive game about being Asian in America," based on a true story, and inspired by David Henry Hwang's play of the same name. The game begins with two facing faces in profile: the one on the left is white, the one on the right is pale yellow, with text bubbles, choices, and a curious "American/Asian" status bar at the top of the screen. The start screen sets the scene: "A college house party in America, 2009; music and indistinct chatter spill from the speakers." Then the first interaction appears as the "White Guy" asks, "Where are you from?" You, as the player-character, have two choices: "North Carolina" and "China." Clicking "North Carolina" elicits the cringe-worthy follow-up question, "No I mean where are you REALLY from?" The remainder of the game moves through a few other interlocutors including a "White Girl" and an Asian girl named "Anna." Different conversation paths reveal further racist and orientalist replies, from "Chinese culture is so zen" to "Do a karate chop" to "I'm not into Asian guys."

Gaming while Asian **43**

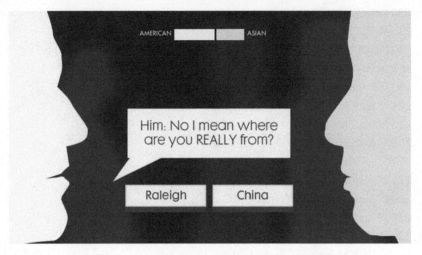

1.1. White and Asian faces talking. Screenshot of *Yellow Face*.

The game dramatizes not only the everyday micro- and macro-aggressions experienced by Asian and other racialized bodies but gestures at the critical potential of games that do more than treat race as a ludic or representational fantasy. What is illuminating about *Yellow Face* is its weaving of the "Where are you from?" conversation so often rehearsed by Asian bodies in white spaces with two curious mechanics. The first is the "American/Asian" status bar (see figure 1.1), which measures how American (i.e., white) or how Asian (i.e., yellow) your responses are perceived to be. The "American" bar critiques the conflation of nationality and citizenship with whiteness and assimilation, recognizing the discursive and ludic violence and impossibility of ever being fully accepted or integrated into normative belonging. Rather than read the mechanic as attempting to quantify "Asianness" (or "Americanness") in a real way, I read it as the algorithmic visualization of the "Where are you from?" game that, as Tara Fickle confirms, "Asian American experience of being made to feel like a 'perpetual foreigner' regardless of birthplace or citizenship" reveals the cultural and procedural logic of Asian American representation as "itself a game."[29] *Yellow Face* shows how the ludic here becomes a way of "representing the problematics of representation in the first place."[30] The second mechanic, bound up with the first, is the way the game takes advantage of the constraints of decision trees, limiting the player to scant choices or a complete lack of adequate responses. There are no good choices, and the player-character ultimately "loses" the "Where are you from?" game trapped in the double-bind and double-consciousness of the gap between Asian and American. Moreover, the "Where are you from?" game critiques a racist temporality and geography that fixes Asian bodies in white spaces only in the past from which they arrived in the United States and forecloses on the present and future. Both mechanics create the illusion that *Yellow Face* is a game that can be won, and like the "Where are you from?" game, there are no good choices.

If you stay at the party, go to 4.
If you zone out to the music, go to 12.
If you decide to leave the party and head into the backyard, go to 13.

9. Game Space

Game spaces, the space *in* games, the space *of* games, is highly regulated, fraught, and always normed. Game space as open, free, and politically or ideologically neutral is a fantasy. McKenzie Wark in *Gamer Theory* (2007) argues, "The game has not just colonized reality, it is also the sole remaining ideal. . . . The reigning ideology imagines the world as a *level playing field*, upon which all folks are equal before God, the great game designer. . . . Everything is evacuated from an empty space and time which now appears natural, neutral, and without qualities—a gamespace."[31] Even gaming spaces themselves, be they at home, at work, in an arcade, around a table, in a back room, in front of a screen, or on a field, divide, discriminate, and define who is a player, who gets to play, what are the rules, what are the boons, and more importantly, who is *not* a player, who does not get to play, who makes the rules, and what are the consequences of winning, losing, and breaking the rules. And since job, school, family, health, leisure, even romance have increasingly become gamified, these problematic logics perpetuate the embedded inequalities and ludic biases already at play in everyday life. Wark continues, "The real world appears as a video arcadia divided into many and varied games. Work is a rat race. Politics is a horse race. The economy is a casino. . . . These games are no joke. When the screen flashes the legend *Game over*, you are either dead, or defeated, or at best out of quarters."[32] Even the language of success, sustainability, and survival has been algorithmically and ludically inflected and reveals the near impossibility for marginalized bodies and identities to compete in, much less win, the game of living.

The End.

10. Roles

In the colorful intro to the 1980s cartoon series *Dungeons and Dragons*, six friends are transported from an amusement park ride to the fantasy realm of D&D. Each is then given a magical item befitting their role. The Dungeon Master, their guide, names them in a creaky, sagely voice, "Fear not, Ranger, Barbarian, Magician, Thief, Cavalier, and Acrobat." The animated series was my first introduction to *Dungeons and Dragons* and the idea and pleasure of character creation, of playing a class, of being a type. The cartoon provided templates for a range of characters but more importantly established an early taxonomy of what characters I might be. Alas, I did not see myself as the blond and brawny Hank the Ranger or Bobby the Barbarian, who was only eight years old. Fabulous were Sheila the Thief and Diana the Acrobat (notably the only character of color on the show), but they were not me either. What did that leave me? The spoiled coward Eric the Cavalier or Presto the bumbling fool of a Magician. I did like Presto the best. Of course, the only main character that actually looked anything like me was Venger the Villain with his vampiric face and slanted eyes. Once again, I could only aspire to whiteness or be despised. Once again, the burden of identification fell to the body not shown, the player not seen, recognizing that most of the time one could not play as or like oneself. I learned these limits of identification early on, often abandoning them, and found other ways to smuggle myself into the scene and in between the lines. Better yet, I created my own world, my own rules. It would be years, many in fact, before I would realize that the one character I at the time never imagined I could inhabit would be the role I now love best: the Dungeon Master.

If you need food badly, go to 5.
If you are looking for players to start a new game, go to 3.
If you decide you'd rather join an existing game, go to the next section.

11. d20

On the hardcover front of the handbook:
a man in a winged helm, bastard sword
aloft, stalwart, muscular, even in armor,
astride a horse in a dun caparison, charging.
Even then I could not see myself as he.

Perhaps I was in the back, in the appendices,
an apprentice, young, scared, sad, small,
hungry, queer, Asian, overweight, hiding,
boxed in by burdened, humid homosociality,
chainmail bikinis, and dice rolls for dick size.
But with the master's tools I made a place
for myself, found ways to pass, hope, pretend:
he was Agicanus, she was named Ayecleare,
he was bitter, sorcerous, ambitious, alone,
she was righteous, wise, glowing, healing.
He loved her but like a brother, partner, teacher.
She loved him, though *not* like a sister, and knew
he poured himself into his studies, his magic
to escape that which he could not know or name.
I saw myself as he, as they, waiting, wishing.[33]

If you want to read the rulebook, go to 7.
If you want to hide in the closet, go to 4.
If you want to make a wish, go to 14.

12. Maze

You are in a text of twisty little paragraphs.

If you are lost, go to 9.
If you are not lost, go to 12.
If you want to be told where to go, go to 7.
If you want to decide where to go, go to wherever you'd like.

13. Infinite Intimacy

Robert Yang's *Intimate, Infinite* (2014) is a reimagining of Jorge Luis Borges's
"The Garden of Forking Paths," mixing first-person shooter (FPS), walking
simulator, puzzle, and role-playing game. The title screen calls *Intimate,
Infinite* a "series of games," a set of interconnected minigames "about gar-
dening, chess, history, infinity, and a murder," which play with time, cause
and effect, genre, and mechanics. The player is thrust *in medias res* into

story and action finding themselves on a dirt road at night, standing over a dead body and gun, being chased by dogs and assailants. Picking up the gun reveals that it is out of ammunition; the expectation is that the player will have to look for and find bullets, but this FPS trope ends being a red herring. Instead, the player-character must run down the road to catch a train about to depart. The player is then taken to the countryside where they eventually find the locked gate to a manor house. The character laments, "I had no key . . . in this life at least." And then the player is taken back to the start screen where they can choose which game, which path, which fork to play next: find a way through garden labyrinth, engage in a glass of wine and game of chess, or return to the chase. Playing one part changes a different part; revisiting a section reveals new details, openings, and possibilities. The game takes to heart "The Garden of Forking Path"'s notion of "an infinite series of times, in a dizzily growing, ever spreading network of diverging, converging and parallel times."[34] In other words, what is not accomplished in one game, in one life, might be accomplished in another.

While not faithful to Borges's short story, the series of games still imagines a Chinese spy who must send word to the German army by killing a British sinologist. However, Yang's beautifully rendered and atmospheric cycle of games offers two provocations. First, in the encounter between Wang and Alber (analogs for Borges's Tsun and Albert), Yang queers the narrative and suggests in one of the lives of the characters they were lovers, not just enemies. This potential is revealed via a brief text and cutscene where Wang acknowledges the relationship (see figure 1.2). Yang writes, "It's also not much of a stretch to read this as a gay relationship between two men arguing about secrecy and shame and possibility. In one of these infinite realities, they are friends—and in another, maybe they are lovers . . . I made this gay subtext more obvious in my game, depending on the randomization [of cutscenes] you get when playing."[35] Second, *Intimate, Infinite* critiques the medium of video games and the interactive fantasy of choice, power, and control. Yang says, "There might be endless dimensions of existence, but as humans, we only experience one. Each time you read this story, it will always be the same story with the same ending, no matter what the ideas promise. The spy will always shoot the sinologist. I push this interpretation in my game: once you shoot my Alber, he's dead in the title screen, hub screen, chess section as well."[36] The game reflects on the explanation of the garden in the short story: "In all fiction, when a

48   Edmond Y. Chang

man is faced with alternatives he chooses one at the expense of others. In the most unfathomable, Ts'ui Pen, he chooses—simultaneously—all of them. He thus *creates* various, various times which start others that will in their turn branch out and bifurcate in other times."[37] Yang's game extends this critique of choice and branching futurities as they intersect with race and nationality commenting on the orientalist relationship between the main character and the sinologist. Yang notes, "It takes a Magical White Guy . . . to make Tsun interested in his own culture again. . . . This Chinese guy has to murder this British guy to supposedly prove to the Germans that the Chinese are a civilized sophisticated people capable of resourcefulness and creativity. . . . There are only two people who know about the Garden, and by the end of the story, they are both dead."[38] Like the garden, like the game, the orientalist logic becomes a trap, a dead end, or at the very least, a fantasy relationship between a fictive West and East, between normative agency and racialized subordination.

If you want to be infinite, go to 1.
If you want to be intimate, go to the next section.
If you want to end the game, go to 15.

1.2. The character of Wang. Screenshot of *Intimate, Infinite*.

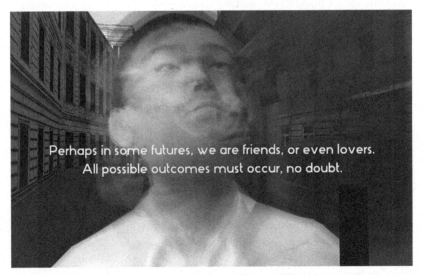

Gaming while Asian   49

14. Hope

I did not start playing tabletop role-playing games till I was well into tenth grade; I was a gaming late bloomer.[39] My first RPG systems are now considered classics: *Advanced Dungeons and Dragons* (also known as Second Edition), *Stormbringer*, *Star Wars: The Roleplaying Game*, *Call of Cthulhu*, and *Champions*. In high school, gaming was an escape, a chance to be someone else and somewhere else. I always played healers or mages, characters that stood in the back, provided support, yet were necessary, even crucial in just the right circumstances. A long weekend's marathon full of dice rolls, smudged character sheets, and Jolt cola bought me respite from the pains of being a shy, overweight, closeted young man of color; it brought me community, camaraderie, and the first thrill of falling in love with one's game master (though not for the last time). For many years, I would be the only nonwhite and openly queer player at the table. In college, gaming became less about escape and more about exploring, about self-expression. College and graduate school is when I discovered live-action role-playing games, when I started tinkering with my own game designs, and when I started learning to be comfortable in my own skin. I also realized that I had a talent for game mastering, for creating and communicating worlds, which dovetailed with my growing aptitude for teaching, for finding confidence at the front of a classroom.

Looking back, I can honestly say that gaming was one of the things that saved my life. It inspired my writing and catalyzed my profession. Gaming is living, loving, learning, and sometimes grieving and coping and escaping. Gaming informs so much of who I am, what I do, and what I believe and fight for. Gaming, in a deep sense then, is practicing utopia and transforming dystopia. It is a longing for a world yet to come; it is a hoping for a world better than this one. Gaming allows us to inhabit the possible and imagine the impossible.

If you want to watch the credits, go to the next section.

Notes

1 Borges, "The Garden of Forking Paths," 93.

2 Aarseth, *Cybertexts*, 3.

3 M.-L. Wong, "The Garden of Living Paths," 104, 106.

4 For more on techno-orientalism, see Roh, Huang, and Niu, *Techno-Orientalism*.

5 Borges, "The Garden of Forking Paths," 94.

6 Borges, "The Garden of Forking Paths," 91.

7 Fickle, *The Race Card*, 3.

8 Borges, "The Garden of Forking Paths," 101, 92.

9 Fickle, *The Race Card*, 14.

10 Borges, "The Garden of Forking Paths," 101.

11 D. Chan, "Being Played," para. 1.

12 Patterson, *Open World Empire*, 62, 64.

13 "How Diverse Are Video Games," paras. 3–4.

14 "How Diverse Are Video Games," para. 5.

15 Nakamura, "User-Generated Media Campaigns," 11.

16 For more on antifeminist, antiqueer, and racist backlashes in gaming cultures, see Quinn, *Crash Override*; Condis, *Gaming Masculinity*; Phillips, *Gamer Trouble*; and Gray and Leonard, *Woke Gaming*.

17 Consalvo, "There Is No Magic Circle," 415.

18 Nakamura, "User-Generated Media Campaigns," 9.

19 Fickle, *The Race Card*, 123.

20 Cook, "Rearing Children of the Market in the 'You' Decade," 23.

21 Cook, "Rearing Children of the Market in the 'You' Decade," 17.

22 Hendrix, "Choose Your Own Adventure."

23 Montgomery, *The Abominable Snowman*.

24 Montgomery, *The Abominable Snowman*, 26.

25 Montgomery, *The Abominable Snowman*, 40.

26 Nakamura, *Cybertypes*.

27 Nakamura, *Cybertypes*, 40.

28 Fickle, *The Race Card*, 3.

29 Fickle, *The Race Card*, 13.

30 Fickle, *The Race Card*, 13.

31 Wark, *Gamer Theory*, 8.

32 Wark, *Gamer Theory*, 6.

33 This is a stanza from E. Y. Chang, "Dice."

34 Borges, "The Garden of Forking Paths," 100.

35 Yang, "Liner Notes: *Intimate, Infinite* (Part 2)."

36 Yang, "Liner Notes: *Intimate, Infinite* (Part 1)."

37 Borges, "The Garden of Forking Paths," 98.

38 Yang, "Liner Notes: *Intimate, Infinite* (Part 2)."

39 Adapted from E. Y. Chang, "Playing Games, Practicing Utopia."

Christopher B. Patterson

The Asiatic and the Anti-Asian Pandemic

On *Paradise Killer*

recognition is the misrecognition you can bear
—Lauren Berlant, *Cruel Optimism*

THE EGO MUST BE SEEN!
APPLY YOUR MARK TO EVERYTHING YOU OWN!
—*Paradise Killer*'s Starlight Computer

There are moments in the game *Paradise Killer* when I incidentally recognize pieces of myself. The game's large public housing architecture places me in the apartment blocks I once occupied in Nanjing, Gimhae, and Hong Kong (see figure 2.1). The game's City Pop–inspired musical score moves me from Korean bars to Hong Kong cafes to the lo-fi study beats on YouTube that feature anime-styled students at work. The game's whodunit mystery told in an over-the-top visual novel format brings me to the Japanese games of *Danganronpa* and *Ace Attorney*, while its slow and open world movement feels directly inspired by the early "F.R.E.E." games of Yu Suzuki's *Shenmue* (2001) and Suda51's *Flower, Sun and Rain* (2001). Yet despite all these recognitions of my Asian/American self, there is not one

Asian-identified face in *Paradise Killer*, even though its cast is dizzyingly diverse: the characters' biographies reveal origins in England, Kenya, Turkey, Scotland, and Romania, and some have Japanese names (e.g., Akiko, Yuri, and Kiwami). The only character with an explicitly Asian background—the fanatical "Witness to the End" from Persia—conceals his face behind a mask and speaks through an echoing ventilation grate. This absence of Asian faces and histories compels me to, almost uniformly, toss the pieces of myself I've found in *Paradise Killer* up as misrecognitions, though perhaps not *mere* misrecognitions. Perhaps, I can bear them just about as well as I can bear Asian American identity itself.

Paradise Killer is a hard game to explain. On one hand, it combines the already-hybridized genre of open world exploration/detective adventure game with the already-hybridized genre of visual novels (as combinations of adventure, romance, eroge). As a low-budget indie game spearheaded by a small British company with a Japanese name,[1] *Paradise Killer* features a queer and campy aesthetic that shows its manufacture everywhere, with its two-dimensional character portraits in three-dimensional environments, and with the player's ability to see multiples of the same recurring character (the demon Shinji) or to happen on major plot points completely at random, sometimes far too early or far too late in the game. Like its vapor-wave soundtrack,

2.1. The Asian-inspired Citizen Housing in *Paradise Killer*. Screenshot by author.

The Asiatic and the Anti-Asian Pandemic   53

there is something hazy about *Paradise Killer*'s ability to be both retro and refreshing, both recognizably Asian in its mood and setting and Western in its characters, designers, and language, both queer in its campy tone and beach sunset color palette, while its narrative focuses sharply on cis-hetero relationships and biological reproduction. These divisions among categories speak volumes about the categories themselves. As I have argued in earlier work, games break many rules of literature and film, where style and content are imagined as both separable and meant to correlate.[2] *Paradise Killer*, like many games, upsets categories, explodes binaries, and proliferates new frames of experiencing a game, so that all recognition becomes misrecognition. But more to the point, *Paradise Killer* also makes me ponder to what extent its Asian and queer forms might either remind players of an other, or as in my own experience, present players with a portal to an open world where they can reminisce upon their many selves.

This chapter will use *Paradise Killer* as a vehicle to revisit and reshape the word *Asiatic*, a troubled term that I attempted to reanimate in my 2020 book, *Open World Empire*, where I used it to characterize games for their "forms, spaces, and personages that many players will find similar to Asia, but that are never exclusively Asian, or are obscured from any other recognizable racial genre, or are not foreclosed to other given identity tropes."[3] Working through theories of erotics, racial embodiment, and virtual otherness from Anne Cheng, Audre Lorde, Lisa Nakamura, Wendy Chun, and others, I conceived of the Asiatic as "a style rather than substance, a technology rather than an essence," as well as a politically charged aesthetic that "shapes the interactions in video games as neither Asian nor Asian American, but as an unrepresentable blend."[4]

Besides the release of *Paradise Killer* in 2020, other events have compelled me to revisit this term: the unexpected capacity of the term to spread across disciplines; the reemergence of yellow peril anti-Asian racism during the COVID-19 pandemic; the book talks where I was often confronted with questions about the term that were not well answered within the book itself: Is *Asiatic* appropriate only to games? How is the term divided from *orientalism*? Is the Asiatic always queer and/or nonserious and/or racist? *Paradise Killer* offers a sideways gaze into these inquiries that allows me to explore these questions lowly, as in, to voice how this term emerged from particular circumstances and experiences, and has continued to grow in my current present.

Before we begin, one context should be clarified: that "the Asiatic" as a term came along within a second book project, after my first book, *Transitive*

54 Christopher B. Patterson

Cultures—a book not about games at all, but about the growth of multiculturalist identities out of Southeast Asian colonial governance—had brought me into a particular way of thinking about identity and race. As a mixed-race Filipino/Chinese/white American with a Hawai'i-based mixed family and even more mixed origins, I've had an ambivalent relationship to Asian American identity, but one I've been able to bear, as I wrote in *Transitive Cultures*, "through active and aggressive imaginative work aimed at reinvigoration, reframing, and remaking."[5] "Asiatic," then was an attempt to remake and to better understand race as transnational processes of racialization that circulate and localize through particular forms of media. To speak of race in this way accounts for how racialization processes both seek to include racialized subjects into socioeconomic systems of neoliberal value, and to leave populations at risk and restriction of life chances in zones of border crossings, incarceration, capitalist exploitation, and healthcare restrictions. "Asiatic" thus sees race as relational processes tied to geopolitical imaginaries, influenced as I am by Kandice Chuh's epistemic shift from thinking about Asian American identities to asking how we can trace Asian racializations, that is, "the production of 'Asian American' as a political and social and racial identity," particularly as they reference other racial forms of whiteness, Blackness, Indigeneity, Latinx, and others.[6] The Asiatic characteristics of games has come to provide one such gateway to remake race, to see otherness otherwise.

Rule #1: *Show Me Your Truth!*

The facts and the truth are not the same. They never were. Perception is reality. Reality is tangible. Reality is intangible. Change a life, change the world. Welcome to paradise.
—*Paradise Killer* marketing byline

For the most part, *Paradise Killer* is a trippy open world adventure game based on vaporwave listening, sauntering exploration, and shit-talking gossip. That is, until the player decides to visit "The Judge" and initiates the ending courtroom scene. In an instant, after the player has become attuned to the queer and colorful Asiatic world of the game's paradise island, the game's mood, tone, and gameplay transform into a courtroom drama that demands their utmost seriousness. The player—as Lady Love Dies—picks up

The Asiatic and the Anti-Asian Pandemic

her gun, collects her facts, and must consider who they are going to accuse of a crime. The punishment for any association whatsoever to the "crime to end all crimes"—murdering the leaders of the island, "the council"—results in execution. Stuck in a room together, the suspects will likely end up betraying each other, especially once one has been condemned to the gun. If the player has collected enough facts about the case, they can use them to expose conspiracies and implicate multiple actors, potentially executing every character in the game. Or the player can select particular masterminds to execute, sparing the low-level criminals. Or the player can just execute those lackeys. Or the player can choose to go along with the most convenient story—that it was all Henry Division, the unfortunate civilian scapegoat. Whatever decision, whatever facts, it is up to the player to create the game's "truth."

Throughout *Open World Empire*, I make the case that the Asiatic is a nonserious, campy, and queer space opened up by the aesthetic forms of video games. However, it is also my truth that the overtly serious mood and consequences of *Paradise Killer*'s trial still exemplifies the Asiatic in the way it conceives of truth itself. Why is this?

To answer, let's turn to the context through which "the Asiatic" emerged in 2020—during a very serious global pandemic in which residual racial formations of yellow peril rose like Goku from the grave for yet another afterlife, and racist attacks on Asian North Americans became too high to reliably establish data (in my own province, British Columbia, racist attacks against Asians were said to have risen over 700 percent).[7] These attacks were buttressed by scientific discourses of public health that held the appearance of objective truth. As Nayan Shah has pointed out, scientific discourses around public health can create firmly held logics "of normal and aberrant" especially when they correlate with "the racial logic of superior and inferior and their reconfiguration over time."[8] Indeed, it was during the 2020 moment of public health reconfiguration, soon after the US president started calling COVID-19 "The China Flu," and just before eight women were killed in Asian-owned spas—six of whom were Asian—by a white man who was reported to be having "a bad day," that I gave a series of book talks about how Asiatic forms of race in video games were "nonserious." This vastly serious moment of racist consolidations and new interethnic collaborations (alongside the resurgence of Black Lives Matter) troubled the ground between "the serious" and "the nonserious." Yet the racism around the COVID-19 pandemic did not seem to me at all "Asiatic." It was, rather, a question of truths.

56 Christopher B. Patterson

In Edward Said's original framing of orientalism, establishing one hegemonic truth as The Truth was foundational to orientalist racisms. As a discourse given validity by academics, proliferation through capitalism and media, and enforcement through the state, orientalism relies heavily on authenticity, essence, and expertise, traits that Said himself sought to resist by framing himself (and the organic intellectual) as an amateur who "refus[es] to be tied down to a specialty."[9] Pivoting from Said, in *Open World Empire*, I describe the Asiatic characters of global games like *Street Fighter II*, *League of Legends*, and *Overwatch* as campy racial depictions that could certainly be called racist and that invoke orientalist tropes but also refuse "the gaze of mastery, expertise, and certainty."[10] Later, I discuss the power of the virtual other or the "Asiatic blur" to resist the production of work "construed as authentic, objective, backed by pedigree and expertise."[11] Similar to Julietta Singh's *Unthinking Mastery*, and Jose Muñoz's and Amber Jamilla Musser's conceptions of Brownness as an already-obscured presence, the Asiatic establishes and helps us confront the obscured digital forms of race where, as John Cheney-Lippold writes, we often presume the presence of air quotes to "emphasize an ironic untruth."[12]

Unlike the racism of the COVID-19 pandemic, and like the end-game trial of *Paradise Killer*, the Asiatic, though often campy and queer, is not entirely "nonserious," though its "truth" *does* differ from the truth-telling of scientific, anthropologic, or state and capitalist discourses that rely on authenticity and essence, whether it is racial or masked through culture or nation. "Asiatic" operates within a realm of divided truths that eludes expertise as facts and figures remain unverifiable. As *Paradise Killer*'s courtroom scene can be triggered at any time during the game, and the all-infallible and objective Judge will agree with whatever the player presents as "your truth" (so long as they can make a strong case), there is always the possibility of "your truth" becoming "the truth," just as there is always the inevitable case of amateur untruths becoming what Stephen Colbert famously called "truthiness," a playful art of not-quite-truth-telling that has become all too common in twenty-four-hour news and social news media. Indeed, *Paradise Killer*'s acceptance of "your truth" is an all-too-tempting premise for the player to present truth through their own biases, and to downplay the presence of contradictory facts. In my final playthrough, I chose not to accuse the game's sympathetic married couple, Lydia and Sam Day Breaks, whose main motivations to collaborate with the conspirators was their desire to free themselves from the island. In effect, I hid facts from the Judge, made a conspiracy look like the fault of a single actor, and denied knowledge. It was no truth at all. Yet my truth became, in the eyes of the state and its citizens, *the* truth. As the game ended there, I could only ponder the potential long-term effects of showing and honoring my truth.

Rule #2: *Oh Baby, Worship Me, Baby!*

Shinji: You guys are the bad guys.

Lady Love Dies: What do you mean?

Shinji: The syndicate worship dying gods that want to rule the world and drown it in a sea of war and blood.

Lady Love Dies: I don't see how that makes us the bad guys.

Paradise Killer's Asiatic realm of multiple truths, unbelievable coincidences, and contradictory facts take place within the insular realm of an island, one masked as a paradise to keep its enslaved citizens happy and forgetful of the "real world." Indeed, the plot of *Paradise Killer* clashes with its Asiatic forms, as well as its queer sun-drenched beach aesthetic and over-the-top sexual mystery. To briefly summarize: ancient gods once ruled the world and controlled mankind until mankind rose against them. Then, sometime around 1000 CE, the Syndicate, a group of radicals who still worshipped these gods, became immortal and, in an effort to entice the gods back to Earth, created islands in an alternative reality, then kidnapped and enslaved people from the real world—"citizens"—and forced them into psychic worshipping rituals. However, as such worship can invite other supernatural forces, one by one, each island was infected by demons, and each had to be ritualistically sacrificed, then replaced by another island. *Paradise Killer* takes place on Island #24. All of its characters, besides the scapegoated Henry, are part of the evil, lunatic cult of the Syndicate.

Slowly unraveling the narrative of *Paradise Killer* can be jarring, as the player only learns of these facts as they are inundated with cute and kitschy symbols of heart shapes, phallic "blood crystals" currency, gorgeous half-naked flirts, and nostalgic references to cassettes and flip phones. Despite your freedom of choice and freedom to roam throughout the island, nothing you do can even remotely affect the cycle of kidnapping, enslavement, and slaughter. Indeed, the ludological dissonance of the game's campy gameplay, with its narrative of enslavement and religious fanaticism, is a revisitation of the cognitive dissonance that classifies Lovecraftian horror, where a person's state of mind will also deteriorate into madness when faced with the harsh, indifferent, and incomprehensible cosmos. But *Paradise Killer* is no horrifying experience. In fact, one could argue that its Asiatic attunement allows the game to present real-world horrors in a way that is comprehensible and approachable, without necessarily being domesticated or gentrified into the palatable and the censored. How, we might ask, does the Asiatic allow such a revisioning?

When *Open World Empire* went in print in late 2019, there was an episode of the Netflix television show *Black Mirror* that seemed to encapsulate the Asiatic's ability to revise the horrors of the world into a queer and approachable media. The episode, "Striking Vipers," follows two old friends, Danny and Karl, two masculine, straight, Black men, who reconnect after eleven years apart by playing a newly released virtual reality version of *Striking Vipers*, a fighting game they once played as college roommates. In previous episodes of *Black Mirror*, virtual and augmented reality appears as a militaristic technology symbolizing techno-paranoia. In the episode "Playtest," augmented reality devices create an actual horror game that can kill the viewer through signal interference. Similarly, in the 2016 episode "Men against Fire," augmented reality technology forces American soldiers to visualize refugees as monstrous terrorists.[13] In "Striking Vipers," though, VR technology is portrayed through the softer forms of video game play and Asiatic cuteness, as Danny and Karl revisit their childhood through inhabiting the virtual characters Lance and Roxanne (see figure 2.2). The game nevertheless remains a threat, not to refugee lives or to technological breakdown but to heteronormative forms of futurity and family, as the Asiatic form of the game permits the two friends to act out their erotic desires for each other by having passionate and repeated virtual sex.

Even as the game *Striking Vipers*—like the real games *Street Fighter* and *Tekken*—features typical racial stereotypes for the purpose of enacting violence, the game's Asiatic associations with bizarreness, silliness, and Asia itself, allow new erotic relations to emerge. The game's homoeroticism feels more taboo when seen from the point of view of the episode's Black male leads, who, since their time apart, have incorporated further into the norms of hetero-patriarchal and capitalist success. As studies have shown, the fighting game community is one of the most diverse in gaming, and its players of

The Asiatic and the Anti-Asian Pandemic   **59**

2.2. Danny and Karl play as Lance and Roxanne in the fictional game *Striking Vipers*. Screenshot by author.

color often gravitate to Japanese-made fighting games that so often depict racial stereotypes.[14] Indeed, the episode's poster patterns the same slash effect and bisexual lighting of the Oscar-winning film *Moonlight*, a text that is also famous for portraying Black male queerness through an Asiatic form, as the film borrows heavily from the visual styles and cinematography of the Hong Kong filmmaker Wong Kar Wai. Through its imperial and Asiatic designation, the fictional *Striking Vipers* video game provides a space for new erotic practices to emerge not against but through practices of a militarized technology.

The Asiatic characteristics in games have often represented an alternative means of approaching new technology that departs from the fears of Western militarism, as well as the techno-orientalist fears of surveillance and control. As Nick Dyer-Witheford and Greig de Peuter argued in *Games of Empire*, the shift from American to Japanese games in the 1980s is often narrated as a political and historical "reclamation" where "video games were rescued not by the military-industrial complex from whence they had sprung but by the victims of its atomic bomb."[15] Indeed, video games as a medium continue to represent the erotic and Asiatic form of the digital as a whole; where social media portrays accountable, transparent, exposed, and meticulously drawn selves, games are envisioned as islands, places of digital anonymity with no direct real-world impact. Through the Asiatic forms of games like *Striking Vipers* and *Paradise Killer*, the "horrors" of the real world's asymmetrical power relations are not merely made approachable but are erotically reanimated into other only-just-imaginable possibilities.

Rule #3: *Breathe Life Back into Paradise!*

I grew up without a dad on a synthetic island in a
different reality, forced to worship gods that want
to rule the world. I needed something to do.
—The citizen Henry Division, when asked about his crimes

While the *Black Mirror* episode "Striking Vipers" illustrates the Asiatic in games, I would hesitate to call it, or any episode of the *Black Mirror* series, Asiatic in the way games like *Paradise Killer* are, because it lacks the futuristic, insular, and islandic space of play and experiment that are so crucial to how the Asiatic appears in games. As Colin Milburn has argued, Huizinga's "magic circle" of experiment and play can better be thought of as islandic, a space that for some invokes a tropical paradise (or a home), and for others the evolutionary insights of Darwin's Galápagos, and for others the atomic nuclear tests of Bikini Atoll. Islands operate as both spaces of queer Asiatic play, "a place for melodrama as much as alien experimentation," as well as spaces for experimental world making that offer "discrete space[s] for prototyping the world of tomorrow: a crucible for futurity."[16] The performance theorist Dorinne Kondo describes world making as the collaborative and productive processes of race and identity making that "evokes sociopolitical transformation and the impossibility of escaping power, history, and culture."[17] Worlds are imagined through repeated interactions that, in time, establish new norms and conventions, and worlds can be remade so long as they always work with the givenness of language and history. If games are world makers, then these worlds are responding to and refracting the "real-world" genres of race, class, sexuality, gender, nation, and so on. As Kondo stresses, in a world structured by race, world making as a frame allows us to trace "the production of race—racialized structures of inequality, racialized labor, the racialized aesthetics of genre, racialized subjectivities, racial affect."[18]

Paradise Killer's making of a queer Asiatic world can seem utopic, an attempt to grasp the queerness on the horizon, as it rejects the militaristic technology and Western cosmologies of the "real world" to envision a future of racially diverse immortals, welcoming the player as a new inhabitant. But even though it takes place on an island, *Paradise Killer* is in no way insular; in fact, one might see it as a critique of insularity itself, a bare refusal of the logics of island thinking. A final question: How does *Paradise Killer* do this?

The smoking gun to this riddle is the sole citizen left on Paradise Island #24, Henry Division, an easy scapegoat for the Syndicate, which blames him for "the crime to end all crimes." And like many scapegoats, Henry may in fact be the only Asian face around (see figure 2.3). Though Henry's face appears East Asian, his racial origins are a mystery, one that the player is never asked to investigate. His father, the immortal councilman Eyes Kiwami, has a Japanese name and lives in a house that mimics a Japanese temple; nevertheless, he is likely not of Asian descent himself, for his other son, Dainonigate, appears totally white. That leaves Henry's mother, the citizen Rina Division, who, despite the Syndicate's dogmatic surveillance of its citizens, has no photos or records about her racial background. If we take another look at the housing where the citizens lived and the graveyards where their massacred bodies lie, we notice that the Asiatic architecture of the game seems to have been built solely for the citizens themselves, while the immortals live in ornate Greco-Roman palaces. Perhaps our protagonist, Lady Love Dies,

2.3. *Paradise Killer*'s Henry Division, "Possessed Citizen Accused of Mass Murder." Screenshot by author.

62   Christopher B. Patterson

could interview more citizens to find *the truth* to the game's mystery of racial origins, but besides Henry, all the citizens—men, women, children—were sacrificed to the gods before she returned to the island. Their presence can only be felt in the whispers of ghosts, in left-behind relics like the diary that complains of "days that go on for months," the pain pills required by workers who must haul all goods by hand, and in the children's stones painted with hopeful wishes for the next life (but, as stated plainly, "Citizens don't have a next life").

So here's my truth, culled from a selection of clues: the kidnapped, enslaved, abused, and then sacrificed citizens of *Paradise Killer* are Asian. They are kidnapped from East Asian regions and forced into labor and worship in housing that mimics the lives they were brutally torn away from so that the queer and diverse "main characters" can continue to play their little games of gossip and intrigue. *Paradise Killer* is thus not a game that seeks to create reparative affects or queer and racial solidarities—quite the opposite. It is a game that encapsulates the often cutesy, queer, and Asiatic ways that the world around us reproduces yellow peril, techno-orientalism, and anti-Asian racism, particularly in the form of Asian debt-slavery within the industry of Information Technology (what I call the "Open World Empire"). Rather than a refusal of H. P. Lovecraft's own anti-Asian and xenophobic racism, *Paradise Killer*'s world is a contemporary reimagining of it, awash in Asiatic pink. To be clear, I am not saying that the game, its developers, or its players are racist—again, quite the opposite. In simulating anti-Asian racism within a queer Asiatic setting, *Paradise Killer* allows us to understand how, through the Asiatic itself, we can continue to reproduce racial and imperial violences by obscuring or dismissing the cheapened life and labor of Asian people, legitimated by their supposed "excess" population growth. In other words, *Paradise Killer* is not a celebration of the queer world-making potential of the Asiatic but a condemnation of it.

This truth was admittedly a revelation to me, who wrote an entire book on the Asiatic. Only after playing *Paradise Killer* was I able to unpack the ambivalences I felt during 2020 at talks, conferences, and laptop surfaces, as I repeatedly confronted my own discomfort with this term. The message that *Paradise Killer* allowed me to conceive was this: yes, the Asiatic can offer new possibilities, more erotic, more queer, perhaps more "woke," than our current dystopias of real-world militaristic and racist horror. Yet this capacity to make worlds through digital media both requires and helps sustain the vast exploitation, precarity, and death of millions of people, many

The Asiatic and the Anti-Asian Pandemic **63**

of whom are centered within the microprocessor factories of Southeast Asia, the "factories of the world" in southern China—whom Jack Linchuan Qiu calls the "iSlaves" of tech megafactories; who live within an "unfreedom of labor"[19]—as well as the low-level designers and coders across the globe experiencing "crunch." Like *Paradise Killer*'s Syndicate, we players and academics tend to stay within the game, treating it as its own isolated island, a futuristic Asiatic wonderland rife for experiment and play, recognizing and misrecognizing pieces of ourselves in it, all the while indifferent to the living and breathing subjects who are present in our real-life worlds but who remain unnamed and unrecognized in our open worlds.

The island laboratory is, as Milburn writes, "an incubator for the future,"[20] and what has become clearer in the time of Donald Trump, COVID-19, and *Paradise Killer* is that an Asiatic future does not bode well for the vast majority of Asian people or for Asian Americans. Indeed, the problem with the Asiatic is less the definitional categories of the term and more the fact that the Asiatic itself is so frequently unrecognized and unnamed and thus remains obscured as a default reference for an alternative to Western militaristic technologies, much like the island utopias of Thomas More and Francis Bacon. Like islands, Asiatic games feel totalizing, isolated, perfect spaces for experimental thinking, while in fact the Asiatic itself helps to fuel the well-oiled machines of capitalism and empire as they continue to operate at full throttle (they are more like the colonized islands of the Pacific, outfitted with both tourist beaches and military bases). *Paradise Killer* participates in Asiatic world making not as utopia but as warning sign. As we investigate and explore the game's series of riddles, accusations, and truths, the real injustices remain in all their evil banality. Games, our islands of paradise, allow us to make new worlds where we feel seen. We recognize ourselves in them because they are built like us: through the logics of capture, control, and death.

. . . and may you reach the moon!

Notes

1 *Paradise Killer*'s UK-based developer is Kaizen Game Works (*kaizen* is Japanese for "change for the better").

2 See Patterson, *Open World Empire*, chap. 5.

3 Patterson, *Open World Empire*, 58.

4 Patterson, *Open World Empire*, 60.

5 Patterson, *Transitive Cultures*, 201.

6 Chuh, *The Difference Aesthetics Makes*, 126.

7 Pearson, "This Is the Anti-Asian Hate Crime Capital."

8 Shah, *Contagious Divides*, 8.

9 Said, *Representations of the Intellectual*, 76.

10 Patterson, *Open World Empire*, 70.

11 Patterson, *Open World Empire*, 233.

12 Cheney-Lippold, *We Are Data*, 19. See also Singh, *Unthinking Mastery*; Musser, *Sensual Excess*; and Muñoz, *The Sense of Brown*.

13 See chapter 4 of *Open World Empire* for my analysis of "Men against Fire."

14 Epps, "Black Lives Have Always Mattered in the Fighting Game Community."

15 Dyer-Witheford and de Peuter, *Games of Empire*, 14.

16 Milburn, *Mondo Nano*, 78, 77.

17 Kondo, *Worldmaking*, 29.

18 Kondo, *Worldmaking*, 25.

19 Qiu, *Goodbye iSlave*, 34.

20 Milburn, *Mondo Nano*, 77–78.

Takeo Rivera

Asian, Adjacent

3

Utopian Longing and Model
Minority Mediation in *Disco Elysium*

The City on the Edge of History

Since the fall of the Berlin Wall in 1989, the hegemonic attitude of much of the Global North across the political spectrum has proclaimed the absolute victory of liberal capitalism as both the final stage of economic and social organization, with any serious challenge to this reigning order rendered futilely quixotic. The truth of the claim notwithstanding, this is the grand narrative best encapsulated by Francis Fukuyama's celebratory claim of the "end of history,"[1] with the lasting effects of liberal capitalism's hegemonic power lambasted on the left, most famously by Fredric Jameson in *Postmodernism* (1989) and the British cultural theorist Mark Fisher in *Capitalist Realism* (2009). Certainly, contemporary global trends toward reactionary far-right authoritarianism in the late 2010s and early 2020s would forcefully rebuke Fukuyama's thesis in regard to liberalism, but the cultural domination of capital remains difficult to unseat. As Fisher puts it succinctly, "Capitalism seamlessly occupies the horizons of the thinkable," erecting both the social and aesthetic limits of the Global North's metropole.[2] Realism has become the aesthetic lingua franca of our age, and the boundary of the thinkable, and with it the truth-claim of capitalism's inevitability.

Fisher's initial formulations of his solution would appear in his introduction to his sequel project, *Acid Communism*, unfinished before his tragic suicide in 2017. In this work, Fisher turns to 1960s Anglophone psychedelic counterculture as a critical cultural potentiality to break free of capitalist malaise. "The crucial defining feature of the psychedelic," writes Fisher, "is the question of consciousness, and its relationship to what is experienced as reality. If the very fundamentals of our experience, such as our sense of space and time, can be altered, does that not mean that the categories by which we live are plastic, mutable?"[3] To resuscitate the aims of the counterculture, Fisher proposes acid communism, which is "the convergence of class consciousness, socialist-feminist consciousness-raising and psychedelic consciousness, the fusion of new social movements with a communist project, an unprecedented aestheticisation of everyday life."[4]

The argument of *Acid Communism*, preliminary and unfinished though it is, is a compelling and organic extension of Fisher's observations in *Capitalist Realism* but relies on a hitherto unacknowledged basis in colonialist orientalism. The countercultural elements to which Fisher alludes heavily exploited South and East Asian spiritualities in order to produce their affects of radical alterity—an alterity relative to capitalist whiteness, but one that has drawn on a logic of commodification by other means. The co-optation of various Asian spiritualities to produce an orientalized mystique for various countercultural forms is so commonplace as to be assumed; for example, as Jane Iwamura has observed, the "Beat Generation and its followers in their own unique interpretation adopted Buddhism as a way to distinguish themselves from 'middle-class non-identity' and to guide and justify their own pursuits."[5] Yet, Iwamura continues, "Zen became something to 'try on' and 'entertain,' rather than something that directly challenged American values. In fact, Zen as *stylized religion* covertly consolidated American national identity and its capitalist orientation."[6] Such a similar dynamic played out throughout the next decades with respect to multiple Asian religions, with "counterculture" adopting such two-dimensional, commodified versions of Asianness to satisfy utopian yearning for oriental mysticism, including in the tech industry, as elaborated extensively by

R. John Williams.[7] This racialized dynamic goes unproblematized in *Acid Communism*, with the central protagonists of the socialist spirit quest as white artists of the Global North.[8]

I do not reject Fisher's central dialectic between capitalist realism and acid communism; in fact, his observations of the hegemonic grip of bourgeois realism and the necessity for an aesthetic break from its logics are difficult to deny. As Fredric Jameson writes in *Antinomies of Realism*, "The realistic novelist has a vested interest, an ontological stake, in the solidity of social reality, on the resistance of bourgeois society to history and to change,"[9] so it logically follows that something like "the psychedelic" offers a disruption of contemporary neoliberal ideology, whose ongoing circumscription of political imagination remains dauntless. Nevertheless, Fisher's critique is incomplete without serious attendance to orientalism, coloniality, and race. One can begin with Christopher B. Patterson's recent theorization of the "Asiatic," a strategy of acknowledged virtual otherness found across Roland Barthes, Michel Foucault, and Eve Kosofsky Sedgwick that enabled them to achieve considerable breakthroughs out of various hegemonic Western normativities.[10] In Patterson's reparative formulation, the Asiatic is an intentionally fantastical Orient, but one that avoids any presumption of epistemological mastery and becomes a necessary component for rethinking queer relations outside Eurocentric grids of intelligibility.

Fisher's acid communism is thoroughly "Asiatic" in Patterson's sense, but it also gestures to a particular kind of political relationality that I term, to borrow a title from a Margaret Cho song, "Asian adjacency."[11] By "Asian adjacency," I refer to a quality found across varying manifestations of Asiatic racial form that arise in articulating communist futurity,[12] a "besideness" that provincializes white epistemology as a position relative to either superego model minoritarianism or mystical, exotified wonder.[13] Rather than the "white adjacency" characteristic of model minority ideology, which places the Asian in a complicit positionality within white supremacist racial capitalism, Asian adjacency instead invokes Asianness as a mediator of utopian political imagination without actually positioning "Asia" as its utopia, fluctuating between idealization, moral comparison, and wonderment, holding together multiple relationalities open for contestation.

It is through Asian adjacency that I analyze *Disco Elysium*, the 2019 indie role-playing game developed by UK-based indie game developer ZA/UM. Written by Estonian novelist Robert Kurvitz, Helen Hindpere, Argo Tuulik,

Cash de Cuir, and Olga Moskvina,[14] *Disco Elysium* arrived on the gaming scene to near-unanimous critical fanfare, nominated for several "Game of the Year" awards and winning Best Narrative and Best Role-Playing Game from the 2019 Game Awards. *Disco Elysium* puts its player in fictional Martinaise, the district of a cosmopolitan, vaguely European city called Revachol, which languishes under foreign occupation by a multinational alliance of liberal-capitalist governments called the Coalition, which had suppressed a communist revolution fifty years prior. Assuming the role of a self-loathing, substance-abusing, amnesiac detective named Harrier DuBois, the player is tasked with solving the murder of a right-wing mercenary who had been sent to break a dockworkers' strike, while simultaneously plumbing the depths of the character's depression and anguish.

Moreover, *Disco Elysium* is a game that embraces, but also supersedes, the political and aesthetic charge of acid communism, including its relationship to race and orientalism. The writers are openly Marxist; during their acceptance speech for the Fresh Indie Game Award at the Game Awards, writer Helen Hindpere said, "I would like to thank all of the great people who came before us . . . Marx and Engels for providing us the political education, thank you!"[15] Correspondingly, Revachol is the city on the edge of history, inundated with a melancholy for a communism that never actualized, currently governed instead by an ideology of centrist normativity, but its political yearnings express themselves through the game's starkly expressionist aesthetics, its mind-altering psychedelics, and its forays into magical realism. Moreover, like the psychedelics of Fisher's acid communism, *Disco Elysium* necessitates the presence of Asian adjacency to negotiate its political affects, but does so with considerable, diasporic difference. In actuality, although drug use and hallucination are rampant throughout the game, *Disco Elysium*'s Asian adjacency lies less in its *psychedelics* than in its *psyche*, its ego-ideal, its projections of fantasy, and its inculcation of wonder. Correspondingly, this chapter focuses attention on three manifestations of Asian adjacency: DuBois's police partner, an "Asian" diasporic man named Kim Kitsuragi; the racial ambiguity of the Marxian Kras Mazov; and the semimythical Insulindian Phasmid. Although deeply flawed in its racial politics, *Disco Elysium* nevertheless presents a racialized dialectic that yearns for a liberatory, postcapitalist futurity to resolve its stark contradictions, utilizing Asianness with and against orientalist clichés to generate its political idealizations.

Difference with a Difference: The Model Minority Ego-Ideal

Unlike many games in its role-playing genre, *Disco Elysium* in many respects disempowers its player through the avatarial vessel of Harrier DuBois, a formerly successful detective in the Revachol Citizens Militia who has, since the departure of his wife, fallen into a bout of self-destructive depression, resulting in a drug-fueled bender just before the start of the game's action.[16] As a consequence of hitting rock bottom, DuBois begins the game with amnesia, prompting the player to effectively reconstruct his personality from the ground up, principally through dialogue choices that allow the player to assume a range of different positions, from aggressive to apologetic, feminist to misogynist, empathetic to cruel. The possible permutations of events in *Disco Elysium* are legion, requiring dozens of playthroughs to fully access every possible short-term outcome, although intriguingly, the conclusion of the game remains unchanged. The paths may vary widely, and the final debrief reflects the player's actions, yet the apprehending of the killer will occur no matter how the player arrives at that point. Meanwhile, the world of the game plays out both in the luscious oil-paint art style of the physical world and the thousands of lines of expository text and dialogue that unfolds on the sidebar of the user interface. Stylistically, the game presents a visual environment of futurist grays of the streets contrasting with the often vibrantly impressionist yellows, reds, greens, and oranges of the clothing, and karaoke and dance halls, visually enacting a dialectic between the whimsy of Muñozian excess and urban-modernist Kafkaesque ennui.[17]

Notably, each of Harrier's levelable skills occupies a schizophrenic place in his mind, talking to his ego-self throughout the game by providing advice and insight, but often also bickering among one another.[18] The skills are grouped into four general categories: Intellect, which includes skills like Rhetoric, Logic, and Encyclopedia; Psyche, which includes the likes of Empathy, Suggestion, and Authority; Physique, which includes Endurance and Pain Threshold; and Motorics, which includes dexterous abilities such as Hand/Eye Coordination and Perception. The twenty-four Skills become characters in their own right, each with a distinct, insistent personality vying for influence within Harrier's mind. Harrier's propensity for hallucination and internal bickering, not to mention the intense brushstrokes and colors of Aleksander Rostov's oil-painting environmental overlays and textures, represents a sense of shattered reality and fractured consciousness reflective of Mark Fisher's psychedelic, all the more intensified by the implication that mind-altering substances are at least partly responsible for his mental state. But it is not so much the centrality of actual psychedelics so much as what they highlight, the psyche itself, that occupies the most verbal presence in the game. The experience of playing through the game, with the twenty-four internal representations of Harrier's psyche bickering and occupying an enormous proportion of the game's CRPG narrative text, has a surrealist acid-trip quality to it, sometimes keeping the player in a haze of competing internal thoughts rather than engaging with the exterior world. But that exterior world is most readily accessible through the figure of Harrier's partner, Kim Kitsuragi.

Shortly after awakening with amnesia in the wake of his drug-filled, suicidal bender, Harrier meets Kim Kitsuragi in the lobby of his hotel. Kim Kitsuragi is *Disco Elysium*'s sole Asian-racialized character, but also the only NPC party member (besides Harry's inner voices) who remains a near-constant presence throughout the game. Kim sports circular teashades, neatly combed short hair, and a wiry build. First described via the in-game text as a "bespectacled man in an orange bomber jacket . . . tapping his foot on the floor," he often keeps his hands folded behind his back in a formal military "at ease." As the deuteragonist, Kitsuragi is undoubtedly the most important and present NPC in the game, representing a paragon of competence and principle that consistently contrasts with DuBois's wildness, excess, and inner psychological torment. But most importantly, Kitsuragi's diasporic Asianness becomes, in fact, a necessary ingredient for DuBois's inner journey. Kitsuragi is Asian, adjacent: he provides not so much a yellow perilist counterpoint to white interiority as he does a semipermeable sounding board on which the player can gauge DuBois's emotional progress. Kitsuragi is not a techno-orientalist bugaboo but a model minority superego to a whiteness characterized principally by failure and ruin. The developers of *Disco Elysium* cast white Belgian actor-musician Jullien Champenois in the role in an unfortunate whitewashed casting; however, Champenois notes that the most necessary ethnic marker for Kim's casting was not Asianness but, rather, a "French accent."[19] Aurally, this is the most distinct feature of Kim, whose French accent permeates his deliberative, restrained vocal performance throughout the game. The effete properness of Kim's vocal presentation suggests a layering of model minoritarian forms, allowing him to assume a hypercivilized position relative to the chaotic Harrier.

Asian, Adjacent   **71**

Although DuBois's political ideology can vary widely depending on the player's dialogue choices, DuBois's masculine whiteness remains fixed, as does Kitsuragi's racial otherness relative to it.[20] Early on, the player/Harrier can choose to tell Kim, "You don't look like other people around here." A dialogue then transpires, and with a high enough Encyclopedia stat, you may learn more about "Seol," Kim's ancestral motherland:

YOU: You don't look like other people around here.

KIM KITSURAGI: That's because I'm half-Seolite. Or quarter. My father's father was from Seol—so was my grandmother, but from my mother's side. . . . [*He shakes his head.*] It's not an interesting topic.

YOU: What is Seol?

KIM KITSURAGI: It's a part of the world, officer. A geopolitical entity— *and* a geographic division. I told you it wouldn't be interesting.

ENCYCLOPEDIA: Seol is a protectionist, isolationist panisiolary state west of the Insulindian isola. Actually, it's *quite* interesting; some would even say mysterious . . .

YOU: You're only making it *sound* uninteresting. I still want to know more about Seol.[21]

KIM KITSURAGI: You're barking up the wrong tree. I don't speak a word of Seolite, I've never met either one of my grandparents. And I've never *been* to Seol. [*He seems almost proud of these things.*] I'm a regular Revacholiere.

Harrier, racked by amnesia, begins the exchange with a presumably innocent but nevertheless microaggressive observation of Kim's phenotypic otherness, followed by Kim providing patient explanation of his Asianness and Harrier's ongoing questions about Seol, which is something of an analog of Korea and Japan, which we can infer from the orientalized description of the isolationist nation and the spellings of the names (Seol ≈ Seoul, Kitsuragi having pseudo-Japanese phonetics). Although Harrier is innocent, the player is not—as an Asian American player, I felt conflicted by the choice of initiating this dialogue, knowing my own irritation at being on the receiving end of such a question, yet eager to delve further into Kim's Asian diasporic

72 Takeo Rivera

background—I sensed that Harrier's bumbling amnesiac inquiry would be the principal means of learning more. Encyclopedia, which ostensibly represents Harrier's internalized voice of book knowledge, describes Seol in thoroughly orientalized terms—protectionist, isolationist, and especially *mysterious*— stoking Harrier's interest more (and thus lending said orientalism epistemic authority). Kim then proudly disavows his ethnic identity, insisting that he is "a regular Revacholiere."

Kitsuragi is a racially familiar figure in ethnic studies, who makes a claim to legitimacy through cultural assimilationism. Within an Asian American context, Kim reflects a well-trodden World War II–era Japanese American Citizens' League–style hyper-Americanness, prideful of his severance from his immigrant background, which the game exoticizes as oriental-barbarous. Kim is, on an individual basis, a model minority, although there does not appear to be any racewide basis for Seolite-Revacholier model minoritarianism as such, but the articulation of his antiracism is principally through assimilationist logics of respectability, a racial strategy that remains prevalent in contemporary continental Europe.[22]

Correspondingly, throughout *Disco Elysium*, Kim is the most exemplary law enforcement agent in the game, outstripping DuBois in terms of competence, professionalism, and reputation. Whereas Seol exists in an ambiguous haze of generic orientalized despotism and the authoritarianism that accompanies it, Kim is less authoritarian than authoritative, leading not through command but through example. Although Kim works in a different precinct, DuBois's disaffected teammates speak to Kim with deep reverence for his accomplishments at the conclusion of the game. Kim does not always comment; rather, he casts a constant, if deliberately understated, judgmental gaze on the range of the player's actions throughout the game. A common recurrence is Kim raising an eyebrow, which often immediately sends a sense of shame down Harrier's spine. While Harrier is a chronically depressed, slovenly, pungent drug addict whose face has been eerily frozen into an otherworldly smile, Kim is a beacon of order, duty, and proper procedure. Here Tara Fickle's astute reading of model minoritarianism is quite illuminating: in her analysis of William Petersen's early articulation of the Japanese American model minority, Fickle observes that the model minority theory is "ultimately less interested in holding up Japanese Americans as a punitive example for blacks. If anything, he considered the former a far more effective parable for white Americans. . . . These were not . . . merely model *minorities*, but model *Americans*."[23] Similarly, Kim is Harrier's ego-ideal, not only a model minority but a model Revacholier, and part of what animates Kim's desire to excel is precisely that sense of feeling out of place. This applies equally to Kim's ethnicity as his sexuality; Kim subtly hints at his own queerness throughout the game when he amusedly reacts to Harrier's bewilderment at homosexual imagery, and through sufficient dialogue and leveling choices, Kim may reveal that he is gay, although this has no additional bearing on the storyline.[24]

In many respects, Kim's competence, detachment, and achievement reflect the type of character most RPG players will usually assume within the genre, as opposed to the slovenly, excessive Harrier. With the dialectic between Kim and Harrier, *Disco Elysium* positions whiteness—often, *leftist* whiteness—as the position of failure relative to model minority Asianness, inviting the player to take on a complex identification mediated by Asian adjacency. Harrier, as the full embodiment of failure, embraces the position of failure even more so by choosing a communist orientation—when the player asks Rhetoric, "What's this *communism* even about," Rhetoric responds, "Failure. It's about failure . . . abject failure. Total, irreversible defeat on all fronts!" but with the hope that, as the comically framed "Last Communist," the player can somehow have different fortunes than their predecessors. Yet regardless of political orientation, players often find themselves yearning to be, or at least be like, the Asian/Asiatic Kim, the character most closely aligned to the RPG's power fantasy—unless the player wishes to go in the opposite direction and abandon all semblance of success, which is its own tacit acknowledgment of Kim's moral and professional superiority.

Perhaps the only instance in *Disco Elysium* in which Kim breaks his generally serene disposition is when he is verbally harassed by a character known only as the "racist lorry driver" (figure 3.1), when the player first initiates dialogue with the driver standing several yards away from the strike:

RACIST LORRY DRIVER: "Welcome to Revachol!" announces the rotund man. The remark isn't addressed to you. It's addressed to the Lieutenant . . .

KIM KITSURAGI: "Don't you *Welcome to Revachol* me," the lieutenant fires back. "My grandfather came here from a three-thousand-year-old racist-isolationist culture, while your ancestors came to this island a mere three hundred years ago."

"Every school of thought and government has failed in this city—but I love it nonetheless. It belongs to me as much as it belongs to you."

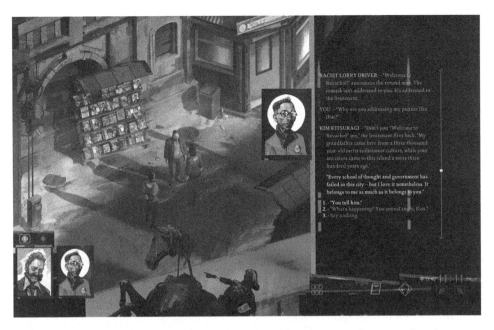

3.1. The Racist Lorry Driver harasses Kim Kitsuragi, who responds. Screenshot from *Disco Elysium* taken by author, courtesy of ZA/UM.

The interaction further cements Kim as a figure whose route to antiracism is through assimilation, and with it an orientalist disavowal of the barbarism from which his ancestors immigrated. In some respects, Kim's assimilationist antiracism reflects Homi Bhabha's oft-cited mimic man, whose assumption of the colonizer's habitus exposes the constructedness of the colonizer's racial superiority to begin with.[25] However, Kim's mimicry/model minoritarianism leaves orientalism intact—Seol is once again cast in terms of exoticized barbarism from which Western civilization has rescued Kim's ancestors. Kim is thus simultaneously racially exceptional *and* avowedly normative, even as he perpetuates exoticism through disavowal. While Kim is the Asian adjacent to Harrier, *Kim positions himself adjacent to Asianness*. The exotic is external rather than internal to Kim, decidedly antithetical to the iconic, vexed sleuth and purveyor of orientalized wisdom, Charlie Chan (while sharing Chan's serenity and logical prowess). In this respect, Kim resists epistemological mastery, even if Harrier's internal voice yearns for colonial knowledge. It is through not racial exceptionalism but exceptional racial mundaneness that Kim aims to distinguish himself, recalling

Asian, Adjacent   75

Ju Yon Kim's argument that the quotidian is a key domain for Asian diasporic self-fashioning.[26]

In terms of social disruption and normativity, despite Kim's sexual preference for men, Harrier is the "queerer" figure relative to insistently lawful Kim.[27] While each of Harrier's personality traits clings to its specific bias, Kim plays the role of deadpan "straight man" (in the comedic sense, *not* a sexual sense, yet remaining essentially homonormative), bemused sounding board. His relationship to the player is adjacency, a constant besideness that neither intrudes nor wholly surrenders.

Yet what is peculiar about Kim's Asian adjacency is the juxtaposition of his assimilationist model minoritarianism with his ironic actual lack of success in the course of the game. As Chris Breault states, "Before the player even learns their own name, they learn to rely on Kim's judgment—he immediately outlines a plan, establishes that Harry's badge is missing, and begins the work of interviewing suspects." Yet, Breault keenly observes, "it takes a while to see that Kim, the voice of reason, is usually wrong."[28] Indeed, as the mystery of the murder of the strike-breaking mercenary unfolds, it becomes increasingly clear that Harrier's messier, sometimes-nonsensical tangents—as opposed to Kim's straightforward, commonsensical approaches—become key to not only solving the murder but also reflecting on the thinkability of political futurity itself. As the final section of this essay will explore, this is particularly true should the player decide to pursue the Insulindian Phasmid, a cryptid with no apparent bearing to the murder case; the player can choose to complete Phasmid side quests (like laying out and restocking bait traps) out of pleasure or amusement while Kim repeatedly bemoans the activity as a waste of time. As a consequence, Kim reflects an inverse of Harrier, the paragon of discipline to Harrier's chaos—a well-worn police procedural cliché, to be sure, but his model minority status coupled with the shadow of orientalist exoticism helps mediate a psychedelic utopian consciousness.

Acid Communism with Asian Characteristics

Rather than the moral alignment that has become a convention in many North American RPGs,[29] *Disco Elysium* instead deploys a political alignment system that allows the player character to embrace one or more of the four principal worldviews: Communism, Moralism (essentially centrist liberalism), Fascism, and Ultraliberalism (neoliberal capitalism). The player can choose any of these alignments through dialogue choices of the game, yet the game's own storyline ultimately embraces a narrative of communist melancholia. Given the overt political stance of the developers, I would assert that the communist political path is the "canonical" one, and the one that best fits the narrative themes of the larger storyline.

Of the four political alignments, Kim claims neutrality, instead embracing his role, above all else, as a model officer of the Revachol Citizens' Militia, though his attempt at apoliticality tacitly makes him a centrist Moralist.[30] Thus, the game's sole Asian NPC represents a figure of multiple levels of normativity: of idealized police behavior, of genre (the detective procedural), of assimilationist culture, and of political alignment. The ideological description of Moralism in the game, as described by the "Thought Cabinet" perk "Kingdom of Conscience," is a searing description of political centrism, which effectively describes Kim's political role throughout the game:

> The Kingdom of Conscience will be exactly as it is now. Moralists don't really *have* beliefs. Sometimes they stumble on one, like on a child's toy left on the carpet. The toy must be put away immediately. And the child reprimanded. Centrism isn't change—not even incremental change. It is *control*. Over yourself and the world. Exercise it. Look up at the sky, at the dark shapes of Coalition airships hanging there. Ask yourself: is there something sinister in moralism? And then answer: no. God is in his heaven. Everything is normal on Earth.

Overall, moralism represents the Fukuyamaist position, humanist liberalism as triumphant default, an ideology of normalcy that contrasts with the utopian dream of communism, the misogynist violence of fascism, and the unfettered avarice of ultraliberalism (neoliberalism). As model minority, Kim represents realism in its ideological and narratological functions alike, having disavowed the orientalist mystique of wonderment to become its exact opposite. However, this is complicated slightly by the fact that Kim also wears an old orange bomber jacket of the communards' Revolutionary Air Corps, for reasons that Kim seems uncomfortable to disclose, suggesting that there is, in fact, a part of him that may have once nostalgically yearned for a left-wing political futurity. Moralism may thus be the position of detached, resigned pragmatism for Kim, as it has been for the post-1990s left at large.[31] Kim's moralism is not so much an enthusiastic passion as psychological management, establishing what Kim has learned to be his horizon of possibility.

Asian, Adjacent **77**

Perpetually the moderate, Kim moderates Harrier's excesses, but in doing so ironically necessitates that Harrier give these ideas verbal form. Eventually, Harrier and Kim discover a bust of Kras Mazov in the apartment of a communard. Described in-game as the founder of scientific socialism and leader of the first major communist revolution, Mazov is an obvious analog for Karl Marx, sporting a wide white mane and thick mustache and beard. Harrier might begin to suspect that he himself is Mazov, to Kim's great annoyance. Gazing on the bust, Harrier insists on his physical resemblance to Mazov, mostly through the excessiveness of the hair. Kim, with a roll of his eyes, points out that Harrier lacks Mazov's birthmark, but, more importantly, adds: "Alright. But here's the big thing—Kras Mazov looks Samaran, and you don't." Harrier claims part Samaran ancestry (though we do not have any prior knowledge of this), and the game describes the response to this claim thus: "The lieutenant closes his eyes. 'Okay, you win. Be Kras Mazov then, I don't care . . .' He opens his eyes again, tilting his head in a quiet wonder. 'Why are you so hell-bent on proving that you're Kras Mazov anyway?,'" to which the player can reply with a choice of responses reflective of the political ideologies in the game (see figure 3.2).

This mention of Mazov's racial otherness raises a question: What does a Samaran "look like"? The game's previous elaboration of Seol suggests that most countries in the world of *Disco Elysium* have real-world analogs, and the island of Samara is no exception—within the game's lore, Samara is described as the sole surviving communist nation, the "People's Republic of Samara." In another segment of the game, the People's Republic of Samara is named as site of manufacture for a set of bootleg speakers. The nonwhite racial otherness, combined with these other iconographic signifiers, seem to suggest that while Seol is a clear analog for Japan and Korea, Samara might vaguely represent China, Southeast Asia, or a Russian/Kazakh border region.[32] Nevertheless, there remains the suggestion of orientalist otherness in Mazov, one that Harrier can claim (albeit quite dubiously, or even facetiously).

This comical moment from *Disco Elysium* represents a moment in which both a socialist futurity and an Asian identity occurs in the space of the whimsical maybe, the what-if, the temporally adjacent. Here Asian adjacency plays out twofold. First, the Asian-diasporic (or perhaps, in Patterson's parlance, Asiatic) Kim Kitsuragi plays the role of deadpan "straight man" to Harrier's wild conspiracies, whose skepticism allows Harrier to elaborate on his grandiose theory, a tragicomic notion that he actually is the Marxian father purported to have killed himself decades prior. Kim regulates Harrier (and thus

78   Takeo Rivera

3.2. Harrier and Kim inspect the communist's apartment, including the bust of Kras Mazov, which is the only physical depiction of Kras Mazov in the game. Screenshot from *Disco Elysium* taken by author, courtesy of ZA/UM.

the player) not so much in political disagreement as in a regular return to "reality," trying to maintain a grip of normativity while Harrier constantly fantasizes, hallucinates, and goes off on tangents. Yet Kim very rarely resists Harrier, either—enabling Harrier even as he occasionally shames him.[33] But the moment in the apartment suggests Asian adjacency with Mazov himself. As an Asian American player, I zoomed as much as I could onto the bust of Mazov, wondering if I could make out phenotypical Asianness in this sole physical representation of the game's author of scientific socialism. Asian/America, as David Palumbo-Liu famously contends, "resides *in transit*, as a point of reference on the horizon that is part of *both* a 'minority' identity and a 'majority' identity," which is a description that equally applies to the liminal racial position of Asian Americans in an antiblack racial order as it does to the affective confusion that arises from this nebulous state.[34] Within *Disco Elysium*'s communist imagination, Asianness exists not essentially but spectrally, an acid communism with ambivalently euphemistic Asian characteristics.

Asian, Adjacent   **79**

Cryptozoology and the Utopian Sublime

The conclusion of *Disco Elysium* presents a compelling transition from Harrier's largely imagined psychedelic interiority to a genuinely magical event that occurs in the material world for even Kim to witness and believe with his own eyes. Harrier and Kim finally deduce that the murder was committed via sniper rifle from an island off the coast of Martinaise, where an old communist revolutionary bunker withers in the bleak wilderness. There they find the murderer, Iosef Lilianovich Dros, an elderly former communard holdout who delivers an extensive, affecting exchange about his traumas, the horrors of anticommunist repression, and his profound melancholy over the failure of the revolution—but who was largely motivated by a libidinal masculinist jealousy over the mercenary's coitus with the beautiful Klaasje Amandou, a corporate spy staying in the hotel. The failure of Iosef's communism appears to have been wedded to this attachment to heteropatriarchal masculinity, a reactionary blind spot within an otherwise dialectical materialist worldview.

Eventually, after this burst of eloquence, Iosef suddenly falls senile, his faculties failing him completely. It is then that Harrier suddenly notices, camouflaged in the reeds behind them, a three-meter-tall mythical cryptid, the Insulindian Phasmid. Throughout the game, Kim doubts the presence of the Phasmid and, if the player decides to complete side quests in pursuit of it, repeatedly expresses his frustration that doing so is a waste of time. The revelation of the Phasmid's actual existence represents a turning point for Kim in particular, humbling proof that his authoritative cynicism was wrong all along. In contrast with a game replete in cynicism, broken dreams, and disappointment (including the scene immediately preceding this one), Harrier and Kim's encounter with the Phasmid is the sole moment of absolute wonderment, vulnerability, and awe. It is also the only supernatural, otherworldly occurrence in the game that Kim actually confirms—it is not one of Harrier's fantasies, not something that Kim hastily dismisses, but an actually occurring figure of resplendent mystery.

As Kim and Harrier are adjacent to one another, so were the Phasmid and Iosef. The game heavily implies that it is the Phasmid's pheromones that enabled Iosef's lucidity and mental youth; Iosef's adjacency is revealed to be alongside not an Asian but an otherworldly creature. Moreover, the Phasmid establishes a telepathic link with Harrier, communicating and conveying the perseverance of the natural world well past the boundaries of coming anthropocentric ecological collapse. The miraculous appearance of the Phasmid

3.3. Kim Kitsuragi takes a photo of the Insulindian Phasmid. Screenshot from *Disco Elysium* taken by author, courtesy of ZA/UM.

represents, at the very conclusion of the game, a glimmer of vulnerable hope, disrupting the futility of futurity in exchange for wonderment. And given the Phasmid's affinity with Iosef, as well as its comedic final advice to Harrier, couched in socialist terms, that he emotionally move on from his lover ("Do it for the working class"), the Phasmid seems to represent a particular kind of socialist possibility.

On Harrier's cue, Kim takes a photo of the Phasmid, providing material proof of its existence in the world, and with it, the possibility of another world, in more ways than one (see figure 3.3). The nonhuman, magical Phasmid represents an otherness that far exceeds the orientalist imagination, taking the place of acid communist wonder that orientalist mysticism would otherwise have occupied.

Although the player experiences the discovery of the Phasmid from Harrier's perspective, Kim's self-shattering awe is perhaps more significant than Harrier's wonderment; the model minority assimilationist, cathected to centrist lawfulness and the realist worldview it demands, suddenly has no alternative but to see, and imagine, otherwise. Just as he had disavowed his own

Asian, Adjacent   81

Asianness, Kim had disavowed the possibility of the Phasmid's existence. In the world of *Disco Elysium*, Asianness is not countercultural commodity, but the figure of diasporic assimilationist exemplariness, who provides the proof of political possibility, allowing the world of the imagination to transmute into the realm of the "real."

Thus, while for the game more broadly the Phasmid represents an imperative to political audacity, for Kim the model minority moralist it provides permission to embrace alterity, racially, politically, and beyond. Although we experience most of the game from Harrier's standpoint, it is from Kim's gaze that we witness the Phasmid in all its glory in the photograph he takes, Harrier in the foreground, reaching out toward it like Gatsby toward the green light (see figure 3.3). Suddenly gone are the logics of normativity that undergird his cathexis to the "regular Revacholier," allowing the Asian diasporic character to experience the totality of strangeness and possibility that had evaded him much of his life. Either by the chemical whisper of the pheromone, or through the sighing skepticism in camaraderie, adjacency opens the utopian imagination for the player, the NPC, the Asian, and the non-Asian alike.

Notes

I would like to thank Jayna Huang (a.k.a. Jeffrey A. Ow), an early pioneer in Asian American video game studies, for exposing me to *Disco Elysium* and remarking on its Asianness. Thanks also to the Boston University Center for the Humanities for supporting the development of this piece through a Junior Faculty Fellowship. And my gratitude to the graduate students in Racial Capitalism and Contemporary Culture, my Fall 2022 seminar at Boston University—especially Lauren Machado—whose discussion provided additional perspectives on *Disco Elysium* and racial capitalism.

1 Fukuyama, "The End of History?"

2 Fisher, *Capitalist Realism*, 8.

3 Fisher, "Mark Fisher | Acid Communism (Unfinished Introduction)."

4 Fisher, "Mark Fisher | Acid Communism (Unfinished Introduction)."

5 Iwamura, *Virtual Orientalism*, 35.

6 Iwamura, *Virtual Orientalism*, 36, emphasis in original.

7 J. Williams, "*Techne-Zen* and the Spiritual Quality of Global Capitalism."

8 In fact, orientalism goes unproblematized in Fisher's mention of the Beatles' "Tomorrow Never Knows," which he says was "minimally adapted from *The Psychedelic Experience: A Manual Based on the Tibetan Book of the Dead.*"

9 Jameson, *The Antinomies of Realism*, 5.

10 Patterson, *Open World Empire*, 235.

11 Cho, "Margaret Cho—Asian Adjacent."

12 For "Asiatic racial form," see Lye, *America's Asia*.

13 I elaborate on the concept of superego model minoritarianism throughout the chapter, but I will also note that this represents an inversion my other elaboration of the superego in relation to model minoritarianism in Rivera, *Model Minority Masochism* (2022), an Afro-Asian superego that represents a moral authority in the opposite, anti-model minority orientation.

14 I should note that, as of this writing in 2023, Kurvitz, Hindpere, and Aleksander Rostov of the original creative team have since departed from ZA/UM, with Kurvitz and Rostov suing the company for fraud and illegal takeover. The legal feud between the original creators of *Disco Elysium* and ZA/UM remains ongoing at this time.

15 The Game Awards (@thegameawards), "Helen Hindpere is back on #TheGameAwards stage to accept award #2!"

16 Revachol Citizens Militia is the principal law enforcement agency in Revachol.

17 "Muñozian excess" refers, of course, to the love of utopian parties and queer dance halls in Muñoz, *Cruising Utopia*. I would moreover argue, however, that the binary between excess/color and gray utilitarianism in *Disco Elysium* is reversed from the usual cliché associations we've seen in the anticommunist West, wherein grayness is associated with Soviet bleakness and color with democratic freedom.

18 Harrier gains experience points almost entirely through dialogue and internal-mental interactions, rather than the conventional RPG procedure of gaining experience through killing enemies.

19 RShuman, "Disco Elysium."

20 North American readers may make the immediate association between Harrier DuBois and the great W. E. B. Du Bois. When the game was first released, a connection between the two was not immediately evident; *Elysium*'s DuBois is pronounced in the French manner, is phenotypically white, and characterized by unkemptness. However, with the advent of *Disco Elysium*'s "Final Cut" in 2021 (authored by Helen Hindpere), all of DuBois's interior voices are now voiced by Black British musician Lenval Brown, effectively making both DuBois and Kitsuragi's English-language voice acting racially asymmetrical.

21 For simplicity, I have inserted the dialogue tree branch of one of two options for dialogue in this line, the other of which is "Okay, I guess it's not interesting then."

22 For example, in Robert Kurvitz's home country of Estonia, the first Black person elected to public office, Abdul Turay, remarked in 2013, "Precisely because there are no blacks here, I have no natural constituency, nobody to speak to as a black person, I cannot have a message that talks about black

issues. . . . So race literally doesn't matter" (de Pommereau, "A First for Estonia"). Turay, who was also a columnist, wrote an article explaining his experiences being stopped for his immigration card, with the principal grievance that as a Black man he is not recognized as the Estonian he is (Turay, "What's Up with the People"). Kim's presence as a quasi-Korean Eurasian may also draw from the cultural memory of Soviet rock icon Viktor Tsoi, ethnically Korean but identified staunchly as Russian (although Tsoi and Kitsuragi, not unlike Harrier and W. E. B. Du Bois, are dispositional opposites).

23 Fickle, *The Race Card*, 90.

24 The homoeroticism between DuBois and Kitsuragi is subtextual but palpable, inspiring a considerable proliferation of fan art and "slash fics" between the two—apparently far more than between DuBois and the game's femme fatale, Klaasje.

25 Bhabha, *The Location of Culture*, 130.

26 J. Y. Kim, *The Racial Mundane*.

27 If the player selects the right "Thought Catalog" leveling choice, Harrier can discover that he is sexually queer, being intensely attracted to a mysterious man called the Smoker on the Balcony. However, if the player does not take this leveling route, Kim will amusedly remark at the game's conclusion that Harrier has never even heard of homosexuality—at least, with his amnesia, he lacks the nomenclature for his own desire.

28 Breault, "Dick Mullen and the Miracle Plot."

29 The games of BioWare are perhaps most emblematic of this tendency. *Star Wars: Knights of the Old Republic* (2003) features a Light Side to Dark Side spectrum based on player choices; the *Mass Effect* trilogy (2007, 2010, 2012) features "Paragon" and "Renegade" sliders. Other games keep track of such moral scores internally without revealing to the player—*Dishonored* (2012) and its sequel (2016) keep track of "chaos" based on the number of voluntary kills the player makes and provide correspondingly different endings. Game morality is perhaps most spectacularly explored in 2015's *Undertale*, in which disciplined, determined pacifism is the only way to acquire the "best" ending. Usually such alignments are determined through accumulation of points depending on the player's moral decisions.

30 The player-run *Disco Elysium* wiki on *Gamepedia* lists Kim as a Moralist, as well, even though it is not a political identity that he explicitly embraces. See "Political Alignment," in *Disco Elysium: A Detective's Wiki*, at *Gamepedia*, accessed February 20, 2021, https://discoelysium.gamepedia.com/Political_alignment.

31 Thanks to Matt York on the Lefty Paradox Plaza Facebook Group (an online leftist gaming community), who pointed this out quite deftly to me on social media. York, "Just one of the details."

32 There does not appear to be a clear answer for which real-world countries the various nations of *Disco Elysium* represent or draw clear inspiration

from, but a spirited debate on the matter unfolded on Reddit, with a general consensus that Samara represents some form of East Asian country: see random_user_1987, "The real world inspirations of the countries in Disco Elysium?" It is also worth noting that, in the real world, Samara is a city in Russia near the border of Kazakhstan, and "Mazov" is a Russian surname.

33 Procedurally, the only action Kim actively prevents Harrier/the player from doing is removing combat boots from the bloated corpse's body for personal use.

34 Palumbo-Liu, *Asian/American*, 5.

Playable Bodies

Part 2

Choose Your Mothership

Designer Roundtable #2

FEATURING:

Sisi Jiang, a game writer, narrative designer, and games journalist, known for *LIONKILLER* (2020), a queer post-colonial game that was nominated for the Independent Games Festival Excellence in Narrative award. They are a recipient of the Game Developers of Color x No More Robots grant, and they occasionally write about Asian games, race, and narrative for outlets such as *Kotaku*, *Vice Games*, and *Polygon*.

Domini Gee, a freelancer/game dev from Edmonton, Alberta, who has done ghostwriting, short stories, articles, and quality assurance testing for both indie and AAA (*Dragon Age: Inquisition*, *Transmogrify*). Her work has been featured on the Unraveled-Chat Stories app, in the *Journal of the Japanese Association for Digital Humanities*, and on Cracked, and she was selected for the IGDA Velocity Program in 2019. Currently Gee is doing narrative quality designer work for Keywords Studios and as narrative designer/colead for her Kickstarted point-and-click game *Camera Anima*.

Toby Đỗ, a game designer, film-maker, and graduate of the NYU

Game Center's MFA in game design. His games include *Grass Mud Horse* (2019), *Meteor-Strike!* (2018), and an upcoming unnamed title about a Vietnamese family living in Southern California. His work has been featured in *Rock Paper Shotgun*, *USgamer*, and *Giant Bomb*. He was an associate producer for the film *Hiếu*, which won the Deuxième Prix award at the 2019 Cannes Film Festival, and in 2020 he was selected as a Game Devs of Color Expo GDC Scholar.

Naomi Clark, a game designer and faculty member at the NYU Game Center. She has been making games for over two decades and has worked at LEGO designing online games and creativity tools (*Junkbot*, *LEGO Digital Designer*), educational games (*Wonder City*, *Josefina's Market Day*) and games for mass-market audiences (*Miss Management*, *Dreamland*). Clark's recent works include *Consentacle* (2018), and contributions to tabletop role-playing games such as *Monsterhearts 2* (2021) and *Honey and Hot Wax* (2020). She's the coauthor of *A Game Design Vocabulary* with Anna Anthropy (2014), and a founding collective member of the Sylvia Rivera Law Project.

Sisi Jiang: I feel like we have to talk about parents in this conversation. Mine were very antigames, so I played games under the covers with a flashlight. It was an uphill climb to even be a gamer. My parents would never buy me video games. I would try to compromise and say, "Hey, instead of giving me this video game, can you get me the strategy guide?" I don't know if that had any effect on how I think about game design. So I've probably gamed the least despite being interested in games just because access was a constant problem. Sometimes I would manage to get bootleg versions from China, though I didn't know they were bootlegs. I just thought they were Chinese editions.

Naomi Clark: I was an early game pirate, too. My family had an Apple II around 1982, and I had a lot of games that we obtained illicitly, all American and European games, because back then the game industry hadn't really taken off in Japan yet. Then I spent several years in Japan with my mom's side of the family, and over there I wasn't allowed to have a Nintendo Famicom, as my parents were suspicious of a dedicated game machine. I got into game design in New York, when the internet content industry started getting big in the '90s. I convinced my boss that we should make a game, and we made one about adolescent girls bullying each other [*SiSSYFiGHT 2000* (2000)]. Everybody had to play as a girl, which we felt was a strong statement in the '90s game world.

Domini Gee: I fell in love with gaming once I started playing things like *Final Fantasy*. My sister got *Final Fantasy IX* [2000], and from then on I was down the RPG rabbit hole. I even wrote a 100,000-word fanfic for *Final Fantasy VIII* [1999]. So when I graduated with my MA, I really wanted to get into the game industry, but unfortunately, it's really hard. So, I went off and did a lot of freelancing, which gave me the opportunity to work on my own game prototype, *Camera Anima*.

Toby Đỗ: I spent a lot of my childhood playing FPS [first-person shooter] games. I originally wanted to be a game designer growing up, so I went into college studying computer science. But I was so bad at coding. Then I went to grad school at Cal Arts for film directing, and there I joined a Game Makers club they had started up the semester I came, and I got into making games. I eventually decided to drop out of the film directing program and apply to game design schools.

Sisi Jiang: Design started for me playing Bioware games and feeling like there were things I wanted to change about them. I tried applying there, but it didn't work out, so I gave up for a while. And then I started making *LIONKILLER*, telling people it was going to be my magnum opus, but I was just making it in-between random hourly jobs. And now that being a narrative designer is my job, around three-fourths of my paying clients end up being Asian American or Asian Canadian. Why is that? I mean, I don't mind it, because working with them is a good time. But I know something's going on. I'm just not exactly sure what it is.

Toby Đỗ: In my experiences with film editing, when I had a hard time getting jobs, most of my clients were Asian as well. So, coming into games, I felt like it would be similar, which is maybe why a lot of my games have Vietnamese characters in them. And when I post them on itch.io, I'm specifically tagging them with Vietnam and Vietnamese. I've gotten a couple people from the Vietnamese game industry messaging me, but I'm also thinking about the blog posts that Marina Kittaka posted a few months ago about divesting from the games industry.[1] I feel like that's where I am at this point.

Sisi Jiang: Yeah, especially when you hear stories about studios refusing to hire people with hard-to-pronounce names and stuff like that. It's especially a problem for narrative designers—I can always find one Asian dude in programming. So it's just this ongoing feeling of "Maybe they just don't want me *here*." When I started out in games, I reached out to a guy, a white guy whose name is actually completely in the mud now. The entire industry hates him for being such an awful person to women. I tried to ask him for advice. And he told me something that is kind of still with me: "Oh, I think you might have pretty okay odds of getting into the industry because you don't look like all the other people in the industry. That's going to give you an advantage." And I just had that constant thought in my head: he thinks I'm a diversity hire. That's literally what he said to my face. And this was my first-ever encounter with a prominent designer in the industry. So sometimes I will just be like, *Hmm, I wonder if my stuff is really good. Or if it's not really that good.*

Naomi Clark: That's real, Sisi. I think there's a general prejudice against East Asian creative professionals. Probably especially Chinese people, but also Japanese and Korean, like, "Oh, you're probably good at programming." And if you're Korean, "You can definitely make artwork, you can do character designs, but we're gonna write the character ideas." As a writer, I think there's a bunch of racism just working against you, and then there are these diversity and inclusion efforts that sometimes make the assumption that Asians are already overrepresented in the game industry.

Sisi Jiang: If we're so well represented, then how come I still see Chinese people depicted with katanas? How come *Cyberpunk 2077* (2020) happened? How did *Ghost of Tsushima* (2020) have exactly zero Asian writers on the team? But sure, we're so overrepresented. Then how come these creative decisions that never include any Asians in character creators just keep happening?

Domini Gee: As a player I always have the weirdest sensation when people say, "It's hard for me not to create myself when I have a game with character creation." I've barely ever had that experience of creating "myself" with character creators. I think the closest I ever got was when I played *Mass Effect Andromeda* (2017). They have this system where your parents are auto-generated based on how you design your main character, so it meant that I could take an East Asian head and modify it a little to what I would consider familiar to myself. Finally, I actually got that feeling for once.

92   Designer Roundtable 2

Likewise, with my own game, what I really want to sneak in are these features that to me would read that this character is very likely interracial. I'm likely gonna be the only one who cares about it; it's not intended to be interesting, I just want it. Because I know that it's not likely to be there otherwise.

Sisi Jiang: Yeah, *Andromeda* has the best character creator ever. I had no idea that this is what [other] people experienced when they played cinematic games. Are you kidding me? I am just now experiencing this? It was mind-blowing. I'm a narrative designer, and I didn't even realize that people could have this kind of emotional connection to the character they see on the screen.

Toby Đỗ: The first time I played *Metal Gear Solid V* (2015), I spent like an hour and a half on the character creator. Basically, they give you a pretty detailed character creator, and you can spend a bunch of time in it, then they tell you that you can't be that character. And instead you have to play as a white guy, as Snake.

Chris Patterson: Thanks to one of our contributors [Keita Moore], I just learned that Snake is actually part Japanese, though he certainly reads as white.

Naomi Clark: Hideo Kojima [creator of the *Metal Gear* series] loves part-Japanese characters for some reason. It doesn't ever really seem to influence his art direction of what the characters look like, though. There was an interview where Jonathan Blow [creator of *Braid* (2008)] described the Japanese industry as a withered soulless husk, which for me was just such a crystallization of a weird inferiority complex and orientalist imagining of Japan as a sort of Ancient Empire—like they just keep repeating the same rituals over and over. And then a whole bunch of people asked me whether I was offended by it, as if I have anything to do with Japanese games!

So for the American game industry, there's long been this feeling that the Japanese game industry is somewhat inaccessible, or, one might say, inscrutable. Because Japanese designers and developers have a reputation for being somewhat tight-lipped and not wanting to say anything critical about their peers or colleagues, or do too much digging into their own process. I don't think it's an entirely fair characterization, but as a result, there's a

Choose Your Mothership **93**

weird mystique around Japanese developers. I have gotten this feeling—and sometimes it's overt—from people that I meet in the game industry, especially when I go to California for events like the Game Developers Conference and they look at me with this double vision. They're like, "Oh, so you're not a Japanese developer, not part of the Japanese industry. But you're part Japanese? Do you know anybody in the Japanese industry?" They're like, "So what's your relationship to the mothership?" I've had to have all these conversations over the years to try to make the point that people in the Asian diaspora are not all exactly the same. You can't just treat everybody as this one giant ball of wax like, "Well, we're not going to include Asian Americans in our considerations when hiring because there are a whole bunch of Asians already in the global game industry."

Sisi Jiang: That's why I've just been hitting really hard about my entire feud with *Ghost of Tsushima*. I wrote this long-form article criticizing it like, "Y'all were literally making a game about Japan with American devs, and y'all had no Asian writers at all." I outline how they project the US-Japan relationship onto the story; for example, they can't represent any kind of Japanese sexuality at all, and the dialogue is so jarring—I was like, *Please stop saying honor or I will go cry in a corner*.

Domini Gee: There is a very weird discourse around the response to games like *Ghost of Tsushima* about white people writing outside their race. Which, yeah, valid, hire more diverse people. But then it starts to lead to the idea that you shouldn't write outside your race that much at all, because you can't depict the experience properly. So then, if you're a minority, you're only capable of writing the mothership analogy, which for me would be extremely flawed. I can guarantee my experiences are very different from other people's. Or you start pigeonholing people by going like, "Well, yes, Sisi, you can only work with Asian companies and games, because that represents your experiences, right?" So it's a kind of progressive exclusionary gesture.

Chris Patterson: I'm curious how you all think about genre now, especially these hybrid genres with blurred boundaries. Like, action or adventure games blurred with visual novels and then being associated with Japan and Japanese cultural norms. It seems most Western-made games can be blurred as Asian in some way.

Sisi Jiang: I have so many thoughts about this. Japan has done better at integrating visual novels into prestige games. *Pokémon* is a visual novel if you really think about it, and so is *Persona*. There are so many games with huge budgets that have portions of the visual novel form. And then meanwhile, in the United States, [visual novels are] seen as kitschy, and I really do think there's a racial component to that—because it's associated with "those weird Japanese games." There are games out there that have basically completely shifted how we think about video game storytelling, like *Zero Escape* (2009), and then in the United States, those are lumped in with "bad games."

Domini Gee: In terms of that stigmatization, there was a game I got asked if I wanted to contract for that was basically a visual novel. And they were saying that they originally had more anime-like sprites, but they were thinking about changing them to be 3D models instead because the game didn't do well initially. And I was like, "Are you sure the art is the problem?" I thought it was interesting that their thought process immediately went to the game's anime art style.

Naomi Clark: There's this malign theory of game design in the West that I blame on Chris Crawford [1980s American game designer and founder of the Game Developers Conference]. He introduced the idea that choice is the central most important aspect of any kind of game. So part of what distinguishes a visual novel in the West, what makes it exotic and different and this weird suspect category, is that there are a bunch of stories that are completely linear. One of the oldest and most boring arguments that game designers have, especially when they're novices, is "How can it be a game if there are no choices?" I'm like, "What are you talking about? You're still just running around inside of the limited set of choices that Chris Avellone [game writer for the *Fallout* series and other RPGs] or whoever gave you. You just turned it into this ideology of 'Western role playing games let you do anything.'"

Toby Đỗ: Yeah, people tell me my games aren't games all the time still. Mostly because they're linear.

Domini Gee: The only way you can really have like a completely customized character experience is if it's a tabletop game and people are customizing it to you. Which, unfortunately, game designers are not gonna be in your house.

Choose Your Mothership **95**

Sisi Jiang: Personally, I'm just so exhausted about having to maintain the illusion. It's such a waste of time to keep pretending that a game is all founded in player choice. We're not giving you a custom experience every time; I mean, even Bioware is not giving you that custom experience. Every time it's what you, your brain, brings into it that is custom. That's why, personally, the more I make games, the less I think about audience. Appeal is such a nebulous concept—you can't anticipate appeal—you have to stick to your guns and understand why your game works. They don't even have to like it; they just have to understand what you were trying to do. With *LIONKILLER*, Asians got what I was doing. After that, I was like, I don't really care if white people get what I'm doing.

Naomi Clark: I think that there's something to the idea that players in the West—or, you know, the people who are drawing these distinctions between visual novel and game, between CRPGs [computer role-playing games] and JRPGs [Japanese role-playing games]—have this idea of agency and free will and being able to express themselves as individuals, to be able to make the game their own and feel important as the player, that they somehow sort of imagine that Asia is a place where people don't care about that.

Domini Gee: And this goes into how people get those assumptions in the first place. People say, "Oh, yeah, in Western games you own your choice. You have to respect choice." And then they get angry when a game shows that your choices ultimately go into a little branch.

Sisi Jiang: It's all fake. I still designed the other path. And if you backtrack, then it's still linear. It's a waste of resources and time to keep pretending that it's free will. When you start off making games, I think there's that insecurity about whether or not something is a game or not. I put puzzles into *LION-KILLER* because I thought having a puzzle is what makes a game a game. And I need to maintain the illusion that this is a game. But I'm not a puzzle designer. I don't even like puzzles.

Toby Đỗ: *Meteor Strike* [Đỗ's game about esports] and *Counter-Strike* (1999) came about because I wanted to make a game where you just press one button the whole time. So the mechanics sort of came first. But I also had recently read an interview with Minh Le [Vietnamese Canadian creator of *Counter-Strike* and a contributor to roundtable 1], and I'd never really known

96 Designer Roundtable 2

about *Counter-Strike*'s origin, so I wanted to make a game that built on my thoughts on that.

In my game *Grass Mud Horse*, a lot of the Asian themes didn't come up until much later. It was originally an idea for a class I came up with where the player got to be a cinematographer loosely based on past experiences I've had on film sets. When I grouped up with other classmates, we combined all of our backgrounds to flesh out the idea. One of our teammates, Julia Wang, was from Chengdu, so we decided to make that the setting because she had never made a game set in China before and our other teammate, Emi Shaufeld, is lesbian and has also worked on film sets so that's how we came up with the characters.

Tara Fickle: Toby, there's an interesting Let's Play video on your itch.io page for *Grass Mud Horse* where the player didn't really seem to get the game's *wuxia* [Chinese martial arts literary and film genre] elements. He seemed startled by the game's callouts to Asian conventions.

Toby Đỗ: The genre of film you're making in the game [as the player] is a *wuxia* Roman Porno film. Roman Pornos were softcore pornographic Japanese films from the '70s produced by a company called Nikkatsu. Basically, they would give directors money, and let them make any movie they want, under the condition that there had to be four sex scenes for every hour of the film. So, we're riffing on that a little bit. Because of that, *Grass Mud Horse* feels more Japanese than Chinese in a lot of ways even though it looks like a *wuxia* game on the surface. Samurai films are oftentimes about heroic warriors, but usually within the system, working under leaders, whereas in *wuxia* films the main characters are usually outsiders, travelling across the countryside, who then encounter corrupt leaders terrorizing their own people. There are parallels in the game, with you playing as a cinematographer working for this annoying, egotistical director. And the director is Asian American, right? So there's that conflation of throwing all these Asian cultures into one monolith, which we were thinking about, too.

Naomi Clark: Back in the 2000s, I was working at a quite diverse studio with a lot of Asian artists. And we got this opportunity to pitch an idea for an East Asian fantasy game. We thought we could put in lots of different myths, some Miyazaki influence, anime stuff, mix it all together. But it was a deeply dissatisfying experience. Because we were just trying to package

Choose Your Mothership **97**

whatever we liked about Asian mythology into some sort of box for an American audience. I think that made me feel like the actual authentic thing to do is to relate to how this stuff has affected you. And if your reaction is ironic, or subversive in some way, then that's the actual authenticity. When I made my tentacle porn card game [*Consentacle*], I was like, "I want this to make people uncomfortable who think that they can masturbate to it." Then I got a bunch of reviews that were like, "This stuff is terrible to masturbate to," and I was like, "Yes!" Aesthetically, it worked out. Because it's not trying to be authentic. It's a weird refraction of the anime art style. For me, that was more real than something "authentically Asian."

Note

1 Marina Kittaka, "Divest from the Video Games Industry!" *Medium*, June 25, 2020, https://even-kei.medium.com/divest-from-the-video-games -industry-814a1381092d. See designer roundtable #4 in this volume for more on Kittaka's discussion of game industry divestment.

Keita Moore

Playable Deniability

Biracial Representation and the Politics of Play in *Metal Gear Solid*

The *Metal Gear Solid* series (Konami, 1998–2015), which follows several covert agents as they infiltrate terrorist bases and active war zones, has received much praise in both academic and popular outlets for its storytelling and clever gameplay. Anglophone game studies has commended the franchise's sophisticated antiwar and anti–nuclear weapon pronouncements—a welcome antidote to American games bound to the military-industrial complex.[1] Derek Noon and Nick Dyer-Witheford, for instance, have read the series' contrast with American military shooters as director Kojima Hideo's reflection on the nuclear bombings of Japan and a "critique of imperial power from within mainstream gaming's culture of 'militarized masculinity.'"[2]

Anglophone work has also looked favorably on the core stealth mechanics: gameplay that involves circumventing confrontation by guiding the player character through different natural or urban terrains, avoiding enemy patrols, and staying out of sight. Although these mechanics foreground nonviolent engagement with the enemy, Noon and Dyer-Witheford note that

Metal Gear Solid (hereafter *MGS*) does not practice simple didacticism: it allows for lethal actions.[3] Indeed, "much of the challenge . . . depends on the tension between the availability of an arsenal of deadly weaponry and the rewards for a 'no-kill' completion" that has been possible from *MGS2: Sons of Liberty* (Konami, 2001) onward.[4] For this reason, Miguel Sicart has seen *MGS3: Snake Eater* (Konami, 2004) as a paragon of gamic media's unique ethical potential. Sicart argues that the provision of player choice, alongside the experience of consequences, enables critical reflection on lethal play at the level of choice in gameplay.[5]

While the Anglophone literature has examined the antimilitary politics of the franchise and Kojima's "antiwar, antinuclear" message, the question of race in the games has received little attention.[6] Noon and Dyer-Witheford's view is paradigmatic: "The game *is* played from a position of 'hegemonic white masculinity.'"[7] I argue against this view for two reasons. First, Solid Snake (hereafter Snake), the protagonist/player character for *Metal Gear Solid* (Konami, 1998), the introductory section of *MGS2*, and *MGS4: Guns of the Patriots* (Konami, 2008)—the three games that form the core of this analysis—is *not* white: he is biracial, half white and half Japanese.[8] This character thus differs from the protagonists of *MGS3* and *MGS5: The Phantom Pain* (Konami: 2015), who are the Caucasian Big Boss and his doppelgänger Venom Snake, respectively.

Second, Snake has largely "passed" as white in the American academic context despite his racialization in the franchise's narrative, in part due to Anglophone game studies' initial inattention to national contexts (see Hutchinson, this volume). This disregard risks replicating the "postracial" rhetoric that attends American representations of mixed-race Asian bodies. LeiLani Nishime argues that the inability to see these bodies in their sociohistorical specificity extends the logic of the Asian American racial formation as "disappearing" (assimilating) along lines that naturalize existing hierarchies of race in the United States. To combat this tendency, she suggests that "grounding contemporary multiracial Asian American visual representations in history and at the intersection of identity categories lays bare the social negotiations that organize our ability to racialize the bodies we see."[9]

By following Nishime's methodological example, this chapter considers Snake's biraciality in the context of Japan, and in terms of discourses around Japaneseness. I argue that Snake's racialization in Japanese political context(s) constitutes a means of engaging with the digital world for the implied Japanese player, a mode of premediating the games' antiwar and antinuclear message in ways that absent Japan itself from the critique. In so doing, I develop the concept of "playable deniability" to describe the processes that allow play to appear free from the politics around militaristic violence in Japan. Here I am indebted to Tara Fickle's observation of "an important and overlooked symmetry between the *racial* logic that undergirds the spatialized systems of oppression and exploitation and the *ludic* logic crucial to securing our perception of games *as* games."[10] I point to a similar symmetry in *MGS*, one that preserves the primacy of play—the political inconsequentiality of action—via a racial logic mediating play.

Paul Martin's work captures the intertwined political problematics arising in the Japanese industry that I am concerned with here: the fraught domestic and intraregional dynamics of war memory in Japan, and the status of playable war in a state that has lacked the constitutional ability to possess an offensive army since 1945, at least on paper.[11] Analyzing *Resident Evil 5* (Capcom, 2009), a game whose narrative draws on "dark continent" colonial tropes, Martin shows how the representation of white and Black bodies allows the Japanese player a racialized power fantasy: the game allows "the non-White-male player to experience being a White-male subjectivity exercising control over Black and female bodies . . . [and] also opens up a space for this player to experience—from a non-White subject position—control over the White-male body of Chris [the player character]."[12] From this nationalized position, the implied Japanese player can perform militarized, white, and neocolonial intervention. This maneuver not only elides Japan's history of imperialism in Asia but also bypasses Japan's postwar "peace" constitution by making military intervention non-Japanese.

The deployment of race in *MGS* echoes Martin's point that racialization externalizes certain questions of war from Japan. Unlike *Resident Evil 5*'s conservative conflation of military capacity with "normal" nationhood, however, *MGS* wears its progressive antiwar politics on its sleeve. Rachael Hutchinson has shown that Kojima's critical engagement with war proceeds from an "observer position [that] preserves the myth of Japan as an uninvolved outsider."[13] *MGS* upholds an exceptionalism where Japan can pass moral judgment on others' wars by means of its exteriority to global conflict—an exceptionality based on "postmilitary" understandings of Japaneseness that obfuscate Japan's own colonialism in the Asia-Pacific. The series thus replicates a political doxa around historical memory that articulates the war through a narrative of Japanese civilian suffering rather than one of imperialist aggression.[14] If *MGS* "has not overcome the 'Japan as victim' stance so problematic

Playable Deniability   **101**

for mainstream/dominant war narratives in Japan—rather, it utilizes this stance as a basis from which to put forward a broader critique of war and violence which is rare in videogames," then I argue that this critique has never earnestly engaged with domestic political debates around war, whether in terms of commemoration or Japan's (defensive) military capability.[15]

Situating Snake

Snake's identity disengages the game from these politics by turning to a problematic conception of Japaneseness, one that Yuko Kawai describes as unmoored from its colonial history as both race and ethnicity. Just as ethnicity in the postwar period "has been used primarily to describe ethnic conflicts outside Japan," so too does "race" exist elsewhere to a Japaneseness that is defined as singular.[16] In the context of this homogenized Japaneseness, Snake's biraciality creates a semantic matrix to glide over the politics of playable war, to transform play's political potential into something deniable.[17] Because biraciality manifests in *MGS* not only as representation or narrative, but also as gameplay, I align myself with Jennifer Malkowski and Trea-Andrea M. Russworm's call to consider racialization in the space between visuality and procedurality, between representation and the core systems of gameplay.[18] If, as Sicart has neatly summed up, Ian Bogost's influential notion of proceduralism "claim[s] that players, by reconstructing the meaning embedded in the rules, are *persuaded* by virtue of games' procedural nature," then Malkowski and Russworm argue that race enters strongly into how rules and play create meaning.[19]

The matrix where play becomes deniable for the implied Japanese player depends on the mass-mediatic bifurcation of masculine biraciality into two particular figures. One is the *konketsuji*, or "mixed-blood child" who resulted from the Allied Occupation of Japan (1945–52) and who emerges historically in society as a maligned domestic minority. The second image is that of *hāfu*, a term that has appeared since the 1970s to connote Japanese internationalism and multiculturalism. Scholars in Asian American studies have shown the contiguity, rather than linear development, of racialized stereotypes; likewise, I would submit that these twin figures of Japanese biraciality run together.[20] In *MGS*, the contiguity emerges on the axis of lethal/nonlethal play as a matter of player choice. If the implied Japanese player chooses the lethally aggressive option, their actions are captured within the semiotic matrix of *konketsuji* that naturalizes violent physicality *as* a biraciality that is aberrant to Japaneseness. Conversely, players who elect a nonlethal strategy imbue Snake with an ability to represent Japan as *hāfu* in juxtaposition to the hegemonic militarized whiteness of the West.

Snake's racialization maintains a formal choice between lethal and nonlethal action, all while avoiding political problematics. The balancing act hangs on the specificity of biraciality in Japan: whereas a fully Japanese avatar might summon past conflicts and divulge the politics of playable war, a stealthy white avatar could challenge the Japanese civilian exceptionalism of *MGS*'s antimilitary and antinuclear message. *Konketsuji* and *hāfu*, as ludo-representational modalities, absent Japan as an object of critical contemplation, maintaining playable deniability. Both lethal and nonlethal styles converge on a singular Japaneseness that finds coherency in play at the moment that Snake's racial difference becomes evident to the implied Japanese player.

Before proceeding, a brief biography of Solid Snake is in order. Snake's story, communicated through cutscenes in *MGS1* and *MGS4*, runs thus: Snake is a clone, born from experiments known as "Les Enfants Terribles" that were aimed at re-creating and perfecting Big Boss (a Caucasian man)—the world's foremost super-soldier. To do so, scientists used Big Boss's DNA and the donated eggs of a Japanese woman and grew Snake and his twin, Liquid Snake, to term in the womb of Eva, an Anglo-American woman.[21] Snake was raised in the United States, eventually joining the military and making his way into the special force unit Foxhound. By the time of *MGS1*, Snake has retired to Alaska after establishing himself as a capable solo operative with a checkered legal past. He is called back to duty when Foxhound, under Liquid Snake, goes rogue and takes over a facility in Alaska that transpires to be a weapons lab for the development of Metal Gears, bipedal nuclear-warhead-equipped tanks. It is during this first game that Vulcan Raven, an Inuit member of Foxhound, identifies Snake as biracial: "Asian blood flows in your veins."[22] After successfully stopping the terrorist plot, Snake goes on to establish the antinuclear organization Philanthropy, having departed the service of the American military. While investigating the continued US development of Metal Gears during *MGS2*, Snake stumbles onto a sinister plot of the Patriots, a shadow organization seeking to control world governments. In *MGS4*, he learns that the Patriots are now artificial intelligences that are running a newly developed "war economy," and he fights through premature aging to disable the AIs and end the struggle "between a dominant, quasi-fascist

Playable Deniability **103**

faction and a dissident libertarian group."[23] The series ends with Snake, having contemplated suicide, deciding to live out his remaining days.

Biraciality as Representation

As this story implies, Snake never organically inhabits spaces where his appearance would allow him to pass unnoticed. In fact, stealth in *MGS* games entails managing Snake's visibility through controlling his physical movements. This visibility manifests differently between the two basic stages of gameplay. In the relatively open areas that pit Snake against rank-and-file nonplayer characters (NPCs), the player can choose between concealing Snake from enemy eyes, or directly engaging them. Boss stages, however, lock Snake into limited arenas, reducing the player's ability to conceal the character. The player progresses through *MGS1*, *2*, and *4* by moving between digital spaces where Snake is always visible and always out of place.

While the series explains this visibility in terms of infiltrating hostile territory, Snake's perpetual liminality resonates with the situation of mixed-race people in a nation that has considered itself predominantly mono-ethnic since the end of the Asia Pacific War (1945). On the one hand, Japanese "blood remains an organizing metaphor for profoundly significant, fundamental, and perduring assumptions about Japaneseness and otherness both within and outside of Japan."[24] On the other hand, to "qualify" as Japanese requires the simultaneous overlap of "nationality, ancestry, language competence, birthplace, current residence, level of cultural literacy, and subjective identity."[25] Biraciality in Japan, then, is ambiguous because many such people born there meet all of these criteria *except* pure-bloodedness—a point evident in the travails of the multiracial children (*konketsuji*) who resulted from the Allied Occupation (1945–52). The contemporary term *hāfu*, which came to particular prominence in the 1990s, has attempted to suture biraciality to the nation through associating it with Japanese internationalism and multiculturalism.[26] Nevertheless, visual difference remains a kind of spectacle, as the large number of biracial individuals working as on-screen talent in the mass media suggests. The oscillation of (multi)culturalized proximity to Japaneseness and racialized distance, frequently signified as "foreignness," makes the question of whether *hāfu* can represent Japan a vexed one. For example, debates raged around whether Ariana Miyamoto, a mixed-race person of Japanese and Black heritage, should stand for the nation when she was elected as Miss Japan in 2015 during the Sixty-Fourth Miss Universe Pageant.[27]

Though *MGS1* was released in 1998, Snake does not visually or biographically correspond to the mass-mediated image of *hāfu*. Rather, there is an ambiguity to his physical appearance, as can be seen in figure 4.1. This ambiguity is particularly visible when he meets his Caucasian "father," Big Boss, at the end of *MGS4* (see figure 4.2).[28] Not coincidentally, this game also fleshes out the earlier invocation of Snake's "Asian blood" in *MGS1*. In one of *MGS4*'s longer cutscene sequences, Eva reveals the source of his Japanese heritage: "In the successful artificial semination, the eggs of a healthy Japanese woman—the doctor's assistant—were used."[29] The subsequent line, a verbatim repetition of Raven's *MGS1* pronouncement, confirms Snake's biraciality.[30] The experimental nature of Snake's birth renders him an orphan. Big Boss was unaware of the cloning, and his "mother," who appears only during this line of dialogue, seems to have had no interest in Snake.[31]

This diegetic depiction makes Snake's closest analog the mediatic image of the *konketsuji*, who resulted from the union of Japanese women with white and Black soldiers during the Allied occupation. As symbols of Japan's defeat, this group of children often found themselves orphaned and effectively stateless. Legal barriers stood on either side of parentage, whether this was the Japanese patrilineal passage of citizenship, or Allied command's discouragement of soldiers' "local" fraternization. Even when they were inclined to claim paternity, GI fathers faced steep challenges in a bevy of anti-Asian exclusion acts, which allowed little migration even after the laws were repealed.[32] Japan's first large-scale population of biracial people entered the public consciousness in both nations as a "problem" trapped between American anti-Asian racism and Japanese discourses of ethnic purity.[33] Carrying forward prewar views of biracial people as more prone to deviant behavior ("hybrid degeneracy") and as a source of discord within Japanese society, these latter beliefs marked *konketsuji* as racially different, leading to their marginalization and stigmatization relative to pure-blooded Japanese children.[34] Simultaneously, their societal spectacularization coincided with the postwar shift from multiethnic empire to mono-ethnic nation, a shift pivoting on a perceived loss of Japanese national self-determinism at Allied hands.[35]

While Snake's biography aligns with *konketsuji*, the science fictional nature of his conception also obscures this history within the game's narrative. Snake's diegetic situation as akin to *konketsuji* is most significant to

Playable Deniability   **105**

Metal Gear Solid (1998)   Metal Gear Solid 2: Sons of Liberty (2001)   Metal Gear Solid 4: Guns of the Patriots (2008)

4.1. The appearance of Solid Snake throughout *MGS*. Image courtesy of Miru *MGS*, YouTube.

4.2. Snake (*left*) meeting Big Boss (*right*) in *MGS4*. Image courtesy of Miru *MGS*, YouTube.

gameplay, where his racialization serves as a de facto explanation for his violent physical capabilities. Examining this association in contemporary media, Yamamoto Atsuhisa has viewed *konketsuji* not as a historical figure per se but as a contemporary modality of representing and policing biraciality. Yamamoto argues that contemporary media constructs an aberrant biracial masculinity exemplified by "an excess of physicality and behavior that anticipates violence, criminality, and aggression."[36] As social figures, the *konketsuji* became disciplinary objects of public discourse and more or less formal discrimination, spectralizing biracial difference in service of a "homogeneous" Japan. By designating biracial people as aberrant, defined in part by a historical association with war and loss, this mode continues to exert a disciplinary effect on mixed-race individuals within mediatic representation. The modality—which I term the *konketsuji* modality, for the sake of clarity—also circumvents questions of Japanese wartime culpability, since it unmarks the implicitly full-Japanese subject and grants them the exceptional power to see, or, in this case, to play.

This function helps explain Snake's biraciality, as it allows for a disarticulation of militaristic violence and Japaneseness. To demonstrate this point, I turn to the original moment and context of Snake's in-game racialization: the cutscene where he meets Vulcan Raven in *MGS1*, and the ensuing boss fight. Raven, an Inuit man, traps Snake in a subterranean frost-filled warehouse. Unlike other boss encounters to this point, the fight against Raven has no narrative rationale beyond making progress. While Snake is a figure of excessive physicality, with developed musculature, the ability to withstand extreme environments, and a trained capacity for lethal violence, Raven visibly and procedurally dwarfs Snake in all of these aspects. The native Alaskan towers over the player character in stature, and his massive machine gun can make short work of Snake's body and weaponry. The fight itself unfolds among rows of shipping containers that divide the space into long, thin corridors. Raven will fire indiscriminately down these passages, requiring the player to avoid his line of sight. In practice, there are two strategies for winning: the player can fire missiles at Raven's back and risk the boss noticing and shooting their ordnance down, or rig explosives along Raven's path. In either case, the player's ability to avoid a head-on conflict ensures their victory.

Diegetically, Raven situates the encounter in terms of survival of the fittest, a deadly competition that pits the Indigenous man against Snake. Snake's triumph, which results in fatally injuring Raven, thus gestures to a *supplemental* quality of the player character over and above Raven's physicality. Raven's final words condemn this quality as an excessive ability to kill, one that he locates in the artificiality of Snake's body: "In the natural world, there is no such thing as boundless slaughter. There is always an end to it. But you are different. . . . The path you walk on has no end. Each step you take is paved with the corpses of your enemies. . . . Their souls will haunt you forever. . . . You shall have no peace."[37] Not only do these lines associate Snake with a ceaseless militarism; they also speak to the *konketsuji* modality of aberrance marking Snake's physicality and aggression. That boss encounters in *MGS1* are fatal (there is no nonlethal way to defeat Raven) links aberrancy to the embodied capacity for a military form of violence—a capacity that,

Playable Deniability   **107**

through Snake's racialization, is externalized from Japaneseness as the object of a disciplining Japanese gaze.

At first glance, the player's skills in strategizing, dodging, and managing Snake's visibility appear to be another source of Snake's supplemental quality. However, this ability is premediated by the *konketsuji* modality: the moment of revealing Snake's biraciality interferes with the immediacy of the implied player's identifications with their actions. Instead, their choices throughout the boss encounter reinscribe the alterity of Japaneseness to the scene of the fight, enacting aberrance to reify its violent difference to "pure" Japaneseness. For this reason, the player's acts are rendered deniable, contained and shaped within the semiotic matrix of *konketsuji* at the moment that Snake's racial difference becomes visible through lethal martial violence.

In *MGS1*, Snake's "biracial" persona aids in the constitution of a Japaneseness that can consume Kojima's "political" message *and* engage in militaristic play without a sense of contradiction. The *konketsuji* modality not only naturalizes the player's violence but also further enables the game's moralizing diegetic message *by* absenting Japan and transforming it into a disciplining presence beyond the game itself. Raven's ominous valediction becomes less a condemnation of the player's actions than an authentication of the *konketsuji* modality, ensuring ludo-narrative consonance—the alignment of play and narrative structures—around the biracial figure of Snake. This consonance extends to the relation of the implied Japanese player and their actions, suturing the gap through a figure that cannot represent Japan even as his "Japanese blood" is confirmed. Thus, the *konketsuji* modality simultaneously nullifies questions of Japanese military violence *and* unmarks Japaneseness while retaining the Japanese player's exceptional power over and above biraciality.

Biraciality as Choice

If the lack of player choice in *MGS1*—the inevitability of Raven's death—thus naturalizes player violence as that of the other, how do we understand the shift from *MGS2* onward, where the games facilitate nonlethal play? Yamamoto's view of the fluidity of mediatic representations of biraciality is key to answering this question: both *konketsuji* and *hāfu*, as images coined by and within the mass media, can be imposed on multiracial bodies ex post facto.[38] In other words, any biracial person can shift from a position of relative

108   Keita Moore

prestige into deviancy that inherits the semiotic matrix of aberrant behavior, without ever being termed *konketsuji*. While *hāfu* ideologically displaces *konketsuji* along a cosmopolitan narrative of historical development, the two are contemporaneous in practice.[39] To play as *hāfu*, then, requires not only sublating *konketsuji*'s aberrant violence but also demonstrating similitude with a disciplining Japaneseness defined in terms of antimilitary nonviolence.

In *MGS2*, Snake can approach *hāfu*—and therefore stand in for a kind of Japaneseness—in the interplay of Japanese difference to militaristic Euro-American whiteness. The game's opening section makes this point by situating racial difference alongside the introduction of player choice between lethal and nonlethal play. Set several years after the events of *MGS1*, the second entry in the series is split into two sections: the brief "tanker chapter," which features Snake as the player character; and the "plant chapter," which introduces a new avatar.[40] The former sees Snake infiltrating a US Marine vessel masquerading as a civilian tanker in New York harbor. At this point, Snake has effectively left the service of the US military; he now works for an anti–Metal Gear NGO, Philanthropy, not unlike an antinuclear NGO. His mission aboard this tanker is to find photographic evidence of a new Metal Gear, and Snake's compatriot stresses the importance of going undetected and avoiding lethal action toward enemy NPCs. For this objective, Snake is given a tranquilizer gun, which serves as one of the main vehicles for nonlethal play throughout subsequent titles.

Snake must use this weapon in the game's first boss encounter with Olga Gurlukovich, a Russian mercenary whose squad storms the tanker to steal the new Metal Gear from the Marines. Olga, who is Caucasian, fights on a stage where she is divided from Snake by an uncrossable wall of boxes. Crucially, the encounter sees a quantitative difference in the use of force. Whereas Olga fights using a live-ammunition pistol, Snake can only use the silenced tranquilizer gun. When the player hits Olga with a dart, a small purple bar under her green "life" bar diminishes; upon reaching zero, Olga slumps over, defeated and asleep.[41] Snake walks away with her lethal gun in hand. In short, the encounter proceduralizes the division between lethal and nonlethal play, and the latter option has the subsequent benefit of incurring lesser penalties even when the player is discovered.[42]

Although this fight lacks the explicit verbal racialization of Raven's, Snake refuses Olga's identification as an "American," instead calling himself stateless.[43] Here Snake's meeting with Olga amounts to an encounter with militarized whiteness *as* deadly force. This connotation to whiteness draws on

Playable Deniability **109**

a long history of Japanese representations of Western aggression that took their most overt depiction in World War II propaganda. Such representations have lasted into the present, recalling the threat of American military pressure against a victimized Japan.[44] In contrast to Olga, the procedural bearer of these significations, Snake comes into legibility as *hāfu*, as representing a Japaneseness that transcends this "Western" belligerence. This legibility builds on the course of action unique to Snake in *MGS2*, which combines the stealth mechanics of the previous game with the possibility of absolute nonlethality.

This possibility reconfigures Snake's supplemental quality from Raven's fight, shifting it from player *ability* to player *choice*. By relieving Olga of her pistol following the fight, Snake and the player symbolically inherit the capacity for lethal force. Henceforth, it is the player's decision whether or not to use it. The logic of inheritance is paramount here: should the player use the deadly weapon, their actions amount to the mimicry of Olga's militarized whiteness, lapsing back into the *konketsuji* modality. The encounter thus sets a precedent by suggesting that Japaneseness becomes aberrant insofar as it copies militarized whiteness. In fact, the allure of deadly force beckons the player via Snake, who can approach *hāfu* only insofar as he withstands this enticement. The pursuit of the "ethical" path inscribes Japanese difference to militarized whiteness as a form of moral refusal, suggesting that Snake's unique ability to succeed through abstaining from lethality wins the day. As a play style, then, Snake as *hāfu* underscores alterity along the axis of nonlethality, implicitly encoded as resistance to the gameplay temptation of using lethal violence.

However, even as *hāfu*, Snake is only ever an incomplete representative of Japan. In this capacity, he premediates player action and vouchsafes player choice within the complex politics of war memory. A violent fully Japanese character, for instance, risks invoking the much-demonized figure of the Imperial Japanese soldier. A stealthy or nonlethal white character, conversely, risks undercutting the exceptionality of Japan's antimilitarism within *MGS*; that is, the supposed *uniqueness* of its response to, and experience of, war. Biraciality solves both of these issues at the level of choice. Snake as *konketsuji* is "naturally" violent *and* different to full Japaneseness, while Snake as *hāfu* can represent Japanese difference without implicating Japan as such. Moreover, the contiguity of these two mediatic modalities allows for containing the meanings of lethal or nonlethal play from one moment to the next. Should the player choose to step off the path of nonlethality, the *kon-*

ketsuji modality premediates questions around why. Player choice never need rise to a higher level of moral or critical questioning because these actions are deniable as play. Snake's racialization reaffirms Japanese exceptionality in matters of war without shining a light on the larger geopolitical conditions of possibility for that exceptionality. Precisely because Snake's actions can be disavowed racially, his biraciality nullifies questions around Japan's place within contemporary and historical global conflicts.

Conclusion

To conclude, I return to Hutchinson's point that Japan as a national actor is always apart from the world of *MGS*—that it never enters the games as an object of contemplation beyond the tamest conceptions of victimhood and externality to global conflict. As I have argued, Japan attains coherence *through* play, defined in action sometimes counter to, and sometimes through, Snake's racialization. The mainline games deploy Snake's biraciality not in its own conflicted terms but, rather, in terms of a singular and unexamined Japaneseness—a point that echoes Nishime's argument that "in popular film, multiracial people often act as a bridge between cultures, representing racial difference without having to address racial issues at any point in the script."[45] The grand irony of Snake's biraciality is its singularizing effect on Japaneseness. By representing what Japan is not, in a sense, Snake flattens the real politics of Japan's (historical) place in global conflict just as it transforms politicized questions of war memory into a unidimensional and abstract refrain of "antiwar, anti–nuclear weapons." Paradoxically, the cost of playable deniability is the undeniability of race as a distancing mechanism, a line dividing play from politics and Japan from a more complex history of war.

Yet Soraya Murray has also shown how games can engage with the specificities of mixed-raced individuals in ways that do invoke larger political questions. Murray analyzes how mixed-race blackness functions to conjoin gameplay and narrative in *Assassin's Creed: Liberation* (Ubisoft, 2012) around the creole player character, Aveline. As the player navigates New Orleans between 1765 and 1777, they have the option to change Aveline's clothing in a way that foregrounds her multiple racial legibilities. These different "personas," in turn, can heighten persuasiveness, mobility, and combat strength. Murray argues this ability to alter Aveline's hybridized racialization foregrounds "larger themes of passing, contingency, the rejection of

Playable Deniability **111**

binaries and the function of context for identity."[46] From this perspective, biraciality—Snake's included—can open new zones of inquiry around the relation of play and politics because racialization opens itself to critical thought as a process in gamic media. Indeed, *MGS*'s chief failing is its dependence on unified and mutually exclusive categories of identity: *konketsuji* or "full" Japanese, *hāfu* or "foreign." This reliance denies the power of play as a hybrid territory, a zone that is, as noted in the introduction to this volume, undeniably political. If play practices can blur boundaries and multiraciality can reconfigure racial meaning, then closer attention to the intersection of the two can generate more penetrating critiques of Japanese and American military entertainment and racial formations through analytical and ludic epistemologies of hybridity, rather than mutual exclusion.

Notes

1 Huntemann and Payne, *Joystick Soldiers*.

2 Noon and Dyer-Witheford, "Sneaking Mission," 92. See also Whaley, "Beyond 8-Bit."

3 For clarity's sake, I will refer to the series as *MGS*, and individual titles by their number.

4 Noon and Dyer-Witheford, "Sneaking Mission," 78–79.

5 Sicart, *The Ethics of Computer Games*, 107–9.

6 In Japanese scholarship, the series generally features in historical accounts of cinematic games in the 1990s more than textual analysis. See Nakagawa, *Gendai gēmu zenshi*, 295–98.

7 Noon and Dyer-Witheford, "Sneaking Mission," 91.

8 While Snake and Big Boss appear in the original *Metal Gear* (Konami, 1987) and *Metal Gear 2: Solid Snake* (Konami, 1990), Snake's appearance in the 3D *Metal Gear Solid 1* (1998) precedes the 3D rendering of Big Boss in *MGS3* (2005). Consequently, the visual similarities between the two constitute a curious case of the "son" prefiguring the "father's" appearance.

9 Nishime, *Undercover Asian*, 18.

10 Fickle, *The Race Card*, 7.

11 While article 9 of Japan's constitution forbids the use of military force, the creation of Japan's Self-Defense Forces in the 1950s has made the legitimacy and scope of national "defensive" capability an ongoing political issue. See Frühstück, *Uneasy Warriors*.

12 Martin, "Race, Colonial History and National Identity," 577–78.

13 Hutchinson, *Japanese Culture through Videogames*, 216.

14 For more on Japan's narratives of civilian victimhood, see Orr, *The Victim as Hero*; and Seaton, *Japan's Contested War Memories*.

15 Hutchinson, *Japanese Culture through Videogames*, 229.

16 Kawai, "Deracialised Race," 37.

17 Needless to say, Japaneseness is always plural and is homogenized only at the expense of its internal diversity. Goodman's "Making Majority Culture" provides a useful overview of this point.

18 Malkowski and Russworm, "Introduction," 3–4.

19 Sicart, "Against Procedurality," para. 13.

20 See Lye, *America's Asia*, 3, for the contiguity between Asian American "yellow peril" and "model minority" stereotypes.

21 Unless otherwise noted, quoted in-game text is my own translation of the Japanese-language editions of the games.

22 Although the revelation of this information in game occurs first in *MGS1*, metagame materials from as early as *Metal Gear 2: Solid Snake* (Konami, 1990) have suggested Snake's biraciality, leaving it unclear whether Snake himself is aware.

23 Noon and Dyer-Witheford, "Sneaking Mission," 81. The same section provide an excellent overview of the series.

24 Robertson, "Blood Talks," 191. See also Frühstück, *Colonizing Sex*.

25 Yamashiro, "The Social Construction of Race and Minorities in Japan," 151.

26 Iwabuchi, "Introduction," 623–25. See also Iwabuchi, *Hāfu to wa dare ka*.

27 Kimura, "Voices of In/Visible Minority," 1–2.

28 "Halfness" is sometimes ascribed through narrative within Japanese visual culture. See J. G. Russell, "Replicating the White Self."

29 "Seikō shita jinkō jyusei niwa hakase no jyoshu de atta kenkō na nihonjin jyosei no ranshi ga tsukawareta."

30 The game implies that, rather than being an exact duplicate of Big Boss, Snake's cloning used embryo splitting to ensure the conjoined passage of maternal and paternal genetics.

31 Snake's exceptional birth also bypasses narratives of Japanese Americanness in Japan. See Yamashiro, "Racialized National Identity Construction."

32 Kovner, *Occupying Power*, 71–72.

33 Koshiro, "Race as International Identity?" See also Arudou, "Japan's Under-researched Visible Minorities," 720.

34 Horiguchi and Imoto, "Mikkusu rēsu wa."

35 Kawai, "Deracialised Race," 36.

36 Yamamoto, "'Hāfu' no shintai," 136.

37 This is the official North American translation.

38 Yamamoto, "'Hāfu' no shintai," 135.

39 Iwabuchi, "Introduction," 624.

40 For more on this Caucasian avatar, Raiden, see Youngblood, "'I Wouldn't Even Know the Real Me Myself.'"

41 For later narrative reasons, it is impossible to kill Olga here.

42 Roth, *Thought-Provoking Play*, 161.

43 Snake says, "Ore nimo kuni wa nai," literally "I too have no country."

44 See Dower, *Japan in War and Peace* and *War without Mercy*.

45 Nishime, *Undercover Asian*, 7.

46 S. Murray, *On Video Games*, 70.

Yasheng She

Designing the Global Body

Japan's Postwar Modernity in *Death Stranding*

The impact of Asian culture and labor on the global gaming industry is immeasurable, yet representations of Asian bodies are not as prevalent as the various labor forces behind the scenes. This chapter expands on this dissonance between Asian labor and the Asian body through a close read of Hideo Kojima's *Death Stranding* (2019), a game produced by Japanese labor but with a mostly white cast and set in a fictional United States. My close reading sheds light on its racial doublespeaks, where those who are familiar with the context can easily spot the hidden Japanese discourse and find some level of catharsis while others can enjoy the game for its more universal and hopeful message about finding comfort in unity when facing future precarity. Furthermore, I will interrogate this practice of embodying and conveying Asian discourse and argue that it stunts the progress of direct representations.

After his decade-long tenure at the world-renowned game publisher Konami, Japanese video game designer Hideo Kojima departed from his beloved *Metal Gear* (1987–2018) series to create *Death Stranding* (2019), a game with spectacular cinematics and a Hollywood cast. Set in the postapocalyptic

United States, *Death Stranding* follows a courier named Sam Porter Bridges (Norman Reedus), who is tasked with transcontinental unification of the broken United States by delivering parcels to surviving communities and reconnecting them via a wireless communications network known as the Chiral Network.

Unlike the *Metal Gear* series, combat and stealth missions are not part of the major gameplay loop (the repetitive activities that a player engages in games) of *Death Stranding*. Instead, players spend most of their time mapping the desolate landscape. Regardless of whether the design choice is intentional, the in-game task of transcontinental unification parallels Chinese migrant workers building the American transcontinental railroad in the middle of the nineteenth century. Sam's white body and Asian coded labor perfectly demonstrate the dissonance between Asian labor and Asian body. Moreover, the game's engagements with nuclear bombs, sublime ruins, and postdisaster bodies resonate with Japan's postwar identity. By representing the United States with an uncanny landscape and removing American cultural signifiers, *Death Stranding* empties the United States to overlay narratives about crisis, trauma, and identity anchored in Japan's postwar discourse. This strategic overlay begins with the prologue, *Porter*, outlining the game's central theme through the juxtaposition between a voice-over narration written by Kojima and a printed quote from Abe Kobo's *Nawa* (*The Rope*): "'The Rope' and 'The Stick,' together, are one of humankind's oldest 'tools.' 'The Stick' is for keeping evil away; 'The Rope' is for pulling good toward us; these are the first friends the human race invented. Wherever you find humans, 'The Rope' and 'The Stick' also exist." Instead of valorizing the stick as a repellent of evil, *Death Stranding* warns of its danger via a monologue about explosions that appears at the beginning as well as the end of the prologue:

> Once there was an explosion, a bang which gave birth to time and space. Once there was an explosion, a bang which set a planet spinning in that space. Once there was an explosion, a bang which gave rise to life as we know it. And then, came the next explosion . . . an explosion that will be our last.[1]

This sentiment toward the stick resonates with Yoshikuni Igarashi's "foundational narrative" in which postwar Japan sees its wartime trauma, namely the atomic bombings, as inevitable and necessary for the birth of a new Japan, a complicated sentiment manifested into feelings of isolation and despair.[2] *Death Stranding* echoes this sentiment and presents the rope as the solution to the problems left by the stick by asking its players to stitch isolated communities of the broken nation back together. Transposing this discourse onto the emptied-out American landscape, *Death Stranding* works through its ambivalence toward the necessity of the bombs in the foundational narrative while serving an ounce of catharsis for the shattered nation: not Japan but the United States.

It is then imperative to ask, How do white bodies help tell a story about Japan's postwar modernity on the global stage? I will elaborate further through an intimate yet uncanny moment of the game, which takes place in the lavatory of the private rooms. The player can discover private rooms in large cities and later fabricate them in the open world, which all share the same interior layout: a bed, a table, a sink, an interactable map, a glass cabinet, and a lavatory. Setting Sam as the pivot point, the camera in the Private Room rotates around him to reveal a variety of interactable actions. Assuming the position of the camera, the player shares the space with Sam, who sometimes breaks the fourth wall by winking or smiling directly at the camera/player (figure 5.1).[3] Norman Reedus shared that Kojima noticed his fidgety

5.1. Sam, played by Norman Reedus, winking at the player in the Private Room in *Death Stranding*.

Designing the Global Body   117

movements in between motion capture and decided to record them.[4] Reedus explained that Kojima incorporated these movements to add authenticity to Sam with the hope of inciting an intimate relationship between the player and Sam. By having Sam acknowledge the player's gaze, the game forces the player to be aware of their positionality as Sam's controller.

Whenever the player guides Sam to use the lavatory, the player/camera follows him, which triggers an intimate shower sequence. Multiple instances of the sequence exist, but the camera always employs a voyeuristic gaze that moves across Sam's body. The camera first reveals the red bruises on Sam's shoulder and feet, which are visualized evidence of his hard labor. It then moves down to Sam's buttocks and lingers on the ghostly handprints tattooed on his smooth, muscular, and masculine body. These handprints testify to Sam's past trauma: he gains a handprint every time he returns to life, or *repatriates*. Repatriation is Sam's unique ability to resurrect himself whenever he dies in the game. Sam, like most video game characters, can die from a variety of causes. However, thanks to his special ability, the player can resurrect Sam by guiding his soul back to his body. This mechanic makes in-game deaths diegetic, while enhancing the relationship between Sam and the player (figure 5.2).[5]

The shower sequence accentuates the red bruises and the ghostly handprints, evidence of hard labor and trauma, which efficiently frames Sam's body as a site of discourse. The body is further complicated through another dimension of objectification. The game encourages the player to trigger these provocative cutscenes by giving them valuable items called EX Grenades that can be used to repel enemies. These grenades are manufactured with Sam's sweat, urine, and feces, collected when Sam uses the lavatory. This function objectifies Sam's body as a mechanical marvel in addition to the psychosexual nature of the camera.

In this chapter, I will situate Sam's body as a site of postwar discourse. The Japanese body as a site of postwar discourse is at the heart of Yoshikuni Igarashi's *Bodies of Memory: Narratives of War in Postwar Japanese Culture, 1945–1970*. *Bodies of Memory* explores Japan's postwar nationhood through Japanese popular culture, in which Igarashi maintains that the postwar Japanese bodies "not only were the site of Japan's reinvention" but also created a gendered relationship that reflected the power dynamic between the United States and Japan.[6] Igarashi notes that Japan assumed the dominant masculine role in its relations to its colonies during wartime.

118 Yasheng She

5.2. Sam steps into the shower in *Death Stranding*, and the camera follows.

However, Japan's later defeat and occupation recast the postwar Japan in the feminine role, with the United States as the powerful masculine role.[7] Igarashi expands on this imagined masculine ideal through his analysis of Akiyuki Nosaka's novel *American Hijiki* (1967). He highlights the power dynamic that the Japanese protagonist, Toshio, perceives between him and an American soldier. When gazing on the muscular physique of the American soldier, Toshio links Japan's defeat to the overwhelming power demonstrated by the GI's body.[8] In his narration, Toshio defines civilization through the white soldier's muscular arms, big hips, wide chest, and impressive buttocks, while finding himself in the smaller Asian bodies surrounding the GI. Igarashi dwells on this homoerotic gaze to frame the white masculine body as the "material evidence of civilization" in the eyes of the postwar Japanese subject.[9] Aesthetically, the white masculine body is to be feared and desired. The white man's muscle as a metaphor for civilization can be traced back to the early days of Hollywood. Richard Dyer employs films

Designing the Global Body **119**

such as *La Battaglia di Maratona* (1959) to identify the built white body as a product of discipline.[10] Dyer maintains that the white male body mirrors the imperial/colonial enterprise that frames the colonized bodies as inferior and in need of discipline.[11]

Here I will highlight the similarity between the camera in *Death Stranding*'s shower sequence and Toshio's homoerotic gaze. The difference here is that *Death Stranding* complicates the white masculine body by texturing it with allegorical Japanese historic trauma and asks the player to simultaneously identify with and objectify the body. Sam's body is metaphorical because it represents an "elevated" or "apolitical" Japanese body, exorcised of Asian characteristics but bearing the discourse of postwar Japan. It is also strategic to use a white body as the vehicle of Asian discourse so that it appears innocuous to the world yet feels somewhat cathartic to those who are still working through the legacy of white supremacy. This strategy is a form of selective self-erasure in which the Asian body is deracialized so the story can remain compelling and universal. I want to contemplate this affordance of the white body and further ponder the lack of Asian representation in games by first establishing the unquestionable Japanese/Asian discourse in *Death Stranding* and then proposing the unintended consequence of such as a practice.

Asian Labor and the White Body

The story of *Death Stranding* progresses as Sam conducts transcontinental unification. Besides delivering parcels, Sam can also fabricate tools, vehicles, and infrastructure. Through these mundane acts of transportation, delivery, and construction, *Death Stranding* provides unity as the salvation to alienation and despair. I interpret this as the game's response to postwar Japan's complex feelings toward the foundational narrative of Japan. By reclaiming control over the hazardous environment through building infrastructure and the constant self-discipline and maintenance of Sam's body, the game presents a productive and caring masculine figure as the ideal subject, which mirrors the gentle and caring postwar Japanese masculine subject.

Sam as the conduit of the *rope* is demonstrated through the interrogation of his body as a cyborg. The game establishes this element in the prologue through Sam's interaction with a baby in a yellow container, which remains one of the most compelling moments. In the cutscene, the camera zooms in on the device to reveal its contents: a floating fetus whose altered umbilical cord is attached to the operator (figure 5.3).[12]

The baby in the yellow container, called a *Bridge Baby* or simply B.B., is the foremost uncanny element of the game, which has been heavily featured in *Death Stranding*'s promotional materials. B.B. as a tool is well established in the prologue, where Sam's caravan is attacked by ghostly beings known as the *Beached Things* or B.T.s, deceased people whose souls have found their way back into the world of the living. B.T.s can trigger a devastating explosion known as a *Voidout* that leaves nothing but a crater behind. They are invisible to the naked human eyes, and their existence can only be deduced by the presence of the toxic rain known as Timefall, which rapidly deteriorates anything it contacts. To counter B.T.s, scientists create B.B.s through human experiments. By attaching themselves to a B.B., the operator can see the B.T.s around them and navigate the world with ease.

The shot of the B.B. suspended in the container establishes the game's critical entanglement with the body as a site of discourse. The eerie fetus

5.3. The reveal of B.B. in *Death Stranding*'s prologue.

Designing the Global Body **121**

floating in the pod, objectified as a tool, is linked to another human via a half-mechanical and half-organic umbilical cord. This motif evokes Donna Haraway's cyborg, "a hybrid of machine and organism, a creature of social reality as well as a creature of fiction."[13] Haraway is concerned with socialist feminism when she conceptualizes the metaphoric function of the cyborg, and here we see a man performing the conventional feminine duty, but the baby is framed as a useful object, and childcare is situated as equipment maintenance. Thus, I want to employ the cyborg metaphor to pinpoint the social reality allegorically re-created in *Death Stranding*. In this vein, this chapter considers how the game makes use of the body's materiality, labor, and aesthetics to interrogate elements of Japan's postwar modernity while focusing on the interplay between Asian labor and white bodies. Since *Death Stranding* features a Hollywood cast, characters of the games are modeled after well-known actors such as Norman Reedus, Lindsay Wagner, Mads Mikkelsen, and Léa Seydoux. Directors Kojima admires, such as Guillermo Del Toro and Nicolas Winding Refn, also make special appearances. It is easy to see that with such a cast, this Japanese video game neither reserves many speaking roles for Asian actors nor features Asian characters in prominent ways. That said, it does remind the audience of the Asian labor behind the scenes through credits. Credits of Japanese names appear during the prologue and epilogue, where they fade in and out alongside the gameplay. The Japanese names appearing alongside the Hollywood cast elicits a sense of uncanniness at the racial dimension and raises the question, Why does a Japanese game decide to tell a story about America?

To answer this, we must visit the intersection between Asian labor, Asian identity, and Asian bodies. Lisa Nakamura examines racial discourse surrounding Asian identity in the massively multiplayer online role-playing game (MMO) *World of Warcraft* by thinking through the anti-Asian sentiment against Chinese "farmers," whom she calls the player workers.[14] Nakamura frames the anti-Asian rhetoric as racism rather than players' justified concern over player workers manipulating the in-game market, and points out that once an Asian player's racial identity is identified by a white player, their play is immediately framed as labor and a threat to the white player's leisure.[15] Though *Death Stranding* does have a multiplayer aspect where random players' fabrications can be seen and used by other players, they do not have any direct means to interact with others. Because players' racial identities are not visible to others, their labor (fabrications) is not racialized. Even so, *Death Stranding* encodes Sam, the player's in-game avatar,

122   Yasheng She

with Asian discourse through his labor of constructing a transcontinental network from the East to the West, which parallels Chinese migrant workers connecting America in the nineteenth century. Asian bodies, remembered for their labor and for yellow peril racism in American history,[16] are relational to the more civilized power of whiteness, a relation that has become techno-orientalist in the popular imagination of the West as Asia's technology growth has become a concern.[17] In these techno-orientalist fantasies, Asian bodies are imagined as automatons that mindlessly carry out tasks. The game turns this techno-oriental fantasy on the United States by designating a white body to carry out the seemingly mechanical labor of transcontinental unification. Unlike the techno-orientalist approach to Asian bodies, the game persuades the player to see Sam as more than a machine, despite the constant disciplining and management of his body. The player comes to understand the importance of human connections through Sam's labor, a subversion of the techno-orientalist trope where Asian bodies are treated as emotionless automatons. *Death Stranding*'s strategic employment of the body as a persuading agent can also be found in Kojima's earlier works. Noting the racially ambiguous design of the *MGS* series' protagonist Snake, Hutchinson argues that the white-passing body welcomes Western players to empathize with its message.[18] Keita C. Moore, on the other hand, argues that Snake's racial ambiguity, what he calls his biraciality, allows Kojima to flatten "the real politics of Japan's place in and apart from global conflict" and to abstract a generalized and unidimensional message about "antiwar, antinuclear weapons" from Japan's postwar metabolizations of war memories.[19] Thinking through Hutchinson's and Moore's perspectives, we could argue that Kojima's strategy of using racial ambiguity to cater to both the Japanese and the Western audience permits him to embody Japaneseness without any historical baggage.

A similar argument about *Death Stranding* is that the game is produced with a double awareness of the internal (Japanese) and external (US) gazes. Kojima shared on Twitter that his initial script was translated into English for facial and motion capture.[20] Then, for the Japanese release, Kojima had the translated English script modified so that the Japanese voice actors could lip-sync with the American actors. Bodies are used interchangeably as well. A promotional trailer shows the early concept of the scene where one of the woman protagonists, Fragile, meets Sam: Kojima Productions' Japanese staff acted out the scene, and all the elements in the previsualizations were then translated into the game with white bodies.[21] The strategic replacement of

Designing the Global Body   **123**

Asian bodies with white bodies underscores what the game thinks is more globally acceptable.

Koichi Iwabuchi suggests that the lack of Japanese signifiers in Japanese popular media is an intentional strategy. Iwabuchi famously coins the phrase "cultural odor" to describe the acute awareness of one's cultural origin and the desire to disassociate from it.[22] Such an odor is "closely associated with racial and bodily images of a country of origin."[23] Reading these design choices through Iwabuchi's odorlessness, it would appear that the game erased the cultural odor of the Asian body so that the white canvas (body) can remain convincing and persuasive. That said, the Japanese names of the production team remind the audience of the Asian labor. The mixture of Asian labor and white bodies creates an ambiguous racial and political awareness. Tzarina Prater and Catherine Fung argue that for the Asian body's labor to be recognized, it must be converted from "the foreign threat to the assimilated model minority."[24] Though the model minority discourse and the postwar Japanese discourse have different ontologies, they share a common complicity in upholding whiteness as the standard. The universalizing effect of whiteness helps *Death Stranding* bring Japanese discourse to the global stage without historical baggage. In contrast, the very same whiteness becomes a totalizing agent that dictates the desired mode of storytelling in the Asian American context.

In 2017, Japanese animation director Oshii Mamoru's *Ghost in the Shell* was adapted into an American live-action film. When Scarlett Johansson was revealed as Hollywood's choice to play the role of Major Kusanagi Motoko, the casting of the US adaptation quickly attracted criticism for its whitewashing.[25] When confronted with the concern of representation in an interview, Oshii rejected the whitewashing allegation by insisting that the film cast the best actors for the job.[26] Stating that he held no political agenda, Oshii first underscored his desire to create art free of politics to distance himself from the racial discourse.[27] He further defended the casting decision by adding that since *Ghost in the Shell*'s protagonist is a cyborg, she can be represented without racial concern.[28] In the same interview, however, Oshii stated his disappointment in not being a part of the Hollywood adaptation.[29] Hollywood interpreted what Oshii imagined as a neutral body as a white body and then stripped Asian bodies and labor from its primary cast and production team. What happened to *Ghost in the Shell* outlines the core issue of Asian representation: the dissonance between Asian representation and the globalization of Asian culture. Oshii's desire to create "apolitical" art using racially ambiguous or empty characters highlights the danger of self-erasure.

Oshii sees the cyborg as an entity free from racial politics, but Donna Haraway's cyborg repudiates such an assumed apolitical nature. *Death Stranding's* Sam is a cyborg whose body is mobilized to reflect the social realities of postwar Japan. Yet whose body gets to bear whose stories and how they are interpreted are two questions at the heart of representation.

Hidden Japanese Discourse and *Mukokuseki* America

Though Japanese popular media, especially video games such as *Pokémon*, are well received globally, it seems that not many of them feature obvious Japanese signifiers. There seems to be an unspoken agreement about what makes a body globally acceptable. I suggest viewing "the global" as a stage where a subject becomes intensely aware of their body as a medium of their performance and a bearer of external gazes. What makes the performance compelling relies on the body, and what makes a body globally acceptable hinges on the negotiation between the internal and external gazes. In short, the global body is a construct that is persuasive, without distraction, and spectacular. Considering Japan's double positions as both the victim and victimizer during and after World War II, it is easy to see how the desire for a new Japan that can rise (and be divorced) from the ashes of wartime trauma helped to shape Japan's postwar media. In the case of media production, the erasure of Japanese cultural odor helps to make them globally acceptable, a process Iwabuchi labels *mukokuseki*.[30] Christine Yano builds on Iwabuchi's work and thinks through what she calls the commodity "whiteface" of Hello Kitty.[31] Remarking on Japanese companies' desires to create globally compatible consumer products in the 1970s by mimicking Euro-American standards, Yano underscores the ambiguity of the international appeal of Hello Kitty, especially her cute white face.[32] Yano links *mukokuseki* to modernity, whiteness, and global acceptance and adeptly points out the Japanese companies' willingness to self-erase for the sake of global marketability.[33]

That said, it is vital not to see Japanese media as a monolith or treat any media artifact that engages *mukokuseki* as a manifestation of Japanese postwar anxiety. *Mukokuseki* should only work as a framework for contextualizing neutral seeming artifacts. Rachael Hutchinson proposes understanding Japanese video games' transnational and global influence through a postcolonial perspective in her *Japanese Culture through Videogames*, where she frames games as a medium through which historic trauma is represented

Designing the Global Body **125**

and metabolized. This is most evident in her analysis of the nuclear discourse in the *Final Fantasy* series and the *Metal Gear Solid* (*MGS*) series. By examining allegories of ethical and environmental concerns over nuclear energy in the *Final Fantasy* series, Hutchinson links the nuclear discourse to Japan's postwar modernity.[34] Notably, she highlights that Kojima delivers his antiwar message through gameplay mechanics.[35] For instance, while the player can craft nuclear weapons in the online multiplayer spinoff of the *MGS* series *Metal Gear Online*, nuclear weapons can be used only for deterrence. Kojima even openly engaged players with the "Disarmament Event" in 2015 by asking them to disarm their in-game nuclear weapons, which led to a sharp decrease of in-game nuclear arms in a short period.[36] These mechanics allow the players from all over the world to critically engage with real-life nuclear discourse, which is at the crux of Japan's postwar modernity.[37]

Igarashi identifies the "foundational narrative" that rationalized Japan's wartime and postwar trauma as the foundation of the new Japan.[38] What crystallized this narrative are the numerous retellings of August 1945, which frame the atomic bombings of Hiroshima and Nagasaki as inevitable and necessary.[39] The foundational narrative, which frames trauma as the onset of identity, is reflected and problematized in the game's prologue, which opens with shots of landscapes that evoke a sensibility that exists between magical realism and uncanniness: open fields with floating objects, raining clouds over an upside-down rainbow, and mossy planes with sprouting hand-shaped crystals. The sublime landscape warns of the danger lurking underneath the beauty. Theorizing the landscape in *MGS: The Phantom Pain*, Soraya Murray highlights Kojima's configuring of Afghanistan "in need of intervention, through its affective connection to representations of actual events and settings."[40] Murray emphasizes the persuasiveness of the game space to highlight the ideology of the game world and the designer.[41] *Death Stranding* moves away from historical realism to prioritize a different relationship between the player and the game world. Though the game uses US geography as the blueprint for the fictional landscape, it removes all obvious American cultural signifiers—or, in other words, renders the United States *mukokuseki*.

Death Stranding textures this emptied-out America with explosions, ruins, and craters—sublime spectacles that seek to overwhelm and over-awe the beholder's senses. Calum Lister Matheson identifies the sublime as "what beckons beyond our unreliable means of mediation to a *Real* we cannot translate perfectly."[42] Motifs such as radioactive waste and nuclear craters are sublime because they "decenter humanity and disrupt the subject by revealing the vastness of the inhuman."[43] Michael J. Shapiro expands on the political and affective affordance of sublimity by detailing how the sublime resists official event-closing narrativization of collective trauma.[44] The sublime serves to "create conditions of possibility for the divided modes of political comprehension that emerge from oppositional communities of sense."[45] Putting Matheson's framework and Shapiro's argument together and applying them to the Japanese context, I argue that *Death Stranding* mobilizes the sublime to visualize Japan's postwar condition and meditate on the postwar trauma or the consequences of the war or the stick. The game imprints reminders of wartime trauma using ruins and craters to illustrate the destructive and corrupting power of the stick. Overlays of historic trauma find their way into the game, making the sublime more overwhelming because they allude to real historical atrocities.

In *Death Stranding*, Kojima illustrates all explosions as a white screen, which can be interpreted as a means to deny the allure of the mushroom cloud and to avoid reencountering wartime trauma. Instead, Kojima works more closely with the sublime aftermath of the explosion. He establishes this through the traumatized body and landscape of the game and specifically through a fictional depiction of atomic bombings in the postapocalyptic United States. When Sam arrives at the biggest map of the game, Central America, the player learns the history of the thermonuclear bombings. *Death Stranding*'s main antagonist, Higgs Monaghan (Troy Baker), smuggles a thermonuclear bomb into Middle Knot City via a private delivery company known as Fragile Express. The bomb kills most residents, and their dead bodies attract B.T.s. Upon consuming the corpses, B.T.s trigger numerous Voidouts that effectively wipe out the remaining population. The ruins of Middle Knot City remain as a reminder of the attack and its lingering effect. The ruin is constantly showered in Timefall, which renders the space hazardous for the parcel-delivering player. While the player can fabricate tools to make their environment less dangerous, they cannot reclaim the ruins or create an infrastructure that would obscure them. As unmetabolized reminders of the past, these sublime ruins lay siege to any unifying narrative of the collective trauma. Identifying the sublime in images surrounding earthquake ruins in Japan, Gennifer Weisenfeld argues that "reconstruction would wipe away the conflicted memories embodied in ruins and replace them with a coherent commemorative narrative of the tragedy."[46] Similarly, *Death Stranding* treats the traumatic landscape of the ruins as a productive site for alternative memories that also destabilizes the foundational narrative of postwar Japan, where the bomb is the precursor of modernity. Instead, the game transposes these reflections of Japan's postwar modernity onto the *American* landscape. This practice, I argue, serves both as a form of catharsis (of inflicting pain onto the victimizer) and an avoidance toward a direct articulation of painful history.

The game furthers its contemplation of the nuclear bomb through the story of the owner of Fragile Express (played by Léa Seydoux), one of the game's main nonplayable characters. Fragile's backstory is a trauma narrative. Realizing Higgs's plan, Fragile decides to prevent the next attack by taking the bomb far away from the next target—South Knot City. Fragile's unique ability allows her to teleport. Familiar with Fragile's ability and her plan to save the city, Higgs captures Fragile and offers her a choice: she can either teleport to safety alone or throw the bomb into a black tar pit to save the city. Higgs strips Fragile to her underwear and tells her that she must run in the toxic rain. Determined to save the city, Fragile cradles the thermonuclear bomb and begins to run. A series of shots follow Fragile running and falling to the ground as her body deteriorates in the rain. The last frame freezes on her determined eyes as she stands up to resume running (figure 5.4).[47]

In this sequence, Fragile's body becomes a site of nuclear discourse. Her rapidly aged body caused by the rain becomes visual evidence of trauma. Instead of letting the second nuclear explosion occur, her body becomes the stand-in for the symbolic second atomic bombing in August 1945. The last freeze-frame on her eyes uncannily utters the feminized postwar Japan's virtue—rebuilding through endurance and perseverance. Fragile's deteriorated body functions similarly to the sublime ruins as a vehicle of postwar discourse. Fragile's body, covered with bruises and a helmet, is the perfect example of the global body where a deracialized body is employed to elevate a racially and culturally coded story.

Death Stranding is a work of complex contemplations of collective memory, trauma, and identity, which engender antihegemonic narratives about collective trauma, all woven into a story about a traumatized white man rebuilding the broken United States. While the work is effective in its critical engagement with postwar trauma, the unfortunate and uncomfortable truth is that the hidden Japanese discourse might serve to tell stories of white nationalism. This is also where the danger of postwar Japanese discourse and model minority mindset intersects—complicity toward whiteness. In an age where video games are increasingly becoming vehicles of cultural discourse, it is vital to think about the racial aspect of the Asian discourse. Keita Moore also thinks through this question in his essay in this volume,

5.4. Fragile's body deteriorates in the rain as she tries to save the city in *Death Stranding*.

"Playable Deniability: Biracial Representation and the Politics of Play in *Metal Gear Solid*," where he notes that biraciality in video games "can open new zones of inquiry around the relation of play and politics because racialization opens itself to critical thought as a process in gamic media."[48] What Asian artists perceive as a globally acceptable body must be interrogated. Only in this way can the Asian body be racialized and visualized to destabilize the default whiteness of the global body.

Notes

1. Kojima, *Death Stranding*.
2. Igarashi, *Bodies of Memory*, 48.
3. Kojima, *Death Stranding*. Screen capture by Yasheng She.
4. Team Coco, "Norman Reedus and Conan."
5. Kojima, *Death Stranding*, 2019. Screen capture by Yasheng She.
6. Igarashi, *Bodies of Memory*, 14.
7. Igarashi, *Bodies of Memory*, 36.
8. Igarashi, *Bodies of Memory*, 171.
9. Igarashi, *Bodies of Memory*, 171.
10. Dyer, *White*, 164.
11. Dyer, *White*, 165.
12. Santosx07, "*Death Stranding*—Prologue All Cutscenes."
13. Haraway, "A Cyborg Manifesto," 5.
14. Nakamura, "Don't Hate the Player," 130.
15. Nakamura, "Don't Hate the Player," 130.
16. Roh, Huang, and Niu, *Techno-Orientalism*, 11.
17. Roh, Huang, and Niu, *Techno-Orientalism*, 198.
18. Roh, Huang, and Niu, *Techno-Orientalism*, 214.
19. Moore, "Playable Deniability," this volume.
20. Garrett, "Hideo Kojima."
21. NeoGamer, "Behind the Scenes."
22. Iwabuchi, *Recentering Globalization*, 28.
23. Iwabuchi, *Recentering Globalization*, 28.
24. Roh, Huang, and Niu, *Techno-Orientalism*, 199.
25. Berman, "A Comprehensive Guide."
26. Osborn, "An Interview with Dir. Mamoru Oshii."
27. Osborn, "An Interview with Dir. Mamoru Oshii."
28. Osborn, "An Interview with Dir. Mamoru Oshii."
29. Osborn, "An Interview with Dir. Mamoru Oshii."
30. Iwabuchi, *Recentering Globalization*, 28.
31. Yano, *Pink Globalization*, 15–16.

32 Yano, *Pink Globalization*, 16.

33 Yano, *Pink Globalization*, 16.

34 Hutchinson, *Japanese Culture through Videogames*, 132.

35 Hutchinson, *Japanese Culture through Videogames*, 229.

36 Hutchinson, *Japanese Culture through Videogames*, 227.

37 Hutchinson, *Japanese Culture through Videogames*, 229.

38 Igarashi, *Bodies of Memory*, 14.

39 Igarashi, *Bodies of Memory*, 48.

40 S. Murray, "Landscapes of Empire," 194.

41 S. Murray, "Landscapes of Empire," 198.

42 Matheson, *Desiring the Bomb*, 19.

43 Matheson, *Desiring the Bomb*, 20.

44 Shapiro, *The Political Sublime*, 172.

45 Shapiro, *The Political Sublime*, 172.

46 Weisenfeld, *Imaging Disaster*, 159.

47 Kojima, *Death Stranding*. Screen capture by Yasheng She.

48 Moore, "Playable Deniability," this volume.

Prabhash Ranjan Tripathy

The Trophy Called "Asian Hands"

On the Mythical Proficiency of Asian Gamers

Introduction: The Death of the Fighting Game Community

In March 2021, Sony Interactive Entertainment and Endeavour (RTS) purchased the Evolution Championship Series (EVO), the largest and oldest fighting game tournament organized by the Fighting Game Community (FGC). The FGC had been organizing EVO since the late 1990s as a community event, depending solely on volunteer labor, with an aim to reduce corporate influence on the community. Though the FGC had actively resisted corporate influence for more than a decade, it was faced with an unprecedented crisis in July 2020: the online EVO event was canceled in the wake of various allegations of sexual misconduct, including pedophilia, by EVO CEO and cofounder Joey Culler, a.k.a. "Mr. Wizard."[1] The accusations against Mr. Wizard started a series of confessions regarding the prevalence of sexual and racial abuse in the FGC. This led to extreme unrest within the community, so much so that many members declared this "the death of FGC," while others welcomed it as a moment of reckoning and called for speculation and self-interrogation.

Discussions started across Twitch.tv, YouTube, and other platforms around topics such as the future of FGC, where the FGC had gone wrong, possible ways to prevent such events from happening in the future, and so on. It is important to note here that the FGC has a long history of misogyny, homophobia, and racism: in June during the same year, amid the Black Lives Matter (BLM) protests, the lead designer of *Skullgirls* (2012), Mike Zaimont, made an "I can't breathe" reference while commentating on a match.[2] A week later, in the same month, the Marvel/Capcom EVO champion Ryan "FChamp" Ramirez received a lifetime ban for posting a picture of a watermelon with the tag "#WatermelonLivesMatter."[3] The month of April was no different: two streamers and community leaders, "LowTierGod" and "CeroBlast," were banned for using homophobic, transphobic, and racial slurs during their live-streams.

Recognizing that these issues were a community-wide problem, two long-time members of the FGC, David "Ultradavid" Graham and James "jchensor" Chen, dedicated a series of episodes on their channel UltraChenTV to address the issues of racial and sexual abuse in FGC; and in one of those shows, an episode titled "The Worst (Most Important?) Week in FGC History," David and James speculated about the historical causes that might have led to these events. The current chapter engages in a similar speculation. Via a close examination of the notion of "Asian hands" within the FGC, the chapter attempts to both demonstrate and provide a theoretical/historical explanation for the coexistence of and interplay between racial discrimination and meritocracy.

The chapter is divided into four sections. The first discusses the orientalist notion of "Asian hands" and the political function it fulfills within the FGC; the second looks at the construction of FGC as a meritocracy, including its masculinity and subsequent color-blind ideology; the third elaborates on the imperial roots of the association between meritocracy and games that one finds in FGC and examines how games, as a meritocracy, have historically facilitated the process of racial profiling and race making and continue to do so by classifying certain forms of play as prerational. The fourth and final section tries to understand the prerational in the play of Asian hands.

Asian Hands

The expression "Asian hands" is used in the FGC to signify the superior skill set of the Asian players (male): that is, quick reflexes, short reaction time, dexterity, and a sense of timing. These attributes are largely understood in either biological terms (small and more dexterous hands) or cultural terms (Asian countries have more vibrant and competitive gaming cultures).[4] Todd Harper and Chris Goto-Jones, who have worked extensively with the fighting game community, have encountered and offered their speculations on the expression "Asian hands." Harper encountered the expression "Asian hands" for the first time while interviewing an American player named Jeff during an EVO event. In analyzing the interview, Harper sees the existence of such a racialized expression within the fighting game community as a contradiction to the claims of meritocracy upheld by the FGC.[5] Given that meritocracy, competitiveness, internationalism, and hypermasculinity are central to the racial color-blind ideology that one observes in FGC, the existence of a notion like "Asian hands" does more than simply contrast with the meritocratic ideal; rather, it reveals how racial discrimination and meritocracy coexist, how meritocracy is deployed as an excuse not to acknowledge the historical socioeconomic construction of race. Yet the role of the ideals of meritocracy, competitiveness, internationalism, hypermasculinity, and color-blindness in the formation of ludic communities has a long history that predates the FGC. The same ideals were evoked to form the modern Olympic Games in the late nineteenth century and continue to fulfill the same function, and the most recent example is the UFC. Goto-Jones, in his essay "Playing with Being Digital Asia: Gamic Orientalism and the Virtual Dojo" (2015), informed by the works of Naoki Sakai and Stephen Hong Sohn, introduces the notion of "gamic orientalism" as a new experimental form of techno-orientalism wherein a Western player can experience the "Orient." He explains gamic orientalism as the ideological appropriation of flow states in games as Asian.[6] The expression "Asian hands" within the FGC serves an aspirational function, as Asian hands are seen as embodying the flow state. However, Goto-Jones views this aspirational quality as something positive and uses it to develop the "Virtual Ninja Code," a martial arts–inspired mode of playing fighting games.[7] This chapter, while indebted to these observations, studies the operation of "Asian hands" as an orientalist notion (even in its aspirational form) within the meritocratic, competitive, and color-blind FGC to understand the politics of its function and how it helps the liberal Western subject maintain its positional superiority.

Harper's interview with Jeff and Goto-Jones's interview with Ap0ca1yp-t1c0 provide a better starting point than any definition would, because even in their brevity the excerpts capture both the evocation of the expression "Asian hands" and the context in which the expression is evoked within the

FGC. In doing so, the interviews provide a sneak peek into the moment of utterance. The excerpts provide a sense of what explanations and meanings the expression "Asian hands" offers to the community. The first is from Goto-Jones's interview with Ap0ca1ypt1c0 on February 1, 2015: "We just got no chance when they hit us with that next-level, otaku, Brucie shit. They're like *into* it, you know? It's like a whole 'nother level."[8] Similarly, Harper's interview with Jeff during EVO 2009 includes this exchange:

TODD: Like I just don't have the experience playing, I don't have the reflexes either, but that's neither here nor there. But like . . .

JEFF: You don't have Asian hands?

TODD: Ha! Is that a . . .

JEFF: You don't have Asian hands.

TODD: Is that a common way of saying it?

JEFF: Oh yeah. I didn't . . . I've certainly been upset that I'm not Asian at certain points, when I just can't, when I *can't* hit a move, I'll throw up my hands and go "Ahh! If only I could have Asian hands!" and I've heard other people say it too, because you just see, like the Korean players and the Japanese players, they're just like "Whatever! Got it first try!" and it's like, "Aaaah! Give me your fingers!"[9]

Ap0ca1ypt1c0's response not only captures the way the Asian other is perceived and how its gameplay is understood—as exotic, "otaku, Brucie shit"—but also how the category of "we" is established and placed in an antagonistic relationship with the exotic other, a point I will discuss further below. The exchange between Harper and Jeff can be read as a discussion between a novice gamer and an experienced gamer, around the themes of aspiration and frustration with/in the game. Interestingly, both aspiration and frustration as notions and experiences belong to the realm of achievement. While aspiration denotes the hope of achieving something, frustration denotes the feeling corresponding to the inability to achieve something. So we may ask: What purpose does the idea of Asian hands serve in this rather brief discourse on achievement? It would not be farfetched to say that the idea of Asian hands is extended to the novice gamer as a therapy/theory, as a pearl of wisdom, in the expectation that novice gamers can both make sense of and

The Trophy Called "Asian Hands"   **135**

come to terms with their frustrations. The notion of Asian hands fulfills three primary functions. First, it establishes a bond between the two non-Asian gamers, as they share the same fate: as gamers devoid of Asian hands, they are left with no choice but to "embrace the grind," or work hard. Second, it establishes the Asian gamer as a biologically/culturally privileged other and thereby also explains why Asian gamers dominate the fighting game scene. Third, it provides a direction to the aspirations of the novice by subtly suggesting that to be good at fighting games means to be able to defeat Asian gamers. It is important to note that this strategy of privileging and then establishing an antagonistic relationship with the other is one of the central features of orientalism, as it helps maintain the West's status as the hero: an agent of enlightenment rationality and liberal values, deemed the hallmarks of progress and civilization. In orientalist discourse, the privileging of the other in one realm usually comes at the cost of explaining the other's deficits in another realm. Sports historian John Hoberman provides an account of the creation of the athletic savage in the scientific discourses of late nineteenth and early twentieth centuries. The athletic advantage of the savage was explained as a result of his or her weak intellect, civilizational inferiority, technological backwardness, the existence of primitive instincts, and so on.[10]

In a 2004 thread titled "Asians and Fighting Games: Exploring the Myth/ Stereotype" on shoryuken.com (the oldest website dedicated to fighting games), one of the discussants, Murakumo, presents a similar pseudoscientific explanation: he argues that an electric charge travels faster between nerve cells in shorter arms of the Asians, which might provide them with a slight/minimal advantage at games.[11] Steve Choe and Se Young Kim, in their discussion on Western reactions to gamer death in Taiwan Korea and China, observe the continuation of similar orientalist tendencies in video game journalism: death by overplaying is understood in terms of an imbalanced existence of the other, in contrast to the balanced existence of the Western subject.[12]

Much like the Black athlete in many American sports, the Asian gamer is portrayed in esports as embodying a biological/cultural advantage as a result of an imbalance. Within this purview, the skills of the Asian gamer have been boosted by an already existing and overwhelming chance—a chance embodied by an entire race. Thus, the contest is to test the chances of skill alone against a skill boosted by chance. Further, this desire for victory of "pure skill" over "skill boosted by chance," although gaming is an individual undertaking, should be understood as a communal act directed at saving the "game" itself or at least upholding the version of the game where pure skill forms the basis of the ideal of meritocracy "inherent" in the game.

The Color-Blind, Meritocratic, Masculine Composition of the FGC

The FGC has imagined and presented itself as a meritocracy and openly sported a color-blind ideology. As revealed by a study in 2018, the FGC has always considered itself highly misunderstood, especially by the media and also to certain extent by academia.[13] This skepticism has led the FGC to take control of its own PR rather than depending on a third party. Various documentary films celebrating the arcade past, meritocracy, and color-blind ideology have emerged from within the community. In one such documentary film, *The Rise of FGC*, one of the featured gamers explains that FGC includes anyone, anywhere in the world who plays fighting games, whether a well-known title or an obscure one, and irrespective of race or gender.[14] FGC has historized itself in popular discourse as emerging from the local arcade scenes in the 1990s: dedicated players (males) would travel locally to different arcades seeking competition, and eventually the desire to compete went global. The fighting game community, apart from being one of the oldest game communities, is without doubt a unique collective of gamers in many ways. The community centers not on a particular game but on a loosely defined genre. With its internationalist aspirations, the FGC represents a congregation of gaming communities from around the world, formed around a certain list of video games. However, the local gaming communities formed around individual games might have no recognition of this global community or fighting games as a category, as was revealed in my MPhil fieldwork in India (New Delhi and Mussoorie), where the interviewed gamers affiliated themselves to a single game and insisted that one game was completely different from any other.[15]

The FGC has no central governing body or institution. It is an imagined international community held together by lore regarding origins, legends about heroes, and stories from the undocumented underground past. Todd Harper identifies "Arcade Ideal," competitiveness, and meritocracy as central features that define the FGC.[16] The ideals of arcade, meritocracy, and competitiveness are political, as they have long enabled the FGC to construct its own identity as a color-blind meritocracy and have also given the FGC power

The Trophy Called "Asian Hands"   **137**

to define fighting games as a genre. On the one hand, these ideals help the FGC to distinguish itself from esports, which many community members regard as too refined, commercial, and phony compared to the rugged, underground, tough FGC.[17] On the other hand, they give the FGC sovereignty over classifications of games as fighting games, as it often separates itself from combat sports simulations like *EA Sports UFC* (2014) series and platform fighters like *Super Smash Bros* (2018) and *Rivals of Aether* (2015). Over the years, the FGC has aggressively chased these ideals and shown its capacity to put an enormous amount of influence on the industry, so much so that it can determine the success or failure of a title. For example, in 2020 the FGC was consulted by the developers of *Samurai Showdown* (2020) during its development phase. This inclusion, involvement, and approval of the FGC was one reason behind the title's huge success.[18]

Mitch Bowman, in "Why the Fighting Game Community Is Color-Blind" (2014), lists its humble arcade beginnings, meritocratic principles, and competitiveness as features that have helped the FGC to become "color-blind."[19] The argument of the article is a classic case of racial color-blind ideology, but it is not a false representation of the beliefs held up by FGC. FGC is racially more diverse than other gaming communities, but that is not due to an absence of racism; rather, it may stem from the affordability and availability of fighting games during the early phases.

Besides its color-blind ideology, FGC is notoriously masculine and homophobic and was known for repeated sexual misconduct even prior to 2021. In 2012, Aris Bakhtanians harassed his teammate Miranda Pakozdi and eventually forced her to drop out of the Cross Assault event. He later defended his actions by declaring that "sexual harassment is part of the culture, and if you remove that from the FGC, it's not FGC anymore."[20] The actions were highly criticized by the FGC, and various articulations of "few bad apples" were duly put forward by game journalists and players. Needless to say, there is more than a grain of truth in Aris's statement.

A glance at the subreddit r/Kappa provides insights into the prevalence of masculinity and exclusivity in the FGC; the group defines itself as "FGC revolution, fight gentrification with shitposts and anime titties." The group description declares, "E-sports is not a part of FGC." By distinguishing fighting games from esports, the community aspires to break FGC masculinity away from the nerd, techno-savvy image of the gamer and appeal to a more traditional trash-talking, tough-guy image or that of the silent stoic martial artist. Goto-Jones observes (and later encourages) the widespread use of bushido philosophy in the FGC and how the gamers imagine themselves as virtual martial artists.[21] It should be noted, however, that while the use of Asian martial arts philosophy is prevalent in the FGC, the notion of a martial arts philosophy is subordinated to the ethos of competition. While competition does form a part of the martial arts training, competition for the "Virtual Ninja" is the sole site of training, being, and becoming. The martial arts philosophy, metaphors, and images are appropriated and subjected to a principle of competition within the FGC.[22]

The Prerational Play of the Asian Hands

The discriminatory aspect of meritocracy in games has been explored by various scholars across disciplines. Christopher A. Paul argues that merit is a "key part of the code within the games," as it becomes the ideology that governs gameplay. While games are celebrated as pure meritocratic spaces, this celebration comes at the cost of ignoring all structural inequalities. Paul identifies video games as a site where the ideals of meritocracy are "actualized and solidified" and propagated.[23] Games thus become pedagogical sites where a meritocratic worldview can be learned, practiced, and assessed. Lisa Nakamura warns against the dangers of the meritocratic way of thinking about social justice prevalent in gaming communities and game scholarship. She argues that a meritocratic way of thinking may hinder the struggle against racial and gender discrimination by making social justice seem like a privilege and not a right.[24] However, the imagination of the ludic as a purely meritocratic space that one encounters in game communities like FGC predates the advent of video games. The genesis of this imagination can be found in the creation of modern sports.

Jo Littler, in her study on meritocracy, finds the early echoes of meritocracy in the self-help traditions of Victorian England, best represented by Samuel Smiles's best-selling book *Self-Help* (1859).[25] Interestingly, sports historians and sociologists alike, including J. A. Mangan, Allen Guttmann, Eric Dunning, Norbert Elias, John Hargreaves, and John M. Hoberman, have identified sports as a modern phenomenon/institution that emerged from the larger philosophical movement of "Muscular Christianity" in late nineteenth- and early twentieth-century Victorian England. Charles Tennyson celebrates this Victorian achievement in his essay "They Taught the World to Play" (1959). Both the self-help tradition and Muscular Christianity were movements

The Trophy Called "Asian Hands"   **139**

dedicated to prescribing moral and physical practices to working-class men, to help them adjust to, cope with, and fight against the changes brought about by industrialization. While the self-help tradition taught the lesson of "pulling oneself up by one's bootstraps" and thrift as a way for social mobility, Muscular Christianity taught discipline, hard work, amateurism, and manliness. The values from both traditions get embodied in modern sports. Unsurprisingly, Littler observes the importance and continuation of ludic metaphors in the discourse of meritocracy, such as "level playing field" and "social ladder" (which she explains through the imperial appropriation of the Indian game of "snakes and ladders"). Sports could accommodate multiple concerns of Victorian society: it could incorporate the meritocratic ideal as a liberal solution to the plight of the working class and could also address the appeal of physical strength against the threat of technological advancement and its discontents and propagate a new form of masculinity. According to Tara Magdalinski, under Muscular Christianity sports was initially imagined as a reaction against industrialization, urbanization, and migration and proposed as an activity essential for physical and moral well-being.[26] Sports was thought of as a carrier of certain values (the games ethic or sports ideal) that were deemed essential to the formation of modern liberal subject.[27] The values learned via sports were expected to translate and govern the behavior of an individual in everyday life. In this period, one also observes a rigorous reworking and standardization of the rules of various sports; various international sports governing bodies were established to host sports under unified rules. Sportisization of the ludic also had a pedagogical dimension, which explains the inclusion of sports in the English education system early on.[28] The question of whether Victorians taught the world to play might be debatable, but they certainly taught the world *through* play, as, sports were spread across the empire as a pedagogical tool to educate or tame the child, barbarian, native, savage—not to teach the savage how to play. The natives of course had their own games, but those games were different from sports: they were neither meritocratic nor separated from the realm of work. The project of sportisization involved both establishing the ludic space as distinct from the workspace and constructing it as a level playing field governed by the meritocratic ideal. The meritocratic ideal that one observes in gaming communities like FGC needs to be understood within the larger and more complex historical connections between the ludic and the meritocratic imaginaries. Ludic space as a meritocracy is a modern European phenomenon, and it actively distinguishes itself from its historical and geographical other.

140 Prabhash Ranjan Tripathy

Allen Guttmann explains how modern sports differ from the games found in ancient society. He ascribes seven distinct features (two values and five processes) to modern sports that distinguish it from ancient games: secularism, equality, specialization, rationalization, bureaucratization, quantification, and record. Within this schema, the five modernizing processes were deployed to preserve and uphold the modern values of secularism and equality. By secularism, he meant that modern sports, unlike ancient games, are not performed to please or appease some divine, transcendental force; rather, modern sports "are activities partly pursued for their own sake or for other ends which are equally secular." He further explains that "we [moderns] don't run in order that the earth be more fertile. We till the earth or work in factories and offices, so that we can have time to play." Secularism in Guttmann's analysis indicates an idea of games dissociated from both the divine and work. By "equality" he means that "everyone should, theoretically, have an opportunity to compete" and the "conditions of competition should be same for all contestants." One can observe that this is a meritocratic definition of equality.[29] The five processes identified by Guttmann work together to create a meritocracy; sustain and propagate it; and chronicle the merit of contestants.

Norbert Elias, in his collaborative work with Eric Dunning, *Quest for Excitement* (1986), extends his theory of the civilization process in the West to the realm of the ludic. He observes that the folk games played in Europe during the Middle Ages underwent a transformation of sentiment and conduct toward violence that was similar to the changes he had observed in other aspects of Western society. In the case of games, the process included the gradual development of stricter rules to sanitize spaces of playful contests, and the purpose of rules was to exclude violence from the space of competition.[30] The civilization of games is marked by an increasing rationalization, making the game space more meritocratic and less violent. Mihai I. Spariosu, in his discourse analysis of the "play concept" in Western scientific and philosophical tradition, provides a complementary analysis to that of Elias when he observes the existence of two forms or ideas of play in discourse (Western): prerational and rational. The prerational play is pre-Socratic, aristocratic, and heroic, embracing the violence that comes with agon. By contrast, according to Spariosu, rational play is Socratic, middle class, and subject to reason. The rational mentality focuses on the productive and nonviolent side of competition and suppresses the violence and destructiveness in it.[31] The rational notions of play attempt to simultaneously suppress and glorify the prerational by treating it as a thing of the past, but the prerational can never be completely suppressed and keeps resurfacing in various discourses. Spariosu and Elias do not see rationalization as a permanent transformation of play. For Elias, the civilizing process he observes in the West is a constant attempt to control and curb what it considers barbaric; similarly, Spariosu posits that the prerational is always in a feud with the rational. It is important to note that both these studies locate themselves in the West and can be accused of overlooking the imperial dimension of the West and how Western subject, society, and civilization were constructed not only against its historical self but also against the geographical other. The prerational (uncivilized) of the historical past found concrete, physical existence in the colony, the "Orient," the East.

If sports were peddled across the empire to educate the natives to increase their productivity and to teach them to work rather than play, then the diffusion of the games ethic or sports ideal also becomes an occasion where the rationalized, meritocratic ludic space of sports encounters the prerational play of the native. In this context, sports becomes both a tool of tutelage and an experimental site to study the native or to produce racialized scientific knowledge, where natives' physiology is recorded, analyzed, and compared with that of whites. The natives then are invited or admitted into the meritocratic space of the ludic, neither as an equal nor to prove their equality but to establish their difference. In notions like "Asian hands," one can observe the continuation of this practice: while the FGC is open to the Asian, his or her play (good or bad) establishes his or her difference. The ludic meritocracy continues to produce racialized, pseudoscientific knowledge and remains an active site for race making.

The admiration shown toward the play of the Asian in gaming communities or for the Black athletes in sports should be seen not as a sign of inclusion but, rather, as emerging from a nostalgia for the prerational, a lost state. Asian hands become appealing only when they are seen as the embodiment of a flow state, just as Goto-Jones argues. The flow state is desirable because it is believed to operate outside the constraints of rationality, a primordial state where actions precede thinking. Asian hands are desirable and feared because they are machinic and nonthinking. They represent the automata.

Moreover, despite the admiration of the play of Asian gamers or Black athletes, their prerational play remains a threat to the meritocratic, rationalized ludic space of the fighting game and sports. Prerational play exposes the inability of the game space to minimize the element of chance or to provide a level playing field for competition; within the rationalized, meritocratic version of the ludic, prerational play assumes the role of a natural adversary and needs to be suppressed via expulsion or defeat. Only the defeat of prerational play ensures the restoration of the ludic as a meritocratic, rational space. The next section explores the perceived threat of prerational play in the discourse regarding play and games.

Locating the Threat of Prerational Play

The prerational play of the other is not located in the other's incapacity to play or create games; the other is deemed capable of both. The locus of the prerational is, rather, in the purposes of and values expressed by the other's play and game creation. Tara Fickle, in her deconstructive reading of Roger Caillois and Huizinga, demonstrates how the orientalist imagination acts as "the formal logic" guiding the hegemonic ludic theories.[32] In her reading of Caillois's paidia/Ludus distinction, she explains how "Ludus," or "the taste for gratuitous difficulty," which is ascribed with positive attributes including a "civilizing quality," is ultimately thought of as a Western mode of "disciplining paidia."[33] Caillois explains that the path from paidia to Ludus is not the "only conceivable metamorphosis"; cultures that are not driven by the "spirit of enterprise and need for progress" might not develop the same pure and excellent games as Western civilization does but might instead pave a different destiny for themselves. Caillois ends the chapter with a warning that a culture's choice regarding how to channel paidia—toward invention (Western ludus) or toward (idle) contemplation (Chinese *wan*)—is a fundamental choice that determines the destiny of said culture.[34] Informed by Fickle's analysis, one might say that the prerational play of the other resides both in the universally shared paidia and in the inability to choose Ludus. The prerational of paidia is understood as a shared heritage of all humanity; it lies in the realm of the biological and can therefore lead to a nostalgic admiration. However, the prerational emerging from the inability to choose Ludus is a cultural/ political decision, a decision to channelize paidia inward (to feed its own desires) rather than outward (to foster progress, civilization, innovation, enterprise, and so on). Within this view, the other is held responsible for remaining a savage, not because they are unable to play or create games or teach via games but because they are unable to teach the right values via games.

Prerational play arises from the way games are used in/for pedagogy. Uday Singh Mehta reminds us how colonization was essentially a pedagogical experiment to remedy the civilizational infantilism of the native even if that task required imperial despotism.[35] I have already mentioned the role sports played in this pedagogical experiment. The question of why prerational play is a threat lies in its pedagogy: because the prerational play/pedagogy of the other neither distinguishes the world of play from the world of work nor assumes that play is subordinate to or an escape from work, this pedagogy creates deviant subjectivities, imbalanced beings. Eugen Fink, in his reflection on play, defines it as "an oasis of happiness" where players can lose themselves and retrieve knowledge; however, this losing oneself into the game needs to happen at a particular intensity, where one can still distinguish between appearance and actuality. A player who plays at this intensity can enter the oasis of happiness and retrieve knowledge (sensual and philosophical), but those playing at a different intensity—for example, lunatics—can lose themselves in the oasis of happiness but without the possibility of return.[36] The distinction between the lunatic and the player proper is another example of how an instrumental view of play operates in the Western discourse on the ludic. The view that play or game is the site from which knowledge can be extracted assumes a subject that inhabits a world divided between work and play. The other is seen as inhabiting another undivided, inefficient world; the prerational play of the other is pathological, lunatic.

To no surprise, then, the "gamer death" in Asia is still understood within this pathological-racial framework. The work ethic of the Asian gamer in the FGC is also understood as a culture's pathological, obsessive play. The Asian gamer is seen as raised in an overtly competitive, obsessive, unforgiving, and violent gaming scene/environment that encourages obsessive play or game addiction. The Asian gaming culture, as a pedagogical site, is seen as encouraging addiction and allowing the gamers (youth) to venture into the game perhaps never to return; "Asian hands" are forged in a culture that permits the youth to take such dangerous risks, like playing till death or playing video games for a living. The Western gamer might aspire to have Asian hands, visit the arcades of Japan and Korea, read the Book of Five Rings, practice the Virtual Ninja Code, but that Western gamer would always return from the oasis of happiness.

Asian gamers playing along in mythologizing their own hands or gaming ethic is also an extremely common phenomenon. While this is sometimes discussed and celebrated as a radical display of agency and subversion, this chapter shares the skepticism of Lisa Nakamura, Toshiya Ueno, and Masanori Oda, for I believe that participation in this racial mythos propagates misconceptions and further contributes to racism.[37] In the realm of games this participation becomes even more dangerous, because while games have functioned as experimental sites to generate racial knowledge, they have also served as a zone of containment or segregation.[38] The belief that one is essentially good at playing video games or sports can discourage a people from exploring other avenues of life or experiencing life as a whole. By accepting and going along with notions like "Asian hands," the gamer by default also accepts the prerationality of his or her play, the ontology of an imbalanced being, the stereotype of the automata and the addict.

Conclusion/Epilogue: The Defeat of Asian Hands

In 2019, an unknown player from Pakistan, Arslan "ArslanAsh" Siddique, defeated the Korean champion Jae-Min "Knee" Bae in the EVO *Tekken 7* finals. The initial rise of Arslan in the tournament was greeted by the trending hashtag #flukestan, but as he made progress, his "claw style" (the way he holds the handle) became a subject of discussion. On live-streams, when players realized that Arslan is a Muslim, "Hold my beer" jokes were promptly converted into "Hold my biryani/kebab" jokes, which soon transformed into "Hold my bomb" jokes.[39] This is another recent example of how the meritocracy of FGC doesn't safeguard it from rampant racism or stop it from manufacturing another hunting trophy in "Pakistani/Arab hands."

Notes

1 Hall, "Evo Online Canceled Following Accusations of Sexual Abuse against CEO." The offline EVO event was canceled because of the COVID-19 pandemic; the organizers decided to hold the event online.

2 Todd, "Skullgirls Lead Designer Makes 'I Can't Breathe' Joke."

3 I. Walker, "Former Evo Champion Banned."

4 Goto-Jones, "Is *Street Fighter* a Martial Art?"

5 Harper, *The Culture of Digital Fighting Games*.

6 Goto-Jones, "Playing with Being in Digital Asia."

7 Goto-Jones declares that even though he understands that doing so might itself be a form of orientalism, he believes that the ethical success of the project depends on whether the project can positively contribute to the society.

The Trophy Called "Asian Hands" **145**

8 Goto-Jones, "Is *Street Fighter* a Martial Art?," 191–92.

9 Harper, "'Asian Hands' and Women's Invitationals," 113.

10 Hoberman, *Mortal Engines*, 54–55.

11 "Asians and Fighting Games."

12 Choe and Kim, "Never Stop Playing."

13 Steltenpohl, Reed, and Keys, "Do Others Understand Us?"

14 Martinez, *FGC: Rise of the Fighting Game Community*.

15 Tripathy, "Playing Cyborg."

16 Harper, *The Culture of Digital Fighting Games*. "Arcade ideal" refers to the insistence of FGC to remain true to the arcade past, i.e., to play offline (face-to-face) on arcade sticks (not gamepads).

17 Groen, "Why FGC Hates the Word Esports."

18 theScore eSports, *What Is the FGC?*

19 Bowman, "Why the Fighting Game Community Is Color Blind."

20 Crossassaultharass, "Day 1: Sexual Harassment on Cross Assault."

21 Goto-Jones, "Is *Street Fighter* a Martial Art?"

22 This is similar to the way martial arts is appropriated in cage fighting.

23 Paul, *The Toxic Meritocracy of Videogames*, 10–11.

24 Nakamura, "Afterword," 246–47.

25 Littler, *Against Meritocracy*, 26–27.

26 Magdalinski, *Sport, Technology and Body*, 17–18.

27 Mangan, *The Games Ethic and Imperialism*.

28 Mangan, *A Sport-Loving Society*.

29 Guttmann, *From Ritual to Record*.

30 Elias and Dunning, *Quest for Excitement*, 20–22.

31 Spariosu, *Dionysus Reborn*, 12–13.

32 Fickle, *The Race Card*, 117–18.

33 Fickle, *The Race Card*, 128–29.

34 Caillois, *Man, Play, and Games*, 27–35.

35 Mehta, *Liberalism and Empire*, 34–35.

36 Fink, *Play as Symbol of the World*, 25–26.

37 See Ueno, "Techno-Orientalism and Media Tribalism."

38 Hoberman, *Darwin's Athletes*.

39 TheMainManSWE, "Knee Mauled 6–0 by Pakistani Player."

Localizing Empire

Part 3

De-Cultural Imitation Games

Designer Roundtable #3

FEATURING:

Joe Yizhou Xu, an assistant professor of media industries at Old Dominion University, who researches the mobile tech industry in China. Yizhou has worked as a documentarian and broadcast journalist based in Beijing, and as part of his dissertation, he worked for over fifteen months as a localizer for several Chinese mobile game companies based out of Guangzhou and Shanghai. His work has been published in *Social Media + Society* and *Communication and the Public*. His feature-length documentary *The People's Republic of Love* (2016) is available for streaming.

Lien B. Tran, an assistant professor of games and design at the DePaul University's School of Design in the College of Computing and Digital Media. She is director of Matters at Play, a lab applying human-centered and iterative design practices for interactive solutions for social impact and player transformation. She is an award-winning designer whose portfolio includes online and game-based tools for organizations such as Open Society Foundations, the World Bank, and the United Nations.

Christian Kealoha Miller (a.k.a. "Silver Spook"), a Native Hawaiian activist and founder of Silver Spook Games, the worker-owned cooperative studio behind the cyberpunk adventure game *Neofeud* (2017). For several years Chris was a social worker and STEM teacher for underserved and at-risk youth in Honolulu; his clients and students consisted disproportionately of impoverished Native Hawaiians, Asians, and Pacific Islanders. The art, stories, and gameplay of *Neofeud* are largely a reflection of his experiences. Chris has spoken at a variety of conferences including the North American Science Fiction Convention and imagineNATIVE Film + Media Arts Festival, on the "Night of the Indigenous Devs" panel.

Paraluman (Luna) Javier, the creative director and cofounder of Altitude Games, the Manila-based studio behind the free-to-play mobile games *Kung Fu Clicker* (2018), *Dream Defense* (2017), and *Run Run Super V* (2016). She started as a game writer in 2002 as part of the pioneer team that released the first Filipino-made game. She has taught game design at De La Salle University, Manila, and is a Women in Games Ambassador.

Luna Javier: You know, I wasn't even sure that I should be on this roundtable, because even though I've been working in the Philippine game industry for a long time, most of our games are still Western or at least global at launch. The reason we do that is because a lot of people here [the Philippines] are still living under the poverty line. But everybody has a phone. So the big mobile game companies, they do their soft-launch testing in the Philippines, because we love to play games, but we just won't pay for it. So they use the Philippines to measure playing behavior like retention, engagement, but they don't use it to measure monetization. That's one problem that I've seen here with people who keep making games that are obviously Filipino. It doesn't make it a good game, just kind of Filipino-looking. What we try to do is let everyone abroad know that the Philippines can make games. When I was with Anino Entertainment, we were the first team that made a computer game out of the Philippines back in 2002, *Anito: Defend a Land Enraged*. And when we started going to conferences, nobody knew that the Philippines had a game industry. So we had to deal with the usual "Oh, you speak English? I'm so amazed." And then, "I didn't know that Filipinos made games." And we're like, "Okay, to be fair, no one had before." But then that kept on for years.

Joe Xu: In China, many developers marketing to the West mask Chineseness through the localization process, hiding the fact that this is a Chinese game. And they do that because of the long-standing issues of people equating China with low-quality or inferior products. If you look up some of the [Chinese game] companies, they would never put their location as China. They would put it as Los Angeles or something like that—again, as a way of masking their actual location. I think they do it to avoid stigmatization. So when

150   Designer Roundtable 3

we localize games, that process is to reskin the game in a way that it doesn't trace back to the original. And I'm the guy who makes sure the various teams' localizations are good enough to pass off as a polished Western game. The games I make are mostly imitation games, which populate much of the app store. It's a massive industry, and these games are extremely lucrative. You could say it's kind of noncreative in that sense, but I think in a way, as an industrial tactic, it *is* creative in terms of extracting money from these markets.

Chris Patterson: Were you ever able to say, "That image that you're putting in the game looks racist"? Or when you talk about making sure the localizations are "good," does that mean politically correct?

Joe Xu: Yeah, in industry that's called culturalization. For example, we have a lot of Middle Eastern audiences in markets like Turkey and Saudi Arabia. So whenever a game deals with drinking alcohol or certain things that might be offensive to those regions, we have a person there to be a kind of gatekeeper to make sure nothing offensive goes through. But for a small or midsized developer where there's only, like, a couple hundred people, things might get overlooked and slip out. That can cause major issues down the line.

A good example is this Wild West game that I worked on [while working in China]. There's a mechanic in the game where you can basically beat up an NPC [nonplayer character], and one of the NPCs can be Native American. And I told them, "Don't do that. That's really problematic." But then the designer basically told me that this is already hard-coded, we don't have time, we need to push this out in a couple of weeks, and it just goes out. So even when we try to convince people not to do certain things, I think either they don't think it's a good use of their time, or they're really pressured during crunch time.

Christian Kealoha Miller: Some of the best reviews for my game *Neofeud* were in China. The game deals with extreme poverty and ghettoization in one of the most beautiful and expensive places in the world to live [Hawai'i] and was inspired by Brazilian favelas, the worst parts of Mexico City, apartheid Africa, the Indian Mumbai shadow cities, and my experiences in Honolulu favelas. A lot of my games deal specifically with economic, political, social inequality, the military-industrial complex, all that kind of fun stuff—empire specifically. But I didn't do any translation; I couldn't afford it. And in the game, I don't come out and say, "This is a political diatribe. This is Silver Spook ranting in C# code." I just say, "This is a cyberpunk adventure game."

But this Chinese reviewer was like, "I see that America has gone down this unfortunate path where their country has been eaten by some of the unfettered, ultracapitalist individuals. And I hope that my country doesn't collapse in this direction." I had Russian reviewers, too. I was surprised how many around the world played it, even with no translation.

Lien Tran: Thinking about localization, as a designer, I think of context as the people, place, environment, as well as the inputs and outputs that are going to stem from your experience. In comparing the social impact games I make to games made strictly for entertainment, I wonder, "Is the point to be authentic to a culture so people learn about that culture, or is it about meeting the expectations of what people think that culture is about?" Kind of like the tourist effect. For example, I created a game [*Toma El Paso / Make a Move* (2014)] for unaccompanied immigrant minors. They're brought into the custody of the US government. And they're in—there are worse words—but we'll call them shelters. And they're in removal proceedings, meaning the government is trying to determine whether or not they should be removed from the country. So localization is important in a social impact context, and you have to be very careful, because it's based in part on reality. So localization for me in that context means making sure you're authentic and not accidentally sending the wrong message.

In game design, many of us talk about abstraction. A lot of games are about war, but their game systems abstract the idea of combat and war in a very simplified mechanic. I always think about how we're faithfully abstracting the real-world system, but not to the point where we're misinforming, or misleading. And, you know, I've had some backlash where people say, "This isn't real, your game isn't about reality." And it's like, no, this is based on research. It's not the entire world, but it's very representative. That's my spin on localization from a social impact stance. It's not about what will [the audience] understand, but about being faithful to the message or the content.

Joe Xu: And there's no such thing as a global game, to some extent, right? You always have to localize. Even within the language, you might localize it to certain regions.

Tara Fickle: What about the role of Japanese games specifically in this local-global context? Is there a connection between Japanese imperialism and Japan's historical dominance in the games industry?

Luna Javier: With the mobile games we make, we kind of accept that our games can easily be published in the US, Australia, Europe. That's the monetizing side. The territory of China, Japan, and Korea, we call that CJK. If we wanted to publish in CJK, we would actually need to—and Joe would know this—pair up with a publisher from that area and localize or culturalize. Because even if our games were made available in Japan or in Korea, it would just be so different from what's popular there. So even if we have games published in China working with a Chinese publisher, in Japan there's a completely different gaming mindset. The UI [user interface] is different, the attention to detail, the complexity of mechanics and controls are different. We would have to understand that to even be able to compete in it. So we've kept ourselves separate from making games that specifically appeal to the CJK market. However, a lot of Filipinos are heavily influenced by Japan and identify with Japan, even though we were occupied by Japan briefly.

Joe Xu: In terms of history and Japan's role as colonial empire in Asia, Japan and China always had a bad relationship politically. Yet culturally, Japan is heavily influential in terms of manga, anime, and pop culture among Chinese consumers. Take for example *Genshin Impact* (2020), a Chinese game that pays homage to a lot of Japanese games and made a lot of money last year, more than a lot of triple-A studios. And China does a lot of that industrial-level work by recruiting Japanese designers. For *Genshin Impact*, a lot of their voice actors are directly recruited from Japan. And Tencent [a Chinese holding company that owns Riot Games and other entertainment companies] recently bought something like three hundred anime titles for exclusive IP rights in China, so now they can basically make any anime game they want. I think Tencent is even making a *Pokémon* game now; Nintendo licensed the Switch to them because of China's massive market potential. So I think we're seeing a bit of a transition in terms of empire in the political sense, to thinking about Japan as a cultural empire. The Japanese industry isn't necessarily declining culturally—Japan still has such a prestigious position in the game industry—but they're declining in terms of revenues. Companies like Konami haven't been doing very well, and a lot of their workforce has been crossing over to China.

Christian Kealoha Miller: I just had a conference with a bunch of Indigenous cyberpunk creators. And we're like, "What is an empire?" To me, the difference between what defines an empire, in the context of Japan, the United

States, and all these other powers, is Indigeneity. When you think of Indigeneity, people think, "Native Hawaiians, that's like being in a grass shack dancing around with the headdress on." But actually, Hawai'i had the most advanced, technologically sophisticated society on the planet. There was a higher literacy rate in the 1850s in Hawai'i than in any country in Europe, by the Europeans' own admission. There were electric lights in the capital of Iolani Palace before the White House had electricity. But there's also mutual coexistence, not beggaring thy neighbor, right? Which is nowhere in the history of these empires. But I'm a quarter Japanese, and it's a very deep and difficult question even for me. What is an imperial relationship, and what is a cultural exchange? To what extent does Japan really dominate when clearly Western planetary and American planetary domination has such a huge impact?

Lien Tran: Going back to this idea of design, and how people use games as an outlet to express themselves, to share their stories and identities, that's definitely big, especially in the indie scene and depending on your intersectionality and so forth. For me, because I consider myself a designer first with games as one of my mediums, I feel you have to know your context. And you may be designing for an audience that you would not necessarily identify as. So it is also important to think about the idea of codesign, right? Like, I have expertise in design, and game design or systems design. But I don't know about the social safety net, I don't necessarily know about how citizen farmers [in Tanzania] understand or try to make decisions. I have to learn all that. And so as a designer, I see myself as a sponge to understand the local context for which I am completely an outsider.

Luna Javier: In terms of making games to share our stories, we tried doing that for *Anito: Defend a Land Enraged* (2003), which was based on the Philippines in precolonial times. We set it in a fictional land and everybody was brown, fighting a fictional race that was obviously the Spanish. And we thought we were the bee's knees, having Filipino weapons and creatures and all that. Looking back at it, it was not well made, and we didn't know what we were doing. We thought, "We're introducing the Philippines to the world," but we did it very poorly. So we were really disappointed. It didn't help that I was female as well. One of my first experiences with selling the game here in the Philippines was at a local all-boys school. These high school kids came up to me, and they couldn't believe that I had made it because there was a

154 Designer Roundtable 3

perception twenty years ago that women didn't make games. Technically, I'm the first female game developer in the country. And what that meant was I got to set a lot of rules moving forward. Like, you have to normalize the fact that you can be Asian, you can be Filipino, you can be female and working on these games.

Joe Xu: In my experience working in China, the racial dynamics were almost reversed. They saw me as a privileged Chinese American. Their racial conception was very different in the sense that Chinese companies want Westerners in the company. A lot of their hiring practices directly target foreigners. They want to be seen as international and cosmopolitan, so they often recruit tokenized foreigners in the company just for looks and to have their images on their company page. I find this interesting because the labor is outsourced to China and Asia, but the way they want to be defined as a game company is still predicated on this White Male Game Designer trope. They hire a bunch of people who look like your typical game designer, but they're not really that experienced. It's just to bring social capital to the company.

Lien Tran: Going through this practice right now as a designer, often you design for other people. We talk about knowing your audience—you're not designing for yourself. I think I've gotten used to being the outsider. I've definitely had microaggressions and collaborations where I felt I got pushed out and people didn't properly acknowledge that I worked on a game. It didn't work out so well for my mental well-being. And there were lots of struggles around how to properly credit things. As we don't sign off on every little rule and aspect of the game, what does authorship mean? What does it mean when you're in academia, where "publication" and "authorship" mean one thing, but in games we're talking about something that is inherently collaborative?

Christian Kealoha Miller: For me, I grew up in the part of Hawai'i that's the not-so-nice side of the coconut tree, the part where you die at the age of thirty-nine from diabetes, where water comes out with chromium-6 and lead in it, where people live sixteen to a house. I've worked with so many, unfortunately, human-trafficked Filipinos, as a social worker and STEM teacher. But then when Silicon Valley billionaires have a midlife crisis, they move to Hawai'i, start a game company, eat pizza with twenty-two-year-olds, hang out and play *Call of Duty* or "Call of Colonialism," *Counter-Strike*, or whatever

De-Cultural Imitation Games **155**

the cool game is, and make a bunch of games. Or Mark Zuckerberg, who's currently colonizing Hawai'i on seven hundred acres, who sued the state of Hawai'i to kick Native Hawaiians off the land that he would like to not have them harvesting their food and medicine from. So Hawai'i is ultra-American in that way, and those experiences shaped everything when I entered the game industry, working for these billionaires.

When I brought these opinions into the game industry, they basically said, "No, you're gonna make *Flappy Bird* clone number seventy-six. And you're gonna make us billions of dollars, doing nothing important for forty years of your life." And then I said, "Maybe I should go, I'm not making enough money to survive in Honolulu." So I made *Neofeud*, and having some amount of agency, sovereignty, being able to at least have some kind of organic control over the way that you're making the games, the community—all that's been really important. And I experience a lot less racism.

For me, it's specifically working on these large teams that seems like the problem. Not really the size of the team, but the economic structure, the political structure. I would call the colonial structure of the team "the digital plantation." It's like, "Here, churn it out." You know, I made a lot of fun of *Cyberpunk 2077* (2020) because you spend all this time crunching your little neofeudal peasants—digital artists, programmers, writers, and musicians—and you couldn't even finish a game that didn't nuke everyone's PS4. So the large teams, and particularly structures that are very dictatorial, that have little or no democratic oversight, were terrible. American teams: terrible. Everyone was fired at one of the teams I worked on. And they were all replaced by rich white Los Angeles assholes. They said, "Oh, good. You've got a nice little startup with Hawaiians and Pacific Islanders and Asian journalists. We're going to take over now: EA is taking you. We're eating you."

Luna Javier: So, gaming was one of the few industries that boomed during COVID, because you had all these people who weren't gamers stuck at home. A bunch of people who weren't gamers suddenly got converted into gaming. And there was a specific genre of games called hypercasual games that really boomed. You've probably seen ads for this kind of game because they're super-aggressive with ads: you're cutting people's hair, you're clipping toenails, you're like, sorting boxes, it's really mundane tasks. Not games the way a typical gamer understands them. There's not even a big mental challenge, like all the levels are meant to be snacked on in less than a minute, it's something that you can play with one hand while watching Netflix. This type of game was already a hit before, but there are studies of just how this went through the charts.

So in terms of mobile gaming, it's been good for engagement, sad to say, because people kind of wanted something to do at home. I would be interested to see if people want COVID in their games, because they're playing games to escape, right?

Lien Tran: I'm just thinking about what Luna said. What if we apply a pandemic layer to these everyday, hypercasual games?

Christian Kealoha Miller: I mean, the xenophobia in particularly the last year against China, right, the Wuhan flu, COVID is this—

Lien Tran:—"Asian" thing. Because it's monolithic, right?

Christian Kealoha Miller: Yeah. And then Indigenous people are getting punched on in Canada, because they look like they might be [Chinese]. It's ongoing: the yellow peril, the Chinese Exclusion Act, the historical, ongoing racism, that's definitely being played up and has been played up to this day. Every time the *New York Times* says, "Oh, there might be a bioterror lab coming out of China," it impacts all of us, right? I mean, even Joe is like, I have to like "de-Chinese" all my games so we can even sell anything.

Lien Tran: What if we were to brainstorm a game in this current moment? You know, these anti-Asian attacks that are happening one after another right now. What voice can we raise, what if we were to make a game to bring attention to these issues and have a message: What would that be?

Christian Kealoha Miller: It's really hard for games to explore that because [AAA game companies] got all the money, all the power; they can talk, they can squash you, often delete you off of Twitter or YouTube. It's "too political." Now you're demonetized or we can't publish it. But I do think that's something that has to, as best as you can manage it, really be explored.

Rachael Hutchinson

Colonial Moments in Japanese Video Games

A Multidirectional Perspective

Dynamics of Asian racialization in video games take a specific turn when the development company is itself based in Asia, the production context generating particular narrative frames. Games from Japan carry a double colonial legacy—that of the oppressor in the Asia-Pacific, and that of the oppressed, under Western imperialism in Asia and the Allied Occupation after World War II. As mentioned in the introduction to this volume, game studies scholars tend to treat region-specific games from a formalist or material perspective, focusing on in-game mechanics or global exports rather than historical perspectives. At the same time, postcolonial scholars tend to use British and French imperialism as their yardstick, analyzing Japanese colonialism in Asia through a singular lens of one-sided oppression. Both approaches indicate a Eurocentric blind spot in the scholarly literature, eliding the doubled realities of Japanese history.[1] What happens when we confront that blind spot head-on?

Following critiques of postcolonial theory by Monika Albrecht and Dwayne Donald, I argue that the Japanese colonial case demands a more relational way of thinking, proposing that Japanese video games offer decolonial moments that read against problematic postcolonial understandings.[2] After outlining Japan's historical experience as colonizer and colonized, I compare early and later readings of the *Street Fighter* (1987–) series to show the benefit of multidirectional analysis. I then explore the double coloniality of Japan through the *SoulCalibur* (1995–) fighting game series before turning to longer narrative games in the *Final Fantasy* (1987–) and *Metal Gear* (1987–) series to see how colonial complexities can function in role-playing and action genres.

When we take Japan's doubled coloniality into account, certain themes, motifs, and imagery in the games come into focus as key points of negotiation with the past. Colonial legacies coalesce in the visual and narrative representations of player characters and nonplayer characters (NPCs) alike, illuminating their diegetic motivation as well as the extradiegetic reasoning for their character design, racialized in specific ways and pointing to specific ideologies of identity, belonging, and ownership of place. Focusing on representation entails understanding games as narrative frames that foreground some elements while eliding others. For this reason I will not analyze gameplay dynamics experienced through player-character actions; rather, I will look at interstitial moments where we glimpse colonial effects, whether through character design, battle dialogue, game maps, or localization strategies. Through this kind of close reading, colonial power dynamics emerge not only between Japan and Asia or Japan and the West but also between Japan and its own Indigenous populations.

Japan's Colonial Legacies

The history of Japan-as-colonizer includes the forced migration of Ainu people northward into Hokkaidō, particularly in the 1800s settler programs of the Tokugawa and Meiji periods.[3] It includes the 1879 annexation of the Ryūkyū Islands and their conversion into Okinawa prefecture and, in the twentieth century, the annexation of the Korean peninsula, incursions into the Chinese mainland, and southward advance through Micronesia and the Philippines.[4] Due to a combination of market factors, collective cultural trauma, and taboos of historical memory, Japanese game designers avoid the direct representation of Japanese colonialism in action, although many games are clearly informed by colonialist thinking in their depiction of places,

160   Rachael Hutchinson

people, and historical events.[5] In contrast, countless video game series from Western studios explore colonialism from the perspective of European imperialist powers, including *Sid Meier's Civilization* (1991–), *Age of Empires* (1997–), *Assassin's Creed* (2007–), and others. *Call of Duty* (2003–) similarly shows America's involvement in foreign wars, invited or otherwise.[6] Echoing orientalist European writing and painting in the eighteenth and nineteenth centuries, Western game companies can depict imperialism this way because they are situated in places that historically held power over other places. This kind of game making is sustained by the continued dominance of Western imperialist capitalism, as Nick Dyer-Witheford and Greig de Peuter argue in *Games of Empire*. On the opposite side of this self/other binary, Japanese game companies occupy a very different position.

The history of Japan-as-colonized includes early encounters with European imperialist forces in Asia and the ideological threat of Portuguese Jesuit missionaries in the sixteenth century. Real fears were engendered by the Opium Wars between China, Britain, and France in the 1800s, while unequal treaties with Japan favored Western nations in the 1860s. These power relations informed depictions of Japan by Rudyard Kipling, Oscar Wilde, Gilbert and Sullivan, and other European artists who traveled to Japan and saw it as an "Orient." The artistic collecting trend of *Japonisme* showed not only an admiration for Japanese artistic styles in calligraphy, woodblock printing, and ceramics but also a sense of ownership and domination over quaint oriental artefacts.[7] This discourse on Japan as Orient continued through and after World War II, with the internment of Japanese civilians on American soil and the Allied Occupation of Japan after 1945. Films such as *Teahouse of the August Moon* (1956) presented an exotic, sexualized Japan, followed by "techno-orientalism," with Japan as the futuristic, dystopian inspiration for *Blade Runner* (1982), *Snow Crash* (1992), and numerous other works.[8] Japan continues to flourish as an Orient in the contemporary Western imagination, with kimono featuring heavily in the pop cultural appropriations of Kim Kardashian and Nicki Minaj, and the popular Victoria & Albert Museum exhibition *Kimono: From Kyoto to Catwalk* (2019–20).[9] Japanese game companies have certainly capitalized on this image, packaging Japan as a marketable commodity open to Western consumption and touristic practice.[10] In this context of Japan as colonizer and colonized, the treatment of Japanese video games in game studies and postcolonial studies illuminates how scholars think of Japan and its history, minimizing the significance of the double coloniality expressed in the Japanese arts.

Disciplinary Elisions

It is now accepted that formalist scholars in game studies have analyzed video games as universal media, erasing cultural content and the context of production. Video games from Japan are frequently aligned with those from North America and Europe, part of the Global North and a dominant site of industry production.[11] When origins are discussed, Japanese games are often treated as mere export products, analyzed for how they mitigate cultural content for smoother global distribution.[12] Tara Fickle ascribes this to "entrenched assumptions about game theories (and games) as inherently disinterested, universal intellectual inquiries having nothing at all to do with race and culture."[13] Paul Martin's analysis of *Resident Evil 5* (2009) as a specifically Japanese artistic product, carrying its own ideological burden of race and racialized history, is an outlier in this regard.[14]

A subsection of game studies that does focus on the cultural and historical context of Japanese games takes a postcolonial approach. Scholars considering Japanese fighting games often place their racial representations within a European orientalist rhetorical structure. *Street Fighter* is the series most mentioned by scholars focusing on visual representations, partly due to its extremes of stereotype construction.[15] In this analysis, Japanese designers represent India and Africa in essentialized ways that follow the Western imagery and rhetorical structures described in Edward Said's *Orientalism*, discounting Japan's own positionality in structures of empire. Monika Albrecht criticizes postcolonial scholarship as "unidirectional," arguing that essentialization, othering, and exoticization can be understood as rhetorical strategies stemming from any place (not just Europe).[16] Albrecht uses the example of the Ottoman Empire as a non-Christian, non-European imperialism to show how postcolonial theory can be expanded and reimagined. Japan provides a useful case study to challenge and expand existing theoretical structures.

Returning to *Street Fighter*, Kishonna L. Gray argues that the game reinscribes "hegemonic structures" of "the default racial setting," seen most obviously in the representation of "second- and third-world characters."[17] The game does not simplistically replicate orientalism but situates Japan in a default superior position defined against Asia and other non-European places. Christopher Patterson observes that *Street Fighter* conveys "power structures across the transpacific, where the desire to equalize Japan as a 'normal country' means balancing Japanese characters alongside other political powers and thus situating Japanese racial constructs closer to American and European power."[18] These formulations read stereotyped and default characters in terms of real-world power relations. Adding the doubled colonial experience of Japan to this analysis, and extending it to include other fighting games like the *SoulCalibur* series (1995–), we see characters from Korea, China, Okinawa, and the Philippines in terms of their othered status in the Japanese creative imagination.[19] Japan is positioned as equal to America, but superior to former colonies, perpetuating the legacy of empire.

On the other hand, Japan-as-colonized is examined by Soraya Murray, who situates Kojima Hideo's *Metal Gear Solid: The Phantom Pain* (2015) in terms of Japan-US power dynamics, understanding the 1980s Afghanistan setting "as an extension of the modern project of US empire."[20] Situating games in their specific historical, economic, and sociopolitical context allows us to understand the narrative content, cultural significance, and thematic concerns of the game text. While the idea of Japan-as-colonized appears in these studies through the specter of the Allied Occupation and postwar US-Japan relations, the ideas of Japan-as-colonizer in Asia and Japan-as-colonized in the 1800s have not attracted the same kind of attention.

Dwayne Donald points out historical and institutional reasons for unidirectional postcolonial analysis. First, a great deal of English-language scholarship applies postcolonial frameworks to India, Africa, and Latin America, thanks largely to the entrenched colonial structures of English-language education and the mobility of artists from colonizing powers who produced vast amounts of material to study.[21] China and Japan attract less attention in this structure than locations in South Asia, as the experience of Western imperialism was vastly different. Second, much Japanese critical theory is written in Japanese and thus less accessible to Western scholars.[22] But the translated works of Ōtsuka Eiji, Karatani Kōjin, and Eiji Oguma provide thoughtful interrogations of Japan's colonial history and how it reverberates in popular culture today. Ultimately, the biggest stumbling block is that highlighted by Fickle, who observes that the foundational texts of game studies, written by Johan Huizinga and Roger Caillois, were premised on orientalist European perspectives:

> We overlook these ludo-Orientalist resonances at our own peril, for doing so produces a series of blind spots in our own analyses that unwittingly reproduce some of the original theories' most problematic ethnocentric assumptions. When we fail to acknowledge the East/West distinction as

Colonial Moments in Japanese Video Games   **163**

both the foundation for and a stumbling block in Huizinga's and Caillois's own binaristic conceptions of play and seriousness, magic circle and ordinary life, competition and chance, and so on, the limitations of their theories become our own.[23]

To combat these effects, we can ask what kinds of discourses are being echoed, replicated, challenged, or problematized in the game text. Just as Paul Martin revealed multifaceted racial structures in *Resident Evil 5*, Ryan Scheiding shows complex counter-discourses at work in Japanese and American game representations of atomic bombs.[24] Fickle's *The Race Card* analyzes geopolitical power dynamics underlying *Pokémon GO* (2016), connecting contemporary digital map augmentation to imperial Japanese mapping of the Asia-Pacific, while Patterson's *Open World Empire* investigates the digitized Pacific Ocean, showing how Google Earth VR and *The Legend of Zelda: Wind Waker* (2002) mimic conquering modes of ocean-crossing and island discovery. These readings open more nuanced postcolonial frameworks applied to the Japanese case. In the remainder of this essay, I consider some additional case studies that offer entry points into decolonial ways of thinking about Japanese games, attempting to read against "unidirectional" postcolonial frameworks.

Imperial Threats in *SoulCalibur*

Whereas Western strategy games reproduce the conquering logics of European powers across the globe, Japanese strategy games play out within the islands of Japan. The focus of the long-running series *Nobunaga's Ambition* (1983–) is not on outward expansion but on inner territorial struggle, with regional warlords pitted against each other in the sixteenth century. The genre of "real-time strategy" differs greatly between the Japanese and Western game industries, a difference based on geopolitical actualities in the sixteenth to nineteenth centuries. Critics of the notion that Japan felt colonized by European powers in the Tokugawa period (1603–1868) argue that Britain and France never established settlements in Japan the same way they did in the Chinese concessions, let alone the established bureaucracies of India and African nations. But it is easy to underestimate the feeling of threat engendered by Japan's close neighbor China falling to Western imperialism. The effects of Western imperialism in Japan are clearly seen in historical

164   Rachael Hutchinson

strategy games set in the feudal and warring states periods, evidenced by the European weaponry used by troops as well as in the spread of Christianity, memorably portrayed through Lord Akashi and Lady Hosokawa Gracia in *Kessen* (2000).[25] In fighting games, an interesting case study is the *SoulCalibur* series, also set in the sixteenth century. The narrative framing of colonial dynamics is clear in *SoulCalibur II* (2002), a breakout hit on the PlayStation 2 after the arcade blockbuster *Soul Edge* (1995) and the first *SoulCalibur* (1998) title on the Sega Dreamcast.

The threat of Western imperialism is shown vividly in the opening cinematics, as we see samurai swordsman Mitsurugi Heishirō facing off against Western soldiers. Dodging arrows as he runs across moored wooden boats, Mitsurugi confronts a line of bowmen with a lone rifleman in the center. The soldier fires his rifle, and Mitsurugi deflects the shot with his katana. Reaching the soldiers, Mitsurugi leaps high in the air with sword raised (figure 7.1). The gunman raises his rifle horizontally to fend off the attack, but Mitsurugi strikes and splits the gun in two as the stirring music reaches a crescendo.

Mitsurugi's face-off with uniformed European soldiers lasts only a few moments on-screen but carries with it a deep binary ideology of Japan versus the West. In the narrative, Mitsurugi hails from Bizen, home of swordmaking and later allied with the Satsuma and Chōshū domains in southern Japan, both of which used European rifles, ships, and artillery for their troops. The Tokugawa years saw the emergence of the *shishi*, or "men of high purpose," fighting for the emperor and older Japanese values in the face of encroaching Western powers. As *SoulCalibur* is set earlier, Mitsurugi may be understood as a symbolic precursor to the *shishi*, living the creed *sonno-jōi*, "Revere the Emperor and Expel the Barbarians."[26] The anachronistic conflation of 1600s action with 1800s ideology fits the emphasis on timelessness in the series, making Mitsurugi's resistance applicable to all time periods up to the present.[27] This kind of Japanese nationalism is not prominent in the narrative or game dynamics but underlies visual representations of characters as well as the privileging of samurai archetype Mitsurugi in the character select screen and user interface.[28] By placing Mitsurugi's act of defiance so prominently in the opening cinematics, the image of Japan-as-colonized is maintained.

On this point, Mitsurugi Heishirō also illuminates the portability of Japanese ideology overseas. *Soul Edge* and the *SoulCalibur* series did not sell well in Asia compared to arcade hits like *Street Fighter* or *King of Fighters* (1994–), which attracted large followings.[29] Unlike the weapons-based *Soul* series, these titles featured bare-handed martial arts fighters. Japanese

Colonial Moments in Japanese Video Games **165**

7.1. Mitsurugi leaps high to cut the rifle in two with his katana in *SoulCalibur II*.

characters in *Street Fighter*, *Virtua Fighter* (1993), and *Tekken* (1994) usually appeared dressed in relatable karate or judo gear (except the sumo wrestler caricature, *Street Fighter II*'s E. Honda). The original *King of Fighters* featured two Japanese school students, Kyo Kusanagi and Benimaru Nikaido, dressed in modern streetwear rather than fighting attire. Although Kyo's backstory evoked traditional Japanese myths of slaying the serpent Orochi in the distant past, he presented visually as an unthreatening and relatable character. In contrast, Mitsurugi's entire visual makeup emphasized his samurai status, an unacceptable and abhorrent figure for the mainland Asian market, recalling banzai charges of Japanese imperial troops in the recent past.

For these reasons, Mitsurugi's character in *SoulCalibur II* was changed to "Arthur" for export to Asia; he retained his physical stature and sword-wielding prowess but acquired blond hair and beard plus an eyepatch, providing some concealment.[30] The art was not well enough developed in *SC II* to denote changes in eye shape based on racial difference, and Mitsurugi's skin tone did not change, as lighter color palettes were used to represent the skin of Asian and Caucasian figures alike. The samurai colonizer of Asia was thus reconfigured into European knight (and, by implication, subduer of non-European peoples through history). It is notable that Arthur's clothing retained distinctly Japanese elements such as *tabi* socks and straw sandals, and his sword is recognizably a katana, bound with *ito* braiding with a *tsuba* guard on the hilt. What interests me about the revised artwork is that Japanese and European imperialism are morphed together, and Japan retains its position of dominance over Asia. This equation of Japan with the West echoes theoretical positionings of Japan as part of the Global North, but the fact that this image was made for export to Japan's previous colonies for the express purpose of erasing Japan's colonial presence in the region and making money from the result points to a more complicated relationship. Mitsurugi Heishirō, simultaneously configured as "man of high purpose" and European knight, provides an opportunity to rethink imperial power dynamics from a multidirectional perspective, as Albrecht proposed.

Imperial Subjects in *Final Fantasy*

Moving from fighting games to the fantasy role-playing genre, the use of European high-fantasy settings in many ways replicates Western imperial rhetorics of mapping, conquering, exploring, saving native inhabitants, an exploiting land for resources—all hallmarks of the adventure game.[31] But this shell acts as a surface container for Japan-specific ideologies, at which the *Final Fantasy* series (1987–) excels. Although each *Final Fantasy* title is a self-contained story, certain items, spells, monsters, and characters recur from game to game, ensuring consistent gameplay. The recurrent character Cid has attracted attention for imperialist connotations. Taking different surnames in each story, Cid is always connected to technology in some way, providing the questing party with rockets and airships or tampering with natural forces to create weapons. Patterson sees Cid as "an allegory for America's role in giving Japan the 'gift of flight' into the modern age and overseeing its ascent from America's own firebombs and atomic warfare into a cultural and economic giant. . . . We can also understand Cid as a critique of the 'madness' of American technological power."[32] Cid is also closely connected to mined resources, energy extraction, and nuclear energy. In *Final Fantasy XII* (2006), Cid is a power-mad user of manufactured nethicite—an engineered version of a naturally occurring crystal much like Magicite in earlier titles. Cid's misuse of these crystals led to destruction and chaos in earlier games, so his narrative asks a moral question: whether to use or abuse technology, and to what ends. *Final Fantasy XII* joins the rest of the series in forming part of Japan's nuclear discourse, stemming from the US bombing of Hiroshima and

Nagasaki.[33] Decolonial thinking allows us to view Cid not only as a symbol of Japan's unease with technology in general and nuclear power in particular but also as a conduit for that Western technology in an Occidentalist critique.

Japan-as-colonizer also plays a large role in the narrative tension of *Final Fantasy XII*. If the player secures the nethicite, party member Ashe may take it and use it against the Archadian Empire, subduing neighboring kingdoms and providing the region with what she sees as benevolent leadership. Japan's Greater East Asia (Dai Tō-A) ideology resonates through Ashe's ambition, the player increasingly uneasy with their own complicity in the plan. Earlier in the series, *Final Fantasy VII* is tied more directly to colonial expansion through the depiction of Shinra Corporation as a military-industrial complex. Cid creates a massive rocket for Shinra's space exploration program, pushing the imperial expansion beyond the confines of the planet. Yuffie Kisaragi and her backstory demonstrate the imperial expansion of Shinra to the end of the world map. The evils of empire appear constantly in *Final Fantasy*, critiquing American and Japanese imperial power alike. Our understanding of the series is diminished if we focus on only one of these aspects.

A closer examination of Yuffie Kisaragi also reveals complex intersections of Japan, China, and an amorphous notion of "Asia." Yuffie's homeland is the

7.2. The main town of Wutai, in *Final Fantasy VII*.

Wutai area (*Ūtai eria*), which sounds Chinese but is written in the katakana script for foreign words rather than in Chinese characters.[34] As seen in figure 7.2, the town's architecture is reminiscent of Chinese style, perhaps after the mode of the Tokugawa dynasty at Nikkō—red-painted wooden pillars and balustrades, a five-tiered pagoda, high pointed roofs with *kawara* tiles, abundant gold leaf and calligraphy. Not pictured here are picturesque canals and bridges crisscrossing the village.

The town's past glory is evident in dialogue, looking back to the "good old days" before Shinra annexed the area. Yuffie describes its trajectory: "Before I was born, Wutai was a lot more crowded and more important. . . . You saw what it looks like now, right? . . . JUST a resort town."[35] In the Paradise Bar, Reno describes the town as "the middle of nowhere." Outside, a villager relates: "Legend has it that the village has been protected by Da-chao, the Water God, and the Five Mighty Gods. But in the last battle, we didn't fare so well. . . . I guess our beliefs were based on nothing more than legends." Wutai is a remnant, defeated in war and looking to the past.

From a gameplay perspective, Wutai is difficult to reach, far out in the corner of the map. A major fight takes place on the sacred Da-chao mountain, a dangerous area for the player without easy recourse to a save point. Yuffie herself is an optional character in the party, marginalized not only from the central plot but also from the player's mission objectives. As a ninja thief, Yuffie obstructs the player's progress, stealing the party's items (although these are later returned). She enjoys hiding in shadows, so the player must expend effort to find her in various places. But it is Yuffie who most vocally opposes Shinra and laments Wutai's diminished position. Defeating her father in the pagoda, Yuffie admonishes: "You turned Wutai into a cheesy resort town peddling to tourists. . . . How dare you!?" He apologizes, but Wutai remains under Shinra's dominion, and the town's future is unclear when we leave the area.

A final note on Wutai shows the complexity of Japan's colonial history, as three bosses in the pagoda have Russian names. The player must defeat Gorky, Shake, Chekov, Staniv, and Godo in turn, prompting some discussion online as to the strangeness of Russian characters in this otherwise stereotypically "Asian" town. The addition makes sense if we consider Wutai in a historical colonial perspective. The northernmost islands of the Japanese archipelago border Russia and are sites of contested ownership. Wutai is in the top northwest corner of the *Final Fantasy VII* map, echoing the placement of Sakhalin and Kuril Islands in relation to Japan. Wutai is thus an agglomeration of China, Japan, Russia, and nameless resort towns. Mechanics, dialogue, boss battles, and the world map thus join with the visual and linguistic depiction of Wutai as a marginal, contested place, a colony.

These instances of colonial commentary in the *Final Fantasy* series are interesting in the ways they emerge in the role-playing genre. Each discrete narrative in the *Final Fantasy* series provides a thematic focus for a clearly unfolding story. Compared to the reliance on visuals and fractured narratives in long-running fighting game series, this can deliver a sociopolitical critique more immediately understandable to the player. On the other hand, character designs point to racialized understandings of colonizer and colonized, with Cid consistently drawn as a bearded, light-skinned man with glasses and Western-style clothing, and Yuffie drawn as an archetypal ninja, with black hair, large dark eyes, and massive shuriken weapon. Visually, Yuffie presents as a Japanese nationalist symbol, but her backstory positions her as an oppressed colonial subject. Perhaps this clash of visual and narrative representation points to the disjunctions of Japan's colonial history, a need for reckoning with the past.

Imperial Elisions in *Metal Gear Solid*

The most obvious place to explore issues of colonialism, imperial expansion, and hostile invasion is the war genre. The longest-running Japanese game series set in the arena of modern war and imperial power is the *Metal Gear* series (Konami, 1987–). The games are set in real-world locations including the United States, Soviet Russia, Costa Rica, Afghanistan, Cyprus, and Cuba, plus fictional locales like Zanzibar Land. The series is often analyzed in relation to empire, masculinity, violence, and in-game mechanics, but what is missing in the majority of this scholarship is the Japanese origin of the game and what that means for representations of imperialism in the franchise. Analysis of empire in the series tends to focus on American power in a US-Japan hierarchy, and Kojima's self-professed anti-American, anti-imperialist stance.[36] But analyzing the series merely in terms of a US/Japan binary privileges Japanese victimhood in the postwar years at the expense of recognizing Japan-as-colonizer, not to mention overdetermining the Allied Occupation as purely American. Outside the US/Japan binary, there remain interesting questions of Indigeneity, the conflation of British and US empires, and the colonial status of Okinawa.

170 Rachael Hutchinson

Indigeneity is first employed in the series to highlight Snake's own racial lineage, revealed by the Inuit warrior Vulcan Raven.[37] With a large raven tattoo covering his forehead, Vulcan Raven is surrounded by ravens in the game environment and calls them his "friends," emphasizing his spiritual connection to animals and totems. Vulcan Raven claims a shared heritage with the player-character Snake: "Blood from the East flows through your veins. Ah . . . your ancestors too were raised on the barren plains of Mongolia. Inuit and Japanese are cousins to each other. . . . We share many ancestors, you and I . . ."[38] Vulcan Raven appeals to Snake as a fellow pawn in games of global powers, sharing a sense of subjugation by white European and North American forces. Their supposed common place of origin, Mongolia, is an ancient civilization now subsumed into modern China. The veneration of ancestors is key to the shaman spirituality Vulcan Raven professes, but modern Japan has shunned its ancestors, spirits, and connections to Asia in favor of American technology and modern science—a system that Vulcan Raven "does not wish to know." Ancient Japan had its own shamanistic practice, now vanished but for the female *yuta* of Okinawa.[39] Vulcan Raven's dialogue posits this premodern spiritual Japan against the military-industrial complex of global empire. In this brief scenario, we see Indigenous peoples treated as an "other" by both Japan and America, with Japan occupying an uneasy position as both colonizer (of the shaman-led peoples) and colonized (by modern forces of Europe, China, and the United States). However, it is notable that the recognized Indigenous people of the Japanese islands, the Ainu, are completely absent from the conversation. In this elision, Japan emerges as a settler-colonial state—although *Metal Gear Solid* was released in 1998, the Ainu would not be formally recognized by the Japanese government as Indigenous people of the archipelago until 2019.

Although imperialism is a clear theme of *Metal Gear Solid*, specificities of empire are often collapsed or conflated, as we see in the backstory of scientist Naomi Hunter, orphaned and raised in Rhodesia. We do not know the scientist's real name, since she took identity papers from a "Naomi Hunter" to pursue life in America. No information is given about her parents, although in the script she wonders whether she might have Indian ancestry due to her skin tone. "Rhodesia" functions as shorthand for a site of empire, without any commentary on the capitalist labor exploitation by Cecil Rhodes, the short-lived nation of Southern Rhodesia (later Zimbabwe), or its continuing racial inequities. Naomi Hunter could have come from any African state, as the specific country has no bearing on the plot. The arbitrary choice glosses over individuating elements of national histories in Africa, as if to say one country in Africa provides the same imperial-shorthand function as any other. Africa and India also merge together as an uncertain place of origin, suggesting the ubiquity and transferability of the British Empire.

Similarly, *Metal Gear Solid V: The Phantom Pain* (2015) makes claims about the global linguistic dominance of English without explicating the historical conditions that led to that dominance. The villain Skull Face plots to wipe out the English language with a vocal parasite, but this is represented as resistance to American linguistic dominance without reference to British expansion and the use of language in bureaucracies and schools across the British Empire. In the logic of *Metal Gear Solid*, Snake, Naomi Hunter and Vulcan Raven are positioned equally as pawns in a bigger global game of bioengineering and military-industrial power, subject to a vague sense of empire unmoored from historical reality. Kojima's Japan positions itself uneasily as part of the technological and scientific advancements of the Global North but also as a victim of those very constructs. The Japanese state is eerily absent from the series, although it does appear in moments such as the treatment of Okinawa.

Okinawa is barely mentioned in *Metal Gear Solid*, although it stands at the nexus of contemporary US-Japan relations. The Allied occupation of Okinawa officially ended in 1972 but continues through the dominance of US military installations on the islands as well as US commercial and security interests in the region. The *Metal Gear Wiki* states: "The Japanese version of *Metal Gear Solid: Portable Ops Plus* (MPO+) features 47 local soldiers based on the prefectures of Japan. . . . Each prefecture soldier has the name of the prefecture written in kanji on the front, a map of the prefecture on the back, and are colored based on the region the prefecture is located."[40] The Okinawan soldier appears in the list of Kyushu prefectures and wears their color clothing, mislocating the Ryūkyū island chain as part of the southernmost island of the main Japanese archipelago. Okinawa is thus subsumed into the "mainland" Japanese governing structure, denying local realities of differences in language, physique, climate, diet, religious practice, and so forth. The overall elision of the Japanese state from one of the most imperialism-focused games made by a Japanese studio points the way back to the original problem: Japan is elided from scholarship applying postcolonial frameworks to video games, partly because its double colonial status is messy and complicated, but also partly because the games themselves work toward an elision of Japan from their colonial representations.

Conclusion

In this essay I have considered games of different genres, which offer some entry points into thinking about Japanese video games in terms of doubled coloniality. I hope to have shown that Japanese games, and their treatment in the scholarly literature, can tell us much about Western understandings of colonial structures, primarily indicating a blind spot at the intersection of postcolonial studies and game studies, which remains fundamentally Eurocentric. Discussing colonialism and empire in games requires discussion of the Asian experience. The "colonial moments" analyzed here show Asia as a complex construction, with the Japanese nation-state as a focal point for intersections with China, Mongolia, Korea, the Ryūkyū Islands, and the Indigenous Ainu as well as Europe and North America. Needless to say, games from Chinese, Korean, or Indigenous designers would offer different visions of Japan-as-colonizer for analysis.

The figures I have chosen to spotlight—Mitsurugi, Cid, Yuffie, Vulcan Raven, Naomi Hunter, and the nameless soldier from Okinawa—offer useful sites of inquiry into colonial structures in Japanese games, although it is notable that they are not main characters. The colonial moments considered here do not form the main plot of the games in which they appear; rather, they exist as interstitial entryways into mainstream ideologies. But it is clear that Japan-as-colonizer and Japan-as-colonized are concepts that reverberate through blockbuster video games from major Japanese studios and offer interesting ways to think about real-world power dynamics and representations. These examples (and many others like them) can expand the scope of game studies and further expand the mission of postcolonial studies from a unidirectional to a multidirectional analytic framework.

Notes

1 On Eurocentric treatments of Japan across various disciplines, see essays by Kaori Okano, Eiji Oguma, and Yoshio Sugimoto in Okano and Sugimoto, *Rethinking Japanese Studies*.

2 Albrecht, "Unthinking Postcolonialism"; Donald, "Indigenous Métissage."

3 B. L. Walker, *The Conquest of Ainu Lands*.

4 Myers and Peattie, *The Japanese Colonial Empire*.

5 See Hutchinson, *Japanese Culture through Videogames*, 189–93; Moore, "The Game's the Thing," 22–27.

6 Patterson observes that *Call of Duty: Modern Warfare* critiques American hegemony and imperialism (*Open World Empire*, 104–11).

7 Napier, *From Impressionism to Anime*.

8 Morley and Robins, *Spaces of Identity*.

9 Alleyne, "What the Kimono's Wide-Reaching Influence Tells Us."

10 *Katamari Damacy*, *Ōkami*, and *Persona 5* are examined as examples in Hutchinson, *Japanese Culture through Videogames*, 21–69.

11 Dyer-Witheford and de Peuter, *Games of Empire*; Penix-Tadsen, *Video Games and the Global South*, 10.

12 Iwabuchi, *Recentering Globalization*; Kelts, *Japanamerica*; Tobin, *Pikachu's Global Adventure*.

13 Fickle, *The Race Card*, 25.

14 Martin, "Race, Colonial History and National Identity."

15 The Indian character Dhalsim is analyzed in an orientalist structure in Mukherjee, *Videogames and Postcolonialism*, 57–58.

16 Albrecht, "Unthinking Postcolonialism."

17 Gray, *Race, Gender, and Deviance in Xbox Live*, 26.

18 Patterson, *Open World Empire*, 55.

19 Hutchinson, "Virtual Colonialism." On colonial legacies in Japanese games see Hutchinson, *Japanese Culture through Videogames*, chap. 9.

20 S. Murray, "Landscapes of Empire," 170.

21 Donald, "Indigenous Métissage," 538–39.

22 Picard and Pelletier-Gagnon, "Geemu, Media Mix."

23 Fickle, *The Race Card*, 118.

24 Scheiding, "Zombies, Vaults and Violence."

25 Fears of Christianity's ideological impact led to the crucifixions, forced apostasy and hidden Christianity (*kakure-Kurishitan*) of the premodern period, resonating in the postwar Japanese imagination through the literature of Endō Shūsaku. Martin Scorsese made a film adaptation of Endō's 1966 novel *Silence* (*Chinmoku*) in 2016.

26 The term *sonno-jōi* has been used since Confucian times to defend the Chinese imperial city from invaders. Japanese nativists popularized the slogan in the 1800s to drive out Europeans from the trading ports and equalize the treaties of the 1860s.

27 On timelessness and the Japan/West binary in the series, see Hutchinson, "Virtual Colonialism."

28 On character design see Hutchinson, "Virtual Colonialism"; on Japanese privilege in the fighting games interface see Hutchinson, *Japanese Culture through Videogames*, 85–87.

29 Ng, "*Street Fighter* and *The King of Fighters* in Hong Kong."

30 Character art may be seen at https://soulcalibur.fandom.com/wiki/Arthur.

31 Harrer, "Casual Empire."

32 Patterson, *Open World Empire*, 118.

33 Hutchinson, *Japanese Culture through Videogames*, chap. 5.

34 There is a real-world Holy Mountain of Wutai in China, generally translated as "Five Plateaus," that echoes the five-tiered pagoda and five gods of the game town.

35 All script quotes are from https://finalfantasy.fandom.com/wiki/Final _Fantasy_VII_script#Homecoming_of_a_Miserable_Daughter.

36 Keita Moore unpacks this stance to show gaping holes in Kojima's logic—see "The Game's the Thing" and his chapter in this volume. See also S. Murray, "Landscapes of Empire"; Dyer-Witheford and de Peuter, *Games of Empire*; and Parkin, "Hideo Kojima."

37 Moore's chapter in this volume analyzes Snake's racial heritage in depth.

38 Greco, "Metal Gear Solid Game Script."

39 Blacker, *The Catalpa Bow*.

40 See https://metalgear.fandom.com/wiki/Metal_Gear_Wiki. This version of the game is available only in Japan.

Souvik Mukherjee

The Video Game Version of the Indian Subcontinent

The Exotic and the Colonized

Introduction: The Indian Subcontinent Vis-à-vis Asian Stereotypes

The earlier version of the cover art of Ubisoft's *Far Cry 4* video game, set in Nepal, ran into some controversy when critics called it out as racist. It seemingly depicted a blond-haired and fair-skinned man wearing a lavish pink suit using what might be a religious statue as a throne while his hand rested on the head of a man of color who is shown kneeling passively, clutching a grenade in his hands.[1] Ubisoft's creative director was quick to point out that the blond-haired man was "not white" and that people had used an incorrect criterion to level criticism; nevertheless, the man of color was soon removed from the cover. The new cover shows only the protagonist with his hands joined in a semi-*namaste*, or the Indian greeting; the way he sits on a broken statue of a Hindu or Buddhist god (the *mudra*, or finger positions, are indicative), with its head beneath his feet and its arms outstretched, makes him look like a four-armed god. One of his legs rests on the other, and a rocket launcher and an assault rifle rest on each side of the statue and the protagonist. Behind him are the Himalayas, Buddhist prayer flags, misty valleys, and half-hidden settlements. The designers may have attempted to erase the racist overtones that offended the critics, but they have taken care to retain the misty (and mystical) notions of the Orient that have been presented in Western accounts of the region since the earliest contact of the Europeans with the Indian subcontinent. The protagonist, Pagan Min (who shares his name with a Burmese king deposed by the British East India Company), is originally from Hong Kong and is purportedly modeled on the Korean dictator Kim Jong Un, thus showing a pan-Asian connection. Speaking of the original controversial image, a commentator on the video game website Kotaku.com observes that "the image and the context surrounding it—or lack thereof—is complicated, people's reactions equal parts bemused and confused" and that "the image itself is a hand grenade that's already going off in slow motion." It is this confusion that makes both the old and new *Far Cry 4* cover images, arguably, an apt metaphor for the representation of the Indian subcontinent in video games and also helps in viewing such portrayals in the context of how Asia is seen from the North American and European perspectives. This chapter aims to situate the representation of the Indian subcontinent in connection with larger discussions of "Asian" video games, especially in terms of the exoticization and sweeping generalizations used to characterize this region.

Although it is one of the most populous regions of the world and is certainly an important part of Asia, the Indian subcontinent is often not immediately associated with the adjective *Asian*, especially in North America, when it comes to cultures and cuisines. As Colleen Lye observes in her *America's Asia*, the "Orient of the American century . . . has predominantly tended to mean East Asia rather than the Middle East."[2] Lye echoes Edward Said when, in *Orientalism*, he observes that the scenario is of course somewhat different in Europe, where the colonial history of European nations has enabled a different understanding of Asia and wherein the subcontinent figures importantly. For Said, orientalism connotes a "Western style for dominating, restructuring and having authority over the Orient." Following this thinking, Lye observes that "where a European Orientalism had disclosed the discursivity of nineteenth-century, territorial-based colonialism, America's Asia thus reflected the discursivity of a neocolonialism that installed the East as a Western proxy rather than antipode."[3] In such a scenario, Lye argues that the cultural production of the Asian American functioned as a geostrategic necessity for maintaining American hegemony and was rooted in the "material history of U.S. relations in East Asia." As far as video game cultures and game studies are concerned, there is a construction of Asia that constructs Japanese video games as the sole representations of Asian video games. Christopher Patterson, in *Open World Empire*, points out how Japan and East Asia "resemble an Asiatic space" where video games,[4] especially those with a certain kind of game art (such as the *kawaii*, or "cute") have become a "medium of Digital Asia."[5]

This chapter aims to address the not-so-well-known narrative of how video games in the Indian subcontinent fare in global perceptions of the culture and industry of video games in Asia. As a rather new arena for studying the games industry and gaming culture(s), the Indian subcontinent illustrates more clearly the othering, the orientalism, and the stereotypes in the way that gaming in the Global North constructs its "Asia."[6] In doing so, it also helps extend and enlarge the idea of Asia and the Asiatic as it applies to the video game industry and culture. The chapter also opens up further possibilities of researching hitherto neglected games culture(s) in different geographies or sections of society that have been subjected to obscurity, silence, and misrepresentation.

Global Flows, Local Cultures, Odorlessness, and Ludo-racism

The Indian subcontinent has attracted international game developers, especially big names in the games process outsourcing (GPO) industry such as Ubisoft, Rockstar, and Zynga, all of which have offices in India. Indian companies such as Dhruva (now a part of Rockstar) and Lakshya Digital also have major clients and have been involved in designing sections of major triple-A video games such as *Red Dead Redemption 2* and *Borderlands 3*. Of course, India is well-known as the BPO (business process outsourcing) hub of the world, and the successes of the Indian software giants such as Tata Consultancy Services, Infosys, and Wipro are also being emulated by much newer game companies such as the ones mentioned. Describing a similar process at work in the games process outsourcing, Anando Banerjee of Lakshya Digital comments:

> The growth potential of GPO industry is much similar to the BPO industry in India, and owes much to the availability of a large trained talent pool in the country at competitive rates. There are additional reasons like familiarity with the English language, inherent cultural flexibility

178   Souvik Mukherjee

of Indians and their ability to quickly absorb and engage with people of other cultures.[7]

The CEO of Dhruva Interactive, Rajesh Rao, has been celebrated by Thomas Friedman as a major figure in his notion of the "flat" world where people are connected and globalized in unthought-of ways, since Dhruva, though based in Bangalore, was poised to become a global player in the video game industry.[8] Of course, in tandem with the global flows and connectivity, one must remember that the global connections are continually deterritorialized:[9] in Arjun Appadurai's words, "Global cultural flows, whether religious, political or market produced, have entered into the manufacture of *local* subjectivities, thus changing both the machineries for the manufacture of local meaning and the materials that are processed by these machineries."[10] Global flows also shape gaming culture in the Indian subcontinent and are increasingly affecting local play cultures and also, indeed, the broader cultural spectrum of the region.

How "Asia" is understood in the video game industry is important in terms of the global flows and as a point of comparison with the scenario in the subcontinent. The Japanese theorist Koichi Iwabuchi suggests the concept of "odorlessness," wherein the object loses its national "odor" and is rendered palatable in a global scenario. Commentators on Japanese games such as Mia Consalvo and Rachael Hutchinson both comment on the cultural odorlessness that pervades some of the games made in Japan.[11] Unlike Western orientalism, which makes a claim toward understanding Japan, according to Iwabuchi, "transnational indifference suggests that 'they' do not even try to understand 'us'" (546). Patterson points to how games today "reflect Japanese cultural aesthetics that . . . deodorize nationalist symbols in order to appear global, while also deploying 'fragrant' racial symbols."[12] Tara Fickle also cautions against such ludo-racial portrayals in *The Race Card*:

> Framed as both the hardest of workers and the most hardcore of players, play for the archetypal Asian is never "just" play: they practice violin until their fingers swell; play *StarCraft* until they drop dead in the middle of the internet cafe; consistently take home the gold, silver, and bronze at every eSports (professional video gaming) championship—and sometimes at the Olympics, too. Indeed, these ludo-racial dualities get at the very heart of what it means to be Asian in America, to be at once yellow peril and model minority, to be constantly misread through stereotypes of "all Asians looking alike."[13]

Video Game Version of the Indian Subcontinent **179**

The concepts of global flows, flatness, and odorlessness necessarily come with problematic concomitant stereotypes that are often connected to race.[14] It ignores the huge diversity of Asian people and their cultures and is thereby also responsible for some sweeping generalizations and stereotypes of the Indian subcontinent and its culture(s). In the complex ways that Appadurai suggests, it is the stereotypes from these global flows that are challenged by local influences, which this chapter will focus on, that prevent the homogenization of the Indian subcontinent; simultaneously, however, the local is also reshaped by the global.

Global Perceptions and Stereotypes from the Indian Subcontinent

In 1991, when *Street Fighter 2* was released on the NES and the Amiga and Atari, very few people in the Indian subcontinent had played the game, as these consoles and computers were not easily available in the country. In 1994, when the *Streetfighter* movie was released in Indian movie theaters, most Indian viewers (including me) did not make the connection with the video game. The film has an Indian scientist, Dhalsim, played by the British Indian actor Roshan Seth who looks completely unlike the original character in the game but nevertheless conforms to stereotypes about Indians as being geeky and bookish. In the game, Dhalsim is depicted with pupil-less eyes and wears saffron shorts and a necklace of skulls, perhaps hinting at being a Tantric. Noting the racial stereotyping, Patterson describes him as an "egregious stereotype of an Indian yogi [who] can be recognized not as an 'odourless' Japanese aesthetic but as a queer exaggeration whose offensive traits signal not realism but a play style, with his ability to strike players from a distance using stretchable arms and legs, as well as his magical ability to incinerate enemies up close by shouting 'Yoga fire!' and spitting out a stream of flame."[15] Both portrayals of Dhalsim, in the film and in the original game, are based on stereotypes that perhaps correspond to the yellow peril and model minority descriptions that have been highlighted both by Lye and by Fickle. In the game, Dhalsim is the rather terrifying-looking yogi (or *kapalika* monk); in the film, he is the rather docile model scientist. *Streetfighter 2* is, however, made in Japan by the company Capcom, and the character of Dhalsim was designed in Asia and rather unimaginatively named after two food items from Indian cuisine, dal (lentils) and *shim* (broad beans). Dhalsim has a wife

180 Souvik Mukherjee

who is called Sari (in the game), after the garment worn by women in the Indian subcontinent. While Dhalsim forms a typical member of the global crew of *Streetfighter 2*, in his case the global flow is characteristically based on Western stereotypes that have been perpetuated in Asia.

Many other such examples abound. Then again, some portrayals may not seem stereotypical, such as the "nuclear Gandhi" in the *Civilization* series, which although not yet the topic of much discussion in India, could be construed as deeply offensive and even racist at many levels. Game designer Jon Shafer seems to have found it funny to make Gandhi a nuclear warmonger in *Civilization V*. Sid Meier, the maker of the original *Civilization* game, writes in his recently released memoirs:

> It is true that Gandhi would—eventually—use nukes when India was at war, just like any civilization in the game, and at the time this did strike a lot of players as odd. The real Abraham Lincoln probably wouldn't have nuked anyone either, but the idea was that every leader draws a line in the sand somewhere. It's also true that Gandhi would frequently threaten the player, because one of his primary traits was to avoid war, and deterrence through mutually assured destruction was an effective way to go about that.[16]

Why representing a globally recognized figure of world peace from the Indian subcontinent as a nuclear warmonger can be considered a joke is something that I am unsure about. It is also an open question whether it is tenable to compare Abraham Lincoln (who presided over the Union forces) with Gandhi, whose philosophy is closer to Henry David Thoreau's. Meier goes on to say that "the Indian political leader Jawaharlal Nehru might have been a more authentic choice, but without Gandhi, the game wouldn't have been nearly as memorable, or as fun."[17] Even Nehru had expressly declared in the Indian Parliament that "we are not interested in making atom bombs, even if we have the capacity to do so," and India's two nuclear bomb tests came long after, in 1974 and 1998.[18] If making Gandhi a nuclear-warmonger is a joke, then it is a cruel one, and one wonders whether the *Civ* developers would have felt the same way about a personage from any other region. If one is to read an appeal to procedural logic (wherein the AI is responsible for the "glitch") in Meier's explanation, then the fact that such a glitch is not rectified is an indication of the game's implicit racism. Although their Gandhi seemingly runs counter to the usual stereotype, the *Civ* games, as I argue elsewhere, actually perpetuate an older colonial stereotype and fear, as embodied in

Winston Churchill's deep-seated resentment against Gandhian civil disobedience.[19] Again, echoing the earlier parallel with the model minority and the yellow peril, Gandhi is seen is both as a model figure of world peace and also, paradoxically, as a threat. Such an idea is not new but is itself a stereotype harking back to colonialism.

Other prominent examples of representations of the subcontinent that are based on uninformed generalizations and stereotypes range from the portrayal of Nepal / Kyrat as a backward and superstitious war-torn country in the *Far Cry 4* example mentioned in the opening paragraph or of an exotic parkour location for Lara Croft in *Tomb Raider*, or a nameless Indian city in *Call of Duty: Modern Warfare 3* as a mere setting for a battle between the United States and Russia, with not a single Indian present.[20] Patterson astutely observes that "as with previous instalments, *Far Cry 4*'s third-world backdrops take advantage of the 'Asiatic' fantasy formed by video games to facilitate a drifting, easy pleasure."[21] Empire is perceived as pleasure. In a similar vein, Samya Brata Roy has recently pointed out how *Hitman 2* presents an extreme orientalist setting and hopes that the game's use of India is satire because, if taken literally, such a portrayal, he feels, "is utterly stupid, borderline offensive."[22] Siddhartha Chakrabarti made a similar comment on an earlier *Hitman* game's portrayal of the Sikh shrine, the Golden Temple in Amritsar.[23] Whether it is Lahore, Pakistan, in *Call of Duty: Black Ops II* or Chittagong in Bangladesh in *Splinter Cell: Blacklist*, the setting is almost alike in that the players either do not encounter any of the local population or merely shoot through the environment, ostensibly to save the world, in another enactment of the "white man's burden," as it was described under colonial rule. The PSP game, *Tom Clancy's Ghost Recon Predator*, shows the US Army intervening in Sri Lanka's civil war and again shouldering the burden of "rescuing" the island nation from terrorism; the reality is more complex, however, and there have been some requests by Sri Lankans to Ubisoft to change the game's location.

Besides these instances, there are also cases of stereotypes that ignore the diversity of culture(s) in the region. For example, in the portrayal of Indians in the *Age of Empires 3: The Asian Dynasties*, considerations of class, historical milieu, religion, and caste (which is common in Hindu communities and also the subject of deeply fraught controversies) are not taken into account. To start with the portrayal of architecture in the game, most of the buildings look like scrunched-down versions of the Taj Mahal, and the very rich diversity of architecture is reduced to one building stereotype that the West identifies with the region. In *Far Cry 4*, besides the other orientalist imagery and the repetition of the "white man's burden," there are some even more overt instances of orientalism—perhaps none more so than the Shangri-La myth as it is experienced by the protagonist under the influence of psychedelic drugs.

Local Histories: Deterritorializing the Stereotypes

It is in such cases that the stereotypes of the global flows are deterritorialized by the local. As Grieve observes, "The fantasy of Shangri-La challenges Nepal game designers, but this myth of isolation has nothing to do with reality," as Nepal has a very high number of people entering from outside the country.[24] In India, as Adrienne Shaw rightly observes, gaming has had a Westernness about it in terms of "history, access and culture" and has been external to Indian media culture, unlike other media industries, but it has been a marker of global progress. Indeed, as she notes, there is no separate word for "gamer" in Hindi (or Punjabi, Gujarati, or Marathi), and this marks out gaming as a very Western and new activity. Nevertheless, with over two centuries of European colonization—mainly British but also French, Portuguese, and Dutch in pockets—much of Indian culture is deeply connected to the West, so it is hard to separate out Western influence. At the same time (and Shaw comes to a similar conclusion), the Indian game industry and markets are quite different and have unique local characteristics: "Diversity was much more central to Indianness than some imagined national community could ever encompass," and mobile gaming markets are of crucial importance in the region.[25] As Appadurai states, the localities themselves may emerge out of the negotiation of globally circulating forms, but I also argue here that they re-form and disrupt these global forms to offset former colonial stereotypes and the very notion of the "global."

The games made in the subcontinent also reflect this deterritorialization of global flows. This section will focus on three representative games from India, Bangladesh, and Sri Lanka to examine how local game development in the subcontinent works as a countercurrent to the stereotypes regarding the subcontinent that have been perpetuated in the global (mostly Western) constructions of the region in video games that often perpetuate earlier colonial stereotypes of race, class, and empowerment. Some other games from the region will also be mentioned but in less detail for the sake of brevity.

During the lockdown that was imposed in India in 2020, the local games industry was able to boast one major success—the release of the video game

Raji, which incorporates art from India's rich temple architecture, Indian classical music, and a story with elements from Hindu mythology. In his review for the *Los Angeles Times*, Todd Martens writes,

> Its tale of a young woman rescuing her brother from forces of the underworld can be told with many backdrops across numerous cultures. But "Raji: An Ancient Epic," a labor of love that was often a struggle to get made by its small team, has a rather specific design intent. Beyond asking players to tackle its demon-like monsters with acrobatic fight moves, the game seeks to highlight a place—ancient India—and the culture it birthed.[26]

In another review, Akhil Arora writes that the game is "proof of what India can contribute to the games industry from its vast culture—with the right eye" and commends the game for having a female protagonist in a "heavily patriarchal society where religion is often twisted to serve misogyny."[27] Nevertheless, the game has been criticized as being a spin-off of a popular console game called *God of War*—Adesh Thapliyal calls it *Goddess of War*.[28] Critics also complain that in trying to make the game accessible to global audiences, the game has lost out on its local appeal (it uses English as its main language and has no Indian-language subtitles), and it also presents an oversimplified version of Hindu mythology, again with global audiences in mind. Finally, Thapliyal faults it for being representative of a political and a Hindu-centric religious bias and "revealing how far conservatism has penetrated the nation's sense of itself."[29] *Raji* nevertheless presents an intriguing case of the global versus the local in the way it presents a local narrative that draws on Indian mythology and yet creates a fiction that relies on conventions of Western popular culture. Of course, among other prominent games from India that address complex social issues regarding caste and religion, Flying Robot Studios' *Missing: Game for a Cause* (2016) and Studio Oleomingus's *Somewhere* (2015) are notable mentions. *Missing* tackles the rather complex and traumatic issue of sex trafficking in eastern India and Nepal; it is probably the only video game from the region that has received international recognition under the "serious game" category. *Somewhere* and its sequels are a rather surreal graphic experience that encompasses subalternity and postcolonial thinking, raising questions regarding how far the voices of the marginalized can be articulated. The Indian diaspora has also inspired games such as *Venba*, which is about southern Indian cuisine but is connected to a sense of loss, memory, and nostalgia. These games, however, are all in the indie genre and have been developed by small studios or groups of people, and there is as yet no major triple-A game produced entirely in India at the time of writing.

Bangladesh and Sri Lanka have also been developing video games that concentrate on their local histories and mythologies. Bangladesh's struggle for independence in 1971 forms the theme of two of its popular games, *Heroes of '71* and *Arunodoyer Agnishikha* (or *The Flame of Sunrise*). The mechanics is that of traditional first-person shooter games such as *Unreal Tournament*, but the backdrop is that of Bangladesh; the difference with the *Call of Duty* and *Splinter Cell* games is that the setting is very relevant to the history of the Bangladeshi people. The Sri Lankan game, *Kanchayudha*, draws on Sri Lankan mythology, and the upcoming *Threta* advertises itself as "a narrative driven fantasy, adventure AAA game which is inspired by Asian & Sri Lankan mythologies and historical characters."[30] In time, with the growth of the video game industries in the region, local cultures will likely have more of an impact on the video games from the Indian subcontinent. Whereas video games from Japan, China, and South Korea are being increasingly discussed in video game research, the games being developed in the Indian subcontinent do not find a place in these global discussions of Asian video games. This will prompt a rethinking of how "Asian" may need to need to be recontextualized in research on the video game industry and player cultures.

The Context of Asia:
Floating Signifiers and Identity Politics

The games from the subcontinent occupy a position of an apparent dichotomy, but in the starker terms of the outsourcing practices, where sections of games from the Global North are outsourced to studios in the subcontinent, as opposed to the games with local content that highlight issues neglected by mainstream triple-A games made in the Global North and also local discourses that resist the sense of "flatness" by identifying the (often colonial) stereotypes and forcible constructions of identity about the regions in the subcontinent.[31] The geopolitical and socioeconomic concerns of the region also play an important role in the gaming culture(s) and industry in the subcontinent. Regarding the complex of the global and the local, the questions that have been seen as relevant for what have hitherto been considered "Asian" video games (or games from Japan and the Asia Pacific) are also applicable once the definition of Asia is extended to include the Indian subcontinent.

Of course, the definite boundaries of Asia have remained contested since the classical past when Herodotus questioned where the borders of Europe were; in recent times, Asia has been described as a "free floating signifier—a term whose exact meaning has not been settled."[32] Roland Barthes, for example, sees Japan "as an immense reservoir of empty signs," and Trinh T. Minh-ha describes it thus: "We read the author reading Asia. He writes, not because he has 'photographed' Japan, but because 'Le Japon l'a etoile d'eclairs multiples' and has placed him in the 'situation of writing.' The unknown he confronts is neither Japan nor China but his own language, and, through it, all of the West."[33] The Orient can only illuminate the Westerner's own truth. In his attempt to address the question of "Asianish games, styles and practices," Patterson has already masterfully shown how such notions of Asia as the void or the excessive are best described as "the virtual other" or the "other produced through recognizing obscurity, silence, and misrecognition."[34] This concept will be invoked further in this section in connection to the Indian subcontinent. Before that, however, it is important to identify the problems of the Western perceptions of the "Asiatic" as Patterson does here:

> As I find in Barthes, Foucault, and Sedgwick, this sense of Asiatic as a placeholder for plurality comes from the desire not to classify others but to understand without knowing, to realize without being certain, to dismantle the self. The Asiatic . . . is rather about the inherent instability of naming, the blurriness of racial thinking, and our experiences within that blur. For this reason, the Asiatic does not translate well into identity politics.[35]

This is, however, only one side of the story, albeit one that is most often in global circulation, especially in the Global North.

In Asian countries, particularly Japan, India, and China, there have been several attempts to establish a sense of Asian identity. Anthony Milner describes some of the early attempts:

> "Asia is one," announced the Japanese art historian Okakura Tenshin (1862–1913). . . . On the other side of "Asia," the Bengali religious leader Vivekananda (1863–1902) was insisting that "on the material plane, Europe has mainly been the basis during modern times," but on the "spiritual plane, Asia has been the basis throughout the history of the world."[36]

The Nobel laureate Rabindranath Tagore from India and Sun-Yat-Sen from China also spoke of the "Asiatic mind." In recent times, organizations such as

186 Souvik Mukherjee

ASEAN (Association of Southeast Asian Nations) and SAARC (South Asian Association for Regional Cooperation) have been formed to represent the interest of Asian nations; they have all made their independent claims for identity as part of Asia. As such, on moving away from the Global North's orientalism or its tendency to view Asia as a void and look from the local perspectives of the Asian countries, the identity of Asia that is seen as being effaced through the Western gaze and through the metaphors of the "flattening" of the world due to globalization is one that persists and keeps challenging the Western stereotypes.

In Conclusion: The Virtual Other and the Games Culture(s) of the Subcontinent

It is now necessary to return to the concept of the "virtual other." The othering that arises through obscurity, silences, and misrecognition has been characteristic of the representations of the Indian subcontinent, whether through the figure of Dhalsim (a Western misrepresentation of India that is perpetuated by a Japanese studio), the politics in the Kyrat of *Far Cry 4*, or how Gandhi is portrayed in *Civilization V*. It is a similar process that results in the ignoring of the subcontinent as anything more than a market for mobile games and the site for outsourcing game art and software. The rendering obscure of the Indian subcontinent in the context of "Asia" as it is perceived by the games culture(s) of the Global North is, arguably, also virtual othering. As commentators have already said, though, even Asia as it is perceived by the Global North (in this case, Japan mainly and now to a lesser extent China and Asia Pacific) is also the virtual other. When viewed only as a function of the global flows, the local "odor" is rendered obscure, and much of the local culture is left to be silent or is reshaped in acceptable Western terms and misrecognized, just like the *Far Cry 4* cover art with which this article began—whether it is the old cover or the new, Asia in its peoples and landscapes is shown as subordinate, exotic, and orientalist. The global and local exist in complex, intertwined ways that need to be studied further and that keep deterritorializing the stereotypes of orientalism, racism, and exoticization.

In this light, reading the games culture(s) of the Indian subcontinent into the "Asia" of video games makes for a big change in perception wherein a much more diverse cultural milieu emerges in games research and, at the same time, the remixing of colonial stereotypes and the reinforcing of a virtual otherness is revealed. The virtual othering of the subcontinent is accompanied by a deterritorialization of the narratives of "flatness" and global flows. The virtual othering of the subcontinent resembles that of other parts of Asia; it also attempts to connect with these other regions of the continent as part of its diverse cultural heritage.

Notes

1 Grayson, "The Problem with *Far Cry 4*'s Box Art."

2 Lye, *America's Asia*, 3.

3 Lye, *America's Asia*, 10.

4 Patterson, *Open World Empire*, 51.

5 Goto-Jones, "Playing with Being in Digital Asia," 39.

6 The term *Indian subcontinent* usually refers to the physiogeographical region comprising the countries of Bangladesh, Bhutan, India, Maldives, Nepal, Pakistan, and Sri Lanka.

7 Mondal, "Gurugram, Bangalore and Pune Have the Potential to Become a GPO Hub."

8 T. L. Friedman, *The World Is Flat*.

9 Deterritorialization is a concept taken from Gilles Deleuze and Félix Guattari's work, where they indicate that the processes of codification are often disrupted to become something that is the opposite of the whole being created. As Claire Colebrook (*Understanding Deleuze*, xii) comments, "Everything, from bodies to societies, is a form of territorialisation, or the connection of forces to produce distinct wholes. But alongside every territorialisation there is also the power of deterritorialisation. . . . The very connective forces that allow any form of life to become what it is (territorialise) can also allow it to become what it is not (deterritorialise)."

10 Appadurai, "How Histories Make Geographies."

11 Consalvo (*Atari to Zelda*, 4) points out two trends regarding Japanese video games—there is either the trend of downplaying the local influence and erasing "unpleasant cultural odours" or the opposite trend of highlighting the "Japaneseness" as a selling point. Hutchinson (*Japanese Culture through Videogames*, 214) observes how *Metal Gear Solid* makes its characters look more Caucasian so as to emphasize the odorlessness. Both of these scholars point at a complexity in viewing video games from Japan and their observations tie into Patterson's comment on racism.

12 Patterson, *Open World Empire*, 53.

13 Fickle, *The Race Card*.

14 In this context, Lisa Nakamura's pioneering work *Cybertypes* is particularly relevant. Rachael Hutchinson's (*Japanese Culture through Videogames*,

235–36) detailed analysis of the lack of Korean characters in the early *Tekken* and *Virtua Fighter* games as well as the portrayal of Korean characters in *SoulCalibur* as objects of sexual exoticization provide interesting comparisons for such stereotypes in Japanese games and would indeed be an intriguing point of comparison.

15 Patterson, *Open World Empire*, 54.

16 Meier, *Sid Meier's Memoir!*

17 Hendrick, "The Influence of Thoreau's 'Civil Disobedience' on Gandhi's Satyagraha."

18 US Arms Control and Disarmament Agency, *Documents on Disarmament*, 338.

19 Mukherjee, *Videogames and Postcolonialism*, 79.

20 Mukherjee, *Videogames and Postcolonialism*, 79.

21 Patterson, *Open World Empire*, 223.

22 Roy, *Games Studies India Adda Talk #7*.

23 Chakrabarti, "From Destination to Nation and Back."

24 Grieve, "An Ethnoludography of the Game Design Industry in Kathmandu, Nepal."

25 Shaw, "How Do You Say Gamer in Hindi?"

26 Martens, "Discover the Joy of a Game That Transports You."

27 Arora, "Review: Made-in-India Raji Is a Feminist Fable and a Strong Debut."

28 Thapliyal, "How 'Raji: An Ancient Epic' Falls into the Indian Far-Right's Trap."

29 Thapliyal, "How 'Raji: An Ancient Epic' Falls into the Indian Far-Right's Trap."

30 "South Asia's First Triple-A Game."

31 It is understood here that the Global North also includes certain Asian countries such as Japan and Singapore; video games from these nations often perpetuate similar stereotypes as European and North American nations, however, as mentioned in connection to cultural odorlessness and, even more so, in the character of Dhalsim, as described above.

32 Milner and Johnson, "The Idea of Asia."

33 Minh-Ha, "The Plural Void."

34 Patterson, *Open World Empire*, 235.

35 Patterson, *Open World Empire*, 235.

36 Milner and Johnson, "The Idea of Asia."

Gerald Voorhees
Matthew Jungsuk Howard

High-Tech Orientalism in Play

Performing South Koreanness in Esports

This chapter looks to esports as a critical site where hegemonic North American cultures engage in techno-orientalist fantasies that conflate conceptions of Asianness with neoliberal rationalities to render Asian-presenting bodies legible and subservient. A global phenomenon with roots in the South Korean gaming scene, esports—the competitive play of digital games—is a dynamic industry with various leagues, each organized around different games and each with their own financial arrangements. But esports are more than an industry; they are a significant element in contemporary game cultures, and they represent a highly stylized form of engagement with games, one that is aspirational and therefore emulated by players broadly. Massive, webbed ecosystems entangling hobby and career, the esports industry brings together professional players, team owners, coaches, journalists, commentators, translators, production teams, and game developers, among others, in physical and digital spaces.[1]

By and large, esports discourses fetishize the Asiatic—specifically Asian players, play practices, and infrastructures—as signifiers of machinic precision, skilled labor, and economic capacity. This fantasy is grounded, in part, on the role of *StarCraft*'s (Blizzard, 1998) Korean professional leagues bringing Western attention to esports, particularly through high-profile events like the government-sponsored 2000 World Cyber Games, and entrenched by nearly a decade of South Korean dominance in *League of Legends* (Riot Games, 2009). Like other configurations of the model minority, the Asian player is useful enough to be included but simultaneously a yellow peril whose genetics and/or cultural background threaten white heteropatriarchy's privileged status as the primary agents and beneficiaries of the neoliberal world system.

Throughout this chapter, we argue that Asian esports professionals' prominence and visibility enables players from around the world to partake in high-tech orientalism and play the techniques of Asian racialization. Our analysis focuses on how North American esports teams tried to adopt South Korean team management, gaming houses (communal housing for professional players and team personnel), play styles, and even players as technologies to subvert South Korean competitive dominance and the already-realized fantasy of a Yellow Future, the future imagined by techno-orientalist rhetorics in which Asians and Asian technologies dominate the West. In our analysis, when performing Asianness fails to materialize expected outcomes, the fantasy is both fulfilled (in that racist otherings are affirmed) and ruined (to the extent that winning remains out of reach). While taking place in the context of techno-orientalist discourses and aesthetics, this high-tech orientalism is made possible by the infrastructure and media apparatus of esports, which segregate players by regions and enable the quantification of Asian play, as well as the material and organizational practices developed by North American teams.

We start by mapping esports' racialization logics entanglements and continuities with Western techno-orientalist fantasies about the Asian other. First, we explain how techno-orientalism is both a continuation and permutation of Western fantasies of the other, and the role of high-tech orientalism in this fantasy. In the context of esports, which are premised in neoliberal rationality, this techno-orientalism is also imbricated with ludo-orientalism. We then turn to how the practices of North American players and teams took shape in the discursive context of the Western gaming press's coverage of South Korean *StarCraft* and later *League of Legends* professional players, and the material context of the infrastructures and institutions of esports that reterritorialize and segregate online players. While we focus on

High-Tech Orientalism in Play   **191**

gaming houses to illustrate how North American players enact high-tech orientalism, we also discuss efforts to "import" foreign players to show how these practices are entangled in a larger assemblage of techno-orientalist thinking. Throughout, we connect this discursive and material formulation of racialized anxiety to the social and economic anxieties of neoliberal capitalism. Our approach aligns with André Brock's critical technocultural discourse analysis to explain the significance of the relations between the affordances of a technology, the forms of activity emerging from users, and the rhetoric and discourse engaged by those communities of practice.[2] For this analysis, we work through critical technocultural discourse analysis to consider both how esports as a media technology—a massive physical-social-aesthetic-economic network—enables high-tech orientalist cultural performances, and how members of the community culturally construct those performances as best practices.

From Techno-Orientalism to High-Tech Orientalism: Race as Technology

While the Western imperial gaze historically imagined the Orient as an ancient, mystical, and mysterious world that inevitably recedes as the West seizes the mantle of history, more recently the Orient is imagined not as the past that will yield to white power but as the future that must be avoided to maintain white supremacy.[3] In the twenty-first century, China is conceived as the existential threat to Western hegemony and has replaced Japan as the primary figure of techno-orientalist discourse. This is facilitated by the complementary role that Japan and China play in the North American social imaginary, where Japan creates technology but China is the technology.[4]

While the figuring of Asians as machine is far from unique to this moment,[5] the "Robotic Asian" figure takes on novel dimensions when theorized in conjunction with Wendy Chun's conception of race as technology.[6] In this formulation, race is conceived from the ground up as a process, a technique of identification and differentiation—in short, a technology of social management. Chun expands Morley and Robins's sketch of cyberpunk to emphasize how the genre thematizes these conjunctions of race and technology in high-tech Asian futures. On a representational level, techno-orientalism's linkage of Asian with technology is made explicit in cyberpunk. As Chun observes, "The human is constantly created through the jettisoning of the

192 Voorhees and Howard

Asian/Asian American other as robotic, as machine-like and not quite human, as not quite lived."[7] But on the level of the corporeal performance of identity, Chun's account of cyberpunk turns to high-tech orientalism to explain a sort of disembodied "passing" by means of global networks of information and communication.[8] This is how cyberpunk thematizes not only the representation of race but the very techniques of constructing, inhabiting, and disturbing racial categories. And critical to this analysis, the high-tech orientalism of cyberpunk also produces a figure of the Western subject that is a victim, one that doesn't seek to overturn the Asian future but, rather, needs it to stage the fantasy of the "console cowboy," the masculinized performance of antihero, or rebel.[9] This is accomplished by piloting racialized people as vehicles to traverse a future hostile to whiteness.

We argue that high-tech orientalism is happening in the North American esports scene and that players and teams are attempting to play well by playing at being South Korean. And while the labor is generative, its payoff is realizing not the sweet success promised by the fantasy but the bitter truth that adopting racialized performance doesn't mean access to the inner world of the raced other. Of course, this failure of high-tech orientalism could enable critical reflection on the part of white North American players, but it is far more likely to embitter them by reinforcing techno-orientalist constructions of Asians as either magically or biologically different.

It should not be surprising that the North American techno-orientalist gaze largely overlooks the particularities of South Korea, with digital games and gaming a notable exception. Though South Korean popular music and culture is increasingly common in North America, South Korea has featured prominently in only a few pieces of North American media. And while films like Tykwer, Wachowski, and Wachowski's *Cloud Atlas* may offer a vivid fantasy of an authoritarian, corporate-controlled Seoul of the future,[10] it is significant that in contrast to the threat constructed of the People's Republic of China's response to COVID-19, South Korea's policy to contain COVID-19 using similar social and digital technologies has been widely praised in the West.[11] But in looking at the myriad cultural discourses circulating around digital games, the techno-orientalist fantasy of South Korea comes into focus.[12] Indeed, it is in the context of gaming and esports, particularly *StarCraft II* and *League of Legends*, that South Korea is made to stand in for all of Asia as the new, universalized, techno-orientalist imaginary.[13] Here South Korea is figured as both the inventor and maker of a form of technology increasingly vital to the global operation of capitalism: management technologies.

Ludo-Orientalism: Esports and the Racialization of Labor

While there has been no small amount of critical attention to the construction and performance of gender norms and roles in esports,[14] comparatively little has focused on how esports is racialized. Outside the competitive fighting game scene, North American esports is almost exclusively a white and Asian space.[15] Even though they are saturated with Asian players and signifiers of Asian cultures, in North America esports are immune to neither the white supremacist culture in which they are situated nor the othering of Asian players.

The Western association of games with Asia predates the digital and can be traced through a long history of "ludo-orientalist" discourses that construct the Orient through the metaphors, logics, and processes associated with games.[16] This is aptly demonstrated in Fickle's analysis encompassing nineteenth-century parlor games, twentieth-century gambling, and the orientalist anthropology at the foundation of game studies. The ludo-orientalism that associates the other with games is strengthened in the context of digital games. This is because digital games are Asiatic; they are suffused with signifiers of Asia, with the "forms, spaces, and personages that many players will find similar to Asia but are never exclusively Asian."[17]

Another vital aspect of this discourse formation lies in the fact that digital games trouble any clear break between gameplay and capitalist production. As Joyce Goggin explains in her survey of the labor of play, game studies considers how play does work, how play and work intertwine, and even how some forms of play have been entirely refigured as work.[18] "Grinding" forms, like gold farming, mark prominent examples of distinctions between work and play so muddied as to lose meaning in most analyses, but gold farming is also a site of racialization. Fickle positions its history as a prehistory of esports' racial capitalism, where Chinese and Southeast Asian players—"the dispossessed subjects of synthetic worlds"[19]—had their labor racially essentialized, tying work/play to raced bodies.[20]

Esports take this further; they are premised on the rationalization of the practices involved in gameplay, the turning of play into instrumentality.[21] As a game is institutionalized as a sport, the experimental and exploratory character of play is truncated and calcifies around the most rationalized, efficient patterns of action. The players' mastery of their gaming technology and their encyclopedic knowledge of the game, which facilitate skilled improvisation, is critical to this instrumentalized performance; they are also critical avenues for the performance of masculinity in these spaces.[22] To play like a man is to have masterful and precise control of both one's body and technology, a juncture that's indexed with metrics like APM (actions per minute) that perpetuate economic and military logics of automation and "noise" reduction within that biotechnical assemblage.[23] Following this thread, roles stereotypically associated with more intensive biotechnical attunements become viewed as more masculine, whereas others are subordinated and effeminized.[24] In this way, the association between economic rationality and a hybrid, sportive, and technological masculinity is sedimented to address neoliberal crises in North American hegemonic masculinity.[25]

The introduction of professional *StarCraft* leagues to North American audiences in the early 2000s through popular press, gaming publications, and online discussion forums provided a site where this othering rhetoric would sediment into several tropes about professional Asian players. This discourse imagines South Korea as a locus where a feminized "cute culture" comes together with the high-tech masculinity of competitive esports.[26] Conflating casual games with intensely complicated games such as *StarCraft* enables the fantasy of South Korea—and thereby Asia as a whole—as simultaneously a weird, unintelligible place and a technological wonderland. This is epitomized in Western news coverage that constructs gaming cafés as dark and seedy places of ill repute, characterized by sloth and excess, which do the symbolic work of reimaging and updating the imagery of the opium den.[27] That image is complemented by generalizations about Korean culture as nurturing "productive obsessions," where this particular phrase can emphasize both the machinic devotion to the task and its contribution to capitalist enterprise.[28]

In short, most North Americans came to know esports through the techno-orientalist framing of it as a particularly Korean obsession, one that is simultaneously an absurd joke and a threat to Western hegemony.[29] This duality not only emerged from the ludo-orientalist discourse of games; it also enabled a specific form of techno-orientalism in the North American esports leagues and communities that emerged in the 2000s and 2010s.

High-Tech Orientalism: Performing Neoliberal Acumen

The techno-orientalism circulating in esports makes it an apparatus for widespread participation in high-tech orientalism—the practices that figure racialized play as the techniques of racial performance. This is most clearly expressed through Western players and teams adopting team building and management practices associated with Korean esports success. Esports are both media technologies and racial technologies, and the emulation of these practices by North American players and organizations illustrates how esports is used to taxonomize and selectively appropriate racialized forms of play to carve out a space for white protagonists in the impending Yellow Future.[30]

Our analysis begins, following Brock's critical technocultural discourse analysis, with the affordances and limitations of a technology: professional *League of Legends* (*LoL*) esports. Taking a cue from Bolter and Grusin, who explain that "media technologies constitute networks[, hence] introducing a new media technology does not mean simply inventing new hardware and software, but rather fashioning . . . a network,"[31] we argue that each moment of professional esports play is situated within an entangled network of systems that produce sportified spectacles, experiences for sale more than goods.[32] We approach professional *LoL* as a physical-social-aesthetic-economic network technology composed of professional gamers, team staff, tournament organizers, broadcast production workers, game developers, and fans, to name some human components. This technology's affordances and limitations are the surface on which the Western imagination plays out its drama of Korean racialization.

One of the world's most viewed esports and a flagship arena for the professionalization of esports competition over the last decade, *LoL*'s professional esport is built around its World Championship, a yearly tournament where the top-ranked teams from regional leagues compete for a prize pool that totaled $2.225 million in 2020.[33] The very architecture of play is intertwined with this structure. Regional leagues and competitive regions are designated based on collections of geographically adjacent servers running online play, thus using professional *LoL*'s technical infrastructure to reborder a globalizing world. Riot Games, *LoL*'s developer, instituted rules governing regionality and international player transfers, concretizing these borders by restricting flows of players between regions.[34] The staging of esports play on the surface of discrete geographies with conditionally permeable borders reifies the Asian professional player as Asiatic other by virtue of technical and rules-based distance.

Atop this networked technological apparatus, professional *League*'s affordances lend itself to the production of interregional drama and rivalry. The esport's rebordering of geographies, competitive centralization around the World Championship, and its constant work producing audiences lend its use to the production of otherness and fierce regionalism. Arguably, the primary narrative over the last several years of *League* play is the heroic Western quest to defeat East Asia.[35] Since the European team, Fnatic, won the first World Championship in 2011, no team from North America or Europe has won a World title despite intense efforts to compete. In South Korea's Worlds debut, Korean team Azubu Frost finished in second place. Teams from the *LoL* Champions Korea (LCK) league have since won six world titles from 2012 to 2020, including five consecutively from 2013 to 2017. Thus, the forms of play and the discourse surrounding professional *LoL* are fraught with not only intense admiration and desire for, but also a bitter, antagonistic conceptualization of, a techno-oriental other.

In a YouTube vlog arguing that Koreans would be essentially competent at any esport that becomes popular on the peninsula, commentator and journalist Duncan "Thorin" Shields argues for and helps maintain the fantasy of an essential, Korean difference through recourse to stereotypes and generalizing Korean work culture in ways that portray Korean workers and gamers as not entirely in control of themselves and thus less human than Western liberal subjects: "The players themselves are still incredibly diligent. . . . They have this cultural thing. . . . It's good in that it produces people that are really successful, but there's this degree to which—unfortunately—people almost overwork themselves, and they feel this compulsion and duty to the degree that sometimes I think they sometimes ruin their lives."[36] Shields reveals a fetishization of Korea bound up in speculation and mystery. This construction of Koreanness authorizes North American esports to manufacture ways of identifying, quantifying, and emulating Koreanness, such as those discussed below, setting the foundation for figuring Korean bodies as technologies that can be reverse engineered domestically or imported from abroad.

Spurred by a combination of international embarrassment at *LoL's* annual World Championship and the desperate industrial jockeying for shares of audiences and sponsor funding, North American esports teams have variously attempted to adopt, import, and acquire the structures that produced Korean esports' success. That is, North American esports organizations studied more than prior matches. By rendering knowable and selectable different aspects of Koreanness by turning them into data, from embodied practices to institutional structures, North American teams approach esports as a racial technology. Thus engaged, esports also facilitates high-tech orientalism in which playing like a South Korean is a vehicle for empowering white subjects in a hostile yellow future.

High-Tech Orientalism in Play   **197**

In the following sections, we look at two distinct but not wholly separate patterns of activity that enact high-tech orientalism—gaming houses and importing players—and focus on how the community frames these activities in its discourse. Significantly, each of these activities is premised on complementary fantasies, and taken together they form a composite picture of South Korea in the North American techno-orientalist imaginary of esports.

Inhabiting the Gaming House

Gaming houses are communal housing provided by esports teams where their players, as well as some coaches and support staff, live, eat, and work together. They originated in South Korean *Brood War* esports, where aspiring professional players banded together to save money and practice intensively.[37] However, these houses became staples of the Western imagination's construction of the South Korean esports ecosystem. Games journalists, casters, talk-show commentary, and vlogs sifted through the scouting reports, statistical breakdowns, coaching regimens, and interviews circulating in Western media and repeatedly concluded between 2012 and 2018 that a combination of hierarchical thinking, discipline, and efficiency, all of which came together in an institution known as gaming houses, were the keys to Korean success. During this period, gaming houses became an increasingly ubiquitous feature for professional teams in the West, lauded for competitive results and leveraged for profit via promotional sponsored house tour videos.[38] However, the desired international competitive results never materialized.

In North American esports, gaming houses represented not only communal living space for esports teams but a particular Koreanness characterized by techno-orientalist conceptualizations of collectivism and regimentation—the subjugation of ego and individuality via the structured tedium of esports as work. Pundits like Shields emphasized a combination of strict oversight and workplace efficiency in Korean esports practice environments enacted by corporate oversight. However, Shields argues elsewhere that gaming houses are vehicles for player burnout, effectively construing them—and their attendant Koreanness—as unsustainable and incompatible with Western esports.[39] In both cases, he responds to long-running stereotypes that Western gamers were unwilling to see *LoL* esports in the same industrial way that their Korean counterparts did.[40] Discussing the struggles of North American teams with gaming houses, Shields talks about Korean team management and player attitudes: "Their coaches want them to accomplish certain goals

198 Voorhees and Howard

and practice certain things, and the coaches themselves are organizing the practice, not the players. . . . They're really efficient, essentially. They're very dedicated, they're very disciplined, and they're efficient . . . and they're going full ball without ego, essentially."[41] In this commentary, Shields reveals the anxiety circulating under the efforts to emulate South Korean esports. He both outlines what is necessary for North American gaming houses to succeed and preemptively excuses white players for not having the cultural capacity to perform as needed. The gaming house was simply *too Korean*.

This construction resonates with figures of Japanese technological innovation and Chinese labor as technology but points to a distinct techno-orientalist fantasy of a Korean future dominated by organizational technologies and management processes that result in dehumanization through gamified or playful labor.[42] The gaming house is a site for the production of esports where the game became work, with workers following the direction of managers in their daily tasks: a highly professionalized, structured work environment of constant practice and competition where the work of professional play is efficiently managed to risk as few spatial or temporal disruptions from human living as possible.

Given this perception, analysts turned to whether or not Western players and teams were capable of subordinating themselves in the same lifeways necessary to achieve Korean levels of ludic noise reduction and neoliberal work. And when adopting the racialized techniques of play associated with South Korea failed both to enable Western players and teams to enjoy success in esports' neoliberal arena and to assuage anxieties about the place of the white subject in an Asian future, the cultural fabric that pundits like Shields see as enabling Koreanness to succeed in gaming houses became an object of simultaneous desire and disgust: the object of fantasy the West managed to acquire that frustrates rather than satisfies.

Importing "Asian Hands"

Complementing efforts to replicate Koreanness through gaming houses, Western teams also acquired Asian players through "importation," precipitating "the Korean Exodus" in 2014, when dozens of Korean pros left South Korea for prolific contracts in other regions. Mirroring the modern neoliberal multiculturalism of skills-based immigration policies, Western teams, players, fans, and pundits used *LoL* esports to identify desirable and undesirable traits of migrant laborers, isolating Koreans as some of the most desirable. Per *LoL* esports' regionality designations, in the spring of 2013 the North American *League of Legends* Championship Series' eight teams fielded one Chinese player (Nyjacky), one Korean (Heartbeat), and one Bulgarian (BloodWater), all of whom were signed locally in North America. In the summer of 2014, the NALCS's first three international transfer players from South Korea, Seraph, Helios, and Lustboy, arrived along with the first Korean coach, Locodoco, who previously had played in North America. In the spring of 2015, the season following the Exodus, there were fourteen Koreans on the league's ten teams.[43] By the summer of 2017, there were twenty-four Korean transfer players and coaches, versus only six from other regions.[44] International transfers between regions aren't new in any sport, analog or digital, but the Exodus was notable because it revealed the Western desire for Korean labor.

The discourse around these international transfers not only otherizes these players but also lingers on the failure of Western athletes to properly sync with their Asian teammates. Pundits and fans referred to international transfer players as "imports," objectifying Korean players but plugging directly into the constructed perception of Korean esports as an ecosystem for the uninterrupted production of players and coaches for international consumption.

Stereotyping can provoke an uncanny valley response and raise questions about a stereotyped person's humanity;[45] imagining Korean people as "imports" does much the same work. Korean esports were praised for their efficiency, productivity, and cultural mobilization to turn games into work and were also described as dehumanizing. Furthermore, outlets like the-Score eSports presented Korean player salaries as disproportionately low,[46] characterizing Korean players as supreme talents exploited by corporate sponsors paying them minimal wages.[47] Even as many Korean players left for China, the discourse evolved to see Korean players as good neoliberal subjects due to their ease of exploitation by corporate interest. That is, the coveted, fetishized, status of Korean esports professionals comes at the cost of fair pay and proper labor conditions. Korean bodies, then, became techno-orientalist constructions: expendable technology to be operationalized by Western industry.[48]

However, as with the gaming houses, importing Korean players did little to change Western fortunes at Worlds. From 2014 to 2017, North American teams topped out at fifth place, and EU teams peaked at third. Korean teams finished in both first and second in 2015, '16, and '17. Western teams' failed attempts to appropriate Korean imports and incorporate them into local teams and training regimens led some pundits to double down on the dehumanized, disembodied imaginary of South Korea as an esports factory rather than individual esports players.

Notably, commentaries presented Koreans as locally engineered and machinic, meaning they could not be uncritically taken from South Korea and plugged into North American contexts and still be expected to "work." ESPN journalist Tyler Erzberger crystallized this techno-orientalist imaginary of Korea after Worlds 2016, arguing that North American team owners failed to recognize Koreans' differing machinic qualities from Western players:

> So many times in the recent past teams have tried to emulate the East. We need to get that South Korean top laner, or we need that South Korean AD carry. Let's get a South Korean coach or try to practice as many hours as the South Koreans do. Yet when you try to implement all those habits and traits, a majority of the time it takes away from the one thing that makes the South Korean giants so great: their ability to work as a single machine working towards the same goal with five separate pieces moving in perfect unison.[49]

In this commentary, Erzberger claims that Western teams did not understand the compatibility between the parts they were importing into their factories and the players they had domestically. Aside from positioning the Korean other as a technological object to be instrumentalized by Western organizations, Erzberger directs blame for the situation toward team coaches and other levels of management.

Once again, this exculpatory discourse points to a distinct techno-orientalist fantasy of Korea as management technology. On first blush, we might think about importing as the return of the fighting game community's obsession with "Asian hands." In that community, players often joke about desiring the essentialized capability of the Japanese gaming body's "Asian hands," which stand in for complicated and shifting social and infrastructural conditions.[50] And while there is undoubtedly some biological essentialism at play, even more crucial is how Asian bodies are racialized as a mobile, transient labor force to be included or excluded at will, but always according to how capitalist market incentives rework political borders to manage the flows of these populations.[51] Somehow, Korea is capable of navigating this esports apparatus and its complex ecosystem of finances, human resource, and logistics that North American organizations and leaders are unable to properly replicate.

Orientalist Fantasies and Neoliberal Anxieties

Using critical technocultural discourse analysis, we have shown that digital games and esports in particular are premised in a high-tech orientalism that imagines the Western subject willfully seeking contamination and commingling with the other, taking up and taking on the Asiatic. This is exactly the case with the North American efforts to field champion *League of Legends* teams. In esports, Western subjects can and should try on Asian ways of being in the world.[52] Like the console cowboys of cyberpunk that Chun writes about, North American professional gamers and those who aspire to play as they do need to perform Asianness in order to succeed in this neoliberal global order. But in esports, unlike popular fiction, there is immediate feedback and the limits of this identity tourism are laid bare: teams can play at Koreanness, but doing so does not appropriate the subject position of the Asian gamer and satisfy the desire to win. If anything, North American players taste the bitter limits of race as play by performing Asian but still achieving as white.

Relative to existing techno-orientalisms, the fantasy of South Koreanness embedded in North American *League* practices combines elements of how Japan and China are imagined. If Japan is constructed in response to techno-orientalist anxiety about technological innovation, and China is imagined as the technology itself,[53] then Koreans are figured in esports discourses as both a technology to be exploited and the creative manipulators of management technology that eludes Western domination. Both the means of objectifying and dehumanizing, and the dehumanized other, this image from esports resonates with the corporate oligarchy run on the backs of androids depicted in *Cloud Atlas* and the praise for South Korean use of technology to manage the COVID-19 pandemic response.

Thus, despite its Asiatic trappings and fetishization of Asian capability, esports is not an amicable site where North America and Asia meet; rather, it exacerbates white anxieties about being replaced by Asians. As we have shown, esports is premised on a ludo-orientalism that constructs Asian players as other, yet a central conceit of North American esports is that Asian hands are not only attainable but also assimilable: in sum, that elements of South Korean technical production and product can be acquired, and the fantasy of performing Koreanness can nominally be fulfilled. However, even though it re-created the organizational structures and forms of professionalization pioneered in Korea, this racialized performance failed to produce the desired competitive outcomes. In this failure, we can see Western esports' bitter desire for Koreanness, in which attaining the object of desire is more frustrating than the desire itself. Obtainable in some ways, but ultimately not fulfilling the orientalist fantasy of professional *League of Legends* esports, Korean players and Koreanness are not the aspirations projected on them.

Notes

Gerald would like to thank friends and colleagues in the Department of Communication Arts and the Canadian Game Studies Association, and my daughter Quinn Voorhees-Nguyen, who will inherit these futures but make her own. Matt is deeply thankful to his partner, Amalia, who has encouraged him to get to know his own Koreanness better, and his brother, Chris, who inspired so many of his interests that led him here. He would also like to thank his friends and mentors in the NCSU Communication and English Departments who support the CRDM program and his colleagues in the School of Communication at Loyola University Chicago.

1 T. L. Taylor, *Raising the Stakes*.

2 Brock, "Critical Technocultural Discourse Analysis."

3 Roh, Huang, and Niu, *Techno-Orientalism*, 7.

4 Roh, Huang, and Niu, *Techno-Orientalism*, 4.

5 Day, *Alien Capital*; Bui, "Asian Roboticism."

6 Chun, "Race and/as Technology."

7 Chun, "Race and/as Technology," 51.

8 Chun, "Orienting the Future," 177.

9 H. Park, "Representing Seoul."

10 H. Park, "Representing Seoul." The film *Cloud Atlas* is based on the novel of the same name by David Mitchell.

11 Kang, "The Media Spectacle of a Techno-City."

12 Hjorth, "Playing at Being Mobile"; Choe and Kim, "Never Stop Playing."

13 Zhu, "Masculinity's New Battle Arena in International eSports," 236–37.

14 T. L. Taylor, *Raising the Stakes*; Taylor and Stout, "Gender and the Two-Tiered System of Collegiate Esports."

15 Fletcher, "eSports and the Color Line."

16 Fickle, *The Race Card*.

17 Patterson, *Open World Empire*, 58.

18 Goggin, "Playbour, Farming and Leisure."

19 Nakamura, "Don't Hate the Player."

20 Fickle, "Made in China."

21 Voorhees, "Neoliberal Masculinity."

22 T. L. Taylor, *Raising the Stakes*.

23 Taylor and Elam, "People Are Robots, Too," 246, 250.

24 Howard, "Esport: Professional *League of Legends* as Cultural History," 108–9.

25 N. Taylor, "Kinaesthetic Masculinity and the Prehistory of Esports."

26 Hjorth, "Playing at Being Mobile."

27 Choe and Kim, "Never Stop Playing."

28 Choe and Kim, "Never Stop Playing."

29 Howard, "Highway to the Golden Zone(fire)."

30 J. C. H. Park, *Yellow Future*, 24.

31 Bolter and Grusin, *Remediation*, 19.

32 Boluk and LeMieux, *Metagaming*, 242; Borowy and Jin, "Mega-Events of the Future," 210.

33 "Worlds 2020," *Gamepedia*, February 28, 2021, https://lol.fandom.com /wiki/2020_Season_World_Championship.

34 Howard, "Esport: Professional *League of Legends* as Cultural History," 56; Monique, "Riot Announces New Rules about Regional Movement"; Leslie, "Riot Tighten Interregional Movement Policy for LCS Players."

35 Zhu, "Masculinity's New Battle Arena in International eSports," 229.

36 Shields, "The Thorin Treatment."

37 Bago, "Dispelling the Myth of the Korean Gaming House."

38 Admin, "Team Houses and Why They Matter."

39 Shields, "The Thorin Treatment."

40 Shields, "Thorin's Thoughts."

41 Shields, "Thorin's Thoughts."

42 Roh, Huang, and Niu, *Techno-Orientalism*, 223.

43 CaliTrlolz8, Dodo8, and KonKwon were designated North American regionals.

44 Dodo, konkwon, Gate, Xmithie, Cody Sun, Inori, and Biofrost were all designated North American regionals.

45 Chu, "I, Stereotype," 78–79.

46 theScore eSports, "The Great Korean Exodus."

47 Deesing, "The South Korean Exodus to China."

48 Bui, "Asian Roboticism"; Roh, Huang, and Niu, *Techno-Orientalism*, 11.

49 Erzberger, "The Gap Is Not Closing in *League of Legends*."

50 Harper, "'Asian Hands' and Women's Invitationals," 114.

51 Day, *Alien Capital*, 31.

52 Patterson, *Open World Empire*, 63.

53 Roh, Huang, and Niu, *Techno-Orientalism*, 4.

Inhabiting the Asiatic

Part 4

The Crumbs of Our Representation

Designer Roundtable #4

FEATURING:

Robert Yang, who makes surprisingly popular games about gay culture and intimacy. He is best-known for his historical bathroom sex simulator *The Tearoom* (2017) and his homoerotic shower sim *Rinse and Repeat* (2015) and his gay sex triptych *Radiator 2* (2016). Previously, he was an assistant arts professor at NYU Game Center. He holds a BA in English literature from UC Berkeley and an MFA in design and technology from Parsons School for Design.

Dietrich Squinkifer (Squinky), a transgender and neurodivergent new media artist who makes weird video games about feelings while somehow continuing to survive in a late capitalist cyberpunk dystopia. After stints in both industry and academia, and gaining recognition for works such as *Dominique Pamplemousse* (2013) and *Coffee: A Misunderstanding* (2014), they cofounded Soft Chaos, a worker coop game studio, while at the same time working on a solo album of short games titled *Squinky and the Squinkettes Present: Second Puberty* (2021).

Rachel Li, an award-winning game designer and new media artist based in Los Angeles, California. With a background in both game design and fine arts, she constantly challenges the border between technology, art, and design. Her games *Hot Pot for One* (2021), *Double R.* (2019), and others are autobiographical simulation games inspired by her observations and reflections on people and the world around her. Her installations and experimental games have been featured in various art exhibitions and major game festivals online and in New York, San Francisco, Chengdu, and Shenzhen.

Marina Ayano Kittaka, an artist, video game developer, and the cofounder of Analgesic Productions. Kittaka is best-known as the cocreator of the *Anodyne* series (2013–19) and *Even the Ocean* (2016). She also wrote the essay "Divest from the Video Games Industry!" (2020) and created the open-source blogging engine Zonelets.

Robert Yang: In my preteens, I got into modding as a design and development practice. I was first making *StarCraft* (1998) maps and adventures and stuff—I wanted to tell stories within *StarCraft*—and then I started getting into making *Counter-Strike* (1999) and *Half Life* (1998) maps. I wanted to get into the triple-A industry. And early on, that meant I had to be closeted or to compartmentalize certain parts of my identity to be more acceptable and palatable. I was like, okay, I'm gonna make this map where we just shoot people, and there's no gay shit, or Asianness, or any of that stuff to distract an employer from hiring me. And then, as I thankfully started interacting with people outside of video games more and more, I realized that life was too short to do all that bottling up or trying to make yourself look more respectable. That's when I started making games that are more gay or sexual or erotic. And now I'm trying to navigate the consequences of those decisions. Like, what does that mean for me? Does that mean I'm—no offense—cursed to be an academic now? Or does that mean I should try to be like some weird indie artist? Does that mean I should try to bring up my East Asianness more? I mean, that's what this whole roundtable thing is about. But yeah, just a lot of questions I'm personally still figuring out. But I do know that I don't want to try to fit some ideal version of what a game developer is. I want to try to be authentic to myself, whatever that means.

Rachel Li: I started to play video games when I got my first PC in high school. I played *Skyrim* (2011), *Minecraft* (2011), open world games like that. I just found myself more and more into the idea of telling a story by navigating a 3D space. I want to be part of that. Even though I was born in the US, I grew up in China, so I don't speak English as my first language. I feel more comfortable speaking Chinese. So one of the challenges in making games is the language, in the way you express humor and some ideas in your games. And I have this tendency of using images and art to replace, or, try to avoid, using writing and text in my games. And because I have Chinese social media and stuff like Weibo and WeChat, there were Chinese game companies reaching out to me, then trying to adapt my games. And when I interviewed as a game designer, they could not understand why I would make a game [*Hotpot for One* (2020)] about personal experience, and that isn't about competition or winning. That didn't really go well.

Squinky: In terms of Asianness, I am enough of a mix of things that I read as definitely not white, but can't tell otherwise. I'm Iranian and Filipino, and from both those sides of the family there are mixes of lots of things like Spanish, Chinese, Jewish, and, as far as I know, probably lots more. So, having spent most of my formative years in very white parts of Canada, the way I have dealt with that is to ignore my race as much as possible, to downplay it and try and act very white. Especially when I started making games on the internet. Nobody really knew what I looked like. They just saw my writing, and they would assume certain things about me based on that. And then I would just never correct those assumptions. Also, because I was raised as a girl, I had to navigate this very awkward relationship with being not a cis man, and early in my career I joined a lot of women in games groups and got really into feminism. And as I kept making more and more games, I figured out a bunch of stuff around my gender, around my sexuality, around neurodivergence. A big part of the neurodivergent part is that games are, in a way, how I communicate and express myself. Sometimes things feel a lot easier to say in a game than they do with words. Meanwhile, I became part of this whole queer games movement, particularly by co-organizing QGCon [Queerness and Games Conference]. So then, bringing it back to race, it's all intersectional for me. All of my experiences inform how I design games, and they all have these parallels of trying to pass as white, pass as a woman or a man or a gender, just pass as an acceptable person within very restrictive categories.

Marina Kittaka: Over time, the part of my relationship with games that has only grown stronger is the sense that in a lot of ways, it's not really about the games themselves, but the kind of potential that they suggest to me. I don't even know what games I like anymore, but I like the idea of games. I don't really consider myself like a big personality, and I don't really notice people talking about me, which is how I want it, for the most part. And I feel like a lot of my experiences as an Asian American person have to do with these kinds of absences. I feel like if I had different ways to move through the world, I wouldn't have this kind of presumed default divestment from community spaces in the way I feel like I do. Or it might have to do with other aspects of my identity or upbringing. My parents are evangelical Christians. And my siblings and I were home-schooled. So there are different axes along which I felt divested from the everyday cultural institutions, and I think about that absence.

Chris Patterson: These comments make me think about how we discuss intersectionality in the academy, where it's about race, gender, sexuality, class, but these are often discussed at a nationalist, English-speaking, classist, and neurotypical table. As Marina said, these are the axes that compel us to invest or divest from particular identities and communities.

Marina Kittaka: Because video games are such a multifaceted form that take a lot of practices from film and animation, they end up uncritically absorbing a lot of the negative aspects of representation in those artistic forms. So the bar is really low. As far as these bigger axes, we have things like race and gender and sexuality, to the point where it doesn't really feel inspiring to me to try to do some kind of representation of a type of person. I would like to see a lot more change in the games industry in general: the structures in place, the tools available, the culture, the platforms through which we talk about games, all that stuff. I would rather have that change than be thinking about, you know, whether Nintendo has some character who's a different race or whatever.

Tara Fickle: This is something we've talked about a lot in trying to think beyond representation or industry diversity, but to think about how we actualize those intersections. This reminds me of how in games, we talk about the relationship between representing something versus simulating how it works, and in the latter case it doesn't even have to look like the thing anymore.

Robert Yang: The word *representation* has been commercialized and co-opted to the point where it's not really meaningful for me anymore. Like, is this *Super Smash Brothers* [1999] character gay or something? Wow. Like, oh, finally, a gay trans Black General, who will keep the troops in Afghanistan.

That's a weird thing to celebrate for me. I avoid the word *representation* when I talk about my own work. And when I use the word *simulation*, instead, I think it's more sarcastic. I think of the way it's deployed in games like *Goat Simulator* [2014], which is not a simulation of what being a goat is like. So I think that's the case with a lot of so-called simulators, which are usually sarcastic and winky. That's why I gravitate toward simulation as a frame, not because I think simulations offer authentic truth power or something. Because they're sarcastic, they're a more irreverent way of thinking about identity or a body in a way that representation always has to assume the best intentions. Instead, we're supposed to be grateful for these representation crumbs.

Squinky: In terms of the capitalist game industry's ideas of representation, over the last year I've been doing professional diversity consulting. I decided to do this so that I wouldn't have to do it for free. Or so that people who work in games understand that this is not work that people should be doing for free. It is work to go through your game and make sure you represented this nonbinary character correctly, whatever that means. So with clients, I end up asking a lot more questions than I give them answers. I ask why they want to do representation. And, obviously, the answer is so that they can sell games to more categories of people. I am generally not that interested in those conversations for their own sake. So if people are going to seek my input on representation-related matters, I'm willing to do it so long as they pay me.

Tara Fickle: The curious idea about diversity consulting is it can assume a kind of singular authority or monolith, right? Which of course is impossible but is also another kind of labor that they're expecting of you, I presume. What are you to do other than occupy that position of expertise and authority?

Squinky: There's a certain thought like, "Why are you making me the authority on this feeling?" But then it's also like, "Holy crap, I *do* have way more authority on this." Because the game industry is that much behind the times. So regarding how we move past that, basically the answer, I guess, is to abolish capitalism. Because there is something about the world right now that has just become incredibly unworkable. Yeah, all roads lead to abolishing capitalism.

Rachel Li: Growing up in China, I was curious when I came to the US and saw this representation focus. I was like, Okay, it's nice to see different groups of people being represented, but is that really the kind of representation we want? Like, take the Asian hands myth. Shenzhen, where I was raised, is the largest southern Chinese city that manufactures computer hardware. Yet when I was an undergrad, nobody knew where Shenzhen was, but suddenly people started talking about it, mainly because of its cheap electronics. But, having grown up there, I was just confused. This is an actual place, but no one talks about the history of Shenzhen, and everyone keeps saying it's a cultural desert. The People's Republic of China says it too. So I started to work on a project about the history of Shenzhen, the city and villages. It made me investigate what it means to be Shenzhener and what kind of people actually live in Shenzhen. More than the money, the electrical parts, the factory.

Robert Yang: Games are a really messed-up rat's nest of all these different politics and cultures intertwining. Like, the tradition of gay male sex culture is very white leaning, usually. And so when I'm trying to call back to that culture in my games, it's hard, because artists have done so much to eroticize white masculine bodies for centuries, and there's not as many eroticized Black bodies, for instance. Or if there is, it can easily slip into this creepy tokenizing fetishizing kind of mode, right? So part of that is my anxiety trying to work with sexualized bodies. This was an issue when I was making that spanking game called *Hurt Me Plenty* (2014) where you can ignore your submissive's boundaries, and basically abuse them. I felt like I had to make the submissive in that game white because I didn't want to make a game where you could abuse Black people. That seemed really messed up to me, and then abusing anyone is also really messed up in the head too. But I feel like it would have been saying something very different.

Marina Kittaka: I just wrote a blog post that feels related to this, called "*Tony Hawk's Pro Skater* and Shape-Meaning Resonance," about how, in action games, characters with certain abilities move about a space and interact with the environment. In my mind, these games create an interesting metaphor for the actions of being a person with a body and with certain experiences. And how that not only limits but gives shape to one's experience with the world. And these metaphors are hard to parse from the very straightforward identity-based social narrative. And they often feel almost kind of cheesy in relation. One of the examples I gave was Kirby. Kirby sucks stuff up and shoots it out or eats enemies to gain their powers. What does that mean with regards to race? It seems unserious, and yet, in my opinion, the capacity to inhabit these absurdist modes of thinking about one's interactions is a really special thing that you can do in games and has a lot to offer. And this is a way for people who have a different perspective on moving through our world to express something vital about that experience in a way that maybe goes beyond surface markers of representation.

Chris Patterson: I love this. What if we saw the kind of actions taken by Kirby, or something in the realm of silliness and absurdity, as speaking to how we express race?

Tara Fickle: Right. Given two objects colliding or just interacting in any given space, what is the meaning of the act that we ascribe to it? One eats the other, one hits the other, or—one simply sits by the other, or they bounce off each other? What are the larger politics of these kind of movements?

Robert Yang: I like trying to slow down movement and pay attention to smaller, slower movements and gestures. What mainstream games care about is traversing a giant landscape but not, like, hugging someone or something. I think that's a commonality across a lot of our games [on this roundtable]. Rachel's *Hot Pot for One* is really good at slowing down and being in a moment. Paying attention to how we move food around is a really interesting thing that games don't really think about usually, and is tricky to do with a video game physics engine, as well. Or Squinky's *Dominique Pamplemousse* (2013): the way the characters wait their turn to talk. That's still a feature that's, like, living in my head. So I think that's where there's a lot of space in games still. Just pick any gesture or moment and enlarge it. And suddenly you have to design the video game body very differently to try to address that space.

Rachel Li: When I first started to work on the controls for *Hot Pot for One*, I focused more on the experience, not the character. Players can use chopsticks to pick up food and move it around.

When people play 3D games, they always expect that they will be able to walk around, but I feel like it doesn't really make sense if your game doesn't require that. So I experimented with throwing player movement away, just letting them stand still by the kitchen table, and that gives me more time to zoom in on the detail related to the core interaction of the game, which is having hotpot. Even though some players don't even know what hotpot is,

The Crumbs of Our Representation   213

they understand feeling that kind of loneliness. *Hot Pot for One* is about me in New York making hot pot alone at home on Christmas night. Even though I'm technically a US citizen, I sometimes identify as an international student, so that game was about me in a foreign country, because all my family are in China.

I feel like I'd never before had questions about my identity, at least not strong enough to make a game about it. But the reason I started to make my new game [about the history of Shenzhen] is because as a US citizen I'm not able to enter China, because they don't let foreigners in anymore [because of the COVID pandemic]. So I haven't been allowed to go back home for the past year. I started to have this anxiety: Who am I? What's my cultural identity? Where do I belong? Games for me are a way to answer those questions, or share my concerns and those issues with other people.

Marina Kittaka: This makes me think of an example from my game *Anodyne 2* [2019], where there are these traditional boss fights toward the beginning of the game, and then those mechanics are altered and recontextualized partway through when you're doing a kind of pro wrestling–style interaction with a friend of yours. You have to pull your punch at the last moment in order to create this performance of a battle. And that kind of recontextualization plays into the broader themes of learning how to be in community and what it means to have a mission in life or to be fighting for justice. Now I'm thinking of Squinky's *Dominique Pamplemousse* and its very abstracted characters, who also read as queer and nonwhite. I think that's an interesting way of navigating some artistic craft concerns with the complicated ways that they're read.

Squinky: Bringing the body more into it came a bit later for me. *Dominique Pamplemousse* is definitely a reflection of how awkward I have always found it to exist in the world as a body. A lot of my games do feature awkwardness in a big way. Since medically transitioning and kind of rediscovering the relationship I have with my body in space—for the better—I'm finding myself having more fun with the way that characters physically move in a space and the ways that you get people to physically do things with their bodies while playing a game. And as somebody who makes games, I feel it is more important than ever to think about processes and structure. How do we find little pockets of community where we can practice these processes and these alternatives, where we take care of each other, instead of constantly competing with each other for resources? So I am finding myself thinking less about my work as an individual. So how does what I have been doing all these years fit into the greater context surrounding us, especially in increasingly dystopian, like, everything?

Huan He

Chinese/Cheating

Procedural Racism in Battle Royale Shooters

In December 2017, the South Korean video game company Bluehold released a multiplayer shooter game titled *PlayerUnknown's Battlegrounds* (*PUBG*), created by Brendan "PlayerUnknown" Greene. Reworking the familiar genre of shooter games, such as the popular franchises *Halo*, *Call of Duty*, and *Gears of War*, *PUBG* introduced a new category of multiplayer shooters known as the "battle royale" (BR). Inspired by the Japanese cult thriller of the same name, the premise of BR games is to be the last player or team standing by collecting combat resources and winning gunfights. Rewarding positioning strategy, quick reflexes, and aim mechanics, BR shooters have dominated the casual, content, and professional gaming scene. Since *PUBG*'s launch, many other video game franchises have produced their own take on the BR genre, including *Fortnite*, *Call of Duty: Modern Warfare*, *Apex Legends*, *Spellbreak*, *Fall Guys: Ultimate Knockout*, *Hyperscape*, and even *Tetris 99*. As a video game trend, battle royale (BR) shooters became a cultural phenomenon across the globe. Given the competitive nature of these multiplayer team-based video games, cheating and hacking became a widespread concern across all skill levels. Common cheat exploits allow for "aimbotting," "speed-hacking," or "wallhacking," granting players godly levels of aim, movement, or enemy awareness. The rampant presence of cheating has been a frustrating issue for both players and developers.

In the global gaming community, there exists a common belief that the most crude and common cheaters are Chinese. For instance, the anticheat software company BattlEye publicly tweeted in 2017 that they were banning at a rate of six thousand to thirteen thousand accounts a day from *PUBG*, with the "vast majority . . . from China."[1] A quick peruse through Reddit gaming forums yields many threads on the topic of Chinese cheating. These discussions range from attempts to identify an innate cultural reason for cheating, anecdotal accounts of encountering cheaters in games, proposed methods for preventing cheating, and outright racist anger toward all Chinese players. Video game hacking is often a difficult topic for gamers to discuss, especially in anonymous forums, as it is both a racial issue (many cheaters are believed to be Chinese) and a nonracial one (anybody can cheat). In a popular gaming subreddit thread titled "What makes online cheating so prevalent in China?," a disclaimer sits in the parent post: *"Racist comments will be flagged appropriately. Some people really want to make this a race issue, so say whatever and the mods deal with you."*[2] Is cheating (really) a "race issue"? If so, how?

This essay examines the racial associations between "Chineseness" and cheating, as a recent phenomenon in BR shooters and as part of a longer sociohistorical legacy of Asiatic hacking. I borrow the term *Asiatic* from Christopher B. Patterson to describe not an identity but a racial form or style. According to Patterson, there is usually something "Asian-ish" that links Asianness and digital games, ranging from the video game's content to its designers, consumers, and industry producers.[3] In a gaming environment of virtual presence, race is detached from embodied subjects and often recoded in covert ways, embedded into the very structure of play itself. If, as Constance Steinkuehler has stated, the designation of "Chineseness" is "aimed more at one's style of play than one's real-world ethnicity,"[4] then Chinese hackers in online competitive shooters extend this claim to the technical dimensions of gaming software, sustained by computational code and global media infrastructures. To be clear, this essay is neither a defense of cheaters nor a defense of the snitches, and it does not cast judgment on the act of cheating. Rather, I mobilize cheating as an analytic for understanding how racial meaning and power shuttles between the gaming world and the social—or so-called real—world. Through an examination of battle royale

218 Huan He

shooters, this essay argues that video game hacking functions as an Asiatic procedure that marks the virtual borders of fair play for global server-based online multiplayer gaming. To illustrate the phenomenon of Chinese cheating as an established discourse, I turn to player-generated textual and media sources on Reddit, Twitter, and YouTube.

Procedural Racism

In a video posted on March 2019 titled "*Apex Legends*—Chinese Player Using Aimbot / Hack," we spectate a player named "China-supre."[5] Along with his fellow teammates in his trio named "china_shuaidaye," and "atuoleigeltong," the player is suspected of cheating via a software hack for ensuring perfect headshot accuracy. Posted on YouTube by an embittered user named "Kylin," the video functions to expose the rampant issue of Chinese cheaters in the popular BR shooter *Apex Legends* (see figure 10.1). Released by Respawn and Electronic Arts in February 2019 for PC, Xbox One, and PlayStation 4, *Apex Legends* is a first-person shooter in the BR format, where gamers team up in squads to fight to be the last remaining team standing in the Apex games. As the video progresses, the viewer sees the player eviscerate online opponents far off in the distance, almost invisible to the human eye. Yellow numbers rack up at the gun crosshairs, indicating that "China-supre" has landed a series of headshot damage on the opponent. In other gunfights shown in the video, we see the player land perfect shots through visual obstacles such as smoke and debris, environmental deterrents that are supposed to momentarily obstruct a player's view. In the background, we hear the Vietnamese commentary of the gamers recording China-supre, who are only able to spectate, having been killed by the cheating player. In the video description, Kylin exclaims his frustration and a plea for help: "I'm so tired of being killed by those CN players, 19/20 games have aimboter [*sic*] like that. Will Respawn & EA do something about it?" Reading into the cheater's racial and national identity through the gamertag "China-supre," Kylin presumes this cheater to be Chinese, one of the many Chinese cheaters encountered in the BR shooter.

These clips of aimbotters are one of many player-uploaded videos documenting the rampant phenomenon of Chinese cheaters in online BR shooters. Not only do these videos often capture negative emotions such as annoyance or rage toward cheaters; they also often comment on the high frequency of encounters with these cheaters. Like the players in Kylin's videos, Chinese cheaters

Chinese/Cheating **219**

10.1. *Apex Legends*: Footage of "Chinese player using aimbot," posted on YouTube by user "Kylin." Screenshot by author.

are often equipped with what Mia Consalvo calls "code-based cheats," hidden software that can allow players to aim automatically at enemy players with inhuman accuracy, detect and see opposing players through walls and natural obstacles, or move through the battleground with unnatural speed.[6] Software hacks like aimbot cheats are relatively easy for players to access, either free or purchased, and come in various forms—whether as a software that runs alongside the primary game or as "foreign" code injected into the game itself. These player-generated videos serve to document and circulate evidence of Chinese cheaters who have installed these software hacks. Often found on public sites such as YouTube or Reddit, they can corroborate other players' similar encounters or warn unsuspecting others of the presence of cheaters. Despite the inability to fully confirm a cheating player's background on the other side of the screen, players often draw from in-game signs to discern identity markers. In Kylin's upload, the gamertag "China-supre" invokes a Chinese nationalism that associates the cheater with a sense of Chineseness, whether racial or national. In the quest to combat cheaters in BR shooters, the line between "cheating" and "Chineseness" is often blurred.

In the world of digital gaming, the association between Chineseness and cheating is not a clear-cut instance of racism, as one might be tempted to conclude (and consequently dismiss as simply "racist"). Rather, this uneasy conflation exemplifies what I call *procedural racism*, in which the technical operations of software malfunction converge with cultural signifiers of invasion. Scholars have argued that computational environments are not simply textual, visual, aural, or even multimedial but, rather, procedural. According to Janet H. Murray, one of computation's defining qualities is its "ability to execute a series of rules."[7] Unlike other media such as novels and films, the underlying logics and processes are central to how computational media produce and maintain their representational effect and experience. Ian Bogost has extended Murray's ideas on the computational to describe digital games as a form of "procedural rhetoric," where its persuasive force draws from "rule-based representations and interactions rather than the spoken word, writing, images, or moving pictures."[8] What Bogost means by "rule-based" is not just any defined set of behaviors or laws but includes the rule-oriented processes of computational and programmatic execution itself that plays a part in shaping user experience. Digital games are procedural in the sense that they are a contraction of code and culture, and analyses of player experiences must account for both dimensions.

Procedural racism builds from Bogost's notion of the procedural because his framework considers the unseen operations of representational effects and, moreover, how process-based media encounters demand new analytics beyond the formal methods for reading text-based, visual, or time-based forms. Procedural racism also describes racialized phenomenon produced by the composite output of multiple factors, some technical and others cultural. Add to this the fact that digital spheres for multiplayer gaming are already a site in which legible markers of identity are disordered, or, as Lisa Nakamura has suggested, "doubly disorienting."[9] Understanding digital games as procedural draws attention to how the technical dimensions of online multiplayer gaming—the computational operations of software, code, server hosting, and so forth—play a critical role in shaping how social meaning emerges and circulates within online gaming spheres. In online competitive shooters, many other variables influence the experience of gameplay that are outside the agency, control, or purview of the individual gaming subject. These include things like latency time (the delay between user input and game response), packet loss (related to how fast data travels from the gaming computer to the data center), server location (which can impact things like latency time and packet loss), and so forth. Even for many dedicated gamers participating in fast-paced shooters, they must become somewhat technically knowledgeable, as amateur computer engineers of sorts, to optimize their gaming

Chinese/Cheating **221**

performance. Otherwise, even a skilled player playing with high lag may inevitably experience defeat due to computational issues. Especially since both digital games themselves and the code that support them are structured by rule-based representations and executions, procedural racism describes how these nondiegetic, technical malfunctions or misuse become racialized in the gaming sphere.

The association between Chinese players and cheating is a common example of procedural racism, as this conflation locates a racial sense of "Chineseness" within the phenomenon of technological hacking. My analysis of Chinese/cheating extends Tara Fickle's notion of "ludo-Orientalism, wherein the design, marketing, and rhetoric of games shape how Asians as well as East-West relations are imagined and where notions of foreignness and racial hierarchies get reinforced."[10] Describing a longer history of how the structure of games and play have framed understandings of Asianness, and vice versa, Fickle's ludo-orientalism helps us conceptualize ideas such as race, nation, and neoliberal capitalism as rule-bound forms. Not only do these "imagined fictions [transform] into a social reality" through their ludic qualities; Fickle suggests that their gamelike attributes also enforce specific formations of social reality as *justified*.[11] In effect, ludo-orientalism emphasizes how Asian racialization can threaten existing social structures (such as the invasion of cheap Chinese laborers) or validate them (i.e., by making US neoliberalism appear "fair" vis-à-vis the model minority myth). In the digital era, ludo-orientalist fantasies and ideologies persist not only through the logic of games but also through the logic of code. Procedural racism, then, brings the rich framework of ludo-orientalism into conversation with the technical dimensions of digital games, the substrata of code, software, hardware, and servers that form the basis of online gaming presence. As the experience and regulation of online multiplayer shooters increasingly accounts for the computational factors of gameplay, race and racism can become coded into the machinic operations of digital play.

Migrating Cheaters

Battle royale shooters are "global games," defined by Patterson as "global commodities produced by transnational companies that seem, initially, to hold no national sentiments or orientations and thus evade the particularities and 'seriousness' of national racial attitudes."[12] Since these games are perceived to be accessible to anyone, anywhere, across the world, they promote a sense of global connection and belonging, where players from Hong Kong can, hypothetically, play with someone from Sweden. Despite the virtual fantasies of online gameplay that artificially separate the digital gaming world from the "real world," online multiplayer shooters rely on computational systems grounded in the geopolitical. The idealization of global digital gaming masks over the media infrastructures sustaining gameplay that are, in fact, quite anchored in the reality of national or regional space. In *Apex Legends*, for instance, most players will play with teammates on their preferred regional server to optimize their technical gameplay attributes, such as latency time and framerate. A player based in Los Angeles would most likely play on a West Coast server through one of the Oregon-based data centers. One can opt to play in a more distant server at the risk of increased lag or lower framerate. This region-based server logic also allows players to be matched with other teammates who are more likely to share the same language and cultural frameworks (i.e., Japanese players in Japan are more likely to be matched with other Japanese players). Yet since data centers and server regions are based in geopolitical reality, any disruption to the purity of servers also draws from a similar geopolitical language. For instance, in Kylin's video documenting Chinese cheaters in *Apex Legends*, one YouTube commenter complains about the aimbotters: "Now they are coming to Oceania servers."[13] Resembling the xenophobic rhetoric that has shaped anti-Asian immigration policies, these Chinese cheaters are framed as unwanted migrants who are finding ways to enter other servers outside their designated region—so much so that the player base called for the *Apex Legends* developers to "region-lock" China to prevent cheaters from migrating to other regional servers in North America, Europe, or other parts of East and Southeast Asia.[14] This demand replicates similar protocol that *PUBG* previously took to curb the overwhelming presence of aimbot hackers from China in October 2018.[15] This discussion of region-locking China reveals that what frustrates many players is not simply that Chinese cheaters exist with undefeatable code-based hacks but that they appear to be a common occurrence spreading across server-based borders. Thus, these discourses codify Chineseness into the procedural dimensions of code-hacking and warn of a potential to multiply and invade servers across the globe.

Precisely since these technical infrastructures are imperceptible to the player yet play a crucial role in maintaining the stability of online gameplay, these concerns are often discussed and narrated using existing cultural

Chinese/Cheating **223**

terminologies that have formed through social histories. As Margaret Morse reminds us, cybercultures often attempt to find cultural frames to imagine the otherwise imperceptible dimensions of information technologies.[16] Region-locking China and preventing server migration for Chinese players parallels the historical precedent of anti-Chinese immigration legislation enacted by the United States in the era of Chinese Exclusion (1882–1943). As more Chinese laborers were needed to fulfill the settler-capitalist demands of US industrialization, Chinese exclusion legislation concretized a growing anti-Chinese sentiment and marked the first instance of race-based US immigration laws.[17] Although the Chinese Exclusion era legally ended with the Magnuson Act in 1943, which replaced exclusion with a quota-based system for migrant entry, the atmosphere of anti-Chinese and anti-Asian sentiment continues to be renewed in contemporary contexts, such as the recent wave of anti-Asian hate and violence in the age of COVID-19.

The stakes and circumstances are, of course, different for all these instances of yellow peril, but there is a common modality subtending these racial fears. In the case of Chinese exclusion, the rhetoric of yellow peril was largely expressed through the terms of labor and economics. Kornel Chang describes how white union laborers were organized against Chinese laborers, "vilified as degraders of labor."[18] Euro-Americans were able to consolidate their own ethnic identities into an abstracted whiteness against the "cheaper" labor offered by Chinese migrants. As financial incentives for entrepreneurs paved room for more Chinese workers, a galvanized sense of whiteness emerged in opposition to Asiatic competition. Perceived as a threat to the honest, integrity-driven ideal of white labor, Chinese labor was deemed corrosive, degenerative, and cheapening. What I am suggesting here is that these economic modalities of racialization could also be considered a type of "hacking," in which yellow peril fears refer not only to Chinese bodies but also to the systemic degradation of Euro-American white labor at the height of industrialization. Chineseness, in this historical instance, signifies a procedural form of hacking, an anthropomorphic figuration of capitalism's invisible and negative competitive force.[19] By thinking of "cheapening" as akin to "cheating," as Fickle has suggested regarding the perception of nineteenth-century Chinese gamblers in the United States,[20] we can better trace social and ludic phenomenon that require the threat of the Asiatic to consolidate normative ideas of labor and gaming.

Although there is a difference between the "cheapening" of Chinese manual labor in the nineteenth century and the "cheating" of Chinese gamers in the twenty-first, they both signify an unwanted Asiatic procedure that can generate racist responses. The similarities between these historically situated phenomena mark an analogy between culture and code, revealing how racial meaning coalesces in this convergence through a demarcation of the boundaries of normative work and play. Despite the variety of processes of software hacking and code-based cheats, online gaming communities often default to calls for cure-all measures that, in effect, categorically inscribe totalizing claims about the presence of cheaters. For example, within two weeks of the *Apex Legends* launch, Reddit threads appeared in which gamers lambasted the pervasiveness of Chinese cheaters. In one thread, the poster cried: "Please Ping lock or REGION LOCK China. Apex is killed by Chinese Cheaters like PUBG."[21] Given that this post surfaced in the early hype of game release, the statement comparing *Apex Legends* to PUBG indicated that the previous trend of cheating in PUBG became a way to narrate what appeared to be a similar phenomenon in this new game. In this sense, the post echoed a plea to game developers to mitigate the problem through technical legislation, such as enforcing a digital "wall" for China-based players. In the thread, commenters affirmed these sentiments with varying degrees of racist speech. One comment stated, "As expected of the Chinese. I live in Japan and also play a lot of PUBG, I'm all too familiar with Chinese cheaters."[22] Another comment said, "Upvoted. Played against a squad of China hackers last night with douyutv names. . . . Guess they migrated from bfv [*Battlefield V*]."[23] The more extreme comments might be captured by this poster, whose frustrations turn explicitly racist: "Chinese is really killing APEX. with their stupid ching chong bots. and cheats. bunch of ching chong cancers."[24] These responses quite viscerally demonstrate how the procedure of cheating becomes coded with racial and racist meaning by figuring "China hackers" as a proliferating entity,[25] as detested "migrants" across different servers and games, or as a degenerative illness such as cancer. Invoking long-standing historical sentiments associating Chinese migrants with infectious disease (as Nayan Shah has pointed out in his study of San Francisco Chinatowns and public health in the late nineteenth and twentieth centuries,[26] and as the contemporary era of COVID has highlighted), these gamers conflate Chineseness and cheating through the rhetoric of contagion and invasion. Yet just as these hackers appear in different servers and shooter games, so do these racist comments. In the same pathways, they spread to different gaming communities and spew racist beliefs for the sake of maintaining the sanctity and purity of rule-based play.

Chinese/Cheating   **225**

As an acute example of procedural racism, the association between Chineseness and cheating draws from but is not contained by existing ludo-orientalist discourse. Although Chinese cheaters are often negatively stereotyped through the language inherited by Euro-American orientalisms, the disdain toward Chinese cheaters circulates in different regions that cannot be reduced to "East" versus "West." For instance, due to the proximity of their data centers, players from Japan, South Korea, Taiwan, Vietnam, Hong Kong, and Singapore are likely to meet Chinese cheaters in their regional servers and harbor similar anti-Chinese feelings. Yet the "Chineseness" of the perceived cheaters can activate a range of responses from comments directed at Chinese people to sentiment targeting the Chinese nation-state, especially since certain hackers (like "China-supre" in Kylin's video) use their gamertag to suggest a type of national supremacy. Like the code-based cheats that range from blatant aimbot (i.e., auto-locking onto enemy targets) to "soft" hacks (i.e., subtler versions of enhanced aim assist), the racial meaning associated with Chinese cheaters span from the explicit to the subdued. Yet what unites these discourses is the phenomenon of code-based hacking, a technical procedure that demonstrates how computational and cultural meaning are mutually reinforcing.

Most Chinese cheaters are accused of using software hacks to enhance their gameplay to inhuman levels, but gamers also report encounters with Chinese "bots" who attempt to sell cheats through the game's team communication platform. For instance, in a YouTube video published less than a month after the release of *Apex Legends*, a player named "ChillTyme" documents his personal encounter with hackers on Asian servers advertising cheats for the game.[27] In his stream-recorded footage, the video begins with light elevator music playing in the audio game chat, the voice communication system for teammates to use during each round. After a few seconds of music, an automated voice recording plays an advertisement in Mandarin Chinese for how to purchase software hacks. The "bot" player also writes a code of letters and numbers in the text chat. In the video, we hear ChillTyme exclaim a mix of confusion and amusement, as it is presumably his first time encountering a nonhuman teammate whose entire purpose is to spam teammates with cheat ads. At the end of the video, ChillTyme asks the viewer if they have experienced any similar experiences, as he believes Chinese "bots" are infiltrating Asian and North American servers. In the form of nonhuman players who join games simply to advertise hacks, this version of Chinese cheaters becomes a similar nuisance with the potential to ruin gameplay across different global servers. If legacies of techno-orientalism have perpetually conflated the Asian and the technological across different social histories,[28] then these fully automated nonhuman player-bots (whose function is not even to participate in gameplay) are a code-based archetype of technical hacking, invading and degrading the "integrity" of virtual presence.

Although I have primarily focused on *Apex Legends* and *PUBG*, the threat of Chinese cheaters is not game-specific but, rather, associated with the genre of multiplayer shooters. A quick search through Reddit's different gaming forums will yield players documenting their experiences with Chinese hackers or Chinese cheat sellers in *Fortnite*, *Call of Duty*, *Battlefield*, *Counter-Strike: Global Offensive*, and other games in this genre. Part of the gamer discourse surrounding Chinese cheaters is that they migrate from game to game, exploiting code-based hacks or selling software through in-game bots. In Patterson's discussion of gaming genres, he describes big-budget first-person shooters as the "least Asiatic game genres out there,"[29] as their game worlds often invoke militaristic, nationalist, and/or imperial themes and mechanics from a Euro-American perspective. At their core, their game environments and narratives are rooted in ideas of combat, conquest, and victory.[30] Considering games like *America's Army*, *Doom*, and flight simulators, Alexander Galloway has asserted that shooters draw heavily from military ideology with varying degrees of realism, where the experience of being a "player" soldier is not unrelated to military recruitment.[31] The presence of Chinese cheaters in this specific genre, then, must also be understood within the rising popularity of first-person shooters in China. If first-person shooters stem from a Euro-American military ideology entrenched in nationalist and imperialist desires, then this popularity among Chinese players may also signal how first-person shooters can mediate these ideologies through a Chinese nationalism. Games like Giant Interactive Group's *Glorious Mission* (resembling the *Call of Duty* franchise) and Shenzhen-based Tencent's *Game for Peace* (a Chinese version of *PUBG Mobile*) represent how the Chinese gaming industry has adapted many Euro-American first-person shooters. In this view, the presence of Chinese cheaters can also be understood as a part of China's entry into the genre of multiplayer shooters, with BR shooters experiencing the most recent uptick in hackers. From the lens of Chinese militarism, the logic of invasion refers to the spread of Chinese neoimperialism, embraced by Chinese gamers who may utilize their gaming presence and skill to celebrate Chinese nationalism across region-based servers.

Chinese/Cheating   **227**

Games studies scholars have examined how Chinese players (or perceived to be Chinese players) are also negatively racialized in other genres, most notably in MMORPGs (massive multiplayer online role-playing games) such as *World of Warcraft* and *Lineage II*. These games contain vast virtual economies that play a crucial role in how a player's avatar levels up and advances in power and privilege, or what Edward Castronova calls "avatarial capital."[32] A player often must dedicate many hours a day to perform tasks, quests, and duties to accumulate in-game currencies, abilities, or status. This play-based labor, or what most gamers call "grinding," is part of the built-in difficulty of these game worlds and separates the casual player from the die-hard gamer, many of whom will have logged thousands of hours of gameplay. Within these MMORPG worlds, Chinese farmers are commonly perceived by gamers to be ingenuine players who level up accounts to sell them to others, or by harvesting in-game virtual currency in exchange for real-world profit. Viewed as a type of Chinese cheating, gold farming, according to Tara Fickle, makes these games not more difficult but too "easy" for those who have the resources to purchase an already "farmed" account.[33] Put simply, it "cheapens" the gaming experience for others. The language racializing gold farming reproduces the anti-Chinese sentiment regarding Chinese laborers during the nineteenth century, in which the threat of Asiatic labor was framed as a "cheapening" of white labor.[34] Lisa Nakamura has also discussed how the phenomenon of Chinese gold farming configures race not as a visible digital identity but as the effect of a style of play, allowing gamers to dislike a particular way of gaming rather than a specific player.[35] Noting similarities in *Lineage II*, Constance Steinkuehler has suggested that within this different MMORPG, many players create an "'us versus them' mentality to wage perpetual field war against all (perceived) Chinese," whereas Chineseness marks the boundaries of fair play.[36]

Thus, the phenomenon of Chinese cheaters is partially defined by an inability to be contained by the virtual borders of any specific game or genre. In these games, both Chinese gold farmers and Chinese cheaters in multiplayer shooters depict how, in the words of Nick Yee, "offline identities and ethnicities are forcibly dragged into online games in which national boundaries do not exist."[37] Yet *how* racial meaning shuttles between ludic and social contexts is different depending on the social-technical systems undergirding each game world. If Chinese gold farmers are racialized by their style of play, a repetitive, robotic embodiment of the player-laborer that denigrates the avatarial "freedom" of other MMORPG players, then Chinese aimbotters are racialized by their conflation with technical misuse. In the server-based play hosted across global data centers, BR shooters demonstrate how technical function and malfunction enact an important role in shaping the gaming experience. As a concept, procedural racism identifies how racial meaning in digital games emerges not only as an effect of style but also as an effect of technical (mal)function and its invasive presence. Ideas of foreignness, a hallmark of Asian racialization in Euro-American histories, are even more complicated in the digital realm, where connection to servers is linked to the stability of a game's avatarial production and procedural mechanics. As computational infrastructures become integral features of multiplayer BR shooters, they also become the terrain in which renewed racial discourse emerges, coded and recoded as a threat lurking at the outskirts of the digital battleground.

China as a "Global Cheater"

The racial marker of "Chinese cheaters" is not unique to gaming communities. In November 2019, the rhetoric of "cheating" characterized much of President Donald Trump's commentary on the US-China trade war. Echoing his anti-China statements that had galvanized his political base, Trump stated at the Economic Club in New York: "Since China's entrance into the World Trade Organization in 2001, no one has manipulated better or taken advantage of the United States more. I will not say the word 'cheated,' but nobody's cheated better than China."[38] Underlying the Trumpian promise to "Make America Great Again" is the use of China as a symbol not only of a nation in direct economic competition with the United States but, indeed, of all that threatens the American fabric of freedom, equality, and fair play. Trump's rhetoric describes China as an economic and national threat, and his comments frame US-China relations as a game. Tara Fickle has argued that there is a structural relationship between games and neoliberalism, in which ludic rhetoric—such as fairness, deservedness, winners, and losers—condition socioeconomic reality.[39] Through the framing of a game with winners, losers, and cheaters, this rhetoric produces a racial proxy—"China" as a national player—that allows racist sentiment to circulate through an avatar of international geopolitics. Insofar as neoliberalism touts a "color-blind" and "postidentity" US nation-state,[40] it appears that processes of racialization are even more gamelike than ever, where racial meaning "flickers" from view in ways that resemble the ephemerality of digital environments.[41]

Chinese/Cheating   **229**

Gaming forms, structures, and logics are all around us, and their avatars and rhetoric actively shape phenomena from the geopolitical to the personal. Although the relationship between games and society is not necessarily deterministic, it is important, as Amanda Phillips has suggested, to look for "parallel developments and mutual constitution rather than linearly for causality."[42] Battle royale shooters dramatize the zero-sum logic that has typified US-China antagonism by casting global capitalism and imperialism as a "last one standing" competitive game. By framing China as the "cheaters"—rather than, say, the nation's "enemies"—the Trumpian rhetoric of Chinese foul play suggests that there is something rigged about the terms of play for modern economic prosperity that perpetually favors the expert manipulators.

Across these cases, the rhetoric of Chineseness refers not only to racial bodies but also to procedures, a system of rules, functions, and operations that exceed visual cognition and capture. Both in the case of global economics and server-based BR shooters, Chineseness signifies the potential for systemic malfunction or misuse, shoring up an anxiety about the socio-technical structure of the "game" itself. Uncomfortably aligned with the procedural's latent threat, these negative encodings of Chineseness become a burden for racial subjects, whether their identities are virtual or real.

Notes

1 BattlEye, "We are currently banning."

2 Arik_De_Frasia, "What makes online cheating so prevalent in China?"

3 Patterson, *Open World Empire*, 27, and "Asian Americans and Digital Games."

4 Steinkuehler, "The Mangle of Play," 209.

5 Kylin, "*Apex Legends*—Chinese Player Using Aimbot / Hack."

6 Consalvo, *Cheating*, 123.

7 J. H. Murray, *Hamlet on the Holodeck*, 71.

8 Bogost, *Persuasive Games*, ix.

9 Nakamura, *Cybertypes*, xv.

10 Fickle, *The Race Card*, 3.

11 Fickle, *The Race Card*, 8.

12 Patterson, *Open World Empire*, 38.

13 "Danny Quach," Re: Kylin, "*Apex Legends*—Chinese Player Using Aimbot / Hack."

14 Banks, "*Apex Legends* Dev Responds."

15 Banks, "*Apex Legends* Dev Responds."

16 Morse, *Virtualities*, 6.

17 For a comprehensive account of anti-Chinese racial violence and law, see Lew-Williams, *The Chinese Must Go*.

18 K. Chang, *Pacific Connections*, 45.

19 Lye, *America's Asia*, 7.

20 Fickle, *The Race Card*, 44.

21 Snoobboons, "Chinese Cheater on *Apex Legends*."

22 DerpHard, comment on Snoobboons, "Chinese Cheater on *Apex Legends*."

23 xzacc91, comment on Snoobboons, "Chinese Cheater on *Apex Legends*."

24 Grudge122, comment on Snoobboons, "Chinese Cheater on *Apex Legends*."

25 Grudge122, comment on Snoobboons, "Chinese Cheater on *Apex Legends*."

26 For more on the racial discourses linking Chineseness and contagion, see Shah, *Contagious Divides*.

27 ChillTyme, "How Chinese Hackers Are Selling Cheats."

28 Roh, Huang, and Niu, *Techno-Orientalism*, 2.

29 Patterson, *Open World Empire*, 196.

30 In 2018, the US Army and Navy even established their own esports team and Twitch streaming channel.

31 Galloway, *Gaming*, 70–71.

32 Castronova, *Synthetic Worlds*, 110.

33 Fickle, *The Race Card*, 183.

34 K. Chang, *Pacific Connections*, 45.

35 Nakamura, "Don't Hate the Player," 130.

36 Steinkuehler, "The Mangle of Play," 208.

37 Yee, *The Proteus Paradox*, 95.

38 Cox, "Trump Says China Cheated America on Trade."

39 Fickle, *The Race Card*, 6.

40 Eng, *The Feeling of Kinship*, 2.

41 Here I am invoking N. Katherine Hayles's notion of "flickering signifiers," in which information technologies reconfigure the relationship between materiality and form, signifier and signified. Hayles, "Virtual Bodies and Flickering Signifiers," 77.

42 Phillips, "Shooting to Kill," 144.

Miyoko Conley

Romancing the Night Away

Queering Animate Hierarchies in
Hatoful Boyfriend and *Tusks*

In April 2011, Japanese artist and game developer Hato Moa released *Hatoful Boyfriend*, a humorous video game about a human who dates pigeons in a postapocalyptic Japan, which rose to unexpected global popularity and commercial success, with overwhelmingly positive reviews from major gaming news outlets in Japan, North America, and Europe. Another testament to the game's success was its numerous spin-offs, such as a sequel game, comic books, and assorted merchandise. *Hatoful Boyfriend*'s success came as a surprise to critics and gamers alike for several reasons, such as its absurd yet intriguing pigeon-dating premise. Most of all, people were surprised by its engaging storyline, because *Hatoful Boyfriend* is a parody of dating games, a somewhat maligned game genre within the gaming community due to its focus on romantic storylines and assumed frothy content. Though the genre originated in Japan, *Hatoful Boyfriend*'s popularity illuminated its dedicated transnational fanbase and spawned an uptick in dating game parodies, from both small and large developers across the globe.

This article examines two independent dating game parodies with nonhuman animal (or animalistic) love interests: *Hatoful Boyfriend*, created by Hato Moa, and *Tusks: The Orc Dating Sim* (2017), created by queer Scottish game designer Mitch Alexander.[1] I define dating games as a genre where love and intimate relationships are the primary narrative focus and where gameplay revolves around dating or other relationship-building activities. The goal of these games is to successfully gain the affection of a partner by choosing the correct options at key points and to end up in a romantic relationship with them. After the player finishes one route, they are expected to replay the game until they partner with every romanceable character.[2] The games encourage replaying through rewards such as unlocking pictures, or sometimes unlocking a final route called the "true" ending. As a narrative- and character-driven style of game, it is impossible to separate narrative from gameplay when discussing dating games; the play *is* the narrative. Therefore, I consider dating game parodies to be any game that somehow subverts the genre's traditional structures through narrative and mechanics.

I build on previous studies of indie visual novels and dating games, which utilize queer frameworks to demonstrate how these games can unsettle heteronormativity and gender roles.[3] My particular interest is how the intersection of nonhuman animals, Asian popular culture, and biopolitics in *Hatoful Boyfriend* and *Tusks* queers notions of animacy—the quality of agency, awareness, and liveness. I argue that *Hatoful Boyfriend* and *Tusks* illustrate how tightly woven race, nationality, sexuality, and animality are in determining which lives are considered more valuable by making the player seriously consider the nuances of dating an animal partner. Through queer game design, they ultimately turn those hierarchies into messy question marks and take pleasure in reforming nonnormative intimacies to resist imperial legacies and imagine future worlds.

Mel Y. Chen's influential works on animate hierarchies—and their argument that sexuality is central to the imagination of our lives[4]—underpins my contention that dating game parodies are a prime site to interrogate the heteronormative and racialized logics that govern the ordering of life. Chen analyzes the linguistic and visual ways these hierarchies have been reinforced to oppress certain groups of people, particularly through animal figures (some familiar examples might be racist images equating Black folks with monkeys or depicting Chinese people as disease-carrying rats). Chen also reminds us that these notions affect real-life systems. They cite how Black, Indigenous, and disabled women have been subject to involuntary sterilization to illustrate reproductive mandates prioritizing certain beings over others.[5] We can also see this in *Dobbs v. Jackson Women's Health Organization*, the 2022 US Supreme Court ruling that overturned *Roe v. Wade*. Many folks were quick to point out that those who can get pregnant now have less bodily autonomy than a corpse—a very *in*animate thing—as organs cannot be harvested without prior consent. (Amanda Lehr skewered the ruling with a parodic article for *McSweeney's* titled "For Bodily Autonomy Reasons, I Now Identify as a Corpse.") Coupled with studies that show how the decision will disproportionately impact Black and brown women, disabled people, and LGBTQ+ communities, it becomes clear that interlocking notions of animacy, race, and sexuality continue to undergird governance. Dating game parodies provide a way for developers and players to engage with and critique these systems, by weaving the overarching game structure into the romantic narratives; the way players understand the game as a whole becomes part of the story, and through interacting with it, they participate in—or disrupt—larger heteronormative narratives.

As part of a genre that developed in Japan and is heavily tied to Japanese pop culture tropes, visual styles, and media mix marketing,[6] dating games are inextricable from the transnational flows of Asian media and are always in relation to Asia, Asianness, and the Asiatic. Christopher Patterson notes that within video games, the Asiatic becomes a technology rather than a representation.[7] Remixing and deconstructing Asian media tropes is one of the core ways dating game parodies queer normative gender and sexual expectations, making Asianness integral to the subgenre, even when the game is not explicitly related to an Asian country. Chen also locates transnational media flows and the recombination of Asian signifiers as productive sites to consider slippages within animate hierarchies; in one example, they analyze how the Fu Manchu figure stitches together a myriad of various and opposing animalistic, gendered, and sexual codes and offers a queer animal-blend of an Asian body that bolsters the stereotype of Asians as inscrutable yet also potentially evades easy categorization.[8]

However, Patterson also locates Asianness as a fraught and understudied area in otherwise queer and inclusive visual novels, where the Asiatic becomes a vehicle to explore queer worlds, but one that could also problematically further techno-orientalist stereotypes or dispense with racial backgrounds all together.[9] Dating game parodies are not immune to these issues either,

234 Miyoko Conley

but the games I consider here deploy a combination of Asian popular culture, animality, and queer romance to show the potentiality of the subgenre to disrupt animate, imperial hierarchies. Specifically, *Hatoful Boyfriend* and *Tusks* build on the themes of contamination and toxicity in relation to Asianness as discussed in the introduction to this volume, particularly around the weaponization of so-called Asian diseases and imperial logics that view Asians as invading hordes. While these dating games illustrate different ways Asianness traverses animate hierarchies, including to reinforce them, they also lean into the potentiality of porous boundaries through their nonhuman datable characters, biopolitical narratives, and subversion of game mechanics.

Heteronormative Structures in Dating Games

Scholars often point out how dating games can reinforce heteronormativity and stereotypical gender roles. One way is through the dominance of heterosexual representation in their narratives. In Japan, dating game subgenres usually target an assumed audience, mainly straight men (*bishōjo* games) or women (*otome* games), and these target audiences carry over when a game is localized for global distribution. The datable characters are also almost exclusively straight, with few representations of LGBTQ+ characters.[10] Additionally, a significant amount of dating games reproduce traditional gender roles in romantic relationships. Sarah Christina Ganzon shows how many otome games formulate the female protagonist's primary role as a "carer" for the men in their lives.[11] Leticia Andlauer describes the traditional otome heroine as pure, sweet, kind, and having a "fragile aspect," and Emily Taylor analyzes how datable women in *bishōjo* games eventually become dependent on male protagonists.[12] However, Patterson and Salter and colleagues argue that indie designers often respond to this lack of representational diversity and strive to incorporate a variety of genders, sexualities, and races in their games.[13] Ganzon has also noted that fans have the power to lobby for more diverse romance options.[14]

It is also not a foregone conclusion that mainstream dating games are *only* heteronormative, and even if they promote heteronormativity in one way, they can also contain narratives and mechanics that complicate it in another. Some ways that scholars see dating games breaking with hegemonic

Romancing the Night Away   **235**

structures include (but are not limited to) the ease and accessibility of visual novel game engines like Ren'py, or distribution platforms like itch.io that offer alternatives to AAA game production;[15] how the looping structure of dating games encourages players to explore different romantic partners;[16] the way historical otome games offer female players the opportunity to assert their presence in historical narratives that often exclude them, effectively "queering history";[17] and the opportunity for intimacies with virtual characters.[18]

I view dating games as largely promoting hegemonic heteronormativity through the idea that romance and sex are "winnable." The point of dating games is to "win" a particular partner and get their "good" ending, which usually means a straight, monogamous relationship. All choices and strategy go toward completing that objective by reading character archetypes to discern what responses will yield the best results. If a player fails, they will get the "bad" ending (usually without romance or even resulting in a character death), or the story may stop early if the player chooses too many wrong options. The only option for the player is to fall in line and choose whatever the game deems the correct option, often along gendered lines. Driving toward a predetermined end of relationship-as-reward echoes Elizabeth Freeman's concept of chrononormativity, or the biopolitical organization of human life toward maximum productivity, where the temporality of "ideal" life stages (school, job, marriage, children) are ordained by the state.[19] The game turns every social interaction into a test of right and wrong that could yield the ultimate win conditions. If the game contains a simulation element, such as raising stats the partner will like, romance also becomes a form of time management and productivity.

The common archetypes found in dating games often reference Japanese popular culture tropes as well. For example, there is usually a *tsundere* character, who is initially cold or even hostile to the protagonist but over time reveals a softer side. Other common tropes are *yandere* (someone who is "lovesick," but to a dangerous, obsessive degree) and the *genki* or energetic character, and there are many more. The use of such set character archetypes can underscore the heteronormative structure in dating games, because while the tropes can be deciphered visually, they are also performative and read through the way the characters act and speak. In turn, the player enacts socialized, normative dating habits when playing the game as they try to successfully romance these set types. Essentially, the characters in traditional dating games are made up of readable elements that can be broken down into component parts, catalogued, and "gamed."

Animality and Blurring Bodily Boundaries in *Hatoful Boyfriend*

One of the primary ways parodies queer dating games is through upending player expectations with seemingly absurd dating options. In *Hatoful Boyfriend*, that means pigeons. The protagonist is a girl named Hiyoko (a pun on both a girl's name and the word for "chick" in Japanese),[20] who is the only human student at an all-pigeon high school in Japan, called St. Pigeonation. Hiyoko is a human representative at the school, serving as an experiment to see if humans and pigeons can live together in harmony. In *Hatoful Boyfriend*'s fiction, a variant of the H5N1 virus (the "bird flu") wiped out most of humankind. Human governments tried to spread a counter-virus to kill the dangerous birds, but this instead resulted in birds gaining human-level intelligence and becoming the dominant life-forms on the planet. In addition to the romance plotlines, *Hatoful Boyfriend*'s story is saturated with a larger biopolitical conflict between birds and humans in a postpandemic world, and the game's continual references to the birds' identities and bodies draw out anxieties around race, nationality, contamination, and the permeability of bodily boundaries.

In one way, *Hatoful Boyfriend* falls into a broader lineage of animal-centric games, and, more specifically, within Marco Caracciolo's formulation of "animal mayhem games," which feature an animal avatar that deliberately hinders human activities.[21] A prime example of this is *Untitled Goose Game* (2019), where the player controls a goose character and completes objectives that largely upset the humans around town. Unlike games that purport to provide an authentic "animal experience" for a human player, which can reinforce Western philosophical notions of human dominance over nature, animal mayhem games do not allow the player full control over the animal avatar and instead disorient them, taking a nonhuman view of the world. Though in *Hatoful Boyfriend* the player does not control a pigeon character until the very last route, the player must consider pigeons as legitimate and attractive romantic partners, which similarly upends anthropocentric views.

Though there are no explicit sex scenes in the game, it is apparent that the protagonist *does* find the birds attractive, although the character never elaborates how a human-pigeon physical relationship would work. For example, in a scene at the school pool the protagonist sees the birds splashing around and thinks: "All these damp, tight-clinging feathers are making my heart race . . ." which emphasizes the pigeons' erotic attributes. Humans often use

Romancing the Night Away **237**

animal figures to represent "our" more animalistic sides, and it is not uncommon for certain animals to represent sex in general (such as a sexually active, virile man being called a "stallion," or an older woman in a sexual relationship with a younger man being called a "cougar"). Chen also shows how animals *become* sexuality through scientific research that uses nonhuman animal biological materials for human-directed reproductive research,[22] indicating how blurry and permeable the line between human animal and nonhuman animal already is both symbolically and biologically. The datable pigeons in *Hatoful Boyfriend* are particularly surprising because pigeons are historically not considered the most erotic of animals in humans' imaginations: they are often called "rats of the skies" and are largely seen as scavengers that carry disease. The character sprites in the game are pictures of real-life birds, which again emphasizes that these are truly birds; they are simultaneously close to our reality as photographs of real animals and made even stranger, as they do not fit into the manga/anime aesthetic typical in dating games. Additionally, the pigeons are just as smart as (or even smarter than) the human protagonist, while retaining their pigeon-ness through references to their bird bodies and birdlike preferences.[23] When dating game parodies utilize outlandish, nonhuman dating partners, they make the player shift their perspective and enact the instability of human/nonhuman boundaries; the player must regard the pigeons as desirable partners and form attachments to them in order to continue the game.

It is worth noting that in the game, the birds' sexuality falls more toward heteronormative, as nearly all the datable birds are male, and the protagonist is female. The one datable female bird, Azami, is treated more like a side quest, as she is not a main character and has a rather short route. Additionally, there is also an option to turn on "human portraits" for the main pigeons. These portraits appear one time when the characters are introduced, fading in behind their pigeon counterparts like a specter. In one way, this can be viewed as anthropomorphizing the pigeons, suggesting that they need to be "humanlike" to be considered fully desirable and not *too* improper as partners. The human portraits are also illustrated in manga/anime style, more firmly seating them in Japanese popular culture tropes, which gives the player a hint regarding the character archetype. However, one pigeon, Okosan, does not have a human portrait; when he is introduced, there's just an illustration of a pigeon in a high school uniform (see figure 11.1). While this is meant to be humorous, Okosan's portrait also indicates the easy slippage between the two portrait styles and the unstable boundaries between

11.1. A comparison of a human portrait and pigeon portrait in *Hatoful Boyfriend*. Screenshots by author.

human and animal. And as the human portraits only appear in conjunction with the pigeon ones, they come to signify a queer refusal to consider them as either/or; instead, they are always both.

Hatoful Boyfriend also points to how this slippage between human animals and nonhuman animals shifts depending on *which* people and/or animals we are talking about, and how animality is tied to race, nationality, and ability. As Antoinette Burton and Renisa Mawani argue, animals are crucial to understanding imperial histories.[24] The authors' bestiary of common animal figures in nineteenth- and twentieth-century British imperialism reveals the ways that animals (both literal and symbolic) were used to reinforce European racial supremacy within transnational imperialist projects and cement conceptions of *who* was more human or animate. One example Burton and Mawani use is the racialization of mosquitoes as Japanese in American propaganda during World War II to symbolize how both were considered the "enemy" at the time (since mosquitoes carried malaria), discursively *lowering* their place on the animate scale and classifying them as subhumans that can somehow "infect" the population.[25]

In *Hatoful Boyfriend*, complex intersections of race and nationality within animate hierarchies play out through its pandemic storyline. The game's setting recalls the ways that viruses become nationalized and racialized, and the xenophobic incidents that happen during disease outbreaks. With the recent COVID-19 pandemic, it is not a stretch to see how a disease becomes racialized, given the rise of anti-Asian and anti-Chinese sentiment around the world, including within other Asian countries.[26] Chen notes other outbreaks—SARS and, apropos for *Hatoful Boyfriend*, bird flu—that were perceived as "Asian" biosecurity threats in the United States.[27] Though it seems Hato Moa has not talked about the bird flu in relation to Asia in *Hatoful Boyfriend*, and it is important to bear in mind that the game draws from a Japanese cultural context (where certain animals may carry different racial connotations), the game's storyline about disease control highlights the association between birds and disease and how, in many parts of the world, bird flu was racialized as "Asian." The game asks us to consider not only who is desirable but also who is framed as a threat to bodily boundaries.

Xenophobia and other prejudices are also present in the game through the characters' ingrained biases, showing that certain hierarchies *are* upheld in this world. Much of the prejudice expressed is based on class, as some pigeons are wealthy and others are not. Some of the pigeons also say derisive things to Okosan, who cannot speak as well as the others and is therefore viewed as less intelligent—notable, considering that Okosan is the only pigeon without a human portrait, making him less "humanlike" and suggesting parallels to the prejudices faced by disabled people. As for xenophobia, the elitist noblebird Sakuya continually disparages fellow student Anghel (the Tagalog word for "angel"), who hails from the Philippines. Sakuya calls him a peasant and tells him to "bang some coconuts together." Sakuya himself is French, which is a common character trope in anime and manga and usually signals that a character is romantic and cosmopolitan. Within the game's Japanese setting, however, Sakuya's prejudice calls up a longer, violent history between

Japan and the Philippines, and shows that anti-Filipino sentiment—and the colonial histories it is tied to—still exists in the game's postapocalyptic future. Even the protagonist Hiyoko is not immune to viewing Anghel in a colonial frame: she admits she has the strange urge to call him "bananaman" (and does so, though only in her narrated thoughts).

Rather than treating all birds as equal or interchangeable, *Hatoful Boyfriend* leans into the discomfort that animate hierarchies bring to the fore. It does not shy away from the language that makes certain "people" more or less human, whether it draws them closer to animals (Okosan is the most "birdlike") or even to things and foodstuffs (coconuts, bananas). The player cannot opt out of these conversations and must contend with these animate divisions, whether by choosing to defend Okosan from Sakuya or figuring out how to keep Anghel away from school doctor Shuu, who is interested in researching him for a bioterrorist plot.[28]

While *Hatoful Boyfriend*'s mechanics follow typical dating game design, the sometimes confounding or silly character choices and outcomes play with their narrative structure. A common trait across many parodies is to upend the standard romance novel trope of the "happily ever after," or, in dating game vernacular, the "good" endings. Dating games' main mechanic is the choice mechanic, where players choose between dialogue options or actions to advance the story. What the player chooses affects the storyline, which gives the feeling of agency. Contrary to the idea of "choice," however, dating games promise happily-ever-afters, so long as the player performs the *correct* actions. If a player wants the "good" endings, they need to choose a specific set of options that will please their romantic partner, which means there is no real choice, as the only way to progress in the game is to choose all the right options and end the game in a monogamous relationship.

Hatoful Boyfriend critiques player choice through the tone in its endings; most of the individual routes have an uncertain, unsettling, or eccentric ending. For example, if the player successfully romances their kind best friend, Ryouta, his ending takes a melancholic turn when his mother passes away, which leads Ryouta to worry about his lifespan compared to the protagonist's. Shy, bookish Nageki turns out to be a literal ghost and fades away. Okosan engulfs the world in pudding. And if the player romances the sinister school doctor Shuu, who is the *yandere* or obsessive archetype, Shuu always kills the protagonist and keeps her brain, no matter the ending. In his "good" ending, Shuu takes his own life, but before he does, he asks Hiyoko if she truly cared for him. The player's choices are "Yes," "Yes," and "Yes."

Romancing the Night Away **241**

This dialogue is simultaneously a critique on how limiting (and potentially dangerous) archetypes like the *yandere* are, and also a comment on how little control the player has; it lays bare how inevitable the ending was based on typically heteronormative game structures.

The illusion of choice dissolves even further in the very last route of the game, titled "Bad Boys' Love." At the start of this route, the player suddenly takes on the role of Ryouta. This is the only time the player plays as a pigeon, and the route begins with Hiyoko getting murdered and Ryouta resolving to figure out what happened to her. The school is simultaneously walled off in an emergency drill, and the player learns that a faction of the bird government has been conducting experiments on pigeons in the school to create a virus that will wipe out the remaining humans, refocusing the story on the sci-fi, biopolitical narrative. Ryouta finds out he was unknowingly infected with the virus and accidentally killed Hiyoko. After unwittingly killing Hiyoko a second time (her brain was transferred to a robot that Ryouta attacks), Ryouta ultimately locks himself in a chamber with Hiyoko's brain, which is still conscious sans body, to await a cure. The player cannot affect the overall outcome of this route; though they still choose options at key moments, there is no way to stop the major events from happening. Overall, the one-to-one couplings the player built prior are not helpful, because no matter what happens, there is still a larger state conspiracy at play, suggesting that though thought-provoking, the previous monogamous, heterosexual pairings do not work in this posthuman future.

Animate NPCs in *Tusks*

Hatoful Boyfriend uses unexpected datable characters (pigeons) to disrupt the human/animal divide by both refusing strict binaries and exposing how race and nationality are tied to fears of contamination. Similarly, *Tusks: The Orc Dating Sim* deploys nonhuman datable characters (orcs) to show how animal-adjacent creatures are used to bring certain groups of people lower on the animate scale. In the game, the player's romantic options are all male orcs or similar species (the group also contains a selkie and a gris), and the protagonist is also a male orc, putting gay relationships front and center. The game is set in a pseudo-mythical, medieval Scotland, and the characters are traveling north together from an annual orcish assembly. Though the game is ostensibly set in the past, the orc characters are on the precipice of their own apocalypse of sorts, as they traverse human lands that are growing ever more hostile toward them. For example, at one point in the game the group runs into a literal human-built wall meant to keep them off the land they must cross; the orcs are supposed to have a formal writ of passage to go through, though this rule was only recently created by the humans and never discussed with the orcs. At another point, orc scholar Brocgin explains how orcs are not allowed to attend human colleges and details the numerous hurdles he has gone through to obtain scholarly material and attend lectures, signaling how cordoned off academia (and therefore official records) are to the orcs.

In a 2015 interview with *Vice*, designer Mitch Alexander said he specifically chose orcs because of their perpetual status as "outsiders" and inherently evil creatures within the fantasy genre.[29] Takeo Rivera notes that depictions of orcs represent a "culmination of masculine chaos and barbarity, coded variously as Hun, Mongol, Islamic, and Black; they are characterized by their massive muscles, warrior culture, protruding canine teeth, green skin, tribal political organization, and, of course, bloodlust."[30] Orcs are not simply "nonwhite" but a "barbaric" and supposedly dangerous amalgamation of races, shifting between stereotypes of Asian, Middle Eastern, and African peoples. In J. R. R. Tolkien's influential *Lord of the Rings* series, orcs are coded as Mongol stereotypes; he describes them in a letter as "squat, broad, flat-nosed, sallow-skinned, with wide mouths and slant eyes: in fact degraded and repulsive versions of the (to Europeans) least lovely Mongol-types."[31] As such, they are linked to racist images of Asians as invading hordes that have been prevalent in Europe since the Middle Ages. Alexander also saw how orcs' depictions othered them in additional ways, connoting "ableism, misogyny, homophobia, cissexism, and classism" in one big bundle.[32] Therefore, the ridiculousness of the game's premise comes not only from dating a mythical creature but also from dating an always already racialized and othered creature who takes on all marginalized codes to represent the lowest of life-forms.

One way the game tackles otherness and animacy head-on is through Aed, the one optically white human character. He is studying orcs, and his conversations involve interviewing the other orcs, including the player. Aed's human-centric worldview is apparent; at one point, he calls the orcs "civilized, like humans," and eventually group leader Ror has to explain the linguistic animacy of words like *humanity* that push all others to the margins of society. The player's choices in Aed's conversations are about how they will respond: Will they directly call out Aed? Will they try to be "nice" and smooth things over? Will they say nothing? For example, in his disastrous interview

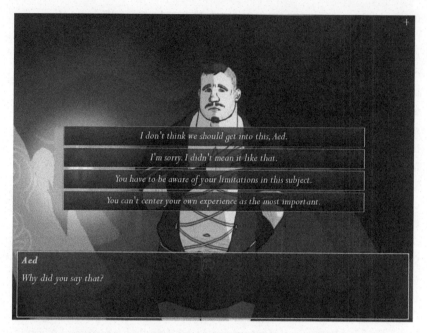

11.2. An example of choice options with Aed. Screenshot by author.

with Ror, Aed centers the conversation on his own feelings. Aed asks Ror what orcs think of humans—which Ror points out is a human-centric question—and Ror gives him a complex answer about orcs being subjugated under humans. Aed misinterprets this as all orcs hating humans, and the player jumps in to mediate the conversation. Eventually, Aed congratulates himself for making progress as an ally, completely centering himself by saying: "The most important thing is, I'm growing a lot as a person with both of your help." If the player calls him out on this behavior, Aed confronts the player about it, and the player's options range from placating Aed to offering various explanations for what he did wrong (figure 11.2). These moments illustrate the ways speech acts create animate hierarchies and make the player decide whether they will reinforce them or reject them.

However, perhaps one of the biggest ways *Tusks* subverts dating game structure is through its approach to player choice and the choice mechanic. First, *Tusks* does away with individual route endings, disrupting the "happily-ever-afters" that exist in most dating games. While the game does not shy away from sex or intimacy (though the player can choose to turn this content off), there are no individual routes for the orc characters, and the romance does not happen at the end of the game. Rather than treating intimate scenes and naked character sprites as a "reward" at the end, these scenes come at different points during the fourteen-day journey. A player could also experience multiple moments like these with different orcs throughout a playthrough, including an intimate encounter with the group's three polyamorous leaders. In fact, the game nearly forces the player to spend time with multiple orcs. The player chooses to spend time with an individual orc at the campsite each night, but after a certain number of encounters, the orc will (gently) refuse to spend more time with the player no matter how close they are. The refusals are not acrimonious but mundane; sometimes the orcs are just tired. This means that unlike with other dating games, the player cannot focus solely on one character, and they have to interact with the other members of the group. Refusals like this interrupt the dominant heteronormative logic of dating games, which rewards players with characters' time if they perform the correct actions. The narrative treats intimate scenes and the ability to partner with multiple characters as acts of closeness where monogamy is not the default. These nonmonogamous queer relationships also shift the focus to how nonnormative intimacies can build community and found family.

Tusks also demonstrates a way to queer the choice mechanic that resists imperialist notions of domination and control through a setting called "NPC autonomy." This means that at key moments in the game, the nonplayer characters will vote on a decision or make their own choices instead of automatically agreeing to whatever the player decides. For example, when the orcs run into the wall that bars them from taking the path they need, the group votes whether to storm the gate or sneak around. If NPC autonomy is turned on, the group can overrule whatever the player decides. Additionally, at the end of each day, two orcs are sent out on guard duty, and if NPC autonomy is on, Ror decides which orcs go out rather than the player choosing. The player won't be able to spend time with the orcs out on duty for that night, which adds an element of randomness to relationships in the game. By granting NPCs autonomy and breaking the reward cycle in dating games, *Tusks* reframes dating as an activity that requires patience, consideration, and consent, not something a person can simply "game." And for the orcs, the NPC autonomy function allows creatures who've been othered and controlled to express resistance to the Western imperialist gaze that codifies them into racialized hierarchies.

Conclusion

I will briefly conclude with a consideration of "walls" as metaphor that permeates both *Hatoful Boyfriend* and *Tusks*. In *Hatoful Boyfriend*, there is visual evidence of walls from the previous world order, as the background landscape is littered with buildings, symbolizing the shift in animate hierarchies from human to bird. Also, the school is literally walled off in the very last route, indicating that just because a hierarchy *shifts*, it does not mean that the new "top dogs" (or birds) will not reproduce former biopolitical controls. In *Tusks*, humans erect walls to keep orcs out of both human-owned land and institutions of higher learning, which act as metaphors for the historical erasure of marginalized folks that persists today. Walls, or boundaries, are what govern the bodies in these two parodies, gesturing also to the rigidity of the rules in the dating game genre, which always steer the player onto a particular, heteronormative path. Importantly, these are state-sanctioned walls, meaning that *Hatoful Boyfriend* and *Tusks* are not simply commenting on personal prejudices; rather, they are highlighting structures of imperialist, racial, and sexual hierarchies that undergird romantic relationships and the overall ordering of life.

There is another wall that these games ask the player to consider: the fourth wall, or the imagined separation between the audience (player) and the actors (or characters) in the story world. On the one hand, any dating game parody would instantly break the fourth wall, because the games constantly reference the player; these parodies run on the assumption that the player understands the structure of dating games and that they'll be able to recognize all the ways the games depart from their norms, creating a metagame for the player through in-jokes, references, and diverted patterns. The resonance of nonhuman intimacies with players is clear through the number of parodies that have come out in the last ten years from both professional game studios and individual fans, creating an ongoing conversation on the potentialities of these relationships. This pool of parodies includes games with datable horses (*My Horse Prince* [2016]), monsters (*Monster Prom* [2018]), weapons (*Boyfriend Dungeon* [2021]), and many other options, including the computer UI (*Date (Almost) Anything Simulator* [2017]).

For *Hatoful Boyfriend* and *Tusks*, their endings turn to repeated queer intimacies as crucial to future survival, through an emphasis on the player's embodied experience. The two games end with similar narrative sections. In *Hatoful Boyfriend*, once Ryouta and the main character's brain are locked in a room, the main character asks Ryouta to fill her in on what has happened. Ryouta replies: "Where do I start? Everything that's happened, what's happening now, and—everything that might happen, one day. We have plenty of time to talk about it all." In these last moments, Ryouta invokes a consideration of "everything that's happened" in the past, present, and possible future, which focuses on the process the player has gone through, or the multiple playthroughs they have performed and will perform.[33] Similarly, in *Tusks*, after the orc group makes it to their destination, the narrator frames the orcs' journey as a historical text. The narrator claims that there have been many versions of this story, which is a meta-acknowledgment of the player's many playthroughs, but importantly, the game ends with a disruption to the authority of the written text. The last lines in the game are "I hope the version of the story you read told you something worth hearing. And if not? You and I can reinterpret it and rewrite it, together or individually, until it works."

In emphasizing repeated playthroughs that will continue, these endings shift the importance away from static, hegemonic authority and onto the player's repeated, embodied experience, or, to use Diana Taylor's terms, they highlight the importance of the *repertoire* (embodied knowledge not captured in written archives, such as gestures, movements, sounds, ceremonies, and other performances) as equal to the archive (written, textual documents).[34] This is significant in games where institutions of higher learning have either shut certain people out (in *Tusks*) or ultimately served as institutions of control (in *Hatoful Boyfriend*). By invoking revision and reperformance, the games acknowledge that replaying is an important aspect of dating games but also suggests that any written record or "true" ending is not what the play is about. The player is not left with straight, linear routes but with a series of queer relationships (with humans, animals, and things) that both resist imperial legacies (within *Tusks* medieval lore) and suggest a way forward (in *Hatoful Boyfriend*'s sci-fi future setting). The games, then, turn to queer intimacy, and the continual formation of them, as a recuperative space for survival in the past, present, and future.

Notes

1 I am analyzing the English-language versions of these games.

2 Dating games are closely related to another style of game called visual novels, which combine on-screen narrative text with 2D backgrounds and character sprites. They also utilize a branching narrative format but can be about any subject matter. Another term that is often used for dating games is

dating sims. Technically they contain simulation elements, though sometimes the term gets applied to all dating games.

3 I am particularly indebted to the work of Reed, Murray, and Salter, *Adventure Games*; Salter, Blodgett, and Sullivan, "'Just Because It's Gay?'"; and Patterson, "Making Queer Asiatic Worlds."

4 M. Y. Chen, "Animacy as a Sexual Device," 2. See also M. Y. Chen, *Animacies*.

5 M. Y. Chen, "Animacy as a Sexual Device," 2.

6 "Media mix" is a business practice in Japan that disperses content across different platforms, such as anime, manga, video games, etc. See Steinberg, *Anime's Media Mix*.

7 Patterson, *Open World Empire*, 58.

8 M. Y. Chen, *Animacies*, 121.

9 Patterson, "Making Queer Asiatic Worlds."

10 There are *yuri* (girls' love) and *yaoi* (boys' love) games as well. However, it is important to note that *yuri* and *yaoi* are specific genres in Japan, and these media cannot be assumed to be made by queer creators for a queer community. See E. Friedman, "On Defining *Yuri*"; and Wood, "Boys' Love Anime."

11 Ganzon, "Making Love Not War," "Sweet Solutions," and "Investing Time."

12 Andlauer, "Pursuing One's Own Prince"; E. Taylor, "Dating-Simulation Games," 201.

13 Patterson, "Making Queer Asiatic Worlds"; Salter, Blodgett, and Sullivan, "'Just Because It's Gay?'"

14 Ganzon, "Sweet Solutions."

15 Salter, Blodgett, and Sullivan, "'Just Because It's Gay?'"

16 Andlauer, "Pursuing One's Own Prince."

17 Hasegawa, "Falling in Love with History."

18 Galbraith, "Bishōjo Games."

19 Freeman, *Time Binds*, 3.

20 The player here, as in most other dating games, has the option to name the protagonist.

21 Caracciolo, "Animal Mayhem Games."

22 M. Y. Chen, *Animacies*, 103.

23 Hato Moa said in interviews that the reason she chose pigeons is because she sincerely likes them. While many people might find the premise ridiculous at first, the choice of these birds was not because they are unappealing but, rather, to demonstrate their attractiveness. M. Nguyen, "Would You Date a Bird?"; Murdoch, "Hatoful Boyfriend."

24 Burton and Mawani, *Animalia*.

25 Burton and Mawani, *Animalia*, 6.

26 Rich, "As Coronavirus Spreads."

27 M. Y. Chen, *Animacies*, 171.

28 In the last route, it is revealed that Anghel releases hallucinogenic phero-mones, which makes anyone in his direct vicinity experience what he does.

29 McCasker, "This Gay Orc Dating Sim."

30 Rivera, "Ordering a New World Orientalist Biopower," 199.

31 Tolkien to Forrest J. Ackerman, June 1958, *The Letters of J. R. R. Tolkien*, 274.

32 McCasker, "This Gay Orc Dating Sim."

33 *Hatoful Boyfriend* contains an epilogue in which Ryouta and Hiyoko are finally released.

34 D. Taylor, *The Archive and the Repertoire*.

Sarah Christina Ganzon

The Fujoshi Trophy and Ridiculously Hot Men

Otome Games and Postfeminist Sensibilities

In the 2011 Anime Expo in Los Angeles, members of Aksys games' marketing team came dressed up as anime versions of historical Japanese samurai Hajime Saito and Toshizo Hijikata. After announcing their localization of Fate/EXTRA, the team played another trailer. Interspersed with images from the game, the trailer text read:

> A historical tale from Japan . . .
> Set at the finale of a grand era
> Filled with honor, courage and sacrifice . . .
> And ridiculously hot men?!
> Aw yeah.

That last two lines in particular triggered numerous laughs and cheers from the audience as the trailer cut to a subtitled version of the opening music video for the game. The trailer in question is for *Hakuoki: The Demon of the Fleeting Blossom*, which they were releasing the following year for the PSP.

Hakuoki was first released in 2008 for the PS2 in Japan. The year before this announcement, the anime adaptation was released, which helped create some interest among anime fans outside Japan. *Hakuoki* is an *otome* game. In its country of origin, otome games are known to be games created for women characterized by a focus on romance, easy controls, and links to media created for women and girls within the context of the anime media mix.[1] While *Hakuoki* is not the first otome game translated to English,[2] there was a lot of speculation about how much this type of game would sell outside its country of origin, especially given that it is a game mostly marketed to women in Japan, and most people who know about *Hakuoki* via the anime are considered very niche audiences even in otaku communities. Moreover, there were no localizations from Japanese otome game companies or their partner companies in English for many years since 2006. While there would be independent makers outside Japan making games—games such as Sake Visual's *Re: Alistair* in 2010 or localizations of Korean online otome games such as Galaxy Games' *Star Project*, in between 2006 and 2012—and fan-made localizations such as the English patch for *Starry Sky in Spring* in 2010, there were no official localizations from Japanese companies or their partner companies from 2006 until *Hakuoki*'s release in 2012. Though otome games from 2006 to 2012 were considered a novelty, discussions on hot men in Japanese games were not. Many years prior to this announcement in 2011, games such as *Final Fantasy VII* also instigated conversations among its players on androgynous men, and these discussions also denote how certain masculine ideals help create perceptions of these games' "Japaneseness" among player communities.[3] Using "ridiculously hot men" as a punchline plays into these ideas.

After its release, *Hakuoki* became the first best-selling otome game, leaning on several ports to Nintendo 3DS, PlayStation 3, mobile, and a later two-part edition released by Idea Factory International. *Hakuoki*'s success allowed Aksys Games to localize more otome games for PSP, PS Vita, PlayStation 4, and the Nintendo Switch, including titles such as *Sweet Fuse* (2013), *Norn9* (2015), *Code Realize* (2015), *Collar x Malice* (2017), and many other titles, as well as otome game fan disks.

Previous scholarship on *Hakuoki* highlights interesting aspects of female-dominated fandoms. Hasegawa, for instance, looks at *Hakuoki* as a case study to show how fans queer history that is male-dominated and heteronormative.[4] Lucy Morris reflects on how the global appeal of the Shinsengumi centers on how the game recycles plot devices and archetypes from popular romantic fiction.[5] More recently, Susana Tosca examines how Western audiences appropriate the world of *Hakuoki* in fan fiction to create hybrid worlds based on their interpretation of *Hakuoki*'s retelling of history that allow women to incorporate these worlds in their lives and their fantasies.[6] This essay rethreads and acknowledges these points on games as texts created for women, and on these points on female fandoms. However, for this essay, I wish to focus on *Hakuoki*'s localization itself as a transcreated text.

Literature on game localization introduces the concept of transcreation. Carmen Mangiron and Minako O'Hagan (2006) point out that the main goal of localization is "to preserve the gameplay experience for the target players, keeping the 'look and feel' of the original" and to make sure the target players feel as if the game was developed for their own language. For this reason, they point out that fidelity for translators means being loyal not just to the language in the game text but to the whole gameplay experience. Thus, they argue, "in game localisation, transcreation, rather than just translation, takes place."[7]

This essay examines *Hakuoki*'s localization as a transcreated text that communicates assumptions about its presumed female player—particularly the ways it wants to insert women into this historical narrative. In the localization, players are addressed as *fujoshis*, a derogatory Japanese term for female geeks who are invested in boy's love or male-male romances. By pointing out how certain creative decisions in the localization, I examine how localization repositions fujoshi identity and desire for men as something that is heteronormative. Ultimately, this rechanneling of desire toward hegemonic masculinity indicates postfeminist and postracist sensibilities embedded within transcreation that mask racism and sexism in the game.

Postfeminism (and Postracism)

A continuously growing body of literature in feminist media studies and literature is concerned with postfeminism—a cultural sensibility made up of several interrelated ideas. Rosalind Gill enumerates the following key ideas within postfeminism: "the notion that femininity is a bodily property; the shift from objectification to subjectification; an emphasis upon self surveillance, monitoring and self-discipline; a focus on individualism, choice and empowerment; the dominance of a makeover paradigm; and a resurgence of ideas about natural sexual difference."[8] Within postfeminism, Angela McRobbie (2004) describes a "double entanglement" of neoliberal values to

252   Sarah Christina Ganzon

discourses of gender and sexuality. In this way, the celebration of women's choice and freedom is tied to individual lifestyle choices and consumer culture, thereby removing the link between agency to feminist political action.[9] Gill further elaborates that this renegotiation of agency and choice points a shift in mass culture toward depicting women as sexual subjects rather than sexual objects. In addressing women as subjects, postfeminism interpellates women to make themselves as desirable sexual subjects for men and the male gaze, and empowerment often articulated via consumer culture and via choosing traditional gender roles.[10]

While the literature on postfeminism primarily concerns texts and discourses from the Western world, Dosekun (2015) extends the analysis of postfeminism toward its manifestations in the non-Western world. Postfeminism, she argues, is "readily transnationalized . . . because it is a fundamentally mediated and commodified discourse and a set of material practices."[11] Though she acknowledges that postfeminist sensibility emerged in the West as a reaction to second-wave feminism, she argues that "because post-feminism is a commodification and hollowing out of this feminist history, . . . under conditions of globalization, post-feminism is sold and consumed transnationally without this history."[12] Furthermore, she explains her usage of the term *transnational*, since it "refers to a critical mode of thinking across borders and thus thinking across multiple intersections, forms, and sites of difference at once. . . . Therefore, to think transnationally about post-feminism is to consider how, as an entanglement of meanings, representations, sensibilities, practices, and commodities, post-feminism may discursively and materially cross borders, including those within our feminist scholarly imaginaries."[13] In relation to Japanese pop culture, Christine Reiko Yano elaborates on how products such as Hello Kitty and cute culture contribute to the Euro-American ideals of girl power by positioning women as consumers.[14] Thus, studies such as these indicate how Japanese popular cultures participate in constructing these constructions of meaning and commodification of female agency.

Recent game studies literature borrows from postfeminist criticism, particularly in the critique of gendered discourses in games and game culture. John Vanderhoef links the feminization of casual games to discourses in popular games media, and points out how postfeminist culture dismisses sexist comments about casual games simply as tongue-in-cheek remarks while simultaneously reinforcing these gendered notions.[15] Sarah Stang, borrowing from Hannah Hamad's critique on postfeminist fatherhood, extends this analysis to constructions of fatherhood in her analysis of father-daughter

The Fujoshi Trophy and Ridiculously Hot Men   **253**

relationships in a number of AAA games.[16] Alison Harvey and Stephanie Fisher call attention to how postfeminist discourse, tied with neoliberalism, constrains women's participation within game industries.[17]

To these, I add how the commodification of women's choices and agency can also mask problematic elements, including historical revisionism and racism. Studies indicating how the notion of a postracial society is part of a political backlash in the post–civil rights era that denies how racism continually figures in structural inequalities and ideological underpinnings.[18] Ralina Joseph, in her case study examining discourses surrounding Tyra Banks, indicates how postfeminism and postracism go hand in hand to deflect race and gender critiques.[19] In my examination of *Hakuoki*, I look into how game localization as transcreation can become a postfeminist way of masking some of the sexist and racist aspects of these games by redirecting them toward desiring heteronormative masculinity. These redirections participate in the discourse of remasculinizing Asian men and position women as desiring subjects in relation to these men. Thus, this form of postfeminism is also postracist.

Emotional Labor and Postfeminist Narrative Choices

Hakuoki (2008) is a visual novel released on PlayStation 2 in Japan, but one that has also received ports to other systems, such as PSP, Nintendo DS, Nintendo 3DS, and PlayStation 3. In 2015, a two-part version of the game was released on the PS Vita, with additional character routes and downloadable content. Set during the Bakamatsu, the game follows the story of Chizuru Yukimura, a girl who dresses up as a boy to go to Kyoto and find her father, who has gone missing.[20] Once in Kyoto, she's attacked by a group of murderous vampire-like men, only to be saved and taken into custody by the Shinsengumi.[21] After she finds out that she's the daughter of a man who has developed a serum called the Water of Life that turns people who drink it into mad, bloodthirsty, vampire-like berjerkers called the *rasetsu*, they enlist her aid to find her father.[22] Things get even more complicated when Chizuru discovers that she's an *oni* (demon) and that there is a group of demons hunting her, led by Chikage Kazama, a demon lord who wants her as his bride. Because this is a game about dating members of the Shinsengumi, such as Shinsengumi captains Toshizo Hijikata and Souji Okita, as well as other historical characters of the Bakamatsu, such as Ryouma Sakamoto and Iba Hachirou,[23] the narrative choices in the game mostly center around

254 Sarah Christina Ganzon

getting a male character's attention during the first half of the game in order to get locked into a character route. If one does not get locked into a route with a character on the first half, one gets the normal ending: in the original version of the game, one ends up with Chikage Kazama; and in the two-part edition, one gets sent away by the Shinsengumi for protection from the war.[24]

Once a route is determined, choices in the second half of the game revolve around getting as much affection as possible from that character, usually by picking choices that demonstrate empathy for the character, and keeping that character sane by making the choice to offer the player character's blood. The reason for this is that halfway through the game, the character whom Chizuru dates mostly ends up becoming a *rasetsu* for various reasons;[25] these reasons usually revolve around protecting Chizuru or prolonging their own existence in the game's narrative longer than the actual historical figures, who may have died before or early on in the Boshin War.[26] In a number of the game's storylines, these characters' decision to become *rasetsu* is usually depicted as a heroic act, something akin to a Faustian imperative, especially when they strive to become more than what they are—men from non-samurai classes rising to become true samurai by upholding the bushido (samurai ideals and codes of honor) and defending the doomed shogunate. However, the consequence for this choice to become *rasetsu* is a slow descent to madness, especially as the *rasetsu* tend to thirst for blood from time to time. For this reason, the correct choice as imposed by the game to get the good endings for these characters always involves Chizuru offering her blood to these men. The game also gives Chizuru the option to make the men endure their bloodlust or give them medicine to suppress it, but continuously choosing both options always leads to bad endings.[27] Interestingly, these moments wherein Chizuru gives her blood are some of those rare moments wherein Chizuru is shown to be very intimate with these men (figure 12.1). Although Chizuru is an *oni*, one almost never sees her in her *oni* form. The only instance in which one sees her in this form is one moment in Souji Okita's route when she chooses to share her blood with him (figure 12.2). As otome game heroines are rarely depicted having sex with their love interests, moments such as these become the substitute for intercourse.[28] In this way, monstrosity in the game also implies repressed sexual urges.

As a player character, Chizuru has very little agency in the narrative even though she dresses up as a man and carries a short sword; she mostly acts as a spectator to the historical events happening around her. None of the game's narrative choices allow her to meddle with history. Despite being a

12.1. Sample image of Chizuru giving her blood in *Hakuoki*.

12.2. Chizuru sharing her blood with Okita in *Hakuoki*.

demon and having powers similar to those of other powerful demons, such as Kazama (e.g., the ability to heal quickly),[29] she fights back only a few times, and does so then only to allow her love interest to gain advantage over his opponent. Her value as a mother figure and life-giver to all the men in the narrative is repeated a number of times in the game. In most of the routes, the narrative places her in dangerous situations so all the men are obligated to save her. In Souji Okita's route, the one route where she drinks the Water of Life (she never makes this choice; her twin brother forces it on her) and gains *rasetsu* powers, she acquiesces to Okita's request to stand back and let him fight for her, even if she clearly is able to hold her ground at this point. Most storylines and branching narrative arcs wherein she displays the most agency are stories outside the historical narrative.[30]

Nonetheless, it is Chizuru's narrative positioning that is the most interesting in the game. Her purpose mostly revolves around collecting intimate moments with these men who are about to die. As Chizuru is the narrator, players see history through her eyes, and the implication of this narrative positioning is that Chizuru outlives these men to tell their story. In this way, it also positions the presumed female player as a collector of historical narratives. It is in this positioning that some find potential in the game. Hasegawa argues that even though the historical narrative in the game is nationalistic and masculine, players can "embrace romance as a new way to interact with history, to imagine their space in the past, as well as to produce alternative narratives."[31] This is especially true with a number of players in Japan, as the game is often mentioned as one that helped trigger a wave of *rekijo* tourism.[32] While there is no denying that players can definitely define their own agency even within a very sexist and heteronormative game, the issue here is that choices in the game encourage postfeminist self-objectification and acknowledge that women's value is measured by the men around them. In this way, the choices are characteristically postfeminist. But player characters need not be doormats to communicate postfeminist sensibilities.

Essentially, almost all of the correct choices to get good endings in the game demonstrate the performance of emotional labor. Arlie Hochschild defines emotional labor as that act of managing feelings and certain expressions, pointing out how differences in social situation, gender, or race can vary the degrees to which individuals are socialized into performing emotional labor.[33] While Hochschild specifically pointed out that her definition excludes those outside a work context, others have expanded this to include invisible labor and emotion work that women are expected to do outside workspaces.[34] The performance of emotional labor in games is of course nothing new. Shira Chess, in her study of time-management games, points out how games designed for women often highlight expectations for women to perform emotional labor.[35] A number of otome games, including *Hakuoki*, are no exception to this, and romance in these games becomes the reason for the performance of emotional labor.

Notably, *Hakuoki* also presents the notion of alternative history. These constructions of alterative narratives demonstrate what Lynn Spigel describes as a nostalgia for a prefeminist past as a way of imagining a future without feminism.[36] All these women need is love, after all. By peppering the world with powerful women and the ability to make choices, they erase histories of oppression and offer a vision of a world wherein feminism is not needed. In these game worlds, choice constructs postfeminist desire because the choices that are always made available are the choices that postfeminist women would make. In this way, the discourse of love as a choice constructs ideal otome girlhoods. Games such as *Hakuoki* indicate how postfeminist sensibilities can emerge in different contexts, without ever needing to acknowledge postfeminism's history and origins. Instead, postfeminism constructs its own heritage, validating its existence in these games and texts made for women, as a way of erasing advancements that women made for themselves in pursuit of equality.

What's even more disturbing is how the game's routes repeatedly retell something akin to a jingoistic Lost Cause narrative. It idealizes these men who notably committed many atrocities for a dictatorial regime and who were ultimately dedicated to bushido. Studies indicate how bushido is actually a concept that was constructed from the late nineteenth century through the 1930s; it would become a fundamental component of Japanese militarism leading to World War II.[37] Narratives about the Shinsengumi were part of the propaganda that fueled this militarism and nationalistic discourse—a way that people defined themselves against foreign "others." While studies on contemporary portrayals of the Shinsengumi in games and anime indicate how the Shinsengumi became floating signifiers depending on how their authors may choose to define them,[38] these narratives are still part of a trend toward historical revisionism and nationalistic nostalgia. As the game system encourages replay, the system positions the presumed female player as an important part of this historical revisionism.[39] Thus, the game's postfeminist celebration of women as collectors of narratives downplays the racism of this form of historical revisionism and nationalistic discourse. This masking of that kind of racism becomes even more prevalent in the localization in the way it redirects players' attention to the "hotness" of these men.

The Fujoshi Trophy: Transcreating Otome Games for the West

Otome games contain postfeminist sensibilities unique to the cultural contexts of their places of origin. The challenges of localizing *Hakuoki* for the West, as well as for other English-language players, include players' lack of knowledge on Japanese history and the games' historical characters, and the absence of the anime media mix's infrastructure to allow dedicated spaces for media consumption around otome games. Nonetheless, in 2010, Aksys Games released a two-part survey on otome games. The first set of questions dealt mostly with people's knowledge about otome games and interest in dating simulators, while the second set of questions dealt with consumption practices around potential otome game releases.[40] Although the results of the surveys were not published, at *Anime Expo 2011* Aksys announced their release of *Hakuoki* for the PSP. Prior to announcing *Hakuoki*, the publisher and localization company released titles from the *Guilty Gear* and *BlazBlue* franchises, and released *999* for Nintendo DS, furthering its reputation among non-Japanese game players for picking up very niche Japanese game titles that many other companies would not localize.

In the case of Aksys Games, in deciding to localize *Hakuoki*, they were not merely commercially localizing one title; rather, they were localizing the otome game category and types of experiences and forms of consumption that go along with otome games. For this reason, this act of bringing *Hakuoki* outside Japan also means defining what otome games are outside their country of origin. Apart from the absence of the anime media mix providing the context of narrative consumption, challenges also include bringing a female-coded category of games to geek cultures and game cultures that is not only male-dominated but also very hostile to women. The year 2011 was, after all, also the year of the Dickwolves controversy.[41]

During the announcement of the game and after playing the trailer, the team described *Hakuoki* as an otome game and explained that otome games are games where one plays a female protagonist dating hot men. Of course, the discussion of hot men in relation to Japanese games is nothing new. Lucy Glasspool, in her analysis of discourses of masculinity in the *Final Fantasy* games and fandoms, points out how many localized Japanese games tend to provide ample "fragrance" for fans to create images of "Japaneseness" that are linked with gender. Borrowing from Judith Butler, she argues that the idea of "Japaneseness" is performative and that fan imaginings of "Japaneseness" often act as promotional tools. She indicates that "bottom-up" transformations of some Japanese games by fans tend to create orientalist associations with androgynous masculinity and same-sex desire, and she points out that these associations often promote Western masculinity and heteronormativity.[42] As seen in the trailer described in the introduction, the game's "hot men" also become markers of its "Japaneseness."[43] More importantly, by

The Fujoshi Trophy and Ridiculously Hot Men   **259**

emphasizing its promotional material featuring hot men,[44] Aksys touches on particular ideas of masculinity in relation to its games' characters, but also turns the discussion more toward the celebration of non-Western masculinity. While much of Aksys's discussion of otome games and hot men points out that these games were made for female audiences, they also point out that men could play these games as well. No doubt this step is intended to make otome games more accessible, extending them beyond their original intended audience. Nonetheless, it is still important to examine this shift in the value of hot men, as the study of shifting values may indicate particular structures of feeling associated with these ideas and images.[45] Research on Asian masculinities tends to indicate how Asian men tend to be emasculated in literature and popular media.[46] Studies also discuss how several critics have deployed the strategy of remasculinization in response to this emasculation.[47] Arguably, the game also deploys this strategy in presenting the game's male heroes and love interests.

Notably, the text translation in the visual novel remained close to the source material. Major changes were seen in later editions of the game, which included PlayStation trophies. The success of Aksys's localization of *Hakuoki* for the PSP made way for multiple ports, including ones for the Nintendo 3DS, mobile, and the PS3. Until the release of Idea Factory International's two-part version, the PS3 version was considered the definitive edition, as it had the most content, including extra and downloadable content. The PS3 version is also the first of the games that featured trophies, and liberties were taken with the translation of these trophies (table 12.1). The translations include a number of intertextual references to North American popular culture references, puns, and phrases. The use of these intertextual references reveals much about their target audience, mostly female fans who have grown up with North American popular culture. Similarly, Idea Factory International's two-part version also uses intertextual references (table 12.2). In some of these examples, humor is used to mask some of the game's sexist elements. Even in some examples, such as the "Does This Mean I Can Go Outside Now . . . ?" trophy in the Idea Factory version, which acknowledges Chizuru's Stockholm syndrome, humor is used as a way of both acknowledging sexism and deflecting criticism.

Out of all the trophies listed, it is Aksys's use of the term *fujoshi* for the platinum achievement that is the most interesting. *Fujoshi*, which literally translates as "rotten girl," refers to female otaku in Japan who are fans of the *yaoi* (boy's love) genre.[48] Studies about fujoshi reveal this to be a self-deprecating

Table 12.1

JAPANESE TROPHY	LITERAL TRANSLATION	AKSYS'S TRANSLATION	DESCRIPTION
プラチナトロフィー	Platinum Trophy	Fujoshi	Got all the trophies. Well done! You're a beautiful person with your whole life ahead of you.
鮮烈な記憶	Vivid Memory	Bark Street Boys	Unlocked all movies
藤堂との思いで	Your Memories with Toudou	Toudou Recall	Unlocked all Toudou images
斎藤との思いで	Your Memories with Saito	Out of Saito	Unlocked all Saito images
原田と・・・	Harada...	Ronin in the Streets, Samurai in the Sheets	Finished Harada's route

yet celebratory term; it had been expanded to encompass female fans of anime and manga.[49] In its original context, according to previous scholarship, the term *fujoshi* harks back to a form of nonproductive sexual desire, framing their relationship to mass media and their desire for boys' love as the cause.[50] In many cases in their usage in anime and manga, the terms *otome* and *otaku* or *fujoshi* are not synonymous.[51] However, Aksys's translation does make some sense, especially if one considers how one could get the Fujoshi trophy in the PS3 version of the game. In order to collect the Fujoshi trophy, one has to finish all the storylines in the game, absorb all the narratives and lore, and collect all the images of Chizuru's love interests. In a lot of ways, to get the Fujoshi trophy, one has to collect a lot of images of hot men, and this may be how the game's English translators perceive the process of becoming a fujoshi. By making this into an achievement, the game makes a term originally

Table 12.2

JAPANESE TROPHY	LITERAL TRANSLATION	IFI TRANSLATION	DESCRIPTION
風ノ章を終えて	After the Wind . . .	Does This Mean I Can Go Outside Now . . . ?	Obtained all trophies
新選組の秘密を知る	Know the Shinsengumi's Secret	Still a Better Love Story than . . .	Cleared chapter 3
鬼の副長の進む道	Ogre Deputy Chief's Path	Just a Small-Town Boy . . .	Hijikata route started
雪村の娘として	As a Daughter of Yukimura	Kazablanca	Kazama route cleared
記憶の全てがここに	Here Are All the Memories	George Lucas Would Be Proud	CG completed

deemed nonproductive into one deemed productive. Instead of describing women fantasizing about men falling in love with each other, it redirects this desire toward the games' heteronormative relationships. The act of collection and aestheticization of idealized male bodies underscores masculinity as a form of bodily property that helps create a particular notion of femininity that corresponds to it. By focusing on the act of collection around hot strong heterosexual Japanese historical characters, the transcreated game system enables what Evans and Riley describe as a "visual economy that turns desire toward hegemonic masculinity."[52] At the same time, by focusing on the men's "hotness," it masks the problematic jingoist elements that I mentioned earlier about these men and the narratives surrounding them. Thus, by redirecting desire toward heteronormative masculinity and by masking the narrative's more nationalistic (and, by extension, racist) elements, the Fujoshi trophy indicates an attempt to popularize and commodify identities seen as other. Rosi Braidotti points out a similar trend of popularizing queerness in consumerist neoliberal youth cultures, maintaining that such frameworks may encourage exploring otherness, but they focus on identities that are marketable. She argues:

> The other complex feature of these new master-narratives is the ability to take "differences" into a spin, making them proliferate with an aim of ensuring maximum profit. Advanced capitalism is a difference engine—a multiplier of de-territorialised differences, which are packaged and marketed under the labels of "new, hybrid and multiple or multicultural identities." It is important to explore how this logic triggers a vampiric consumption of "others," in contemporary social and cultural practice. From fusion-cooking to "world music," the consumption of "differences" is a dominant cultural practice.[53]

While games can provide liminal spaces for the exploration of identity, what the transcreated game system does is channel these in directions that are most beneficial to capitalism, commodifying women's choices and denying the existence of racism. The transcreated game system can thus underlie the transformation of selves in line with postfeminist sensibilities. In this way, game localization makes a text produced in one particular postfeminist and postracist context adaptable to another.

Conclusion

This examination of *Hakuoki* and its localizations shows how postfeminist sensibilities are transnational and postracist, adapting to different contexts as a way of directing discourses of both femininity and masculinity to make them appear productive and mask the game's sexist and racist elements. The discourse of "hotness," as it remasculinizes Asian men, distracts players from the game's nationalistic nostalgia. The creation of the "Fujoshi trophy" disregards the complexities of how female fandoms (particularly Japanese female fans of boy's love) redefined this identity. As players of otome games are usually presumed to be women, even as it positions women at the center of the game narrative and the act of collecting, the game commodifies women's choices. Titles that have followed *Hakuoki*, such as *Code Realize*, *Norn9* and *Collar x Malice*, continue to mask some of the games' sexism and heteronormativity by shifting the focus to "badass" women.

Although this analysis focuses exclusively on the game and its localization, it also raises the question of how we can examine predominantly female fandoms within postfeminist media cultures. While *Hakuoki*'s fans can use the game as a way of queering history and can appropriate this world to create their own versions in fan fiction, the discussions within these female fandoms also omit the subjects of race and racism. Rukmini Pande, in particular, argues that fandom algorithms or fandom protocols often contribute to silencing discussions of race among fans.[54] Future scholarship on *Hakuoki* and otome game fandoms can look into the various ways they mute talk of racial issues.

Notes

1 H. Kim, "Women's Games in Japan."

2 The first otome game localized in English is *Yo-jim-bo* (2006), a PC-based game by Hirameki International. Little is known to what happened to this game or the company that localized it, but years later, fans and bloggers would replay this and talk about this as the very first title localized in English. Examining blogs and forum discussions around 2011–12 prior to *Hakuoki*'s release, one would find fans encouraging each other to support and purchase *Hakuoki* to show companies that there is a market for otome games outside Japan, and so *Hakuoki* won't "fail" like *Yo-jim-bo* did.

3 Glasspool, "Making Masculinity."

4 Hasegawa, "Falling in Love with History," 136.

5 Morris, "Love Transcends All (Geographical) Boundaries."

6 Tosca, "Appropriating the Shinsengumi," 176.

7 Mangiron and O'Hagan, "Game Localisation."

8 Gill, "Postfeminist Media Culture," 149.

9 McRobbie, "Post-feminism and Popular Culture."

10 Gill, "Postfeminist Media Culture," 149.

11 Dosekun, "For Western Girls Only?," 961.

12 Dosekun, "For Western Girls Only?," 968.

13 Dosekun, "For Western Girls Only?," 965.

14 Yano, *Pink Globalization*, 37–39.

15 Vanderhoef, "Casual Threats."

16 Stang, "Big Daddies and Broken Men."

17 Harvey and Fisher, "Everyone Can Make Games!"

18 Teasley and Ikard, "Barack Obama and the Politics of Race."

19 Joseph, "Tyra Banks Is Fat."

20 The Bakamatsu was the period in Japanese history that marked the end of the Edo period and the Tokugawa shogunate.

21 The Shinsengumi were Kyoto's elite police force, most of whom died fighting in the Boshin War.

22 In some routes in the game, it is explained that the Water of Life was developed from the blood of "Western Oni," and in Keisuke Sanan's route, which is part of the expanded edition, vampires are named to be the original *rasetsu*. In a lot of ways, one could surmise that the *rasetsu* plot in the game borrows heavily from vampire fiction, such as *Twilight* and the shojo manga *Vampire Knight*.

23 The list of datable characters in the original game are Toshizo Hijikata, Hajime Saito, Souji Okita, Toudou Heisuke, Sanosuke Harada, and Chikage Kazama. In the two-part version of the game, the list is expanded to include Ryouma Sakamoto, Iba Hachirou, Kazue Souma, Keisuke Sanan, Susumu Yamazaki, and Nagakura Shinpachi. Hijikata's route is mostly regarded as the "canon" route, as his storyline reveals him to be the titular Hakuoki, or Demon of the Fleeting Blossom.

24 Changes were made in the two-part edition: because Chikage Kazama's route was changed to a character route, this time one has to make choices to end up with this character, just like the rest of the other datable characters.

25 Almost everyone except Sanosuke Harada becomes a *rasetsu*.

26 Hijikata and Saito's routes revolve around protecting Chizuru. The routes of Toudou Heisuke, Souji Okita, Keisuke Sanan, and Ryouma Sakamoto revolve around prolonging their existence in the game's narrative longer than that of the actual historical figures. For example, the historical Toudou Heisuke died during the Aburakoji Affair in 1867, and Souji Okita died from tuberculosis sometime in the middle of the war. The *rasetsu* plot keeps them longer in the game's narrative, which roughly ends around 1869 after the fall of the Ezo Republic. The Boshin War was the Japanese civil war (ca. 1868–69).

27 Bad endings usually lead to Chizuru and/or her love interest dying in horrible deaths, in comparison to good endings, where they mostly live happily ever after following the war.

28 The amount Chizuru gets to have sex varies in both versions of the game. In the original version, the only time she has sex is in Harada's route. In the two-part version of the game, in addition to Harada's route, Chizuru also sleeps with Ryouma Sakamoto and Kazue Souma in their character routes.

29 This is slightly amended in the two-part edition, where the game adds an explanation why Chizuru does not fight: according to the game's lore, male demons are always more powerful than their female counterparts.

30 For example, in Kazama's route, Chizuru can choose to take responsibility for her father's actions and hunt him down, thus claiming her position as the head of her *oni* clan, but this is a storyline that exists outside the historical narrative that's usually front and center in this game. Chizuru in Ryouma Sakamoto's route is given a similar choice. But even in those two routes, she almost always needs to partner with these men in hunting her father down.

31 Hasegawa, "Falling in Love with History," 136.

32 Sugawa-Shimada, "Rekijo, Pilgrimage and 'Pop-Spiritualism.'"

The Fujoshi Trophy and Ridiculously Hot Men **265**

33 Hochschild, *The Managed Heart*, 35.

34 Chess, *Ready Player Two*; Hartley, *Fed Up*.

35 Chess, *Ready Player Two*.

36 Spigel, "Postfeminist Nostalgia for a Prefeminist Future."

37 Benesch, "Bushido."

38 Lee, "Becoming-Minor through Shinsengumi."

39 In a lot of ways, it is not too dissimilar to US groups such as the United Daughters of the Confederacy.

40 Ishaan, "Here's Another Aksys Survey on Otome Games."

41 The Dickwolves controversy was an incident involving the *Penny Arcade* online comic and its perpetuation of rape culture.

42 Glasspool, "Making Masculinity."

43 Interestingly, the trailer they showed before *Hakuoki* was *Fate/Extra*. While *Hakuoki* has so much focus on "hot men," there was no mention of "hot women" in the case of *Fate/Extra*.

44 See also their two-part interview with Siliconera: "Aksys Roundtable Interview," *Siliconera*, June 21, 2011.

45 Skeggs, "Values beyond Value?"

46 T. H. Nguyen, *A View from the Bottom*, 2–3; Eng, *Racial Castration*, 28–29.

47 V. T. Nguyen, "The Remasculinization of Chinese America," 133.

48 The male equivalent of the term *fujoshi* is *fudanshi*.

49 Suzuki, "The Possibilities of Research on 'Fujoshi' in Japan."

50 Galbraith, "Moe Talk."

51 Take, for example, in the anime *Watashi ga Motete Dōsunda* (*Kiss Him, Not Me!*) a hilarious scene depicts its protagonist's personality as scale as one that slides from otome to otaku quickly when she gets lured into buying merchandise from her favorite BL anime. Since the protagonist is a fujoshi, she also laments that when she suddenly attracts a lot of boys in her school that her life is suddenly turned into an otome game.

52 Evans and Riley, "'He's a Total TubeCrush,'" 11.

53 Braidotti, "Feminist Epistemology after Postmodernism," 66.

54 Pande, *Squee from the Margins*, 116.

Mobilizing Machines

Part 5

How Do We Talk about Things That Are Happening without Talking about Things That Are Happening?

Designer Roundtable #5

FEATURING:

Mike Ren Yi, a game designer and filmmaker based in Shanghai, working at the intersection of games, animation, and films. He is currently a video producer at RADII China, and before that he was a level designer at Ubisoft Shanghai. He also runs Branches: Interactive Storytelling, a community and workshop series centered around narrative-driven interactive stories. His independent video game projects about China-US relationships include *Hazy Days* (2016), a breathing simulator set in China; *Novel Containment* (2020), a docu-game reflecting the COVID outbreak; and *Yellow Face* (2019), a game about casual racism targeted toward Asian Americans.

Pamela Punzalan, a Nebula Award–nominated queer Filipina game designer, editor, writer, cultural consultant, and sensitivity reader based in Metro Manila. She has pursued a master's degree in literary and cultural studies at the Ateneo de Manila University and taught at high school and university levels. Beyond producing her own games, Pam has been part of the team for projects like *The Islands of Sina Una* (2021), the *D&D Cultural and Ancestry Zine*, *Spire: Shadow Operations* (2020), and *Thirsty Sword Lesbians* (2021).

Melos Han-Tani, a Tokyo-based game developer, composer, and programmer who is the cocreator of the *Anodyne* series (2013–19), *Even the Ocean* (2016), and *Sephonie* (2022). Previously a game design and game music lecturer at the School of the Art Institute of Chicago, he also created the game *All Our Asias* (2018) and enjoys walking outdoors and writing about games on his blog. He runs the

game studio Analgesic Productions with Marina Kittaka.

Yuxin Gao, a Chinese game developer and producer based in the United States and an MFA in game design from New York University. Her work explores the intersection of journalism and games. During the Hong Kong extradition bill protests in 2019, Gao curated the Year of the Pig exhibition at Babycastles gallery in New York, showcasing indie games made in mainland China, Hong Kong, and Taiwan. In 2020, she directed and programmed *Out for Delivery*, a 360-degree interactive documentary following a food delivery courier at the start of the pandemic in China.

Mike Ren Yi: After I joined some game jams in New York, I moved out to Shanghai in 2014, and within a month I got a job at a mobile game company that was doing free-to-play games. After that, I worked at Ubisoft [the French game company known for the *Assassin's Creed* series, the *Far Cry* series, and others] Shanghai for two and a half years—I was about four years in the video game industry and in Shanghai—and then I left. Now a lot of my work talks about China, but it's also not talking about China. I think it's a valid point to ask if I'm gonna get in trouble for making these games, and I think, honestly, I do have a certain amount of privilege that's offered to me because even though I'm living in China, I'm not a Chinese citizen. And in my games, I try to not actively reference China. The games have an aesthetic of what the city looks like to me, and I use games to view things happening around me. It's a way for me to process thoughts. I'm a Chinese immigrant, and when I first got to America, it was quite difficult. But I think having a Gameboy Color really changed that. I was growing up at a time where *Pokémon* was the thing, which, thank God for that, because in the very beginning it was the only way I could communicate and connect with people.

Pamela Punzalan: For video games, Filipinos are primarily the invisible hands of development. So nobody really talks theory, they only produce; even the

270   Designer Roundtable 5

big universities do not have a formal game design course. Instead, we have our equivalent of blue-collar vocational schools that do game design. I grew up thinking that game design was merely a hobby—thinking this was a mix, of course, of traditional Filipino upbringing where they think that art is pretty, but you don't actually go into it for a career unless you want to starve. The Square Enix store does not have the Philippines listed as a country. There are a lot of game studios that just forget we even exist: there's an idea that Filipinos do not play games. Because beyond being the invisible hands, we are also the invisible market. We speak English very well, we consume primarily English media, and yet most big companies ignore us. I want to change that. And the first way of doing that is to actually have publishing studios and means that will let people put their games out.

To Mike's point: Ubisoft hit Manila too. Well, not Manila, actually. They went down to a province in 2015. And their hiring policy was fascinating. They did not get experienced people very often. They built from the ground up. They were specifically looking for a few experienced heads to manage projects and bring a local face. But the main hiring base were all straight out of college. And those kids moved on to develop, I think, [the *Assassin's Creed* games] *Odyssey* [2018] and *Valhalla* [2020].

Mike Ren Yi: Yeah, they're very global focused. The heads from France or Montreal would basically find locals to hire. There's a thing in Shanghai where everyone who works in the industry has done time at Ubisoft because it's the best school you can go to learn a specific type of design, which is open world design, or the Ubisoft philosophy on that genre.

Melos Han-Tani: What are the local views on game design? Do they tend to agree with what Ubisoft teaches? Or do they go against that?

Mike Ren Yi: Ubisoft has a very specific methodology for open world design, which is also one of the reasons everything feels quite copy-and-paste between their games. I don't want to generalize too much, but that was my feeling at Ubisoft Shanghai when we were working on some projects. But every studio around the world has a different way of working, and with these big projects, the methodology needs to go across all these teams. It's a really interesting way of fragmenting parts of a game, to basically not outsource per se but to have an entire company over here doing one little element of a big open world. One of the fun things that Ubisoft Shanghai loves to say is that almost every animal in Ubisoft games—the AI, the behavior, the gameplay—is made in Ubisoft Shanghai.

Yuxin Gao: Mike's point about getting in trouble for making games about China makes me think about how people look at *Out for Delivery* [Gao's 2020 360-degree documentary game about a courier's life during early COVID time in Beijing]. When people see a political game, they think it must be to criticize the government. But that's something I'm not trying to do directly, for a specific reason. I feel the purpose of the work is for people to be able to experience a small trace of history in my home country, where newspaper censorship has been so tight that it's difficult to figure out what has actually happened. So my focus is not really to anger or point fingers. And I still don't want the games to be banned in China. So a lot of times my approach is to reflect individual stories. People come across my work and ask, "Why are you making this? This is going to endanger you." But I tell them I just want to preserve the moment, or in some way leave traces of it.

Melos Han-Tani: I wonder how others have dealt with the kind of pressure that comes about when, for example, a white person plays a game by someone from China and may read it as representative of every Chinese person. How do others think about that unreasonable view that a single person can represent entire groups of people? Do you choose to ignore it?

Pamela Punzalan: That is a question that preoccupies a lot of the indie tabletop [nondigital games] space in the Philippines, because the barriers of entry are massive. My group, Play without Apology, got involved with Gamers and Gaming Meets Philippines (GnG), who were into organizing miniconventions specific to tabletop gamers, and who later helped us set up the first minicon for gamers who were women and/or queer. But actually producing a game where you can see yourself is hard. You will have no audience in the Philippines; they will not understand you. You'll barely have an audience in North America unless you want to put up with constantly being told, "Oh, this is such a unique Filipino theme," which is a very strange statement given that we don't even know what "Filipino" is.

Melos Han-Tani: There's a lot of ways of going at Asianness through games. What tends to be common is some aspect of preserving either past or present history within the game. So that could be researching the past of the country, or portraying a present-day event. I think that's one unifying thread I see amongst creators who are not just making games for the commercial status quo. Asian creators tend to be concerned with putting history or their reality into the game in some form. So, for me, for a long time, I wondered, "How do I talk about being Asian?" But then eventually I realized this is a question that has no answer because there's no fixed group or culture of Asianness. So I feel the best thing I can do, perhaps, is to pick certain aspects of history. Marina [Kittaka] and I both had a similar experience of growing up in insulated parts of the USA, when the virtual space of Twitter during Black Lives Matter and Ferguson exposed us to lots of ideas, and at a far faster rate than our schools. So our goals now are to give new experiences to people playing our games that get them to think more in depth about America and themselves.

Mike Ren Yi: When I was making *Yellow Face* [Yi's 2019 game about anti-Asian microaggressions], it was coming from a place of hatred. I was really frustrated with a lot of things—in my personal life, and also in media representations of Asians. Making the game was cathartic for me. I remember I had a white guy afterward who was like, "Hey, great game. I wanted to share it, but it's kind of weird." Then he threw one of the jokes in the game back at me. He said, "I guess you really do look like the guy from *The Hangover*." And I thought, this is so fascinating: this person thinks they're not the person I'm talking about in the game. Like, "Oh, that's not me, that's bad white people. I'm a good white person." The way that they generalize Asians is the same way that they can separate themselves from other white people.

Yuxin Gao: Sometimes I ask myself if I'm making games just because I came to New York and met friends who are curious about Asian and Chinese experiences. Sometimes I wonder if my work is intentionally made "too Chinese" to satisfy the craving for Chinese content. "Would *Out for Delivery* be interesting to play for someone who lives in China and speaks Chinese?" "Would *Year of the Pig* be as well received if it were exhibited in China?" I think about these questions. I am self-conscious about telling Chinese stories in the English language. I want to make sure they are true to what I experienced and how I feel, not ideas I get from reading English media. Since I speak both languages and spend time in both countries every year, it's easy to recognize that two powerful ideology/propaganda machines are constantly blasting their realities at me. When making anything social or political, I need to be careful about these things. When I was making *Out for Delivery*, I was pretty confident

How Do We Talk about Things?   **273**

about my motivation. I care about migrant workers. When I lived in Beijing, I really felt for them when I read about the massive cleanup—or demolishing—of suburban Beijing in 2017 that forced a lot of people out of the city. The stories of these people touched me, and I always wanted to pursue it. There are times, though, when the idea of specializing in Chinese stories is stifling.

Mike Ren Yi: It's really fascinating to be a designer in China now. How do we talk about things that are happening without talking about things that are happening? One of the interesting things about working in China is everyone seems to have an understanding of what is socially and politically acceptable and what isn't. Games are interesting because people don't really take them that seriously here. Even when I talk to industry designers in Shanghai, they're shocked and appalled that you can make games about serious things. And one of the cool things I love about games is that through interaction, we can express our feelings and emotions. Like, you can put the player into a situation where they're not empowered, and what if the verb is not "to shoot"? These little indie games I make are experiments on the form of games, attempts to take things the player is familiar with and ascribe new goals, which is sometimes uncomfortable.

Pamela Punzalan: That resonates with me, because I am on the fringes as the person of color in the region. The question I'm getting from you, Mike, is people telling you that you will get in trouble for making a game about China. But what me and my colleagues tend to get is, "Where's the Filipino in your game? I thought you were Filipino. Why are you not writing Filipino narratives?" And one of the issues that we have in our BIPOC spaces is that many designers in tabletop who are people of color insist that they can speak for *all* people of color. They feel their otherness allows them to do that because they are an other in a white space, completely forgetting the fact that people like me exist [in the Philippines]. And I really like how you pointed out, Mike, that games evoke feelings and actions and simulation, because in tabletop we play games, but they are not programmed. They don't have particular algorithms, and there is no set path for you. In tabletop, we can decide that whatever is written in the rule book is wrong. The tabletop is supposed to be fully collaborative and completely mutable. And that type of immersion merits a lot more study than what's currently given to it. And on a discursive level, we have to move away from using video game studies frameworks to study tabletop.

274 Designer Roundtable 5

Melos Han-Tani: I think it's important to allow people to explore history or write about more recent topics—like, Asian creators who just want to show what it's like living in 2021 in Taiwan, or want to talk about the Japanese colonial period of Taiwan. At Analgesic Productions, we make commercial games, but they tend to be much more informed by particular aspects of history, and in thinking about ourselves and where we're living. Compared to the average commercial game developer, Marina and I do a lot more reading and research, even if it doesn't necessarily make its way into the final games. In some ways our work is trying to get people to think about life outside of America—partially informed by how I'm from the USA but living in Tokyo now. Or how there are complex relations between countries, and how "countries" are not even a fixed or timeless concept.

Yuxin Gao: In my own work, in retrospect, I often ask, "Who am I making this for?" In *Out for Delivery*, the choice of following a courier and that opportunity of witnessing the shutting down of Wuhan city at the very morning that the lockdowns happened was just because I was looking for footage that would be visually interesting for 360-degree video. I was scouting in all different places in China, shooting sixteen hours of footage trying to tell stories about migrant workers in quickly urbanizing Chinese cities. Two days before my flight back to the US, I couldn't sleep and was anxious because I filmed all these amazing locations, but I wasn't sure that I would be able to connect them. I decided to try to follow someone on a vehicle. A courier would be the perfect subject because they are gig economy workers, and a lot of them are migrant workers. Also, they bike around the city, providing a visual treat of the constantly changing city landscape. They interact with the locals in close proximity and reveal their struggles through everyday conversations. So when I heard about the [COVID-19] lockdown that morning, I was already on my way to film the couriers. Wuhan was shutting down, and couriers were having these conversations, just joking about going home to play games all day. I felt that it was like being at the right place at the right time. But also, it was the technical decision that led me there.

Pamela Punzalan: In terms of personal design, I am very interested in seeing what has not been explored yet. My game *Asian Acceptance* (2020) came from wanting to show people the unique, quiet terror of living in a country that feels that you shouldn't exist. Because—this is gonna sound very blunt—white people like to think that they know what protest games are. But I don't

How Do We Talk about Things? **275**

think they do. Not when you've got an antiterrorism bill in Manila that could literally have people at my door right now if they found out that I was talking about this. Nobody talks about that. Nobody writes about that. And some people also accuse my country of being passive. "Why don't you protest? Why don't you talk about it more, and why don't you create more games?" But I like to throw the question back: "How, when we don't even have the words?" It's a collective experience of trauma. How do you begin with that when your own history is a patchwork? It has been for centuries. We were colonized five times. Where do you begin? What is culture? Who are you? And how do you define that for yourself when everyone will tell you you're doing it wrong? I want to impress the idea that fun also means profoundly disturbing. If it disturbs you, then there is an interesting kind of enjoyment to that, because it made you step out of yourself. If I could make more games that have those moments, I've done my job.

Anthony Dominguez

Hip-Hop and
Fighting Games

Locating the Blerd between New York and Japan

Introduction: Theorizing the Blerd

> A man from Texas[] had told me how astonished he was when he went to Shibuya. He said: "I thought I was in Harlem or someplace, all those kids walking around looking like black hip-hop artists.... What was amazing was, here they are completely copying the fashions of African-American kids."
> —Ryu Murakami, *In the Miso Soup*

The formulation of this essay begins with my personal experience as a Black nerd (Blerd) growing up in New York City who watched anime, played Japanese fighting games, and listened to East Coast hip-hop during the early 2000s. For this generation of millennials of color, these interests were not unusual. In his now-seminal article "Japan's Gross National Cool," Douglas McGray argues that despite economic stagnation, by the year 2002 Japan was becoming a cultural superpower through the global exportation of pop culture phenomena like *Pokémon* (1996) and *Hello Kitty* (1974).[1] Missing from McGray's analysis, however, are the ways in which Black culture and producers have also influenced and remixed Japanese pop culture, and for the purposes of this essay, the crossovers between Black culture and Japanese fighting games.

As media scholar Yoshimasa Kijima details, Japanese fighting games evolved from the arcade genre of side-scrolling beat-'em-ups, like *Final Fight* (1989). In side-scrolling beat-'em-ups, players battled enemies in fictionalized settings based on real environments, such as *Final Fight*'s Metro City being a stand-in for New York City. Kijima highlights that the beat-'em-up, and soon thereafter the fighting-game genre, were distinct in the large scale of their settings, which reflected a sightseeing impetus.[2] *Street Fighter II* (1991) features stages ranging from a casino in Las Vegas, to a flamenco tavern in Spain, to a feudal castle in Japan.

Despite their Japanese production, by reflecting a global influence through sightseeing, fighting games and beat-'em-ups offered early representations of Black characters and culture in video games. Games like Sega's *Streets of Rage* (1991) franchise or Capcom's *Street Fighter* series allowed players to pick a multitude of Black characters. Furthermore Capcom's *Street Fighter III: 3rd Strike* (1999), *Marvel vs. Capcom 2: New Age of Heroes* (2000), and *Capcom vs. SNK 2* (2001) featured soundtracks composed of jungle, hip-hop, R&B, and jazz music. Black hip-hop artists like MF Doom and Madlib would also go on to sample sound clips from *Street Fighter II* on their landmark album, *Madvillainy* (2004), whereas the American television-programming block Adult Swim would air commercials for anime set to trip-hop music by the likes of legendary Black producer J Dilla.

From these events and mixed media emerge the historical presence and influence of Black communities within the Japanese pop culture of fighting games. In this chapter, I demonstrate how the metaphysical environment of an arcade and its community functions as an intersectional social space. By developing a brief historical overview of the Blerd identity in relation to New York City's fighting-game community (FGC), I argue that this specific instance of Blerd culture in New York City during the early to mid-2000s was formed by the synthesis of New York City's hip-hop culture and Japanese otaku culture.

278 Anthony Dominguez

More than Just Black

Game studies scholars Michael Ryan Skolnik and Steven Conway link the space of the video game arcade to masculinity, arguing that video game arcades are both physical spaces for play and metaphysical spaces in which identities form.[3] Facets of arcade culture, like competing over high scores, led to the emergence of machismo attitudes, and even when the popularity of arcades seceded to home consoles, the machismo attitude persisted across mediums, leading to the tired trope of video games as a masculine hobby. TreaAndrea Russworm points out, however, that video games are also perceived as a white masculine hobby by fans who police the borders of fandom.[4] My own intervention here lies in dispelling this myth by demonstrating how the Blerd identity, and Blerd communities and culture, can form at the crossroads between physical and digital spaces.

The Black media scholar Anna Everett argues that online spaces have been key to the creation of Blerd communities. As Everett details, early discussions of the internet portrayed the frontier of cyberspace as a primarily white space; Black people seldom if ever appeared in specialized computer magazines like *Wired* and *Mondo 2000*.[5] My research therefore focuses on how Black social spaces centered around nerd culture can dismantle racist ideologies, such as what Everett calls, "black technophobia," the belief that Black communities don't participate in digital spaces.[6]

As Kishonna L. Gray contends, Black gamers often struggle with being perceived as more than gamers who are "just black." Rather, Gray continues, the identity of Black gamers operates within a nexus that includes "skill sets, intellectual contributions, and technical expertise."[7] The Blerd must be understood as more than just a Black nerd; the Blerd is a Black nerd whose identity forms at the intersection of their race, gender, class, and cultural consumption—in this case Japanese fighting games and anime.[8]

The modern Blerd as an identity in the United States emerged toward the late 1980s and early 1990s in the character of Steve Urkel from the American television show *Family Matters* (1989–98). Yet in the next section I also complicate this reading of Urkel through my own personal experience of "discovering" the Blerd identity at a panel on the subject at the Anime NYC 2017 convention, thereby exposing the shortcomings and limitations of Blerd characters like Urkel. It is through this personal experience that I shift to discussing the FGC, a community I participated in as a fan, playing Japanese fighting games and watching video game streams online.

Historicizing the Blerd within the FGC

In 2006, the streaming group known as "Team Spooky" would begin spearheading early cultivation of New York City's FGC through grassroots efforts like tournament gatherings, and later online streaming on platforms like Twitch and YouTube. Key moments in Team Spooky's history include the "Battle by the Gazebo" (BBG) tournament series centered on the Japanese anime fighting game *Melty Blood* (2002). Held in a public park adjacent to the Chinatown Fair Arcade, BBG continued the practice of repurposing public space that grew from the practice of hip-hop block parties in the South Bronx during the 1980s.

As arcades throughout New York City closed down, such as Playland in Times Square, Chinatown Fair Arcade emerged as the premiere hub for New York City's FGC to gather. Chinatown Fair Arcade would also close in 2011, but in 2012 it would reopen under the new ownership of Lonnie Sobel, who wished to rebrand the arcade as more family friendly. Lobel's remarks regarding the old Chinatown Fair atmosphere, the arcade's subsequent rebranding, and the removal of the fighting games that made the arcade popular become part of a longer history concerning moral panics over arcades and their demographics.

In 2011, following the closure of Chinatown Fair, former employee Henry Cen would go on to open the Next Level Arcade in Sunset Park, Brooklyn, with the goal of providing a new space for the community who used to gather at Chinatown Fair. Operating within Next Level, Team Spooky would begin streaming a variety of tournaments online. The fusion of Next Level's physical space with the digital platform of Twitch served as the metaphorical nexus between New York and Japan, a space where members of the Blerd community could gather and create their own unique culture.

At tournaments held at Next Level, players like IFC Yipes would become even more notable for their commentating prowess. While commentating has always been a part of the FGC, streaming practices on Twitch and YouTube would bring commentating into the wider public. I argue that this commentary harks back to the performance of masculinity found in arcade spaces but also, as with '90s hip-hop, references the local culture. In this case, the commentary of IFC Yipes explicitly references the culture of New York City and yet becomes remixed by the commentary's application to Japanese fighting games, thereby producing a new subculture. If commentary can be linked to the hip-hop MC through signifying, then by commentating on *Marvel vs Capcom 2*, a

Japanese fighting game, Yipes's commentary also serves as an example of how this specific subculture of the FGC fits between hip-hop and otaku culture.

What Is a Blerd?

Originally slated to appear in only one episode of *Family Matters*, the character Steve Urkel turned out to be wildly popular and soon became the protagonist of the series. With his suspenders, thick glasses, and high-pitched voice, Urkel served as an emblem of American nerds during the late 1980s. Yet Urkel's identity as a Black man must be considered in relation to his identity as a nerd. Ron Eglash emphasizes Urkel as a prime example of the Blerd within American media and points toward Urkel's appeal in how he "[opposes] the myth of biological determinism" and "must pull himself up . . . the social status rungs of youth subculture."[9]

While Urkel may be proof against certain racial stereotypes, however, he becomes indicative of others. Urkel's a scientific genius, but his dorky personality puts him at a disadvantage in his love life, and he begins to attract the attention of women only after he develops a potion that allows him to switch personalities. Under this new guise Steve Urkel becomes Stefan Urquelle. Stefan doesn't slouch; he speaks in a cool baritone, and, perhaps most important, lacks Steve's scientific genius. While Stefan recalls Black R&B or soul musicians, his performance of Black masculinity serves as visual codes for the type of Black masculinity that would emerge alongside hip-hop and gangster rap in the early 1990s.

Robin Boylorn highlights that films influenced by hip-hop and gangster rap, like *Boyz N the Hood* (1991), *Juice* (1992), and *Menace II Society* (1993), "dictated black masculinity in real life."[10] In these films, Black men were expected to be heterosexual, demeaning toward women, aggressive, and virile, traits that resurface in Stefan. Yet these two personalities of Steve and Stefan reinforce notions that Black people cannot be nerds without sacrificing supposed notions of what it means to be Black. Judith Roof positions Urkel within a lineage of scientists who gain sexual prowess but in turn give up their intelligence.[11] In *Family Matters*, Urkel must choose between being "Black" and being a nerd. Consequently, Urkel must either be a genius or sublimate his sexual desire, thus he fails in being a more complex representation of the Blerd, one who can be a nerd without needing to reaffirm their Black racial identity.

Redefining the Blerd as Otaku

In 2017, I attended a panel at Anime NYC titled "Nerds on Hip-Hop: Bridging Anime and Hip-Hop." Hosted by Victoria Johnson and Marcus Wolfe and featuring three guest speakers—Detroit-based rapper Noveliss, cultural critic Valerie Complex, and graphic novelist Stephane Metayer—the panel discussed the intersection between hip-hop and anime culture. In recounting how she got into anime, Complex describes discovering the series *8 Man After* (1993): "I saw one that really changed my perspective. . . . It was called 8 Man After. It was one that really impacted me cuz [*sic*] it was the first time that I saw a Black character in anime cuz I didn't know Black people were in that [anime] at the time."[12] In becoming a global product, by the 1980s, anime began to reflect a global audience by blurring cultural origin and loosening the requirements of cultural representation.[13] Just as in the earlier examples of beat-'em-up and fighting games, in having Black representation, anime like *8 Man After* crosses the borders between global production and national identity and thus offers an alternative of Black representation found in characters like Urkel or those populating New Black Hollywood films—a representation defined by either the suppressing of Black male sexual desire in order to be seen as an authentic nerd, or the incitement of Black male sexual desire in order to be seen as authentically Black.

By banding together to talk about our shared interests and the difficulties we've experienced due to our identities as Black gamers/anime fans, we were forming a network of support and resistance. Yet we were also a specific category of Blerds who had gathered to form this community at an anime convention; we were also otaku, a Japanese word first coined in the 1970s to describe a nerd, usually a nerd obsessed with anime. To be an otaku, however, one doesn't necessarily need to be a fan of anime. Japanese scholar Izumi Tsuji describes the "train otaku," an otaku utterly devoted to the study of Japanese trains;[14] Yoshimasa Kijima, on the other hand, outlines the "fighting-gamer otaku," an otaku devoted to playing fighting games competitively.[15] These identities should be thought of not as hierarchical and fixed but, rather, as horizontal and amorphous, with communities that frequently overlap. Furthermore, while the word *otaku* originates from Japan, Japanese scholars like Azuma Hiroki have drawn attention to how the otaku identity is not exclusive to Japan, once again reminding us how Japanese pop culture traveled beyond the borders of Japan via globalization.[16]

282   Anthony Dominguez

Those of us at Anime NYC had been exposed to imported Japanese pop culture at some point in our lives, whether anime such as *Dragon Ball Z* (1989) and *Pokémon*, or video game consoles from Japanese companies like Sony (PlayStation), Sega (Genesis, Dreamcast), and Nintendo (SNES, Nintendo 64, GameCube). Our communities were products of globalization, but each succeeding generation had been defined by different communication infrastructures. For the Blerds at Anime NYC 2017, it was access to the internet, which alerted us that we were indeed not alone. We were not simply consuming Japanese pop culture, however, but also filtering it through our personal experiences as Blerds, thus finding connections between Black culture and Japanese media, such as the myriad of connections between hip-hop music and Japanese pop culture: Kanye West's homage to Katsuhiro Otomo's *Akira* in his music video for *Stronger* as well as his collaboration with Japanese artist Takashi Murakami on his third album, *Graduation* (2007); Lupe Fiasco directly referencing the character Dhalsim from *Street Fighter II* on his track "Yoga Flame"; or RZA from Wu-Tang Clan reading Goku from *Dragon Ball Z* as the contemporary Black man in America. These examples alongside the anecdote I've examined here denote how Blerd communities remix Japanese pop culture through a Black lens to produce new forms of culture and fandoms. In doing so, the Blerd as an otaku significantly differs from a stereotype like Steve Urkel, because it allows the Blerd to be *both* Black and a nerd.

Locating the Blerd within the FGC

I've talked about your parents' responsibility for making sure you stay on track and you get your homework done, and don't spend every waking hour in front of the TV or with the Xbox.
—former US president Barack Obama

My experience at Anime NYC led me to rethink the shaping of my own Blerd identity and consequently my role within New York City's FGC as a participant-observer. Like the community I had encountered at the Nerds on Hip-Hop panel, the FGC held an important role in shaping contemporary Blerd identity through the representation of Black characters in fighting games and the presence of Black fandoms in the community. While I grew up playing fighting games, I did not become aware of the wider FGC until

Hip-Hop and Fighting Games **283**

the advent of video game streaming around the year 2011 on platforms like UStream and Twitch. On Twitch I watched the streaming channel Team Spooky, because they were also based in New York and featured players and commentators like the team's founder, Victor "Spooky" Fontanez; Sanford Kelly; Justin Wong; Arturo Sanchez; and Mike "Yipes" Mendoza.

Here was a multiracial group of people from New York City who embodied the city's hip-hop braggadocio in their playstyle and commentary but also, through the practice of streaming, openly consumed Japanese media and thereby challenged conventional notions of Black identity. In essence, watching Team Spooky was unknowingly also my first encounter with a wider Blerd community. Yet this encounter was not entirely accidental. While anyone interested in the FGC would perhaps stumble on Team Spooky, there were specific material, cultural, and technological shifts that led to the popularity of both Team Spooky and fighting games at large around the year 2011.

The basis for Team Spooky had been around for years before the establishment of Twitch, but it would be wrong to argue that Team Spooky's production shifted from a physical to digital space much like the shift from arcades to console gaming at home. Rather, Team Spooky's streaming practices highlight the overlap between physical *and* digital spaces. As I previously mentioned in the introduction to this chapter, in 2008 Victor Fontanez hosted the fighting-game tournament series Battle by the Gazebo (BBG), centered on the anime-fighter *Melty Blood*. Fontanez held BBG in a public park next to Chinatown Fair, because the arcade did not have a *Melty Blood* cabinet. To facilitate the tournament, Fontanez and other attendees would gather their laptops and arcade sticks and congregate around a nearby Snapple machine, whose outlet they siphoned for power.

Although the park was not an arcade, by hosting the tournament in the park Fontanez and the other players re-created the arcade environment. In essence, the BBG tournament gave players interested in playing *Melty Blood* a space to gather when there wasn't one available. In his essay *Times Square Blue*, Samuel Delany highlights the importance of public space for communal building. For Delany, public spaces in the city could facilitate the gathering of interracial and interclass gatherings.[17] By repurposing the space of the park and its outlets, BBG had a similar function in creating an interclass and interracial otaku community around *Melty Blood*.

BBG can also be linked to previous practices of repurposing public space in New York City—the tournament shares an affinity with hip-hop block parties held in the Bronx during the early '70s. At this point in time, hip-hop had not emerged into the mainstream and consequently lacked any formal space to be celebrated. Instead, parties were held on the street, and DJs would bring their equipment to these public areas and station themselves near outlets whose power they could use for their turntables.[18]

Although the events of BBG and hip-hop block parties are separated by space and time, they both demonstrate Delany's argument while also being rooted within the specific geography and history of New York City. Similar to the shift of hip-hop from block parties to clubs and dancehalls, *Melty Blood* in America would eventually move from the streets to the sanctioned spaces of the arcade and hotel ballrooms, where bigger tournaments like the Evolution Championship Series would be held. Still, however, by hosting the informal BBG, Fontanez allowed for the growth of both the FGC and Blerd communities.

Chinatown Fair and Next Level

While BBG evinces the importance of public and informal spaces in the formation of Blerd communities, New York City's FGC also had the Chinatown Fair Arcade. By 2008, Chinatown Fair remained the only traditional arcade left in New York City after rising rent costs led to the closure of Playland in Times Square. Owned by Sam Palmer, an Indian immigrant, Chinatown Fair focused its business on competitive Japanese fighting games like *Street Fighter*, *Tekken*, and *Marvel vs. Capcom*. Consequently, it was at Chinatown Fair that prominent FGC players from New York City would gather, such as Sanford Kelly, Arturo Sanchez, Mike Mendoza, and Justin Wong. Chinatown Fair thus served as a point of origin for the Blerd community and subculture emerging from New York City's FGC, such as the Battle by the Gazebo tournament series previously held next door.

In 2011, though, Chinatown Fair would also close down. It reopened the following year under the new ownership of Lonnie Sobel. Unlike Palmer, Sobel did not express interest in the historical background of Chinatown Fair as a grassroots community for New York City's FGC. Rather, under Sobel's ownership, the Japanese fighting games that attracted the FGC to Chinatown Fair and led to Chinatown Fair's reputation were removed. In an interview with *The Verge*, Sobel expressed his desire to transform Chinatown Fair into "a cross between Dave & Busters and Chuck E. Cheese."[19] In Kurt Vincent's

Hip-Hop and Fighting Games   **285**

documentary on Chinatown Fair, *The Lost Arcade* (2015), Sobel's grandson reveals that Sobel wished to rebrand the arcade to be more family friendly in order to deter the "teenagers hanging out there."

Sobel's rebranding of "Chinatown Fair Arcade" into "Chinatown Fair Family Fun Center," which included the removal of Japanese fighting games and thereby the previous FGC audience, marked the loss of a Blerd space. Dmitri Williams contends that news media often reported arcades as breeding grounds for crime that threatened conservative social values,[20] so Sobel's remarks about the old Chinatown Fair become situated into a history of moral panic regarding the metaphysical space of arcades as intersectional spaces.

In *The Lost Arcade*, while attendees do attest that Chinatown Fair often reeked of cigarettes and that its basement walls were dank, thus producing an atmosphere of "grime" not too dissimilar from the rest of New York City, they also fondly maintain that Chinatown Fair served as a communal space, especially for players of color from working-class backgrounds. The closure of Chinatown Fair would subsequently lead its former manager, Henry Cen, to establish the Next Level arcade in Sunset Park, Brooklyn, in 2011. Next Level would serve as the spiritual successor to Chinatown Fair, though it would also differ from it. Twitch and UStream were emerging online as the first platforms to embrace live-streaming, and as a grassroots space, Next Level would be key in the growth of the FGC/Blerd community through streaming practices.

At Next Level, Team Spooky would emerge as a prominent streamer within the FGC, handling production and streams for tournaments held at the arcade. It was precisely these same streams that led me to discover the wider FGC and retrospectively, a Blerd community. Although I lived in New York City, I had never been to Next Level, but through Twitch I could metaphorically inhabit Next Level alongside other viewers. In this regard, Twitch, like the public park where Fontanez held BBG, became an extension of the arcade environment. While home consoles were now the dominant way to play fighting games, streaming illustrated a new way that arcades could still survive despite shifts in gaming culture and rising rent costs in the city. Streaming therefore encompassed a fusion of physical and digital spaces and, in the case of the FGC, a fusion of New York City's hip-hop culture and Japanese otaku culture.

In the creation of this Blerd community, the labor behind streaming practices must also be acknowledged. At Ultimate Fighting Gamer 8, Fontanez held a panel on the origins of Team Spooky and discussed the technological logistics behind streaming production. Fontanez revealed that with the growth of streaming in 2012, Team Spooky also expanded their production, shifting from just streaming gameplay footage to including a web camera that could also live-stream commentators and players. Through the streaming of players, commentators, and gameplay, Team Spooky offered representations of the Blerd not found elsewhere. Take, for example, the epigraph that opens this section. For then–US president Barack Obama, playing video games ran antithetical to notions of Black excellence. Instead, Obama encouraged a focus on performing well academically, perhaps at the risk of erasing different Blerd identities. By contrast, in watching Team Spooky's streams I found Blerd representations that existed between New York City hip-hop culture and Japanese otaku culture but also within Everett's concept of Black cyberspace.

Commentating as Signifying

Ostensibly, the commentator works to provide a play-by-play analysis, but within the FGC, the commentator also controls the atmosphere of the room—whether they are working to excite the crowd for an upcoming match or taking a more casual approach by making jokes about the game or the players on stream. Through the practice of signifying, FGC commentators can be linked to the hip-hop MC. Building off the work of Henry Louis Gates Jr., who defines signifying as saying one thing and meaning another, Crystal Belle elaborates that signifying allows the MC to "bring in cultural and historical links to their creativity."[21] Belle uses the example of Jay-Z, who uses wordplay to allude both to his home neighborhood of Bedford Stuyvesant and to the dangers of Black working-class life in New York City.

In this regard, the commentator—like the MC—brings their local and cultural background to their commentary. In his own study of the FGC, Todd L. Harper provides an anecdote of the commentator Yipes, praising Yipes for his showmanship but also questioning how New York / East Coast culture has influenced Yipes's commentary.[22] The answer to Harper's question lies in examining how Yipes, a New York–based commentator, practices signifying.

In one famous YouTube video titled "mahvel baybee!," Yipes's unique commentary for *Marvel vs. Capcom 2* can be heard throughout. In one match, a player can be seen controlling the character Sentinel, but this specific player has chosen the orange-and-blue color scheme for the character. Consequently, Yipes dubs the Sentinel "the New York Knicks" and,

Hip-Hop and Fighting Games   **287**

when the player loses, yells, "Fuck the Knicks."[23] At another point, Yipes compares a combo—a string of individual hits—to Häagen-Dazs ice cream because the player on the receiving end is launched into the air and is thus "scooped."

Yipes's commentary has now become intrinsic to the *Marvel vs Capcom* community: terms Yipes ad-libbed while commentating have become standard phrases for players. In the earlier example, "Häagen-Dazs" referred to aerial combos, but we can also draw attention to the term *Pringles*, a different way to describe a player who has weak defense and thus, like the Pringles potato chip, breaks easily. In referencing the New York Knicks, Häagen-Dazs, and Pringles to define gameplay in *Marvel vs. Capcom 2*, Yipes employs signifying but does so in a way that brings his specific cultural background into his commentary.

Conclusion

By arguing that the New York City's FGC culture draws influence from hip-hop and otaku communities, I have demonstrated how arcade spaces can be intersectional but also expand beyond the space of the arcade, whether a public park, a Twitch stream, or a YouTube video. Consequently, in examining how the metaphysical space of the arcade can exist in online spaces, we can dispel myths of gaming spaces being perceived as largely white and also reaffirm the existence of a digital Black space. Within this digital Black space—between New York and Japan—the hip-hop otaku can be found.

It would be naive, however, to believe that the infrastructure that makes these Blerd communities possible are intrinsically built for that purpose. As the rebranding of the Chinatown Fair arcade demonstrates, an arcade cannot be designated a Blerd space simply by virtue of being an arcade. Similarly, we must also question the infrastructure of online platforms like Twitch and YouTube. In May 2021, Twitch announced the introduction of "tags" to their platform. Tags include race, gender, and sexuality, and they allow for streamers to signal toward their identity. Tags can thus potentially curb the influence of the algorithm by allowing something like the Blerd community to become more visible, thereby making the platform more inclusive.

It becomes equally imperative, however, to question how inclusive spaces within the FGC and wider gaming communities actually are. Although Black gamers are more visible within the FGC, Skolnik and Conway remind us that the nostalgia for the techno-masculine arcade space also persists within contemporary attitudes of the FGC.[24] The overlap between performances of masculinity within the FGC/arcade space and hip-hop communities highlights the fact that although these fandoms *can* be inclusive, they are far from utopian. Ultimately, though, the FGC does still in some ways foster a sense of community across overlapping identities, whether the otaku, Blerd, or hip-hop fan.

Notes

1 McGray, "Japan's Gross National Cool," 48.

2 Kijima, "The Fighting Gamer Otaku Community," 256.

3 Skolnik and Conway, "Tusslers, Beatdowns, and Brothers," 743.

4 D. Kim et al., "Race, Gender, and the Technological Turn," 156.

5 Everett, *Digital Diaspora*, 19.

6 Everett, *Digital Diaspora*, 19.

7 Gray, *Intersectional Tech*, 24.

8 Although I employ the framework of the Blerd throughout this chapter, I wish to note the diversity of the FGC. The FGC contains intersections beyond just Black American and Japanese culture, yet I begin this discussion using the framework of the Blerd because of its roots in my own personal experience.

9 Eglash, "Race, Sex, and Nerds," 55.

10 Boylorn, "From Boys to Men," 147.

11 Roof, "Sex and the Single Nerd," 219.

12 Nerds on Hip-Hop, "Nerds on Hip-Hop."

13 Darling-Wolf, *Imagining the Global*, 121.

14 Tsuji, "What Are Train Otaku?," 3.

15 Kijima, "The Fighting Gamer Otaku Community," 256.

16 Azuma, *Otaku*, 10.

17 Delany, *Times Square Red, Times Square Blue*, 111.

18 Diallo, "Hip-Hop Cats in the Cradle of Rap," 3.

19 Kopfstein, "New York's Chinatown Fair Arcade Reopens, but the Game Has Changed."

20 D. Williams, "A Brief Social History of Game Play," 235.

21 Belle, "From Jay-Z to Dead Prez," 295.

22 Harper, *The Culture of Digital Fighting Games*, 112.

23 Gabby Jay, "mahvel baybee!"

24 Skolnik and Conway, "Tusslers, Beatdowns, and Brothers," 758.

Haneul Lee

"This Is What We Do"

14

Hong Kong Protests in *Animal Crossing: New Horizons*

It's essential for HKers to maintain momentum & raise global awareness. Even though Gov has abused the coronavirus measures to suppress any form of protest, we will try every means to call for changes. #AnimalCrossingNewHorizons is one of the means for us.
— Joshua Wong, "It's Essential for HKers to Maintain Momentum & Raise Global Awareness"

Introduction: "This Is What We Do in #AnimalCrossing . . ."

On a clear night, eight people are huddled on the seashore of an uninhabited island. They are each wearing a formal black dress, a yellow hard hat, a surgical mask, and a black gas mask. Beside them lies an erected gravestone adorned with a candle, a white cosmos, and a woman's portrait. Although the portrait appears blurred, it is not difficult to recognize Carrie Lam, who served as the chief executive of Hong Kong from 2017 to 2022. She became an antidemocratic figure when she proposed an extradition bill in early 2019 that "would allow criminal suspects to be sent to mainland China for trial."[1] Although the bill was withdrawn later that same year, it triggered massive prodemocracy movements on the streets of Hong Kong against the administrative action to surveil and suppress dissent.

The group of eight mourning Lam are in fact gamers inhabiting virtual bodies in the social simulation video game *Animal Crossing: New Horizons* (2020), and the gamers holding a virtual funeral service are young Hong Kong protesters. Their in-game performance looks far removed from any of the great solemnity, tension, or sense of emergency in street protest scenes captured by mainstream news media. Perhaps this is because the fake funeral was orchestrated as a form of protest action by a small number of people acting as game characters in a virtual space. However, the political activity in the digitally animated island of *Animal Crossing: New Horizons* (*AC*) still subverted the antidemocratic authoritarian status quo by securing the protesters against real-world police brutality while also offering a public and highly visible platform for dissent. Moreover, the protest occurred during the peak of the COVID-19 crisis, making it a way to shelter in place for protesters.

Joshua Wong, a leading activist figure in the Hong Kong protest movements since 2014, was one of the participants in the virtual funeral service for Lam and tweeted the image described above with the following comment (figure 14.1): "This is what we do in #AnimalCrossing . . . maybe it's why these people are so anxious to go back to the game!!"[2] Besides the staging of Lam's funeral, Hong Kong protesters participated in a variety of other performances of political protest in the game, such as putting up a virtual banner displaying the message "Liberate Hong Kong" and launching a harmless (but still resentful) attack with butterfly nets against pictures of antidemocratic personages like Carrie Lam or Xi Jinping, president of the People's Republic of China (PRC) (figure 14.2).[3] Wong and his fellow activists used the online space of *AC* to stage their protest against the state. In doing so, they were able to avoid the dangers both of offline protest and of COVID-19. That is, they occupied and used this space to perform various modes of protest sheltering from real-life clashes with the Hong Kong riot police. However, this also means they had to adhere to the rules of the game.

What do the *AC*-based Hong Kong protests tell us about gaming-as-protest, or protest-as-gaming? The way gamers circumvent the issue of political suppression must be examined within the framework and rules of *AC*. I will thus investigate how *AC* engages players through its mechanism of creating a fictional world that is also socially real. Here Ian Bogost's reading of *AC*

14.1. *Animal Crossing* characters' fake funeral for Carrie Lam. Screenshot from Joshua Wong (@joshuawongcf), "This is what we do in #AnimalCrossing..."

14.2. Protester players whipping Carrie Lam's face with butterfly nets. Screenshot from Studio Incendo (@Studioincendo), "This is how #hongkong ppl spend our time during coronavirus lockdown..." *Note*: Studio Incendo's Twitter page is currently unavailable.

is useful, allowing us to see the *AC*-based virtual Hong Kong protests as a form of (re)invention of a space where antistate activities can exist unsuppressed. According to Bogost, *AC* as "a political hypothesis" is a place to experiment with life routines, including social interactions with family members or friends, to see "how a different kind of world might work—one with no losers."[4] In the context of the virtual Hong Kong protests, the protesters, inhabiting a virtual island in *AC*, made their own safe space, one where they could stay connected with other fellow protesters in different places or time zones by communicating across game consoles, smartphones, social media, and online forums.

The Hong Kong protesters' networked activities in *AC* should be viewed as a form of political participation that occurs in a virtual space, a world free from police brutality and the pandemic. Thus, I will pay attention to *AC*'s "network play mode," which is available only for Nintendo Switch's annual membership holders. Playing *AC* in network play mode, which allows eight *AC* players to gather at one time, does not simply mean that players can hang out with fellow players. To be able to socialize virtually, players must share a personal Dodo code with trusted people to visit them on or invite them to the site. It keeps the protesters' communications and political actions private and secure.

Moreover, it is noteworthy that many protesters during the 2014 Occupy movement in Hong Kong also communicated via "closed" text apps, which used individual cellular signals, rather than public ones, which used data or Wi-Fi. This fact is useful for understanding how the protesters use *AC* in a radically playful way as a protest site. As Zhongxuan Lin posits, the rise of social media as a new protest tool points to the rise of a younger generation of protesters who are skilled in using digital media technology, and suggests changes in the styles and scales of mobilizing, staging, and participating in social movements.[5] The protesters' abilities to develop their protest tactics by using digital media technologies—including not only social media but also video games—have decentralized the social movements in Hong Kong.

Even before the *AC*-based Hong Kong protests, political activism had already intersected with online life-simulation games such as Linden Lab's *Second Life* (2003) or Electronic Arts' *Sims* series (2000–2023). These games have provided alternative venues for many social movements, from the 2007 virtual protests of IBM workers in Italy to the Black Lives Matter rallies that have occurred since 2013 (figure 14.3).[6] Protesters have held political events in virtual spaces to allow a large number of players to see what they are doing in them. From designing or buying virtual protest gear (banners, pickets, or

14.3. Ebonix's "Black Lives Matter Rally Pack" for *The Sims 4*. Image courtesy of Ebonix.

clothes) to decorating their game characters to hold or participate in a virtual sit-in demonstration, the protesters have appropriated gaming technologies to playfully express their grievances about real-life problems. Their protesting as gaming—or gaming as protesting—has made game spaces function as alternative protest sites.

That is, the sheltered spaces the protesters have created within virtual game worlds differ from the protest sites they can physically attend. These spaces also differ because of the protesters' awareness of their positions in them. By dissecting the virtual Hong Kong protest scenes captured in *AC*, I will discuss how the *AC*-based protesters' playful activities contributed to space-making for their own purposes. Also, through a comparison with other virtual Hong Kong protests that have been mobilized in the larger game world, I will explore the insulated nature of the networked gaming that the trusted protesters who play *AC* use. Through a close analysis of gaming-as-protest, or protest-as-gaming, I will argue that the closed networked gaming space of *AC* became a place where radically playful protest activities were enacted in and beyond *AC*.

The Hong Kong Protests in the Digital Media Space

Since the handover of Hong Kong to the PRC in 1997, the PRC's control over the region has increasingly tightened despite the reunification slogan, "One Country, Two Systems." Following past social movements, the Hong Kong Federation of Students and Scholarism, a student activist group organized by

Agnes Chow, Joshua Wong, and others in 2014, led the Umbrella Movement. These young protesters have used digital media—from social media outlets (Facebook or Twitter) to video games (*AC* or *Liberate Hong Kong* [2019])—in diverse ways, with varying degrees of success, to conduct protest tactics against the state. The growth of digital media employment has expanded the range of potential shapes of protest spaces, and varied protest tactics have become available in digital spaces.

However, as scholars like Zhongxuan Lin and Laikwan Pang have argued, the Hong Kong protests were provoked not solely by digital media itself but by protesters who could employ its technology and device for their own use.[7] As Lin points out, young activists who were "sophisticated media users" and highly skilled in engaging with various digital media advanced the Umbrella Movement.[8] The "inconspicuous" media users (activists) and their "disorganized" tactics regarding social media technologies made them "reorganized in every occupied area at the micro level."[9] The decentralizing of the power of larger social movements was possible because, as Pang states, "social media can mediate and liaise political concerns and private emotions," which proliferate its impact on the larger society or related communities.[10] The sharing of frustration, anger, and aspiration on social media often provokes a countermovement in and beyond the given media platforms as well.[11]

Here the Blitzchung incident is a good example of how an individual political comment made live on YouTube was drawn into a larger political controversy. At the 2019 Grandmaster Finals for *Hearthstone* (2014), an online card game from Blizzard Entertainment, Ng Wai Chung, also known as "Blitzchung," appeared in a postmatch live-stream interview. He was wearing goggles and a gas mask—a direct visual reference to the Hong Kong protests. And he made an explicit verbal comment about liberating Hong Kong. The interview immediately went viral. Blizzard Entertainment disqualified Blitzchung, banned him for one year from the *Hearthstone* League, and deprived him of his rank and prize money.[12] In response to public resentment, J. Allen Brack, president of Blizzard Entertainment, reduced the period of suspension to six months and explained that the corporate decision was made "to bring the world together through epic entertainment, celebrate our players, and build diverse and inclusive communities."[13] Yet, Brack's utopian account indicates the weakness of decentralized protest activity, which the platform owner can censor and eliminate from the game. The corporate threat disclosed the counterpower of independent protest activity to provoke a chain reaction of other protest actions.

As an immediate countermove to his ban, Blitzchung live-streamed a play-through of *Liberate Hong Kong* (*LHK*) on the live-streaming platform Twitch. Produced by a group of Hong Kong–based game developers, *LHK* centers on a frontline protester defying police brutality on the streets of Hong Kong and includes gameplay tools and mechanics such as rubber bullets, tear gas canisters, and arrests (figure 14.4). As Josh Ye states, the game was developed to be "a part of the protest movement, taking the fight beyond the streets of Hong Kong."[14] In response to *LHK*, a mobile game called *Fight the Traitors Together* (*FTT*, 2019) was produced and released in China (figure 14.5). The game induces players to launch an attack against a group of high-profile Hong Kong protesters, including Joshua Wong and Martin Lee, who were disparagingly marked as "traitors" or "useless youth" carrying weapons.[15] The confrontation between these protest games indicated that video game activism had entered a new phase in which a protest game was being designed to influence players to change their behavior.

Despite the intentions behind them, these sorts of independent games, created by either protesters or propolice developers, has not made much of an impact except as a propagandistic tool.[16] That throws further doubt on expectations regarding educational video games' creation and use as an "activist medium."[17] As Taylor Anderson-Barkley and Kira Foglesong note, educational games center on fostering a feeling toward others, making players aware of a sociopolitical message at stake in the course of play, and representing players' corporeal experience and observations on specific circumstances in an immersive setting.[18] So the newly developed games are significant as a device for influencing players' behaviors offline. Still, given that some games, including *LHK*, should come with their own set of affordances, such games also have limitations for lacking the accessibility and viability to develop protest tactics or use them in the external world.

Virtual Hong Kong protests are taken more playfully by inconspicuous gamers as "leaderless" protesters in multiplayer online games than in independent activist games.[19] Looking at the Hong Kong protests mobilized around Blizzard's team-based first-person shooter game *Overwatch* (2016), the conversion of the game's Chinese character, Mei, into a Hong Kong protester could be an example of the protesters' creative associations with commercial online games. When Blizzard clamped down on Blitzchung, a Reddit user, u/batture, posted a meme of Mei on r/Hong Kong with the following caption: "It would be such a shame if Mei from *Overwatch* became a pro-democracy symbol and got Blizzard's games banned in China."[20] In the game, Mei is a

14.4. *Liberate Hong Kong* (2019). Image courtesy of Liberate Hong Kong Game Team.

14.5. *Fight the Traitors Together* (2019). Screenshot from Josh Ye, "China Has Its Own Hong Kong Protest Game That Lets You Beat up Activists." Abacus, *South China Morning Post*, December 6, 2019, https://www.scmp.com/abacus/games/article/3040864/china-has-its-own-hong-kong-protest-game-lets-you-beat-activists.

14.6. u/FloL0OL, "Pro Hong Kong Mei Inspired by a Post on Here. Fuck Blizzard," Reddit, October 8, 2019, https://www.reddit.com/r/HongKong/comments/df5tx1/pro_hong_kong_mei_inspiered_by_a_post_on_here/.

female climatologist and adventurer from Xi'an, China, and her catchline is "Our world is worth fighting for."[21] u/batture's post stirred up other Reddit users, and they began to produce a variety of memes of Mei with the message "Free Hong Kong" to express their support for the protests (figure 14.6).

However, turning Mei into a Hong Kong protester took more than simply adding political comments to her image. It required unsettling the lurking racist and nationalist fantasy represented through Mei, which is "the optimism of mainland China burgeoning with wealth and global prowess."[22] In the memes that Reddit users created, Mei became an antihero disowning the nationalistic reverie of the PRC, undercutting the given narrative. In other words, Reddit users disoriented the rationale of Mei via their unconstrained reworking of racial politics as virtual protest measures. They also circulated memes through other social media platforms using the hashtag #MeiSupportsHongKong. Consequently, the unorganized protesters' collective redevelopment of Mei as a supporting symbol of the Hong Kong protests demonstrated the scalability of their radically playful protest activities across media platforms.[23]

Online multiplayer-game-based protests indicate that online video games are a new space of collaborative and collective actions for challenging the ongoing suppression of the people of Hong Kong in the real world. As observed in previous cases, *AC* gamers also fought against suppression in their virtual islands by unsettling the politics and mechanics of the game and redeveloping them into a new form and style of mobilization of political protests in the virtual space. However, the ways *AC* gamers circumvented the issue of political suppression differed from previous attempts in open world games and their related media platforms. The gamers' political gaming on a virtual island in *AC* was networked but gated, as they did not allow untrusted others to participate in the protest scenes.

Virtual Political Protests Emerging from *Animal Crossing*

From the siege of Hong Kong Polytech University in 2019 to the subsequent street clashes between protesters and police in 2020, the violent police crackdowns on the Hong Kong protests were part of the reason that protesters went online. Moreover, the PRC's order to lock down Hong Kong in response to the pandemic, prohibiting crowds from gathering in public and forcing people to stay indoors, made protesters take to an online/virtual space as an alternative protest space. This way they used digital technologies to not only circumvent but also challenge the situation.

The fifth edition of the *Animal Crossing* franchise, *Animal Crossing: New Horizons* (*AC*), is an open-ended and real-time social simulation game Nintendo developed and released in 2020, designed to be played on the Nintendo Switch. Like many video games, it has a user-friendly mechanism and interface allowing you to turn a deserted island into "your dream getaway."[24] The possible social interactions also made *AC* more popular when the pandemic happened, and many people, including politicians, started playing it. For example, Alexandria Ocasio-Cortez's call for invitations from random *AC* users and visits to a few selected users' islands at the time showed that *AC* was conceived as a kind of social media platform rather than just a video game.[25] Uninterested parties hardly acknowledge any social activities enacted by a group of trusted players in the world of *AC*.

This restricted openness was a crucial framework of *AC* for Hong Kong protesters to create a "digitally networked public sphere" in the game's gated virtual island.[26] That is, as Zeynep Tufekci posits, a digital media platform like *AC* "help[ed] people reveal their (otherwise private) preferences to one another and discover common ground."[27] Tufekci's reference is to political protests on social media platforms, where "the boundaries of private and public, home and street, and individual and collective action" are blurred.[28] However, her argument is still helpful to explicate the *AC*-based Hong Kong protests because they were organized based on trusted protesters' shared political consciousness. The in-game protests against the PRC's autocracy further obscured the line between the virtual and the actual. Like social media platforms, *AC* was transformed into a sphere of political protest, where the fantasy and the real intersected through its seemingly apolitical mechanics and gameplay.[29]

AC asks a player to develop a deserted island economically and culturally. In the economic aspect, the player as an inhabitant of the island engages in long hours of virtual manual labor—growing fruits and plants, mowing grass, fishing and hunting bugs, digging up fossils and iron/gold nuggets, and felling trees. The players are regularly given "DIY Recipes" as a form of reward for their labor to make a new item (furniture, ornament, or implement) for their living space. Here each player's labor power is interchangeable; players can barter in-game items for what they need. Selling items gathered through such labor is a necessary part of the game for the player to pay back a loan for building a house from Nook Inc., a virtual development company owned by the raccoon character Tom Nook. Players can use the money remaining after the debt has been paid off to construct the island's infrastructure with materials purchased in the Nook Shop, a virtual store in the game.

However, the player is never actually able to free themselves from debt because Tom Nook encourages them to continue taking out new mortgages for better houses in terms of size and design. *AC*'s debt-capitalism economics, as Naomi Clark explains, epitomizes the village debt system in premodern Japan, which was "what made villages continue to function" without direct income coming in from indigent villagers.[30] In *AC*, the mortgage system forces the indebted player to continue to engage in relentless labor to work off their debt, develop a personal paradise, and nourish its culture.[31] At the same time, the game requires the player to do gratuitous tasks such as collecting fossils, marine life, and insects and donating them to a virtual museum founded to promote the cultural development of the game's island.

Interestingly, as Ian Bogost asserts, the game's debt-capitalism economics mingled with volunteerism allowed players to "reclaim [the] structure and routine" of their social activities in the virtual space during the lockdown.[32] The Hong Kong protesters re-created the structure and routine of their protest activities in the game space by taking the in-game tools for their own use. For example, the "Pro Design" app that players can purchase for Nook Miles, a virtual currency acquired in *AC*, provides players with a set of tools for customizing their own items. To identify themselves as protesters, the players produced and carried protest gear—yellow hard hats and gas masks, for instance.

In addition to these more obvious objects, yard signs—replacing placards or banners hung on Hong Kong streets—were used to publicly display messages like "Free Hong Kong Revolution Now." Such political messages served as shared objects among specific groups of islanders in the game. Like the virtual banners, all the items retooled for political use were the protesters' private possessions in *AC*. These self-owned game items were made playable for a specific group of players only. However, they were also distributed using free QR or special codes through social media or online forums by the creators of the items, who "want to spread awareness" of the movement.[33]

From displaying a virtual banner and buying protest gear to decorate their game characters to organizing a virtual sit-in, the series of protest activities made it plain that the protesters were reacting against the present state of the real world. In addition, they reinvented their protest tactics to make them appear more moderate in the virtual space. The spatial and formal reorganization of their political actions in *AC* shows the utility of the game for carrying out political protests in Hong Kong to cope with the existing difficulties of administrative oppression, police brutality, and the COVID-19 pandemic.

Proliferating Networked Protests on the Gated Islands of *Animal Crossing*

Playing *AC* in network play mode is allowed only for those who subscribe to Nintendo Switch Online. With a shared Dodo code, which is a mix of letters and numbers, trusted players (up to eight) can assemble in a gated island of *AC* for social gaming based on affinity without random interruptions. Gated network play is an important factor of *AC* with regard to the new protest culture independent Hong Kong protesters have cultivated.

Yet digital protests have robust similarities in terms of how protesters use digital technology as a protest tool. As discussed in the context of video game–based protest movements, gamers as decentralized protesters have created protest items (e.g., signs and costumes) and shared those items with others. The ability to modify items in this way allows them to challenge the

"This Is What We Do"   **301**

politics of the games they play. However, as Tufekci states, each protest has its own "grievances," and the various issues require different responses.[34] She also notes that "protests are also locations of self-expression and communities of belonging and mutual altruism."[35] If Tufekci's account is valid, then Hong Kong (HK) protesters' struggles and frustrations were acknowledged in *AC*, and the game allowed the protesters to give voice to themselves, take creative and collaborative action, and—most important—protect their community based on shared material.

Because the networked protests were performed in a closed public sphere, the protesters could protect themselves against disruptive influences, including police violence and propolice protesters' retaliation. However, the ability to protect one's own community is rarely available in virtual protests in massively multiplayer online role-playing games. For example, when a gamer-organized protest group, "Stand with Hong Kong," launched a virtual protest in the open world game *Grand Theft Auto V* (*GTA*), the group's action triggered a counterreaction from mainland *GTA* players, who showed hostility to the protests.[36] The confrontation provoked wild "virtual scuffles" between the two parties in the online game space and related online forums.[37] The way in which the *GTA*-based protesters politicized the game platform to reveal their grievances differed little from how activists carried out protests in *AC*. However, whereas protesters' struggles were redressed by reenacting real-life clashes between them and riot police in the open world game space, the protests on the gated virtual island of *AC* circumvented this issue by politicizing in-game leisure activities and proliferating their gated plays.

In one *AC*-based protest scene in HoSaiLei's Twitter posts, seven *AC* characters don protest gear (gas masks, goggles, and hard hats); form a musical band; play instruments (piano, saxophone, drum, and violin); and sing "Glory Be to Thee, Hong Kong," the HK protesters' anthem, by spreading the lyrics through the game's chat function with their consoles or smartphone apps (figure 14.7). Players must perform a considerable amount of labor in *AC* to acquire musical instruments. Possessing them allows gamers to take pleasure in strengthening ties among each other.

When rendering the protest anthem in the gated game world, the seven players displayed their ability to politicize the game's apolitical nature for demanding social change. It carried the significance that the civic anthem was performed on other media platforms or in public spaces, such as Hong Kong's streets and shopping malls. By gathering to sing the anthem on the virtual

14.7. HK protester characters' rendering of "Glory Be to Thee, Hong Kong." Screenshot from HoSaiLei (@hkbhkese), "願榮光歸香港(動物之森版)."

island, the protesters avoided the physical threat they would have dealt with in a real-life demonstration, including the riot police's clubs, water cannons, and surveillance cameras. The group of trusted protesters' in-game musical demonstration did not function just as a playful protest; their networked political gaming in such a gated space also became a way to deepen the sense of intimacy and care for their survival and resistance.

In other words, *AC* players reassembled their virtual manual labor as a source of sociopolitical power to transform the gated game world into a place of shielding their collective political voice from the PRC's antidemocratic suppression of dissent. By unsettling the debt-capitalist politics of *AC*, the protesters reclaimed the right to carry out sit-in demonstrations in the in-game virtual islands for maintaining opposition to oppression. Their networked gaming manifested itself as an exigent skirmish over their political subsistence without any epic clashes with Hong Kong riot police on campuses or streets.

Yet the fragility of the political actions conducted in the gated virtual game space cannot be ignored: the collective struggles and playful resistance to the situation in Hong Kong were hardly recognized beyond the sphere of the game. Nonetheless, despite their ephemerality, these microscaled virtual

"This Is What We Do"   303

protests have allowed cross-platform media activism beyond *AC*—especially when protesters promoted screen captures of protest scenes on social media using hashtags, such as #AnimalCrossing with #LiberateHongKong, #Stand-WithHK, or #RevolutionOfOurTime. As Sarah Jackson and her colleagues insist, hashtags are useful tools for protesters to "bridge political consciousness across oceans and cultures" by specifying the time, space, and initiative of their political activities.[38] For young Hong Kong protesters, the cross-platform mobility of these microscaled political movements became a way to build new ground to take their messages about their unending resistance to state-sanctioned violence to the external space of the game, and to social media or online forums like Twitter or Reddit.

There, *AC*-based political protests and activities that were once decentralized and blockaded have been made available for general viewers to witness protesters inhabiting cute characters and transforming the game into a protest site. This has spurred the construction of an alternative network with potential fellow protesters and supporters beyond the virtual world. Thus, the radically playful Hong Kong protests in *AC* are not a mere simulation of political protests in the virtual world but a socially potent movement.

Conclusion: Have You Seen What We Do in *#AC*?

It should be kept in mind that *AC* is no longer a popular medium for the Hong Kong protests (or any political activism in general) because its blockaded protests have been isolated from the corresponding larger social movements. Despite its transience, for young Hong Kong protesters *AC* and its closed system for networked gaming among trusted players were effective in helping their political protests continue in the virtual world without physical clashes with the riot police. The *AC*-based protesters reinvented street protest tactics through their playful subversion of the game's escapist narrative, rules, and mechanism entangled with debt capitalism. As a radically playful political activity, their networked gaming allowed their political consciousness and voices to be expressed and heard on the gated virtual islands the police could not access. At the same time, the *AC*-based protesters circulated the captured or recorded in-game protest scenes across social media or online forums, and that circulation enabled them to proliferate beyond the game's simulated boundaries. The way the protesters made their own safe places in *AC* to keep their voices alive further suggests an alternative way to build a political community that is not fragile and ephemeral—that strengthens political activism in Hong Kong and expands its scope.

Notes

1 Reuters, "Timeline: Key Dates for Hong Kong Extradition Bill and Protests."

2 J. Wong, "This Is What We Do in #AnimalCrossing..."

3 From the virtual fake funeral to the whipping performance, that Carrie Lam became the subject of collective resentment was conspicuous in *AC*-based protest scenes at the time. See Ong, "*Animal Crossing: New Horizons* Is Fast Becoming a New Way for Hong Kong Protesters to Fight for Democracy."

4 Bogost, "The Quiet Revolution of *Animal Crossing*."

5 Lin, "Contextualized Transmedia Mobilization," 55.

6 Prompted by the 2020 murder of George Floyd by Minneapolis policemen, a *Sims* player, Ebonix, and fellow gamers organized an antiracism rally in *Sims 4*. They created protest items such as BLM signs, costumes, skins, and hairstyles and made them downloadable through a shared code for other gamers to encourage them to join the virtual rally. BLM protesters entered into *AC* as well. Some Reddit users created BLM signs and costumes and shared the codes on Reddit; see u/Emilyx666, "Black Lives Matter!"

7 Pang, "Retheorizing the Social," 71; Lin, "Contextualized Transmedia Mobilization," 48.

8 Lin, "Contextualized Transmedia Mobilization," 54.

9 Lin, "Contextualized Transmedia Mobilization," 65.

10 Pang, "Retheorizing the Social," 75.

11 Pang, "Retheorizing the Social," 89.

12 Blizzard Entertainment, "Hearthstone Grandmasters Asia-Pacific Ruling." While giving a shout-out supporting the Hong Kong movement, two Taiwanese casters hid themselves under their desks in solidarity with him. Of course, the casters were also suspended.

13 Blizzard Entertainment, "Regarding Last Weekend's Hearthstone Grandmasters Tournament."

14 Ye, "A New Steam Game."

15 Ye, "China Has Its Own Hong Kong Protest Game That Lets You Beat Up Activists."

16 The fact that the independent games haven't made much impact also shows how such games are not necessarily political or intrinsically progressive.

17 Anderson-Barkley and Foglesong, "Activism in Video Games," 253.

18 Anderson-Barkley and Foglesong, "Activism in Video Games," 262.

19 Ming Ming Chiu, "Are Video Games Making Hong Kong Youths Delinquents, Loners . . . or Better Protesters?," *Hong Kong Free Press*, September 15, 2019; quoted in Davies, "Spatial Politics at Play," 5.

20 u/batture, "It would be such a shame if Mei from *Overwatch* became a pro-democracy symbol and got Blizzard's games banned in China."

21 Blizzard Entertainment, "Mei," accessed July 28, 2023, playoverwatch.com/en-us/heroes/mei/.

22 Patterson, *Open World Empire*, 65.

23 Some of the Reddit users on r/Hong Kong also conferred about putting messages of/about the Hong Kong protests in the live chat box of the game on the comment board.

24 Animal-crossing.com/new-horizons/.

25 Wilson, "AOC Is Sharing Pears with Randoms on 'Animal Crossing' Because This Is Who We Are Now."

26 Tufekci, *Twitter and Tear Gas*, 26.

27 Tufekci, *Twitter and Tear Gas*, 26.

28 Tufekci, *Twitter and Tear Gas*, 26.

29 Pang, "Retheorizing the Social," 89.

30 NYU Game Center, "Naomi Clark: Why Tom Nook Symbolizes Village Debt in 18th Century Japan."

31 NYU Game Center, "Naomi Clark: Why Tom Nook Symbolizes Village Debt in 18th Century Japan."

32 Bogost, "The Quiet Revolution of *Animal Crossing*."

33 u/Emilyx666, "Black Lives Matter!"

34 Tufekci, *Twitter and Tear Gas*, 88.

35 Tufekci, *Twitter and Tear Gas*, 88.

36 Ye, "Hong Kong Protesters and Mainland Gamers Clash in *Grand Theft Auto V* Online."

37 Ye, "Hong Kong Protesters and Mainland Gamers Clash in *Grand Theft Auto V* Online."

38 Jackson, Bailey, and Welles, *#HashtagActivism*, xxxi.

Christopher B. Patterson
Tara Fickle

Coda

Role / Play \ Race

> Identity itself is a complex system—one whose
> potential ontological affinities with the medium of
> video games have not yet been fully grasped.
> —TreaAndrea M. Russworm and Jennifer Malkowski

During the three-year process of editing and organizing this collection, we were consistently challenged with the same inquiry coming from contributors, roundtablists, and even the reviewers of the final manuscript: How do games fundamentally disrupt our normative ways of understanding race? More precisely, what if we were to see the racial logics in video games— particularly in games that situate players into racialized roles alongside racialized others—not just as subjects of ideological critique but also as offering modes of reimagining "race" itself? How is the world making we see in games also a form of race making?

While this inquiry has been marginal to game studies, it has been attended to critically by multiple authors, including Lisa Nakamura, Anna Everett, Adrienne Shaw, TreaAndrea Russworm, Jen Malkowski, and others. More recently, this question emerged in response to one of the most tenacious problems of game studies: namely, as Russworm wrote in 2018, "the fact that whiteness remains a defining feature of the continuing formation of game studies" as well as within the games industry.[1] However, critiques of white and male dominance in both game studies and game industries frequently turn to a commonly proposed solution: to diversify games through the inclusion of more nonwhite and queer characters, a shift that seems positive on first blush but that Adrienne Shaw, in 2014, importantly emphasized came as much from a market logic as from marginalized gamers themselves. As Shaw wrote, "Arguing for the representation of cleanly defined, marketable identity groups excludes those at the margins of representation, those who do not sit comfortably in demographic categories, and those who exist outside the market."[2] Since the transformations in game cultures toward more marketable forms of progressive and antiracist politics (post-indie, post-#Gamergate), Shaw's cautionary remarks seemed to have predicted the shift in games from erasing discourses of race to quickly foreclosing these discourses by envisioning "racial issues" as ends in themselves—that is, as a diversity "win condition" that makes for a successful game (or a successful work of game studies).

Second, this inquiry on how games can reimagine race must also be charged for its underlying assumptions: that racial difference can be generalized to such an extent as to make any broad claims on its meanings, that video games represent a medium so exceptional as to disrupt the very core of racial discourses, and that we—two Asian/American gamers and editors—would be so bold as to answer it. Or perhaps a more common charge against this inquiry is the disbelief that the low art of video games, known for perpetuating racial stereotypes and imperial violence, can say anything unique about how racializing processes work. Yet what if, despite or even within these problem(atic)s, we still ventured boldly into the radical possibilities that games may offer, allowing them to take us beyond discussions of diversity toward more antiracist and abolitional political practices? Given that the medium of games is so focused on simulations, experimentations, and systemic views of race and identity, how could we not pursue its potential meanings for our ever more gamic future?

This brief coda, inspired by the chapters and roundtables in this collection—as well as our own experiences editing it—plays with the ways that games can transform our understandings of race through their procedural logics of racial management. While our introduction focused on the insularity of game studies, we use this concluding space to explore how this collection makes urgent a gamic relation to studies of race, revealing how games note limitations in perceiving and accounting for racial (in)justice. We ask how games can offer ways of understanding race as not merely structural but also an epistemic force guiding our perceptions and describing our experiences within the wider social and political "game."

Because race is a fundamental organizing rule of our "real world" (our "afk" society), it is inevitably, not incidentally, baked into cultural productions that represent or simulate that society (whether implicitly or explicitly). Thus, instead of attempting to treat race as a form of quality control by explaining away, supplementing, or substituting for "bad" representations, we ask: How does race get implemented as not a bug but a feature of games? How do games, not despite but because of their own racist representations, simulate the problems of racial hegemony and, through play, present alternatives to the failed solutions of multicultural "diversity"? Given the extent to which players and game communities have productively modded, hacked, or "metagamed" games, can games offer us a theoretical approach to exploiting rather than attempting to eliminate their racial features?[3] In what follows, we attempt to answer these questions by examining three gamic racial logics that, beneath the particularities of their character representations, govern the *Mass Effect* trilogy (BioWare, 2007–12), *Genshin Impact* (miHoYo, 2020), and *Divinity: Original Sin 2* (Larian Studios, 2017).

1 / Multiculturalist Manager (*Mass Effect*)

In role-playing series like *Final Fantasy*, *Fallout*, *The Witcher*, and *Mass Effect*, the player tends to occupy a position of relative superiority or neutrality in relation to their nonplayable friends and teammates, who are often cast as either explicitly racialized human others or implicitly racialized aliens, elves, monsters, mages, and so on. *Mass Effect* games, as the contributor to this collection Gerald Voorhees writes, professes "the unmitigated superiority of neo-liberal multiculturalism as a form of dealing with difference."[4] They do so, as Patterson has argued elsewhere, by asking players to play the role of a "multiculturalist umpire":[5] a human literally named "Shepard" who is meant to learn and reinforce the rules of tolerance in order to exercise their own quest to ensure the supremacy of "glorified space cops."[6]

Coda **309**

As scholars have noted, *Mass Effect* is a particularly apt game for conversations about race, because many of its alien species resemble encoded racial types within the context of the War on Terror, and because the game seems to lay the groundwork for its own problematics. Players are not merely presented with choices that train them to police difference; rather, they are made to recognize how their own managerial roles reiterate histories of violence *despite* their abilities to produce a diverse and tolerant squad. In the original *Mass Effect*, players must convince their nonhuman teammate, Wrex, to abandon the interests of his own species by allowing them to suffer forced sterilization.[7] In *Mass Effect 2*, the player becomes a puppet of Cerberus, a violent organization vying for human (read: white) supremacy of the galaxy. In *Mass Effect 3*, the player discovers that the synthetic race they spent the entire first game killing—"the Geth"—have been capable of self-sacrifice and motivations that reveal sentience and free will.

Taken less as flawed representations and more as simulations of a form of racial management, games like *Mass Effect* compel us to question the motivations of tolerance and multiculturalism as a means of perpetuating, not mitigating, our militaristic present of empire and permanent war. In turn, we as editors are brought by this managerial form to consider our own decision-making in editing this collection, which, as a collection organized around a racial identity ("Asia America") has the ambiguous role of diversifying the field of game studies (and the media associated with Asian American studies), but also urges us throughout this volume to decenter Asian American identity as the primary logic guiding our editorial and writing practice. As mixed-race Asian American professors who work mainly on games, we may appear and indeed feel marginalized in our own contexts, yet when it comes to video games globally, our positions feel anything but marginal. Like *Mass Effect*'s humans, our roles as editors have felt in danger of being so concerned with managing (and even radicalizing) "Asian American identity" that we overlook the ways that our entire project might be complicit in imperial and colonial violence (like the racial exploitation of factory work in games and the IT industry writ large or, more locally, the exploitation of contingent faculty labor and the racialization of personnel hierarchies at our institutions). In short, the "multiculturalist manager" role of these games alert us, as editors, to the limitations of a familiar center/periphery model of race, one in which the inclusion of more peoples within our borders is the ultimate goal, while the mission and sanctity that exists within those borders remain intact.

2 / Racial Empath (*Genshin Impact*)

While the "multiculturalist manager" role in games like *Mass Effect* focuses on diversity management as a form of distraction that feels like progress, another subgenre of role-playing games encourages players to regard exotic representations as voyeuristic opportunities to play with the pain of, or as, others. Such play frequently takes on the language of empathy as a means to appreciate rather than appropriate difference. Though it might appear to be a form of border-crossing, such gamic identity tourism, as Nakamura notes, reflects "a desire to fix the boundaries of cultural identity and exploit them for recreational purposes."[8] The desire to cloak this exploitation as empathy is especially visible in the marketing of virtual reality games, which, as our contributor Robert Yang has stated, marks them as "appropriation machines" that "are fundamentally about mining the experiences of suffering people to enrich the self-image of VR users."[9] Such cross-racial play thus might identify as antiracist while also assuming what Bo Ruberg has called a form of "embodied colonialism."[10]

The Chinese-made 2020 role-playing game *Genshin Impact* can make an illuminating case study in understanding race as a form of cross-racial play that overlays the exotic, the empathetic, and the erotic, as it repeats many of the same familiar racisms of identity/empathy tourism on an even more explicit level. In the game, players can inhabit forty-eight playable characters as they explore a vast open world whose regions are based on particular national medieval imaginaries (an English-style kingdom, Chinese-style villages, Japanese-style temples, "Middle Eastern"–style gardens). As each playable character originates from a particular region, players can play as and with these racialized others while discovering more of their (often tragic) backstories, which promise deeper empathetic attachment. At the same time, the game asks players to do so while massacring enemies who are indisputably hybrid caricatures of Black and Indigenous populations (as emphasized by a video of one designer basing enemy character movement on Native American dances).[11] This "ludo-dissonance" might seem a "bug" in the machine, yet it is precisely *Genshin Impact*'s unabashed racism—and its foreignness as a Chinese product—that has allowed so many gamers and games journalists to look past its racist representations and to instead enjoy its racialized characters as figures of empathy and eroticism. Similar to the commonplace sexualized bodies and attire of female avatars found in most games, the racisms in *Genshin Impact* are so explicit that conversations about them have become

Coda **311**

moot, a thing too obvious to mention, freeing games journalists and fans to focus on the attachments they feel toward the game's many playable heroes. Often, too, these attachments are tinged with erotic desire, as *Genshin Impact* pornography has been a phenomenon in itself, with over a thousand videos on Pornhub, and *Genshin Impact* communities have been known to (often uncomfortably) create space for queer desire and trans representation (particularly through the playable god, Venti, a being who has mourned the loss of his dear friend for over a century, and whose depression has caused him to spiral into a century-long alcoholic bender).

In short, racial difference in *Genshin Impact* is treated as an opportunity to satisfy (and, for us, to reveal) the overlapping desires of empathy and erotics that enable ludic climax (all for the price of participating in the game's Gacha pay mechanics). *Genshin Impact*'s entangling of sexual fetishes with fetishes for racial otherness further emphasizes the mechanics of desire whereby racism functions: how it expects something, some deeper truth, or some magical cure, that can only be provided through a racialized other. Thus, it is not despite but through the game's racism that we experience its pleasurable pull. Such intimate entanglements of sexual and racial pathologization are intrinsic: as Patricia Holland has argued, the "erotic life—a desiring life" will always carry a relationship with "the messy terrain of racist practice."[12]

Genshin Impact can easily be accused of reproducing racist tropes; at the same time, the game expands our perspective of how race works by extending racial logics into the overlapping realms of empathy and erotics—that is, it helps us see identity tourism and racial empathy as themselves speaking to the widespread logics of racial fetishization, the combined pleasures of which constitute the appeal of cross-racial play. As Olúfémi O. Táíwò has argued, such fetishizations also lie at the heart of diversity projects in academia today, where committees and those with power habitually "defer to" / "have deference for" those whom they name as "the most marginalized in the room" but whose perspectives also must be authenticated and deemed worthy of empathy by those in privileged positions.[13] As a "casual" mobile game rather than a "real" PC or console game, *Genshin Impact* can also escape deeper critique on the basis of genre and format alone.[14] Such critique reveals a further warning: while *Genshin Impact*'s perceived foreignness as an Asian-made game provides evidence of these racial logics' global circulation, rather than something exclusive to North American or European game developers, it also provides a ready-made excuse for Western game journalists, or for scholars outside Asian and Asian/American studies, to avoid addressing

312 Patterson and Fickle

its racial representation in the name of honoring contextual diversity (i.e., a narrow and isolationist interpretation of "cultural relativism").

3 / Cosmic Avatar (*Divinity: Original Sin II*)

The word *avatar* has long been used in games discourse as a neutral term to describe a character or other in-game player proxy. Yet as one of our contributors, Souvik Mukherjee, has argued elsewhere, the original Sanskrit usage of *avatar* carried a particular meaning in its adoption by early game developers as "the manifestation of divinity that descends on Earth to destroy evil," with its most common English translation as " 'incarnation' (literally 'the being made flesh')."[15] The borrowing of this term from Hinduism into video games continues a long history of Silicon Valley technocultural fascination with "the East," meant both to orientalize and mystify a familiarly Christian messianic trajectory of heroes "invested with a sense of divine right, as their role is to restore a sense of order to the game world."[16] While the avatar is often read within technoculture's broader project of deincarnation (of a virtual shedding of the physical racialized and gendered body), role-playing games can allow us to dwell further in the potential of the avatar as the opposite: a re-incarnated, re-inhabitation of the body as a racial form.

Most contemporary role-playing games, such as the *Mass Effect* series, see the avatar as a digital incarnation of the player themselves, as both individual (in the sense that they come from a player's imagined and perhaps desired self) and diverse (in the sense that each avatar can be as unique as its player). Games usually enact this through some form of character customization that allows players to choose their race (often including a plethora of granular options related to appearance, skin tone, hair, etc.). Such a perceived choice promises the player a chance not to play as another but to finally play "as themselves"—to create an avatar "as diverse as you are." Yet avatar racialization can also be enacted in games where characters are racialized but are intentionally *not* customizable; it is through such perceived programming limitations, in fact, that race is made meaningful as an in-game simulation rather than merely a representational "skin." Games in the *Elder Scrolls* series, the first and second *Dragon Age*, the *Pillars of Eternity* games, and the *Divinity* series not only cater the dialogue, plot, nonplayer character (NPC) behavior, and even the camera positioning to the player's selected racialized experience, but, as in traditional conceptions of the avatar itself, these games

Coda **313**

are also commonly predominated by a messianic plot, where the player, no matter their race, will be set on a journey to become divine, to approach godhood or sainthood, or to become renowned as a god-killer.

It is through these divine experiences as a racialized avatar that understandings of race can reach a more "cosmic" realm, a term Legacy Russell has used to emphasize how some users—in her discussion, Black queer women—find fulfillment in online identities despite their perceived fakeness.[17] Russell centralizes the body as a means to defeat the "digital dualism" that sees afk (away from keyboard) bodies as real (carnate) and virtual bodies as merely imagined (as without true form), which for Russell have led to discourses of identity tourism that see online identities as fake or problematic, even when Black queer women find new forms of flourishing within them. In turn, Russell envisions the "cosmic body" as a concept of the body that blurs the real and the virtual by reinvoking Edouard Glissant's "right to opacity," the refusal by the racialized subject in the face of colonial powers to meet their demand to express their whole and transparent being.[18] The cosmic body is neither real nor virtual; instead it is marked (or more accurately, *un*marked) as "inconceivably vast," pushing players to speculate on a world of proliferated multiplicity rather than collected and coherent unity.[19]

In *Divinity: Original Sin 2*, a cosmic sense of race emerges in the way players control and experience a motley crew of characters with different racialized backgrounds—Beast (dwarf), Sebille (elf), Fane (undead), and Red Prince (lizard)—while its two human characters smuggle along difference with them: Ifan Ben-Mezd talks to animals and can summon them by his side; Lohse is possessed so strongly by a demon that their characteristics and voices can become inseparable. But, again, this is the realm of representation. What makes the game interesting for us is not the particularity of the avatars but that the player's experience inhabiting them will always be conditioned by the knowledge that the game has gone to great lengths to tell each racialized group member's story differently—indeed, that the meaning of racial difference *is* narrative divergence. The player's experience is thus always limited racially, as no single avatar can represent the universal—that is, all of the multiple aspects of the divine. One can never be presented with all the stories simultaneously; one can only see the particular, the limitations of flesh, and then speculate on the other lives and thoughts that they've been excluded from. In other words, it is not the virtual body but the cosmic body that the player becomes aware of through this racial form, even as it serves to make the game feel more "real" and replayable (an argument often made about nonlinearity as a defining game appeal). At the same time, the fantasy setting itself begins to resemble a "skin" of contemporary liberal multiculturalism as practiced in North America and Europe: when playing as the Red Prince, a lizard, one is consistently presented with dialogue options with unfriendly NPCs that are literalizations (lizardizations?) of "playing the race card": "You're only treating me this way because I'm a lizard!"

Beyond focusing on racialized avatars as (failed) attempts to simulate race as vicarious identity tourism—to let the player experience "what it's like" to be an other—such role-playing games ask us to consider how the avatar creates a cosmic (rather than a particular or universal) racialized logic, which uses race as the expression of the limitations of a knowable, transparent body. Rather than see the body as a material given, Russell encourages the use of *bodied* as a verb, meaning "giv[ing] material form to something abstract"—a process that the avatar promises in its re-incarnation of the body that can also "make room for other realities."[20] In *Divinity*, players are "bodied" through a constant feeling of embodied limitation that is exaggerated by the trope toward divinity itself: as the game proceeds, each player is informed that the other characters might each be one of the "Godwoken" and, as such, must be viewed as threats rather than allies, whose thoughts and intentions will remain (at least for this playthrough) opaque. Thus, every racialized interaction is laden with the constant sense of missing out on the experience of others, making the player feel their singularity, their positionality, while also the vast, cosmic potentials of the world around them. Every experience is deuniversalized, refracted from the one to the many. At the same time, every interaction with the five other playable characters is infused with a similarly cosmic feeling: this character could have been me, I could have been them. Each other represents a different possible self, and even the nonplayable others are either kin (i.e., the same race as the avatar) or people who could have been kin.

Shifting the focus away from race as a managerial exercise or a fetishistic opportunity for empathy, the racial logics of games like *Divinity: Original Sin 2* focus not on the player learning from the other but, rather, on learning how much they cannot understand, and how this limitation structures the way that they navigate the world. In the game studies world, perhaps recognizing the limitations posed by our professional avatars could help us better reveal the limitations of the various magic circles that we've created to define "us," and to reconfigure how we see (or do not see) those who could not be included or even regarded as belonging with "us."

Coda **315**

Closing the Loop: How Games Can (Really) Unmake "Us"

As with our meditations on the limits of game studies in the introduction, we end this brief inquiry on gamic race making by considering what remains beyond the walls of the kingdom, who is not found in the room, and how the world making we see in games is also world ending: that is, abolitional. Here we understand our investments in race as part of an abolitional practice that seeks to shift from the institutionalized terms and logics of our present racial formation into something new and imagined, something our experimentations in interaction might reveal. At the end of this experiment, we have come to see interaction not merely as an editorial method but as a refusal of the competitive attitudes that compel us to respond to a racial injustice somewhere with the anger of our own injuries. Rather, interaction invites us to engage in ways that can make new and unpredictable forms of collaboration, coalition, and solidarity.

The racial gamic logics explored in this coda urge us out of a dominant racial formation that privatizes racial justice by pinpointing racism onto seemingly anachronistic acts: racial slurs, personal traumas, and microaggressions that can be reinterpreted or reinforced on social media. As others have argued, such privatizations of racism can threaten abolitional praxis when they give legitimacy to the state and institutions (and, indeed, promise inclusion in them).[21] The gamic forms of race we have analyzed here give us a systemic view of race and help us understand its algorithms, its processes, its operations. Games give us ways not only to read but also to abolish these systems through forms of disruptive world making, of imagining what can happen after we hit the reset button, when power might shift forms and we might run the risk of the rebels turning against acts of rebellion.

Guided by our attachments as Asian/Americans and as players ourselves, this book has swayed against giving definitive generalizations of games or "Asia America," refusing the identitarian frameworks that provide the grist of state and institutional planning. Instead, we have sought to trace the ungovernable and the unnamable ways of feeling, living, and playing, that pulse along the racial traces of Asia/America. To do so, we have understood video games as a grippable, archival ballast in the vast viscosity of our context of technological empire. Where other mediums—literature, film, performance—might see this empire's rocky shores and lapping waters, video games are in the thick of the technological mass; they are its fun, cute, childish, Asiatic, and well-adorned scions. Dressed up as they may be, video games can help us see what writhes within empire's murk: the unseen work, the unheard deaths, and the possibilities of our collective struggle. When asked "What use are video games?," we reply, "Nothing but the collective unmaking of our violent, deadly world."

Notes

Part of this coda was published previously as Tara Fickle and Christopher B. Patterson, "Diversity Is Not a Win-Condition," *Critical Studies in Media Communication* 39, no. 3 (2022): 211–20.

1 Russworm, "A Call to Action for Video Game Studies."

2 Shaw, *Gaming at the Edge*, 8.

3 Boluk and LeMieux, *Metagaming*.

4 Voorhees, "Neo-liberal Multiculturalism in *Mass Effect*," 259.

5 Patterson, "Role-Playing the Multiculturalist Umpire."

6 Cole, "*Mass Effect*'s Revival Reminds Us It's Time to Abolish the Space Police."

7 For a close reading of this scene with Wrex, see Patterson, *Open World Empire*, chap. 3.

8 Nakamura, *Cybertypes*, 42.

9 Yang, "If You Walk in Someone Else's Shoes."

10 Ruberg, "Empathy and Its Alternatives," 61.

11 Messner, "Here's Why 'Boycott Genshin Impact' Is Trending on Twitter."

12 Holland, *The Erotic Life of Racism*, 46.

13 Táíwò, "Being-in-the-Room Privilege."

14 Consalvo and Paul, *Real Games*.

15 Mukherjee, "Vishnu and the Videogame."

16 Wildt et al., "(Re-)Orienting the Videogame Avatar," 967.

17 L. Russell, *Glitch Feminism*, 41.

18 Glissant, *Poetics of Relation*.

19 L. Russell, *Glitch Feminism*, 46.

20 L. Russell, *Glitch Feminism*, 41.

21 As Eric Stanley writes, "The managed translation of cultures of attack into personal incidents" produces the citizen human as "the sole beneficiary of rights before the law" (*Atmospheres of Violence*, 6).

Bibliography

Published Sources

1023119780. "A Long-Ass Thread about Chinese Cheaters." Reddit, February 17, 2018. https://www.reddit.com/r/PUBATTLEGROUNDS/comments/7y7lyj/a_longass_thread_about_chinese_cheaters/.

Aarseth, Espen J. *Cybertexts: Perspectives on Ergodic Literature*. Baltimore: Johns Hopkins University Press, 1997.

Admin. "Team Houses and Why They Matter." *ESL Magazine*, January 6, 2014. https://www.eslgaming.com/article/team-houses-and-why-they-matter-1676.

Albrecht, Monika. "Unthinking Postcolonialism: On the Necessity for a Reset Instead of a Step Forward." In *Postcolonialism Cross-Examined: Multidirectional Perspectives on Imperial and Colonial Pasts and the Neocolonial Present*, edited by Monika Albrecht, 181–94. New York: Routledge, 2020.

Alleyne, Allisia. "What the Kimono's Wide-Reaching Influence Tells Us about Cultural Appropriation." *CNN Style*, March 6, 2020. https://www.cnn.com/style/article/kimono-fashion-history-cultural-appropriation/index.html.

Anderson-Barkley, Taylor, and Kira Foglesong. "Activism in Video Games: A New Voice for Social Change." In *Woke Gaming: Digital Challenges to Oppression and Social Injustice*, edited by Kishonna L. Gray and David J. Leonard, 252–69. Seattle: University of Washington Press, 2018.

Andlauer, L. "Pursuing One's Own Prince: Love's Fantasy in Otome Game Contents and Fan Practice." *Mechademia* 11, no. 1 (2018): 166–83.

Apex Arena. "13 Minutes of *Apex Legends* Crashing and Streamers' Reactions." YouTube video, 12:56, posted January 30, 2021. https://www.youtube.com/watch?v=eZAstfv9yDE.

Appadurai, Arjun. "How Histories Make Geographies." *Journal of Transcultural Studies* 1, no. 1 (2010): 4–13.

Arik_De_Frasia. "What makes online cheating so prevalent in China?" Reddit, February 16, 2018. https://www.reddit.com/r/Games/comments/7xz9cf /what_makes_online_cheating_so_prevalent_in_china/.

Arora, Akhil. "Review: Made-in-India Raji Is a Feminist Fable and a Strong Debut." *NDTV Gadgets 360*. N.p., n.d. Accessed February 28, 2021. https:// gadgets.ndtv.com/games/reviews/raji-an-ancient-epic-review-nintendo -switch-2286347.

Arudou, Debito. "Japan's Under-researched Visible Minorities: Applying Critical Race Theory to Racialization Dynamics in a Non-white Society." *Washington University Global Studies Law Review* 14 (2015): 695–799.

"Asians and Fighting Games: Exploring the Myth/Stereotype." Shoryuken.com, October 2004. https://forums.shoryuken.com/t/ asians-and-fighting-games-exploring-the-myth-stereotype/8412.

Azuma, Hiroki. *Otaku: Japan's Database Animals*. Minneapolis: University of Minnesota Press, 2009.

Bago, John Paolo. "Dispelling the Myth of the Korean Gaming House: What Lessons the Philippine eSports Industry Can Learn from Our Korean Overlords." *Inquirer.net*, February 24, 2016. https://esports.inquirer.net/13920 /dispelling-the-myth-of-the-korean-gaming-house-what-lessons-the -philippine-esports-industry-can-learn-from-our-korean-overlords.

Banks, Marcus. "*Apex Legends* Dev Responds to Calls to Region Lock China to Stop Cheaters." *Dexterto*, April 10, 2019. https://www.dexerto.com /apex-legends/developer-responds-apex-legends-region-lock-china -532277/.

BattlEye (@TheBattlEye). "We are currently banning at a rate of 6K–13K per day, nearly 20K within the last 24 hours alone. The vast majority is from China." Twitter, October 13, 2017, 3:06 a.m. EST. https://twitter.com /thebattleye/status/918734703183659008.

Belle, Crystal. "From Jay-Z to Dead Prez: Examining Representations of Black Masculinity in Mainstream versus Underground Hip-Hop Music." *Journal of Black Studies* 45, no. 4 (2014): 287–300.

Benesch, Oleg. "Bushido: The Creation of a Martial Ethic in Late Meiji Japan." PhD diss., University of British Columbia, 2011.

Berlant, Lauren. *Cruel Optimism*. Durham, NC: Duke University Press, 2011.

Berman, Eliza. "A Comprehensive Guide to the *Ghost in the Shell* Controversy." *Time*, March 29, 2017. https://time.com/4714367/ghost-in-the-shell -controversy-scarlett-johansson/.

Bhabha, Homi. *The Location of Culture*. London: Routledge, 1994.

Blacker, Carmen. *The Catalpa Bow: A Study of Shamanistic Practices in Japan*. London: Allen & Unwin, 1986.

Blizzard Entertainment. "Hearthstone Grandmasters Asia-Pacific Ruling." Blizzard.com, October 8, 2019. https://playhearthstone.com/en-us/news/23179289/hearthstone-grandmasters-asia-pacific-ruling.

Blizzard Entertainment. "Regarding Last Weekend's Hearthstone Grandmasters Tournament." *Blizzard Entertainment News*, October 12, 2019. https://news.blizzard.com/en-us/blizzard/23185888/regarding-last-weekend-s-hearthstone-grandmasters-tournament.

Bogost, Ian. *Persuasive Games: The Expressive Power of Videogames*. Cambridge, MA: MIT Press, 2007.

Bogost, Ian. "The Quiet Revolution of *Animal Crossing*." *The Atlantic*, April 15, 2020. https://www.theatlantic.com/family/archive/2020/04/animal-crossing-isnt-escapist-its-political/610012/.

Boluk, Stephanie, and Patrick LeMieux. *Metagaming: Playing, Competing, Spectating, Cheating, Trading, Making, and Breaking Videogames*. Minneapolis: University of Minnesota Press, 2017.

Bolter, Jay David, and Richard Grusin. *Remediation: Understanding New Media*. Cambridge, MA: MIT Press, 1998.

Borges, Jose Luis. "The Garden of Forking Paths." In *Ficciones*, edited by Anthony Kerrigan, 78–101. New York: Grove Press, 1962.

Borowy, Michael, and Dal Yong Jin. "Mega-Events of the Future: The Experience Economy, the Korean Connection, and the Growth of eSport." In *Mega-Events and Globalization: Capital and Spectacle in a Changing World Order*, edited by Richard Gruneau and John Horne, 206–19. London: Routledge, 2016.

Bow, Leslie. *Racist Love: Asian Abstraction and the Pleasures of Fantasy*. Durham, NC: Duke University Press, 2021.

Bowman, Mitch. "Why the Fighting Game Community Is Color Blind." *Polygon*, February 6, 2014. https://www.polygon.com/features/2014/2/6/5361004/fighting-game-diversity.

Boylorn, M. Robin. "From Boys to Men: Hip-Hop, Hood Films, and the Performance of Contemporary Black Masculinity." *Black Camera* 8, no. 2 (2017): 287–300.

Braidotti, Rosi. "Feminist Epistemology after Postmodernism: Critiquing Science, Technology and Globalization." *Interdisciplinary Science Reviews* 32, no. 1 (2007): 65–74.

Breault, Chris. "Dick Mullen and the Miracle Plot." *Bullet Points Monthly*, November 6, 2019. https://bulletpointsmonthly.com/2019/11/06/dick-mullen-and-the-miracle-plot.

Brock, André. "Critical Technocultural Discourse Analysis." *New Media and Society* 20, no. 3 (2018): 1012–30.

Bui, Long. "Asian Roboticism: Connecting Mechanized Labor to the Automation of Work." *Perspectives on Global Development and Technology* 19, nos. 1–2 (2020): 110–26.

Burton, Antoinette, and Renisa Mawani. *Animalia: An Anti-imperial Bestiary for Our Times*. Durham, NC: Duke University Press, 2020.

Byrd, Jodi. "Beast of America: Sovereignty and the Wildness of Objects." *South Atlantic Quarterly* 117, no. 3 (2018): 599–615.

Caillois, Roger. *Man, Play, and Games*. Chicago: University of Illinois Press, 1961.

Caracciolo, Marco. "Animal Mayhem Games and Nonhuman-Oriented Thinking." *Game Studies* 21, no. 1 (2021). https://gamestudies.org/2101/articles/caracciolo.

cárdenas, micha. *Poetic Operations: Trans of Color Art in Digital Media*. Durham, NC: Duke University Press, 2021.

Castronova, Edward. *Synthetic Worlds: The Business and Culture of Online Games*. Chicago: University of Chicago Press, 2005.

Chakrabarti, Siddhartha. "From Destination to Nation and Back: The Hyperreal Journey of Incredible India." *Journal of Games and Virtual Worlds* 7, no. 2 (2015): 183–202.

Chan, Dean. "Being Played: Games Culture and Asian American Dis/Identifications." *Refractory: A Journal of Entertainment Media* 16 (2009). https://refractoryjournal.net/being-played-games-culture-and-asian-american-disidentifications-dean-chan/.

Chan, Dean. "Playing with Race: The Ethics of Racialized Representations in E-games." *International Review of Information Ethics* 4, no. 12 (2005): 24–30.

Chang, Alenda Y. *Playing Nature Ecology in Video Games*. Minneapolis: University of Minnesota Press, 2019.

Chang, Edmond Y. "Dice." In *Roll for Initiative*, edited by Suzanne Richardson and Daniel Shank Cruz. Forthcoming.

Chang, Edmond Y. "Playing Games, Practicing Utopia." *Gamers with Glasses*, September 26, 2020. https://www.gamerswithglasses.com/features/playing-games-practicing-utopia-a-life-in-tabletop-games.

Chang, Kornel. *Pacific Connections: The Making of the US-Canadian Borderlands*. Berkeley: University of California Press, 2012.

Chen, Kuan-Hsing. *Asia as Method*. Durham, NC: Duke University Press, 2010.

Chen, Mel Y. *Animacies: Biopolitics, Racial Mattering, and Queer Affect*. Durham, NC: Duke University Press, 2012.

Chen, Mel Y. "Animacy as a Sexual Device." In *The Oxford Handbook of Language and Sexuality*, edited by Kira Hall and Rusty Barrett. Oxford: Oxford University Press, 2021. https://doi.org/10.1093/oxfordhb/9780190212926.013.10.

Cheney-Lippold, John. *We Are Data: Algorithms and the Making of Our Digital Selves*. New York: New York University Press, 2018.

Chess, Shira. *Ready Player Two: Women Gamers and Designed Identity*. Minneapolis: University of Minnesota Press, 2017.

ChillTyme. "How Chinese Hackers Are Selling Cheats in *Apex Legends*." YouTube video, 3:54, posted March 5, 2019. https://www.youtube.com/watch?v=VO9p0azfAtM.

Chin, Frank, and Jeffery Paul Chan. "Racist Love." In *Seeing through Shuck*, edited by Richard Kostelanetz, 65–72. New York: Ballantine, 1972.

Cho, Margaret. "Margaret Cho—Asian Adjacent—featuring Grant Lee Phillips." YouTube video, 2:19, posted November 2, 2011. https://www.youtube.com/watch?v=8MxFYpIubeU.

Choe, Steve, and Se Young Kim. "Never Stop Playing: *StarCraft* and Asian Gamer Death." In *Techno-Orientalism: Imagining Asia in Speculative Fiction, History, and Media*, edited by David S. Roh, Betsy Huang, and Greta A. Niu, 113–24. New Brunswick, NJ: Rutgers University Press, 2015.

Chu, Seo-Young. "I, Stereotype." In *Techno-Orientalism: Imagining Asia in Speculative Fiction, History, and Media*, edited by David S. Roh, Betsy Huang, and Greta A. Niu, 76–88. New Brunswick, NJ: Rutgers University Press, 2015.

Chuh, Kandice. *The Difference Aesthetics Makes*. Durham, NC: Duke University Press, 2019.

Chun, Wendy Hui Kyong. *Control and Freedom: Power and Paranoia in the Age of Fiber Optics*. Cambridge, MA: MIT Press, 2008.

Chun, Wendy Hui Kyong. "Race and/as Technology." *Camera Obscura* 24, no. 1 (2009): 7–35.

Chun, Wendy Hui Kyong. "Race and/as Technology, or How to Do Things to Race." In *Race after the Internet*, edited by Lisa Nakamura and Peter A. Chow-White, 38–60. New York: Routledge, 2012.

Cole, Yussef. "*Mass Effect*'s Revival Reminds Us It's Time to Abolish the Space Police." *Polygon*, May 17, 2021. https://www.polygon.com/22436615/mass-effect-legendary-edition-police-ea-bioware-brooklyn-99.

Colebrook, Claire. *Understanding Deleuze*. New York: Routledge, 2002.

Condis, Megan. *Gaming Masculinity: Trolls, Fake Geeks, and the Gendered Battle for Online Culture*. Iowa City: University of Iowa Press, 2018.

Consalvo, Mia. *Atari to Zelda: Japan's Videogames in Global Contexts*. Cambridge, MA: MIT Press, 2016.

Consalvo, Mia. *Cheating: Gaining Advantage in Video Games*. Cambridge, MA: MIT Press, 2007.

Consalvo, Mia. "There Is No Magic Circle." *Games and Culture* 4, no. 4 (2009): 408–17. https://doi.org/10.1177/1555412009343575.

Consalvo, Mia, and Christopher A. Paul. *Real Games: What's Legitimate and What's Not in Contemporary Videogames*. Cambridge, MA: MIT Press, 2019.

Cook, Eli. "Rearing Children of the Market in the 'You' Decade: Choose Your Own Adventure Books and the Ascent of Free Choice in 1980s America."

Journal of American Studies 55, no. 2 (2020): 1–28. https://doi.org/10.1017/S0021875819001476.

Cox, Jeff. "Trump Says China Cheated America on Trade, but He Blames US Leaders for Letting It Happen." CNBC, November 12, 2019. https://cnbc.com/2019/11/12/trump-says-china-cheated-america-on-trade-but-he-blames-us-leaders-for-letting-it-happen.html.

Crossassaultharass. "Day 1: Sexual Harassment on Cross Assault." YouTube video, 13:35, posted February 28, 2012. https://www.youtube.com/watch?v=0SLDgPbjp0M.

Danico, Mary Yu, and Linda Trinh Vo. "'No Lattes Here': Asian American Youth and the Cyber Café Obsession." In *Asian American Youth: Culture, Identity, and Ethnicity*, edited by Jennifer Lee and Min Zhou, 177–89. New York: Routledge, 2004.

"Danny Quach." Re: Kylin, "*Apex Legends*—Chinese Player Using Aimbot / Hack." YouTube video, 3:18, posted March 4, 2019. https://www.youtube.com/watch?v=aW6fAXhZRR4.

Darling-Wolf, Fabienne. *Imagining the Global: Transnational Media and Popular Culture beyond East and West*. Ann Arbor: University of Michigan Press, 2014.

Davies, Hugh. "Spatial Politics at Play: Hong Kong Protests and Videogame Activism." DiGRA Australia Conference, February 10, 2020.

Day, Iyko. *Alien Capital: Asian Racialization and the Logic of Settler Colonial Capitalism*. Durham, NC: Duke University Press, 2016.

Deesing, Jonathan. "The South Korean Exodus to China." *RedBull Esports*, December 12, 2014. https://www.redbull.com/us-en/the-south-korean-exodus-to-china.

Delany, R. Samuel. *Times Square Red, Times Square Blue*. New York: New York University Press, 2001.

de Pommereau, Isabelle. "A First for Estonia: An Elected Black Politician." *Christian Science Monitor*, October 26, 2013. https://www.csmonitor.com/layout/set/print/World/Global-News/2013/1026/A-first-for-Estonia-an-elected-black-politician.

DerpHard. Comment on Snoobboons, "Chinese Cheater on *Apex Legends* OMFG Too First!!!!:(:(:(" Reddit, February 12, 2019. https://www.reddit.com/r/apexlegends/comments/apr77f/chinese_cheater_on_apex_legends_omfg_too_first/egqu75w/.

Diallo, David. "Hip-Hop Cats in the Cradle of Rap: Hip Hop in the Bronx." In *East Coast and West Coast*, vol. 1 of *Hip-Hop in America: A Regional Guide*, edited by Mickey Hess, 1–30. Santa Barbara, CA: Greenwood, 2020.

Donald, Dwayne. "Indigenous Métissage: A Decolonizing Research Sensibility." *International Journal of Qualitative Studies in Education* 25, no. 5 (2012): 533–55.

Dosekun, Simidele. "For Western Girls Only?" *Feminist Media Studies* 15, no. 6 (2015): 960–75.

Dower, John W. *Japan in War and Peace: Selected Essays*. New York: New Press, 1993.

Dower, John W. *War without Mercy: Race and Power in the Pacific War*. New York: Pantheon Books, 1986.

Duggan, Maeve. "Public Debates about Gaming and Gamers." Pew Research Center, December 15, 2015. https://www.pewresearch.org/internet/2015/12/15/public-debates-about-gaming-and-gamers/.

Dyer, Richard. *White*. New York: Routledge, 1997.

Dyer-Witheford, Nick, and Greig de Peuter. *Games of Empire: Global Capitalism and Video Games*. Minneapolis: University of Minnesota Press, 2009.

Eglash, Ron. "Race, Sex, and Nerds: From Black Geeks to Asian American Hipsters." *Social Text* 71, vol. 20, no. 2 (2002): 49–64.

Elias, Norbert, and Eric Dunning. *Quest for Excitement: Sport and Leisure in the Civilizing Process*. Oxford: Basil Blackwell, 1986.

Eng, David. *The Feeling of Kinship: Queer Liberalism and the Racialization of Intimacy*. Durham, NC: Duke University Press, 2010.

Eng, David. *Racial Castration: Managing Masculinity in Asian Americans*. Durham, NC: Duke University Press, 2001.

Epps, De'Angelo. "Black Lives Have Always Mattered in the Fighting Game Community." *Polygon*, June 26, 2020. https://www.polygon.com/2020/6/16/21292108/black-lives-matter-fighting-game-community-blm-fgc-majin-obama-tasty-steve.

Erzberger, Tyler. "The Gap Is Not Closing in *League of Legends*." ESPN, October 14, 2016. https://www.espn.com/esports/story/_/id/17794800/gap-not-closing-league-legends.

Evans, Adrienne, and Sarah Riley. "'He's a Total TubeCrush': Post-feminist Sensibility as Intimate Publics." *Feminist Media Studies* 18, no. 6 (2017): 1–16.

Everett, Anna. *Digital Diaspora: A Race for Cyberspace*. Albany: State University of New York Press, 2009.

Fickle, Tara. "Made in China: Gold Farming as Alternative History of Esports." *ROMchip* 3, no. 1 (2021). https://www.romchip.org/index.php/romchip-journal/article/view/132.

Fickle, Tara. *The Race Card: From Gaming Technologies to Model Minorities*. New York: New York University Press, 2019.

Fickle, Tara, and Christopher B. Patterson. "Diversity Is Not a Win-Condition." *Critical Studies in Media Communication* 39, no. 3 (2022): 211–20.

Fink, Eugen. *Play as Symbol of the World*. Bloomington: Indiana University Press, 2016.

Fisher, Mark. *Capitalist Realism: Is There No Alternative?* Winchester: Zero Books, 2009.

Fisher, Mark. "Mark Fisher | Acid Communism (Unfinished Introduction)." *Blackout ((poetr&politics))*, April 25, 2019. https://my-blackout.com/2019/04/25/mark-fisher-acid-communism-unfinished-introduction/.

Fletcher, Akil. "Esports and the Color Line: Labor, Skill, and the Exclusion of Black Players." Proceedings of the 53rd Hawaiʻi International Conference on System Sciences, 2020. https://pdfs.semanticscholar.org/638b/7405b44bfa22c0058406852ead94094aad0f.pdf.

Freeman, Elizabeth. *Time Binds: Queer Temporalities, Queer Histories*. Durham, NC: Duke University Press, 2010.

Friedman, Erica. "On Defining *Yuri*." In "Queer Female Fandom," edited by Julie Levin Russo and Eve Ng, special issue, *Transformative Works and Cultures*, no. 24 (2017). http://dx.doi.org/10.3983/twc.2017.831.

Friedman, Thomas L. *The World Is Flat: A Brief History of the Globalized World in the Twenty-First Century*. London: Allen Lane, 2005.

Frühstück, Sabine. *Colonizing Sex: Sexology and Social Control in Modern Japan*. Berkeley: University of California Press, 2003.

Frühstück, Sabine. *Uneasy Warriors: Gender, Memory, and Popular Culture in the Japanese Army*. Berkeley: University of California Press, 2007.

Fukuyama, Francis. "The End of History?" *National Interest* 16 (1989): 3–18.

Gabby Jay. "mahvel baybee!" YouTube video, 0:59, posted December 7, 2007. https://www.youtube.com/watch?v=sZZUMjoxfZA.

Galbraith, Patrick W. "Bishōjo Games: 'Techno-Intimacy' and the Virtually Human in Japan." *Game Studies* 11, no. 2 (2011). https://gamestudies.org/1102/articles/galbraith?utm_source=twitterfeed&utm_medium=twitter.

Galbraith, Patrick W. "Moe Talk: Affective Communication among Female Fans of Yaoi in Japan." In *Boys Love Manga and Beyond: History, Culture, and Community in Japan*, edited by M. McLelland, K. Nagaike, K. Suganuma, and James Welker, Kindle ed., 153–68. Jackson: University Press of Mississippi, 2015.

Galloway, Alexander R. *Gaming: Essays on Algorithmic Culture*. Minneapolis: University of Minnesota Press, 2006.

The Game Awards (@thegameawards). "Helen Hindpere is back on #TheGameAwards stage to accept award #2!" Twitter, December 12, 2019, 11:16 p.m. EST, https://twitter.com/thegameawards/status/1205340759823540224.

Ganzon, Sarah Christina. "Investing Time for Your In-Game Boyfriends and BFFs: Time as Commodity and the Simulation of Emotional Labor in *Mystic Messenger*." *Games and Culture* 14, no. 2 (2019): 139–53. https://doi.org/10.1177/1555412018793068.

Ganzon, Sarah Christina. "Making Love Not War: Female Power and the Emotional Labor of Peace in *Code: Realize—The Guardian of Rebirth* and *Princess Arthur*." In *Digital Love: Romance and Sexuality in Games*, edited by Heidi McDonald, 225–44. Boca Raton, FL: CRC Press, 2018.

Ganzon, Sarah Christina. "Sweet Solutions for Female Gamers: Cheritz, Korean Otome Games, and Global Otome Game Players." In *Digital Love: Romance and Sexuality in Games*, edited by Heidi McDonald, 37–58. Boca Raton, FL: CRC Press, 2018.

Garrett, Eric. "Hideo Kojima Discusses Death Stranding's English and Japanese Dialogue Differences." comicbook/gaming, July 8, 2019. https://comicbook .com/gaming/news/hideo-kojima-death-stranding-english-japanese -dialogue/.

Gill, Rosalind. "Postfeminist Media Culture: Elements of a Sensibility." *European Journal of Cultural Studies* 10, no. 2 (2007): 147–66.

Glas, René. *Battlefields of Negotiation: Control, Agency, and Ownership in World of Warcraft*. Amsterdam: Amsterdam University Press, 2012.

Glasspool, Lucy. "Making Masculinity: Articulations of Gender and Japaneseness in Japanese RPGs and Machinima." In *Transnational Contexts of Culture, Gender, Class, and Colonialism in Play*, edited by Alexis Pulos and S. Austin Lee, 99–125. London: Palgrave Macmillan.

Glissant, Édouard. *Poetics of Relation*. Translated by Betsy Wing. Ann Arbor: University of Michigan Press, 2010.

Goggin, Joyce. "Playbour, Farming and Leisure." *Ephemera Journal* 11 (2011): 357–68.

Goodman, Roger. "Making Majority Culture." In *A Companion to the Anthropology of Japan*, edited by Jennifer Robertson, 59–72. Malden, MA: Blackwell, 2005.

Goto-Jones, Chris. "Is *Street Fighter* a Martial Art? Virtual Ninja Theory, Ideology, and the Intentional Self-Transformation of Fighting-Gamers." *Japan Review* 29 (2016): 171–208.

Goto-Jones, Chris. "Playing with Being in Digital Asia: Gamic Orientalism and the Virtual Dōjō." *Asiascape: Digital Asia* 2, nos. 1–2 (2015): 20–56.

Gray, Kishonna L. *Intersectional Tech: Black Users in Digital Gaming*. Baton Rouge: LSU Press, 2020.

Gray, Kishonna L. *Race, Gender, and Deviance in Xbox Live: Theoretical Perspectives from the Virtual Margins*. Amsterdam: Anderson, 2014.

Gray, Kishonna L., and David J. Leonard, eds. *Woke Gaming: Digital Challenges to Oppression and Social Injustice*. Seattle: University of Washington Press, 2018.

Grayson, Nathan. "The Problem with *Far Cry 4*'s Box Art." Kotaku, May 22, 2014. https://kotaku.com/the-problem-with-far-cry-4s-box-art-1579810068.

El Greco. "Metal Gear Solid Game Script." *IGN*, August 24, 2003, last updated August 28, 2004. http://www.ign.com/faqs/2004/metal-gear-solid-game -script-506035.

Grieve, Gregory Price. "An Ethnoludography of the Game Design Industry in Kathmandu, Nepal." *Gamevironments*, no. 8 (2018). https://media.suub .uni-bremen.de/bitstream/elib/3483/1/00106967-1.pdf.

Groen, Andrew. "Why FGC Hates the Word Esports." *Penny Arcade Report*, August 2013. Accessed July 2021. https://www.penny-arcade.com/report /article/why-the-fighting-game-community-hates-the-word-esports#.

Grudge122. Comment on Snoobboons, "Chinese Cheater on *Apex Legends* OMFG Too First!!!!:(:(:(" Reddit, March 14, 2019. https://www.reddit.com/r /apexlegends/comments/apr77f/chinese_cheater_on_apex_legends_omfg _too_first/egqu75w/.

Guttmann, Allen. *From Ritual to Record: The Nature of Modern Sports*. New York: Columbia University Press, 1978.

Guttmann, Allen. *Games and Empires: Modern Sports and Cultural Imperialism*. New York: Columbia University Press, 1994.

Hall, Charlie. "Evo Online Canceled Following Accusations of Sexual Abuse against CEO." *Polygon*, July 3, 2020. https://www.polygon.com/2020/7/3 /21312536/evo-online-canceled-joey-cuellar-mr-wizard-sexual-abuse.

Haraway, Donna J. "A Cyborg Manifesto: Science, Technology, and Socialist-Feminism in the Late Twentieth Century." In *Manifestly Haraway*, by Donna J. Haraway with Cary Wolfe, 3–90. Minneapolis: University of Minnesota Press, 2016.

Harper, Todd. "'Asian Hands' and Women's Invitationals." In *The Culture of Digital Fighting Games: Performance and Practice*, 108–33. New York: Routledge, 2014.

Harper, Todd. *The Culture of Digital Fighting Games*. New York: Routledge, 2014.

Harrer, Sabine. "Casual Empire: Video Games as Neocolonial Praxis." *Open Library of Humanities* 4, no. 1 (2018). https://olh.openlibhums.org/articles /10.16995/olh.210/.

Harris, Owen, dir., and Charlie Brooker, writer. *Black Mirror*. Season 5, episode 1, "Striking Vipers." Netflix, June 5, 2019.

Hartley, Gemma. *Fed Up: Emotional Labor, Women and the Way Forward*. New York: HarperCollins, 2018.

Harvey, Alison, and Stephanie Fisher. "Everyone Can Make Games! The Postfeminist Context of Women in Digital Game Production." *Feminist Media Studies* 15, no. 4 (2014): 576–92.

Hasegawa, Kazumi. "Falling in Love with History: Japanese Girls' *Otome* Sexuality and Queering Historical Imagination." In *Playing the Past: Digital Games and the Simulation of History*, edited by Andrew B. R. Elliott and Matthew Wilhelm Kapell, 135–50. New York: Bloomsbury Academic, 2013.

Hayles, N. Katherine. "Virtual Bodies and Flickering Signifiers." *October*, no. 66 (1993): 69–91.

Hendrick, George. "The Influence of Thoreau's 'Civil Disobedience' on Gandhi's Satyagraha." *New England Quarterly* 29, no. 4 (1956): 462–71.

Hendrix, Grady. "Choose Your Own Adventure: How *The Cave of Time* Taught Us to Love Interactive Entertainment." *Slate*, February 17, 2011. https://slate.com/culture/2011/02/choose-your-own-adventure-books-how-the-cave-of-time-taught-us-to-love-interactive-entertainment.html.

Hjorth, Larissa. "Playing at Being Mobile: Gaming and Cute Culture in South Korea." *Fibreculture* 8 (2006). https://doaj.org/article/38c24dd608c746c485cc48a3a297cc6d.

Hjorth, Larissa, and Dean Chan, eds. *Gaming Cultures and Place in Asia-Pacific*. New York: Routledge, 2009.

Hoberman, John Milton. *Darwin's Athletes: How Sport Has Damaged Black America and Preserved the Myth of Race*. New York: Houghton Mifflin Harcourt, 1997.

Hoberman, John. *Mortal Engines: The Science of Performance and the Dehumanization of Sport*. Caldwell, NJ: Blackburn, 1992.

Hochschild, Arlie. *The Managed Heart: Commercialization of Human Feeling*. Berkeley: University of California Press, 1983.

Holland, Sharon P. *The Erotic Life of Racism*. Durham, NC: Duke University Press, 2012.

Horiguchi, Sachiko, and Yuki Imoto. "Mikkusu rēsu wa dō katararete kita ka: 'Hāfu' ni itaru made no gensetsu wo tadotte." In *Hāfu to wa dare ka: Jinshu konkō, media hyōshō, kōshō jissen*, edited by Koichi Iwabuchi, 55–77. Tokyo: Seikyusha, 2014.

HoSaiLei (@hkbhkese). "願榮光歸香港(動物之森版)" (Glory to Hong Kong [Animal Crossing Version]). Video, 1:56. Twitter, April 30, 2020, 5:10 a.m. EST. https://twitter.com/i/status/1255786603215073283.

Howard, Matthew Jungsuk. "Esport: Professional *League of Legends* as Cultural History." Master's thesis, University of Houston, 2018. https://uh-ir.tdl.org/handle/10657/3298.

Howard, Matthew Jungsuk. "Highway to the Golden Zone(fire): PC Bangs and Techno-Orientalism in the *StarCraft II Visual Novel*." *Journal of Games Criticism* 5, bonus issue A (January 2022). https://gamescriticism.files.wordpress.com/2023/07/howard-5-a.pdf.

"How Diverse Are Video Gamers—and the Characters They Play?" Nielsen, March 24, 2015. https://www.nielsen.com/us/en/insights/article/2015/how-diverse-are-video-gamers-and-the-characters-they-play/.

Huggins, Mike, and J. A. Mangan. *Disreputable Pleasures: Less Virtuous Victorians at Play*. Oxon, UK: Frank Cass, 2004.

Huizinga, Johan. *Homo Ludens: A Study of the Play Element in Culture*. Boston: Beacon, 1950.

Huntemann, Nina, and Matthew Thomas Payne. *Joystick Soldiers: The Politics of Play in Military Video Games*. New York: Routledge, 2010.

Hutchinson, Rachael. *Japanese Culture through Videogames*. New York: Routledge, 2019.

Hutchinson, Rachael. "Virtual Colonialism: Japan's Others in *SoulCalibur*." In *Transnational Contexts of Culture, Gender, Class, and Colonialism in Play: Video Games in East Asia*, edited by Alexis Pulos and Austin Lee, 155–78. New York: Palgrave Macmillan, 2016.

Igarashi, Yoshikuni. *Bodies of Memory: Narratives of War in Postwar Japanese Culture, 1945–1970*. Princeton, NJ: Princeton University Press, 2000.

Ishaan. "Here's Another Aksys Survey on Otome Games." *Siliconera*, October 7, 2010. http://www.siliconera.com/2010/10/07/heres-another-aksys-survey -on-otome-games/#tapqiygAeWYOX0Q8.99.

Iwabuchi, Koichi, ed. *Hāfu to wa dare ka: Jinshu konkō, media hyōshō, kōshō jissen*. Tokyo: Seikyusha, 2014.

Iwabuchi, Koichi. "Introduction." *Journal of Intercultural Studies* 35, no. 6 (2014): 621–26.

Iwabuchi, Koichi. "Lost in TransNation: Tokyo and the Urban Imaginary in the Era of Globalization." *Inter-Asia Cultural Studies* 9, no. 4 (2008): 543–56.

Iwabuchi, Koichi. *Recentering Globalization: Popular Culture and Japanese Transnationalism*. Durham, NC: Duke University Press, 2002.

Iwamura, Jane. *Virtual Orientalism: Asian Religions and American Popular Culture*. Oxford: Oxford University Press, 2011.

Jackson, Sarah J., Moya Bailey, and Brooke Foucault Welles. *#HashtagActivism: Networks of Race and Gender Justice*. Cambridge, MA: MIT Press, 2020.

James, C. L. R. *Beyond a Boundary*. 1963. Reprint, Durham, NC: Duke University Press, 2013.

Jameson, Fredric. *The Antinomies of Realism*. London: Verso, 2013.

Jameson, Fredric. *Postmodernism, or, The Cultural Logic of Late Capitalism*. Durham, NC: Duke University Press, 1989.

Joseph, Ralina. "Tyra Banks Is Fat: Reading (Post-)Racism and (Post-)Feminism in the New Millennium." *Critical Studies in Media Communication* 26, no. 3 (2009): 237–54.

Kang, Jaeho. "The Media Spectacle of a Techno-City: COVID-19 and the South Korean Experience of the State of Emergency." *Journal of Asian Studies* 79, no. 3 (2020): 589–98.

Kawai, Yuko. "Deracialised Race, Obscured Racism: Japaneseness, Western and Japanese Concepts of Race, and Modalities of Racism." *Japanese Studies* 35, no. 1 (2015): 23–47.

Kelts, Roland. *Japanamerica: How Japanese Pop Culture Has Invaded the U.S.* New York: Palgrave Macmillan, 2006.

Kijima, Yoshimasa. "The Fighting Gamer Otaku Community: What Are They 'Fighting' About?" In *Fandom Unbound: Otaku Culture in a Connected*

World, edited by Mizuko Ito, Daisuke Okabe, and Izumi Tsuji, 249–74. New Haven, CT: Yale University Press, 2012.

Kim, Dorothy, TreaAndrea M. Russworm, Corrigan Vaughan, Cassius Adair, Veronica Paredes, and T. L. Cowan. "Race, Gender, and the Technological Turn: A Roundtable on Digitizing Revolution." In "Women Digitizing Revolution," edited by Anna Everett and Guisela Latorre, special issue, *Frontiers: A Journal of Women Studies* 39, no. 1 (2018): 149–77.

Kim, Hyeshin. "Women's Games in Japan: Gendered Identity and Narrative Construction." *Theory, Culture and Society* 26, nos. 2–3 (2008): 165–88.

Kim, Ju Yon. *The Racial Mundane: Asian American Performance and the Embodied Everyday*. New York: New York University Press, 2015.

Kimura, Keisuke. "Voices of In/Visible Minority: Homogenizing Discourse of Japaneseness in *Hafu: The Mixed-Race Experience in Japan*." *Journal of Intercultural Communication Research* 50, no. 3 (2021): 254–72.

Kittaka, Marina. "*Tony Hawk's Pro Skater* and Shape-Meaning Resonance." *The Marinazone*, February 14, 2021. https://marinakittaka.com/posts/2021-02-14-Shape-Meaning-Resonance.html.

Kondo, Dorinne. *Worldmaking: Race, Performance, and the Work of Creativity*. Durham, NC: Duke University Press, 2018.

Kopfstein, Janus. "New York's Chinatown Fair Arcade Reopens, but the Game Has Changed." *The Verge*, May 7, 2012.

Koshiro, Yukiko. "Race as International Identity? 'Miscegenation' in the US Occupation of Japan and Beyond." *Amerikastudien / American Studies* 48, no. 1 (2003): 61–77.

Kovner, Sarah. *Occupying Power: Sex Workers and Servicemen in Postwar Japan*. Stanford, CA: Stanford University Press, 2012.

Kylin. "*Apex Legends*—Chinese Player Using Aimbot / Hack." YouTube video, 3:18, posted March 4, 2019. https://www.youtube.com/watch?v=aW6fAXhZRR4.

Lee, Rosa. "Becoming-Minor through Shinsengumi: A Sociology of Popular Culture as a People's Culture." Paper presented at 18th Biennial Conference of the Japanese Studies Association of Australia, Australian National University, July 8–11, 2013.

Lehr, Amanda. "For Bodily Autonomy Reasons, I Now Identify as a Corpse." *McSweeney's*, May 9, 2022. https://www.mcsweeneys.net/articles/for-bodily-autonomy-reasons-i-now-identify-as-a-corpse.

Leslie, Callum. "Riot Tighten Interregional Movement Policy for LCS Players." *Dot Esports*, August 2, 2016. https://dotesports.com/league-of-legends/news/riot-regional-residency-changes-lcs-3746.

Lew-Williams, Beth. *The Chinese Must Go: Violence, Exclusion, and the Making of the Alien in America*. Cambridge, MA: Harvard University Press, 2018.

Lin, Zhongxuan. "Contextualized Transmedia Mobilization: Media Practices and Mobilizing Structures in the Umbrella Movement." *International Journal of Communication* 11 (2017): 48–71.

Littler, Jo. *Against Meritocracy: Culture, Power and Myths of Mobility*. London: Routledge, 2018.

Lye, Colleen. *America's Asia: Racial Form and American Literature, 1893–1945*. Princeton, NJ: Princeton University Press, 2005.

Magdalinski, Tara. *Sport, Technology and Body: The Nature of Performance*. New York: Routledge, 2009.

Malkowski, Jennifer, and TreaAndrea M. Russworm. "Introduction: Identity, Representation, and Video Game Studies beyond the Politics of the Image." In *Gaming Representation: Race, Gender, and Sexuality in Video Games*, edited by Jennifer Malkowski and TreaAndrea M. Russworm, 1–16. Bloomington: Indiana University Press, 2017.

Mangan, J. A. *The Games Ethic and Imperialism: Aspects of the Diffusion of an Ideal*. London: Routledge, 1998.

Mangan, J. A. *A Sport-Loving Society: Victorian and Edwardian Middle-Class England at Play*. London: Routledge, 2006.

Mangiron, Carmen, and Minako O'Hagan. "Game Localisation: Unleashing Imagination with 'Restricted' Translation." *Journal of Specialised Translation* 6 (2006): 10–21.

Martens, Todd. "Discover the Joy of a Game That Transports You into the Mythologies of Ancient India." *Los Angeles Times*, September 10, 2020. https://www.latimes.com/entertainment-arts/story/2020-09-10/discover-the-joy-of-a-game-that-transports-you-into-the-mythologies-of-ancient-india.

Martin, Paul. "Race, Colonial History and National Identity: *Resident Evil 5* as a Japanese Game." *Games and Culture* 13, no. 6 (2018): 568–86.

Martinez, Esteban, dir. *FGC: Rise of the Fighting Game Community*. 2016.

Matheson, Calum L. *Desiring the Bomb: Communication, Psychoanalysis, and the Atomic Age*. Rhetoric, Culture, and Social Critique. Tuscaloosa: University of Alabama Press, 2019.

McCasker, Toby. "This Gay Orc Dating Sim Is All about Inclusivity and Diversity" (interview with Mitch Alexander). *Vice*, April 14, 2015. https://www.vice.com/en/article/xd7q94/orcs-are-the-immediate-future-of-gay-gaming-culture.

McGray, Douglas. "Japan's Gross National Cool." *Foreign Policy*, May–June 2002, 44–54.

McRobbie, Angela. "Post-feminism and Popular Culture." *Feminist Media Studies* 4, no. 3 (2004): 255–64.

Mehta, Uday Singh. *Liberalism and Empire: A Study in Nineteenth-Century British Liberal Thought*. Chicago: University of Chicago Press, 1999.

Meier, Sid. *Sid Meier's Memoir!—a Life in Computer Games*. Illustrated ed. New York: W. W. Norton, 2020.

Messner, Steven. "Here's Why 'Boycott Genshin Impact' Is Trending on Twitter." *PC Gamer*, April 6, 2021. https://www.pcgamer.com/heres-why-boycott-genshin-impact-is-trending-on-twitter/.

Milburn, Colin. *Mondo Nano: Fun and Games in the World of Digital Matter*. Durham, NC: Duke University Press, 2015.

Milner, Anthony, and Deborah Johnson. "The Idea of Asia." Faculty of Asian Studies, Australian National University. November 22, 2000. https://openresearch-repository.anu.edu.au/bitstream/1885/41891/1/idea.html.

Miru MGS. "Miru *Metal Gear Solid*." YouTube video, 4:15:32, posted January 11, 2015. https://www.youtube.com/watch?v=erTgzZPW94I&t=4207s.

Miru MGS. "Miru *Metal Gear Solid 2 Sons of Liberty*." YouTube video, 5:49:48, posted February 23, 2015. https://www.youtube.com/watch?v=1WwlXHezteU.

Miru MGS. "Miru *Metal Gear Solid 4 Guns of the Patriots*." YouTube video, 7:57:32, posted January 12, 2015. https://www.youtube.com/watch?v=_fRVftmNanM.

Mondal, Poonam. "Gurugram, Bangalore and Pune Have the Potential to Become a GPO Hub: Lakshya Digital." *AnimationXpress*, June 29, 2020. http://www.animationxpress.com/latest-news/gurugram-bangalore-and-pune-have-the-potential-to-become-a-gpo-hub-lakshya-digital/.

Monique, Rhea "Ashelia." "Riot Announces New Rules about Regional Movement." *RedBull Esports*, September 6, 2014. https://www.redbull.com/us-en/riot-announces-new-rules-about-regional-movement.

Montgomery, R. A. *The Abominable Snowman*. Waitsfield, VT: Chooseco, 1982.

Moore, Keita. "The Game's the Thing: A Cultural Studies Approach to War Memory, Gender, and Politics in Japanese Videogames." Master's thesis, University of Hawai'i at Mānoa, 2017.

Morley, David, and Kevin Robins. *Spaces of Identity: Global Media, Electronic Landscapes, and Cultural Boundaries*. New York: Routledge, 1995.

Morris, Lucy. "Love Transcends All (Geographical) Boundaries: The Global Lure of Romance Historical Otome Games and the Shinsengumi." In *Digital Love: Romance and Sexuality in Games*, edited by Heidi McDonald, 253–63. Boca Raton, FL: CRC Press, 2018.

Morse, Margaret. *Virtualities: Television, Media Art, Cyberculture*. Bloomington: Indiana University Press, 1998.

Mukherjee, Souvik. *Videogames and Postcolonialism: Empire Plays Back*. Basingstoke, UK: Palgrave Macmillan, 2017.

Mukherjee, Souvik. "Vishnu and the Videogame." In *Proceedings: 6th Philosophy of Computer Games Conference*, 29–31. ArsGames, January 2012.

Muñoz, José Esteban. *Cruising Utopia: The Then and There of Queer Futurity*. New York: New York University Press, 2009.

Muñoz, José Esteban. *The Sense of Brown*. Durham, NC: Duke University Press, 2020.

Murdoch, Julian. "Hatoful Boyfriend." Gamers with Jobs, February 4, 2014. https://www.gamerswithjobs.com/node/1016261.

Murray, Janet Horowitz. *Hamlet on the Holodeck: The Future of Narrative in Cyberspace*. Cambridge, MA: MIT Press, 2017.

Murray, Soraya. "Landscapes of Empire in *Metal Gear Solid V: The Phantom Pain*." *Critical Inquiry* 45, no. 1 (2018): 168–98.

Murray, Soraya. *On Video Games: The Visual Politics of Race, Gender and Space*. London: I. B. Tauris, 2017.

Musser, Amber Jamilla. *Sensual Excess: Queer Femininity and Brown Jouissance*. New York: New York University Press, 2018.

Myers, Ramon H., and Mark R. Peattie, eds. *The Japanese Colonial Empire, 1895–1945*. Princeton, NJ: Princeton University Press, 1984.

Nakagawa, Daichi. *Gendai gēmu zenshi: Bunmei no yūgi shikan kara* (*A Complete History of Contemporary Games: A Historical View of Ludic Civilization*). Tokyo: Hayakawa Shobō, 2016.

Nakamura, Lisa. "Afterword: Racism, Sexism, and Gaming's Cruel Optimism." In *Race, Gender and Sexuality in Videogames*, edited by Jennifer Malkowski and TreaAndrea M. Russworm, 245–50. Bloomington: Indiana University Press, 2017.

Nakamura, Lisa. *Cybertypes: Race, Ethnicity, and Identity on the Internet*. New York: Routledge, 2002.

Nakamura, Lisa. *Digitizing Race: Visual Cultures of the Internet*. Minneapolis: University of Minnesota Press, 2008.

Nakamura, Lisa. "Don't Hate the Player, Hate the Game: The Racialization of Labor in *World of Warcraft*." *Critical Studies in Media Communication* 26, no. 2 (2009): 128–44.

Nakamura, Lisa. "'It's a Nigger in Here! Kill the Nigger!': User-Generated Media Campaigns against Racism, Sexism, and Homophobia in Digital Games." In *The International Encyclopedia of Media Studies: Media Studies Futures*, edited by Kelly Gates, 1–15. Hoboken, NJ: Blackwell, 2013.

Nakamura, Lisa. "Race in/for Cyberspace: Identity Tourism and Racial Passing on the Internet." *Works and Days* 13, nos. 1–2 (1995): 181–93.

Napier, Susan. *From Impressionism to Anime: Japan as Fantasy and Fan Cult in the Mind of the West*. New York: Palgrave Macmillan, 2007.

NeoGamer—the Video Game Archive. "Behind the Scenes—Death Stranding [Making of]." YouTube video, 7:00, posted December 1, 2009. https://www.youtube.com/watch?v=faatWOs2c5c.

Nerds on Hip-Hop. "Nerds on Hip-Hop: Bridging Anime and Hip-Hop Panel at Anime NYC 2017." YouTube video, 34:49, posted November 25, 2017. https://www.youtube.com/watch?v=U8bJZm44cWA.

Ng, Benjamin Wai-ming. "*Street Fighter* and *The King of Fighters* in Hong Kong: A Study of Cultural Consumption and Localization of Japanese Games in an Asian Context." *Game Studies* 6, no. 1 (2006). http://gamestudies.org/0601/articles/ng.

Nguyen, Mai. "Would You Date a Bird? Interview with *Hatoful Boyfriend* Creators." Asia Pacific Arts, February 21, 2016. https://asiapacificarts.org/2016/02/21/would-you-date-a-bird-interview-with-hatoful-boyfriend-creators/.

Nguyen, Tan Hoang. *A View from the Bottom*. Durham, NC: Duke University Press, 2014.

Nguyen, Viet Thanh. "The Remasculinization of Chinese America: Race, Violence, and the Novel." *American Literary History* 12, nos. 1–2 (2000): 130–57.

Nielsen. "How Diverse Are Video Gamers—and the Characters They Play?" Last modified March 24, 2015. https://www.nielsen.com/us/en/insights/article/2015/how-diverse-are-video-gamers-and-the-characters-they-play/.

Nishime, LeiLani. *Undercover Asian: Multiracial Asian Americans in Visual Culture*. Urbana: University of Illinois Press, 2014.

Noon, Derek, and Nick Dyer-Witheford. "Sneaking Mission: Late Imperial America and *Metal Gear Solid*." In *Utopic Dreams and Apocalyptic Fantasies: Critical Approaches to Researching Video Game Play*, edited by J. Talmadge Wright, David G. Embrick, and András Lukács, 73–95. Lanham, MD: Rowman and Littlefield, 2010.

NYU Game Center. "Naomi Clark: Why Tom Nook Symbolizes Village Debt in 18th Century Japan." YouTube video, 5:44, posted March 27, 2020. https://www.twitch.tv/videos/575962902.

Okano, Kaori, and Yoshio Sugimoto, eds. *Rethinking Japanese Studies: Eurocentrism and the Asia-Pacific Region*. New York: Routledge, 2018.

Ong, Alexis. "*Animal Crossing: New Horizons* Is Fast Becoming a New Way for Hong Kong Protesters to Fight for Democracy." *USgamer*, April 1, 2020. https://www.usgamer.net/articles/animal-crossing-new-horizons-is-fast-becoming-a-new-way-for-hong-kong-protesters-to-fight-for-democracy.

Orr, James Joseph. *The Victim as Hero: Ideologies of Peace and National Identity in Postwar Japan*. Honolulu: University of Hawai'i Press, 2001.

Osborn, Alex. "An Interview with Dir. Mamoru Oshii on the Live-Action Adaptation of *Ghost in the Shell*." [In Japanese.] IGN Japan, March 22, 2017. https://jp.ign.com/ghost-in-the-shell-live-action-movie/12278/news/.

Palumbo-Liu, David. *Asian/American: Historical Crossings of a Racial Frontier*. Stanford, CA: Stanford University Press, 1999.

Pande, Rukmini. *Squee from the Margins: Fandom and Race*. Minneapolis: University of Minnesota Press, 2018.

Pang, Laikwan. "Retheorizing the Social: The Use of Social Media in Hong Kong's Umbrella Movement." *Social Text* 35, no. 3 (2017): 71–94.

Park, Hyungji. "Representing Seoul." *Wasafiri* 33, no. 4 (2018): 20–26.

Park, Jane Chi Hyun. *Yellow Future: Oriental Style in Hollywood Cinema*. Minneapolis: University of Minnesota Press, 2010.

Parkin, Simon. "Hideo Kojima: 'Metal Gear Questions US Dominance of the World.'" *The Guardian*, July 18, 2014. https://www.theguardian.com/technology/2014/jul/18/hideo-kojima-interview-metal-gear-solid-phantom-pain.

Patterson, Christopher B. "Asian Americans and Digital Games." In *Oxford Research Encyclopedia of Literature*, July 30, 2018. https://oxfordre.com/literature/view/10.1093/acrefore/9780190201098.001.0001/acrefore-9780190201098-e-859.

Patterson, Christopher B. "Making Queer Asiatic Worlds: Performance and Racial Interaction in North American Visual Novels." *American Literature* 94, no. 1 (2022): 17–47.

Patterson, Christopher B. *Open World Empire: Race, Erotics, and the Global Rise of Video Games*. New York: New York University Press, 2020.

Patterson, Christopher B. "Role-Playing the Multiculturalist Umpire: Loyalty and War in BioWare's *Mass Effect* Series." *Games and Culture* 10, no. 3 (2015): 207–28.

Patterson, Christopher B. *Transitive Cultures: Anglophone Literature of the Transpacific*. New Brunswick, NJ: Rutgers University Press, 2018.

Paul, Christopher A. *The Toxic Meritocracy of Videogames: Why Gaming Culture Is the Worst*. Minneapolis: University of Minnesota Press, 2018.

Pearson, Natalie Obiko. "This Is the Anti-Asian Hate Crime Capital of North America." *Bloomberg*, May 7, 2021. https://www.bloomberg.com/features/2021-vancouver-canada-asian-hate-crimes/.

Penix-Tadsen, Phillip. *Video Games and the Global South*. Pittsburgh: Carnegie Mellon University Press, 2019.

Phillips, Amanda. *Gamer Trouble: Feminist Confrontations in Digital Culture*. New York: New York University Press, 2020.

Phillips, Amanda. "Shooting to Kill: Headshots, Twitch Reflexes, and the Mechropolitics of Video Games." *Games and Culture* 13, no. 2 (2018): 136–52.

Picard, Martin. "The Foundation of Geemu: A Brief History of Early Japanese Video Games." *Game Studies* 13, no. 2 (2013). http://gamestudies.org/1302/articles/picard.

Picard, Martin, and Jérémie Pelletier-Gagnon. "Geemu, Media Mix, and the State of Japanese Video Game Studies." *Kinephanos* 5, no. 1 (2015). http://www.kinephanos.ca/2015/introduction-geemu-media-mix-en/.

Qiu, Jack Linchuan. *Goodbye iSlave: A Manifesto for Digital Abolition*. Urbana: University of Illinois Press, 2017.

Quinn, Zoë. *Crash Override: How Gamergate (Nearly) Destroyed My Life, and How We Can Win the Fight against Online Hate*. New York: PublicAffairs, 2017.

random_user_1987. "The real world inspirations of the countries in Disco Elysium?" Reddit, January 16, 2020. https://www.reddit.com/r/DiscoElysium /comments/eprvi8/the_real_world_inspirations_of_the_countries_in/.

Reddy, Chandan. *Freedom with Violence*. Durham, NC: Duke University Press, 2011.

Reed, Aaron A., John Murray, and Anastasia Salter. *Adventure Games: Playing the Outsider*. New York: Bloomsbury, 2020.

Reuters. "Timeline: Key Dates for Hong Kong Extradition Bill and Protests." June 30, 2019. https://www.reuters.com/article/us-hongkong-extradition -timeline/timeline-key-dates-for-hong-kong-extradition-bill-and-protests -idUSKCN1TW14D.

Rich, Makoto. "As Coronavirus Spreads, So Does Anti-Chinese Sentiment." *New York Times*, January 30, 2020. https://www.nytimes.com/2020/01/30 /world/asia/coronavirus-chinese-racism.html.

Riot Games. *"League of Legends" Championship Series 2015 Season Official Rules*. January 8, 2015. Accessed through *Gamepedia*. https://lol .gamepedia.com/File:LCS_2015_Rulebook.pdf.

Rivera, Takeo. *Model Minority Masochism: Performing the Cultural Politics of Asian American Masculinity*. New York: Oxford University Press, 2022.

Rivera, Takeo. "Ordering a New World Orientalist Biopower in *World of Warcraft: Mists of Pandaria*." In *The Routledge Companion to Asian American Media*, edited by Lori Kido Lopez and Vincent N. Pham, 195–208. New York: Routledge, 2017.

Robertson, Jennifer. "Blood Talks: Eugenic Modernity and the Creation of New Japanese." *History and Anthropology* 13, no. 3 (2002): 191–216.

Roh, David S., Betsy Huang, and Greta A. Niu. "Technologizing Orientalism: An Introduction." In *Techno-Orientalism: Imagining Asia in Speculative Fiction, History, and Media*, edited by David S. Roh, Betsy Huang, and Greta A. Niu, 1–19. New Brunswick, NJ: Rutgers University Press, 2015.

Roh, David S., Betsy Huang, and Greta A. Niu. *Techno-Orientalism: Imagining Asia in Speculative Fiction, History, and Media*. New Brunswick, NJ: Rutgers University Press, 2015.

Roof, Judith. "Sex and the Single Nerd: The Schizo Saga of Genius, and Finally Getting Some." In *The Year's Work in Nerds, Wonks, and Neocons*, edited by Jonathan P. Eburne and Benjamin Schreier, 195–222. Bloomington: Indiana University Press, 2017.

Roth, Martin. *Thought-Provoking Play: Political Philosophies in Science Fictional Videogame Spaces from Japan*. Pittsburgh: Carnegie Mellon University Press, 2018.

Roy, Samya Brata. *Games Studies India Adda Talk #7: Samya Brata Roy*. Game Studies India Adda, 2021. Film. https://www.youtube.com/watch?v=Kox_vg3OhrM.

RShuman. "Disco Elysium: Interview of Jullian Champenois, Kim Katsuragi's Voice Actor." French Stranding, August 12, 2020. https://frenchstranding.fr/disco-elysium-interview-of-jullian-champenois-kim-katsuragis-voice-actor.

Ruberg, Bo. "Empathy and Its Alternatives: Deconstructing the Rhetoric of 'Empathy' in Video Games." *Communication, Culture and Critique* 13, no. 1 (2020): 54–71.

Ruberg, Bo. *The Queer Games Avant-Garde*. Durham, NC: Duke University Press, 2020.

Ruberg, Bo. *Video Games Have Always Been Queer*. New York: New York University Press, 2019.

Russell, John G. "Replicating the White Self and Other: Skin Color, Racelessness, Gynoids, and the Construction of Whiteness in Japan." *Japanese Studies* 37, no. 1 (2017): 23–48.

Russell, Legacy. *Glitch Feminism: A Manifesto*. London: Verso, 2020.

Russworm, TreaAndrea. "A Call to Action for Video Game Studies in an Age of Reanimated White Supremacy." *Velvet Light Trap*, no. 81 (2018): 73–77.

Said, Edward. *Orientalism: Western Concepts of the Orient*. New York: Pantheon, 1978.

Said, Edward. *Representations of the Intellectual: The 1993 Reith Lectures*. London: Vintage, 1994.

Salter, Anastasia, Bridget Blodgett, and Anne Sullivan. "'Just Because It's Gay?': Transgressive Design in Queer Coming of Age Visual Novels." In *Proceedings of the Foundations of Digital Games (FDG '18)*, 1–9. New York: ACM, 2018. https://doi.org/10.1145/3235765.3235778.

Santosx07. "Death Stranding—Prologue All Cutscenes." YouTube video, 34:49, posted November 11, 2019. https://www.youtube.com/watch?v=AUGQi6egMHw.

Saturday Night Live. "E-Sports Reporter—SNL." YouTube video, 5:15, posted October 26, 2019. https://www.youtube.com/watch?v=DlnwZzK2Ngo.

Scheiding, Ryan. "Zombies, Vaults, and Violence: Collective Memory and the Representation of Atomic Fears in Video Games." PhD diss., Concordia University, 2021.

Seaton, Philip A. *Japan's Contested War Memories: The "Memory Rifts" in Historical Consciousness of World War II*. New York: Routledge, 2007.

Shah, Nayan. *Contagious Divides: Epidemics and Race in San Francisco's Chinatown*. Berkeley: University of California Press, 2001.

Shapiro, Michael J. *The Political Sublime*. Thought in the Act. Durham, NC: Duke University Press, 2018.

Sharif, Solmaz, and David Naimon. "Between the Covers Solmaz Sharif Interview." *Tinhouse*, March 3, 2022. https://tinhouse.com/transcript/between-the-covers-solmaz-sharif-interview/.

Shaw, Adrienne. *Gaming at the Edge: Sexuality and Gender at the Margins of Gamer Culture*. Minneapolis: University of Minnesota Press, 2015.

Shaw, Adrienne. "How Do You Say Gamer in Hindi? Exploratory Research on the Indian Digital Game Industry and Culture." In *Gaming Globally*, edited by Nina B. Huntemann and Ben Aslinger, 183–201. New York: Palgrave Macmillan, 2013. https://link.springer.com/chapter/10.1057/9781137006332_13.

Shaw, Adrienne. "What Is Video Game Culture? Cultural Studies and Game Studies." *Games and Culture* 5, no. 4 (2010): 403–24.

Shibusawa, Naoko. "Where Is the Reciprocity? Notes on Solidarity from the Field." *Journal of Asian American Studies* 25, no. 2 (2022): 261–82.

Shields, Duncan. "Thorin's Thoughts—Koreans Would Dominate any Esports Game." YouTube video, 24:49, posted January 15, 2015. https://youtu.be/00LjRaBtxcs.

Shields, Duncan. "The Thorin Treatment—Team Houses and Burn Out." *Dot Esports*, June 15, 2016. https://dotsports.com/league-of-legends/news/the-thorin-treatment-team-houses-and-burn-out-5837.

Sicart, Miguel. "Against Procedurality." *Game Studies* 11, no. 3 (2011).

Sicart, Miguel. *The Ethics of Computer Games*. Cambridge, MA: MIT Press, 2009.

Singh, Juliette. *Unthinking Mastery: Dehumanism and Decolonial Entanglements*. Durham, NC: Duke University Press, 2017.

Siliconera. "Aksys Roundtable Interview Pt. 1: About 999, Anime Expo, and Choosing Games" and "Aksys Roundtable Interview Pt. 2: BlazBlue Vita, Visual Novels, and E3 Picks." *Siliconera*, June 21–22, 2011. https://www.siliconera.com/aksys-roundtable-interview-pt-1-the-part-about-999-anime-expo-and-choosing-games/.

Siliconera. "On Bringing Hakuoki: Demon of the Fleeting Blossom Overseas." *Siliconera*, July 11, 2011. https://www.siliconera.com/on-bringing-hakuoki-demon-of-the-fleeting-blossom-overseas/.

Skeggs, Beverly. "Values beyond Value? Is Anything beyond the Logic of Capital?" *British Journal of Sociology* 65, no. 1 (2014): 1–20.

Skolnik, Michael Ryan, and Steven Conway. "Tusslers, Beatdowns, and Brothers: A Sociohistorical Overview of Video Game Arcades and the *Street Fighter* Community." *Games and Culture* 14, nos. 7–8 (2019): 742–68.

Snoobboons. "Chinese Cheater on *Apex Legends* OMFG Too First!!!!:(:(:(" Reddit, February 12, 2019. https://www.reddit.com/r/apexlegends/comments/apr77f/chinese_cheater_on_apex_legends_omfg_too_first/egqu75w/.

"South Asia's First Triple-A Game." *Prodigi Interactive / Gaming*, February 28, 2021. http://prodigi.lk/gaming.html.

Spariosu, Mihai I. *Dionysus Reborn: Play and the Aesthetic Dimension in Modern Philosophical and Scientific Discourse*. Ithaca, NY: Cornell University Press, 1989.

Spigel, Lynn. "Postfeminist Nostalgia for a Prefeminist Future." *Screen* 54, no. 2 (2013): 270–78.

Stang, Sarah. "Big Daddies and Broken Men: Father-Daughter Relationships in Video Games." *Loading* 10, no. 16 (2017): 162–74.

Stanley, Eric A. *Atmospheres of Violence: Structuring Antagonism and the Trans/Queer Ungovernable*. Durham, NC: Duke University Press, 2021.

Steinberg, Marc. *Anime's Media Mix: Franchising Toys and Characters in Japan*. Minneapolis: University of Minnesota Press, 2012.

Steinkuehler, Constance. "The Mangle of Play." *Games and Culture* 1, no. 3 (2006): 199–213.

Steltenpohl, C. N., J. Reed, and C. B. Keys. "Do Others Understand Us? Fighting Game Community Member Perceptions of Others' Views of the FGC." *Global Journal of Community Psychology Practice* 9, no. 1 (2018): 1–21.

Studio Incendo (@Studioincendo). "This is how #hongkong ppl spend our time during coronavirus lockdown—villain hitting in #animalcrossing, the villain is #CarrieLam, the worst governor in #hongkong history." Twitter, April 1, 2020. https://twitter.com/i/status/1245414753058426881. Page no longer available.

Sugawa-Shimada, Akiko. "Rekijo, Pilgrimage and 'Pop-Spiritualism': Popculture-Induced Heritage Tourism of/for Young Women." *Japan Forum* 27, no. 1 (2015): 37–58.

Suits, Bernard Herbert. *The Grasshopper: Games, Life, and Utopia*. Toronto: University of Toronto Press, 1978.

Suzuki, Midori. "The Possibilities of Research on 'Fujoshi' in Japan." In "Transnational Boys' Love Fan Studies," special issue, *Transformative Works and Cultures*, no. 12 (2013): http://dx.doi.org/10.3983/twc.2013.0462.

Táíwò, Olúfémi. "Being-in-the-Room Privilege: Elite Capture and Epistemic Deference." *The Philosopher* 108, no. 4 (2020): 61–69. https://www.thephilosopher1923.org/post/being-in-the-room-privilege-elite-capture-and-epistemic-deference.

Taylor, Diana. *The Archive and the Repertoire: Performing Cultural Memory in the Americas*. Durham, NC: Duke University Press, 2003.

Taylor, Emily. "Dating-Simulation Games: Leisure and Gaming of Youth Japanese Culture." *Southeast Review of Asian Studies* 29 (2007): 192–208.

Taylor, Nicholas. "Kinaesthetic Masculinity and the Prehistory of Esports." *ROMchip* 3, no. 1 (2021). https://romchip.org/index.php/romchip-journal/article/view/131.

Taylor, Nicholas, and Jessica Elam. "'People Are Robots, Too': Expert Gaming as Autoplay." *Journal of Gaming and Virtual Worlds* 10, no. 3 (2018): 243–60.

Taylor, Nicholas, and Bryce Stout. "Gender and the Two-Tiered System of Collegiate Esports." *Critical Studies in Media Communication* 37, no. 5 (2020): 451–65.

Taylor, T. L. *Raising the Stakes: E-Sports and the Professionalization of Computer Gaming*. Cambridge, MA: MIT Press, 2012.

Taylor, T. L. *Watch Me Play: Twitch and the Rise of Game Live Streaming*. Princeton, NJ: Princeton University Press, 2018.

Team Coco. "Norman Reedus and Conan on Their Roles in 'Death Stranding.'" YouTube video, 3:00. Posted March 11, 2020. https://www.youtube.com/watch?v=DhoTxTtd8jg.

Teasley, Martell, and David Ikard. "Barack Obama and the Politics of Race: The Myth of Postracism in America." *Journal of Black Studies* 40, no. 3 (2010): 411–25.

Tennyson, Charles Mar. "They Taught the World to Play." *Victorian Studies* 2, no. 3 (1959): 211–22.

Thapliyal, Adesh. "How 'Raji: An Ancient Epic' Falls into the Indian Far-Right's Trap." *Vice*, October 27, 2020. https://www.vice.com/en/article/m7ajbv/raji-ancient-indian-epic-far-right-hindu-nationalism.

TheMainManSWE. "Knee Mauled 6–0 by Pakistani Player." YouTube video, 11:52, posted October 14, 2018. https://www.youtube.com/watch?v=ICqK37g0zuM.

theScore eSports. "The Great Korean Exodus: How Huge Chinese Contracts Gave Us LoL's Craziest Offseason Ever." YouTube video, 9:37, posted November 29, 2018. https://www.youtube.com/watch?v=olpBaV6Eavo.

theScore eSports. "What Is the FGC? How Hype, Sweat and Tears Saved Gaming's Oldest Scene." YouTube video, 12:15, posted July 28, 2019. https://www.youtube.com/watch?v=TY176IOvS_c.

Tobin, Joseph, ed. *Pikachu's Global Adventure: The Rise and Fall of Pokémon*. Durham, NC: Duke University Press, 2004.

Todd, Isaac. "Skullgirls Lead Designer Makes 'I Can't Breathe' Joke on Stream to 13 Seconds of Silence." *thegamer.com*, June 5, 2020. https://www.thegamer.com/skullgirls-lead-designer-i-cant-breathe-joke-twitch-stream/.

Tolkien, J. R. R. *The Letters of J. R. R. Tolkien*. Edited by Humphrey Carpenter. New York: HarperCollins, 2000.

Tosca, Susana. "Appropriating the Shinsengumi: *Hakuoki* Fan Fiction as Transmedial/Transcultural Exploration." In *Transmedia in the Asia and* the Pacific: Industry, Practice and Transcultural Dialogue, edited by Filippo Gilardi and Celia Lam, 157–80. New York: Palgrave Macmillan, 2021.

Trinh T. Minh-ha. "The Plural Void: Barthes and Asia." Translated by Stanley Gray. *SubStance* 11, no. 3 (1982): 41–50.

Tripathy, Prabhash Ranjan. "Playing Cyborg: A Study of the Gamer in the Video Game Parlours of Delhi and Mussoorie." MPhil diss., Jawaharlal Nehru University, 2017.

Tsing, Anna Lowenhaupt. *The Mushroom at the End of the World*. Princeton, NJ: Princeton University Press, 2015.

Tsuji, Izumi. "What Are Train Otaku? At the Bottom of the Social Ladder of Boys' School Culture." In *Fandom Unbound: Otaku Culture in a Connected World*, edited by Mizuko Ito, Daisuke Okabe, and Izumi Tsuji, 3–29. New Haven, CT: Yale University Press, 2012.

Tuan, Mia. *Forever Foreigners or Honorary Whites? The Asian Ethnic Experience Today*. New Brunswick, NJ: Rutgers University Press, 1998.

Tufekci, Zeynep. *Twitter and Tear Gas: The Power and Fragility of Networked Protest*. New Haven, CT: Yale University Press, 2017.

Turay, Abdul. "What's Up with the People Who Are in Charge of Immigration?" *Estonian World*, November 19, 2013. https://estonianworld.com/opinion /cut-whats-people-charge-immigration/.

u/batture. "It would be such a shame if Mei from *Overwatch* became a pro-democracy symbol and got Blizzard's games banned in China." Reddit, October 8, 2019. https://www.reddit.com/r/HongKong/comments/df2rz7 /it_would_be_such_a_shame_if_mei_from_overwatch/.

u/Emilyx666. "Black Lives Matter!" Reddit, June 2, 2020. https://www.reddit .com/r/AnimalCrossing/comments/gvg5t7/black_lives_matter/.

Ueno, Toshiya. "Techno-Orientalism and Media Tribalism: On Japanese Animation and Rave Culture." *Third Text* 47 (1999): 95–106.

Uperesa, Lisa. *Gridiron Capital: How American Football Became a Samoan Game*. Durham, NC: Duke University Press, 2022.

US Arms Control and Disarmament Agency. *Documents on Disarmament*. Washington, DC: US Arms Control and Disarmament Agency, 1968.

Vanderhoef, John. "Casual Threats: The Feminization of Casual Video Games." *Ada* 6, no. 2 (2013). https://adanewmedia.org/2013/06/issue2-vanderhoef/.

"Video Game Industry Statistics, Trends and Data in 2021." *We PC*, June 12, 2021. https://www.wepc.com/news/video-game-statistics/.

Voorhees, Gerald. "Neoliberal Masculinity: The Government of Play and Masculinity in eSports." In *Playing to Win: Sports, Videogames, and the Culture of Play*, 63–91. Bloomington: Indiana University Press, 2015.

Voorhees, Gerald. "Neo-liberal Multiculturalism in *Mass Effect*: The Government of Difference in Digital RPGs." In *Dungeons, Dragons, and Digital*

Denizens: The Digital Role-Playing Game, edited by Gerald A. Voorhees, Joshua Call, and Katie Whitlock, 259–77. London: Bloomsbury, 2012.

Walker, Brett L. *The Conquest of Ainu Lands: Ecology and Culture in Japanese Expansion 1590–1800*. Berkeley: University of California Press, 2001.

Walker, Ian. "Former Evo Champion Banned from Multiple Fighting Game Events after Racist Tweet." Kotaku, June 6, 2020. https://kotaku.com/former-evo -champion-banned-from-multiple-fighting-game-1844059754.

Wark, McKenzie. *Gamer Theory*. Cambridge, MA: Harvard University Press, 2007.

Weisenfeld, Gennifer S. *Imaging Disaster: Tokyo and the Visual Culture of Japan's Great Earthquake of 1923*. Asia: Local Studies / Global Themes 22. Berkeley: University of California Press, 2012.

Whaley, Benjamin. "Beyond 8-Bit: Trauma and Social Relevance in Japanese Video Games." PhD diss., University of British Columbia, 2016.

Wildt, Lars de, Thomas H. Apperley, Justin Clemens, Robbie Fordyce, and Souvik Mukherjee. "(Re-)Orienting the Videogame Avatar." *Games and Culture* 15, no. 8 (2019): 962–81.

Williams, Dmitri. "A Brief Social History of Game Play." In *Playing Computer Games: Motives, Responses, and Consequences*, edited by Peter Vorderer and Jennings Bryant, 229–47. Mahwah, NJ: Lawrence Erlbaum Associates, 2006.

Williams, John. "*Techne-Zen* and the Spiritual Quality of Global Capitalism." *Critical Inquiry* 38, no. 1 (2011): 17–70.

Wilson, Cameron. "AOC Is Sharing Pears with Randoms on *Animal Crossing* Because This Is Who We Are Now." *BuzzFeed News*, May 7, 2020. https:// www.buzzfeed.com/cameronwilson/alexandria-ocasio-cortez-animal -crossing.

Wong, Joshua (@joshuawongcf). "It's essential for HKers to maintain momentum & raise global awareness. Even though Gov has abused the coronavirus measures to suppress any form of protest, we will try every means to call for changes. #AnimalCrossingNewHorizons is one of the means for us." Twitter, May 20, 2020, 12:20 a.m. EST. https://twitter.com/joshuawongcf /status/1262961248360161281.

Wong, Joshua (@joshuawongcf). "This is what we do in #AnimalCrossing . . . maybe it's why these people are so anxious to go back to the game!!" Twitter, April 10, 2020, 2:43 a.m. EST. https://twitter.com/joshuawongcf /status/1248501778703761408?s=20.

Wong, Mou-Lan. "The Garden of Living Paths: Interactive Narratives in Global Geek Culture." In *Digitalizing the Global Text: Philosophy, Literature, and Culture*, edited by Paul Allen Miller, 103–25. Columbia: University of South Carolina Press, 2020.

Wood, Andrea. "Boys' Love Anime and Queer Desires in Convergence Culture: Transnational Fandom, Censorship and Resistance." *Journal of*

Graphic Novels and Comics 4, no. 1 (2013): 44–63. https://doi.org/10.1080/21504857.2013.784201.

xzacc91. Comment on Snoobboons, "Chinese Cheater on *Apex Legends* OMFG Too First!!!!:(:(:(" Reddit, February 25, 2019. https://www.reddit.com/r/apexlegends/comments/apr77f/chinese_cheater_on_apex_legends_omfg_too_first/egqu75w/.

Yamamoto, Atsuhisa. "'Hāfu' no shintai hyōshō ni okeru danseisei to jinshuka no porichikusu." In *Hāfu to wa dare ka: Jinshu konkō, media hyōshō, kōshō jissen*, edited by Koichi Iwabuchi, 114–42. Tokyo: Seikyusha, 2014.

Yamashiro, Jane H. "Racialized National Identity Construction in the Ancestral Homeland: Japanese American Migrants in Japan." *Ethnic and Racial Studies* 34, no. 9 (2011): 1502–21.

Yamashiro, Jane H. "The Social Construction of Race and Minorities in Japan." *Sociology Compass* 7, no. 2 (2013): 147–61.

Yang, Robert. "'If You Walk in Someone Else's Shoes, Then You've Taken Their Shoes': Empathy Machines as Appropriation Machines." *Radiator Design* (blog), April 5, 2017. https://www.blog.radiator.debacle.us/2017/04/if-you-walk-in-someone-elses-shoes-then.html.

Yang, Robert. "Liner Notes: *Intimate, Infinite* (Part 1)." *Radiator Design* (blog), last updated August 26, 2014. https://www.blog.radiator.debacle.us/2014/08/liner-notes-intimate-infinite-part-1.html.

Yang, Robert. "Liner Notes: *Intimate, Infinite* (Part 2)." *Radiator Design* (blog), last updated September 12, 2014. https://www.blog.radiator.debacle.us/2014/09/liner-notes-intimate-infinite-part-2-on.html.

Yano, Christine Reiko. *Pink Globalization: Hello Kitty's Trek across the Pacific.* Durham, NC: Duke University Press, 2013.

Ye, Josh. "China Has Its Own Hong Kong Protest Game That Lets You Beat Up Activists." *South China Morning Post*, December 6, 2019. https://www.scmp.com/abacus/games/article/3040864/china-has-its-own-hong-kong-protest-game-lets-you-beat-activists.

Ye, Josh. "Hong Kong Protesters and Mainland Gamers Clash in *Grand Theft Auto V* Online." *South China Morning Post*, December 23, 2019. https://www.scmp.com/abacus/games/article/3043211/hong-kong-protesters-and-mainland-gamers-clash-grand-theft-auto-v.

Ye, Joshua. "A New Steam Game Lets You Fight as a Hong Kong Protester." *South China Morning Post*, November 9, 2019. https://www.scmp.com/abacus/games/article/3037019/new-steam-game-lets-you-fight-hong-kong-protester.

Yee, Nick. *The Proteus Paradox: How Online Games and Virtual Worlds Change Us—and How They Don't.* New Haven, CT: Yale University Press, 2014.

York, Matt. "Just one of the little details I discovered. . . . He seems like the ultimate sympathetic portrayal of someone who becomes disillusioned with radical politics but decides to try to act as a force for good within the existing system." Facebook, June 3, 2021. https://www.facebook.com/groups/1984944608449267/permalink/3034227380187646.

Youngblood, Jordan. "'I Wouldn't Even Know the Real Me Myself': Queering Failure in *Metal Gear Solid 2*." In *Queer Game Studies*, edited by Bo Ruberg and Adrienne Shaw, 211–22. Minneapolis: University of Minnesota Press, 2017.

Zhu Lily. "Masculinity's New Battle Arena in International eSports: The Games Begin." In *Masculinities in Play*, edited by N. Tylor and G. Voorhees, 229–47. New York: Palgrave Macmillan, 2018.

Ludography

Aksys Games. *Hakuoki: Stories of the Shinsengumi*. Aksys, 2014. PlayStation 3.

Alexander, Mitch. *Tusks: The Orc Dating Sim*. Itch.io, 2017. PC, Mac.

Analgesic Productions. *Anodyne 2: Return to Dust*. Analgesic Productions, 2019. PlayStation 4, Nintendo Switch, PC.

Anino Games. *Anito: Defend a Land Enraged*. Anino Games, 2003. PC.

Anonymous. *Fight the Traitor Together*. Anonymous, 2019. Mobile.

Arimac. *Kanchyudha*. Arimac, 2017. PC.

Bandai Namco. *Super Smash Bros*. Nintendo, 2018. Nintendo Switch.

Bandai Namco. *Tekken 7*. Bandai Namco Entertainment, 2019. Arcade, PlayStation 4, Xbox One.

Bioware. *Mass Effect Andromeda*. Electronic Arts, 2017. PlayStation 4, Xbox One, PC.

Blizzard Entertainment. *Hearthstone*. Blizzard Entertainment, 2014. Multiplatform.

Blizzard Entertainment. *Overwatch*. Activision Blizzard, 2016. Multiplatform.

Capcom. *Final Fight*. Capcom, 1989. Arcade.

Capcom. *Marvel vs. Capcom 2: New Age of Heroes*. Capcom, 2000. Arcade, Dreamcast, iOS, PlayStation 2/3, Xbox, Xbox 360.

Capcom. *Street Fighter II: The World Warrior*. Capcom, 1991. Arcade.

Capcom. *Street Fighter III 3rd Strike: Fight for the Future*. Capcom, 1999. Arcade, Dreamcast, PlayStation 2/3/4, Xbox, Xbox 360, Xbox One, Nintendo Switch, PC.

Clark, Naomi. *Consentacle*. Itch.io, 2014. Board game.

Digital Eclipse. *Samurai Shodown NeoGeo Collection*. SNK, 2020. PC, PlayStation 4, Xbox One.

Đỗ, Toby, Emi Schaufeld, and Julia Wang. *Grass Mud Horse*. Itch.io, 2019. PC.

EA Canada and SkyBox Labs Sports. *EA Sports UFC*. EA Sports, 2014. PlayStation 4, Xbox One.

Electronic Arts. *The Sims*. Electronic Arts, 2000. Multiplatform.

Ensemble Studios. *Age of Empires III: The Asian Dynasties*. Ensemble Studios, 2007. PC.

Flying Robot Studios. *Missing: Game for a Cause*. Flying Robot Studios, 2016. Android, iOS.

Fornace, Dan. *Rivals of Aether*. Dan Fornace, 2017. PC, PlayStation 4, Xbox One, Nintendo Switch.

Gao, Yuxin. *Out for Delivery*. Itch.io, 2020. PC.

Hato Moa and Mediatonic. *Hatoful Boyfriend*. 2011. Devolver Digital, 2014. PC, Mac.

Hideaki Itsuno. *Capcom vs. SNK 2: Mark of the Millennium 2001*. Capcom, 2001. Arcade, Dreamcast, PlayStation 2, Xbox Nintendo GameCube.

Hong Kong Protesters. *Liberate Hong Kong*. Hong Kong Protesters, 2019. Multiplatform.

House House. *Untitled Goose Game*. Panic, 2019. Nintendo Switch.

Idea Factory International. *Hakuoki: Edo Blossoms*. Idea Factory International, 2018. PC, Steam.

Idea Factory International. *Hakuoki: Kyoto Winds*. Idea Factory International, 2017. PC, Steam.

Jiang, Sisi. *LIONKILLER*. Itch.io, 2020. PC.

Kaizen Game Works. *Paradise Killer*. Fellow Traveler, 2020. PC, Steam.

Karin Entertainment. *Eikoku Tantei Misuteria* (London Detective Mysteria). Marvelous USA Inc., 2013, PSP; XSeed Games, 2019, Steam, PlayStation Vita.

Kojima, Hideo. *Death Stranding*. Kojima Productions, 2019. PlayStation 4.

Kojima, Hideo. *Metaru gia soriddo* (*Metal Gear Solid*). Konami, 1998. PlayStation.

Kojima, Hideo. *Metaru gia soriddo 2: Sanzu obu ribati*. Konami, 2001. PlayStation 2.

Kojima, Hideo. *Metaru gia soriddo 4: Ganzu obu za patoriaotto*. Konami, 2008. PlayStation 3.

Li, Rachel, and Qin Yin. *Hotpot for One*. Itch.io, 2020. PC.

Liberate Hong Kong Game Team. *Liberate Hong Kong*. Liberate Hong Kong Game Team, 2019. Multiplatform.

Linden Lab. *Second Life*. Linden Lab, 2003. Multiplatform.

miHoYo. *Genshin Impact*. miHoYo, 2020. PC.

Mindfisher Games. *Heroes of '71*. Mindfisher Games, 2017. Android.

Nintendo. *Animal Crossing: New Horizons*. Nintendo, 2020. Nintendo Switch.

Nodding Heads. *Raji: An Ancient Epic*. Super.com, 2020. PC, Nintendo Switch, PlayStation 4.

Noriyoshi Ohba. *Streets of Rage*. Sega, 1991. Mega Drive/Genesis, Sega CD, Game Gear, Master System, Nintendo 3DS.

Prodigi Interactive. *Threta*. Prodigi, in development. PC.

Ren Yi, Mike. *Yellow Face*. Mike Ren Yi, last updated June 21, 2019. https:// mikeyren.itch.io/yellowface.

Rockstar Games. *Grand Theft Auto V*. Rockstar North, 2013. Multiplatform.

Silver Spook Games. *Neofeud*. Silver Spook Games, 2017. PC.

Squinky. *Dominique Pamplemousse in "It's All Over Once the Fat Lady Sings!"* Itch.io, 2013. PC.

Studio Oleomingus. *Somewhere*. Studio Oleomingus, 2014. PC.

Sucker Punch Productions. *Ghost of Tsushima*. Sony Interactive Entertainment, 2020. PlayStation 4/5.

Tran, Lien B. *Toma El Paso / Make a Move*. New School, 2014. Board game.

Trimatrik Inc. *Arunadoyer Agnishikha*. SHOM Computers, 2004. PC.

Type-Moon and French-Bread. *Melty Blood*. Type-Moon and French-Bread, 2002. PC.

Ubisoft. *Far Cry 4*. Ubisoft, 2014. PC, Xbox, PlayStation 3.

Unknown. *Fight the Traitors Together*. Unknown, 2019. Multiplatform.

Valve. *Counter-Strike*. Valve Corporation, 1999. PC.

Yang, Robert. *Intimate, Infinite*. Robert Yang, last updated 2014. https:// radiatoryang.itch.io/intimate-infinite.

Zachtronics. *Eliza*. Zachtronics, 2019. PC.

ZA/UM. *Disco Elysium*. ZA/UM, 2019. PC, Mac.

Contributors

EDMOND Y. CHANG (he/they) is an assistant professor of English at Ohio University. Recent publications include "Imagining Asian American (Environmental) Games" in *AMSJ*, "Why Are the Digital Humanities So Straight?" in *Alternative Historiographies of the Digital Humanities*, and "Queergaming" in *Queer Game Studies*. He is an editor for *Analog Game Studies* as well as the website *Gamers with Glasses*.

MIYOKO CONLEY (she/her) is an independent scholar and games writer. She researches transnational media, theater, and fan cultures, with a focus on Japanese and South Korean popular culture, and she has been published in the journal *Transformative Works and Cultures*.

ANTHONY DOMINGUEZ is a PhD candidate in cinema studies at NYU Tisch School of the Arts. His dissertation focuses on Times Square and the influence of global capitalism on public space, architecture, corporate advertising, and military powers. His research includes urban screens, Japanese media, and Black nerd culture.

TARA FICKLE is an associate professor of English at the University of Oregon, and her first book, *The Race Card: From Gaming Technologies to Model Minorities* (2019), won the Before Columbus Foundation's American Book Award. Fickle is currently working on a digital archive and analysis of the canonical Asian American anthology, *Aiiieeeee!* (Aiiieeeee.org).

SARAH CHRISTINA GANZON is an assistant professor of communication studies at Simon Fraser University. She is a member of the mLab and TAG research networks. Her research revolves mostly around the areas of game studies and digital fandom. Recently she finished her doctoral thesis on otome games in English and otome game players.

HUAN HE is an assistant professor of English at Vanderbilt University. His research engages Asian/American literature and culture, digital studies, critical game studies, and poetics. His writing has been published in *College Literature: A Journal of Critical Literary Studies* and *Media-N*. He also writes poetry, which can be found in *A Public Space*, *Beloit Poetry Journal*, *Colorado Review*, and elsewhere.

MATTHEW JUNGSUK HOWARD is a PhD candidate in communication, rhetoric, and digital media at North Carolina State University. His research mobilizes Asian/Americanist critique and feminist new materialist studies of race in contexts of globalization and transnational cultural industries. His dissertation is a media history of Korean/Americanness that implicates the Korean Wave in the racialization of Korean/American diaspora.

RACHAEL HUTCHINSON is a professor of Japanese and game studies at the University of Delaware. Her work on representation and identity in Japanese video games appears in *Games and Culture*, *Game Studies*, *Japanese Studies*, *Replaying Japan*, and various book chapters. Her books include *Japanese Culture through Videogames* (2019) and the coedited *Japanese Role-Playing Games: Genre, Representation and Liminality in the JRPG* (2022).

HANEUL LEE (she/her/her) is a PhD student in cinema studies at Tisch School of the Arts, New York University. Her research focuses on informal media production, circulation, and consumption among migrant workers, immigrants, and other sociopolitical precariats.

KEITA MOORE (he/him) is a PhD candidate at the University of California, Santa Barbara, in the East Asian Languages and Cultural Studies program who is interested in the politics of temporality, place, and play that emerge at the intersection of video games and their critiques. His dissertation ethnographically analyzes game design and the production of social spaces and times in Japan.

SOUVIK MUKHERJEE is assistant professor in cultural studies at the Centre for Studies in Social Sciences Calcutta and a pioneering South Asian games studies scholar. His research looks at video games as storytelling media and as postcolonial media. He is the author of three monographs, including *Videogames in the Indian Subcontinent* (2022). Souvik is a DiGRA Distinguished Scholar.

CHRISTOPHER B. PATTERSON is an award-winning author and associate professor of social justice at the University of British Columbia. His academic works are *Transitive Cultures: Anglophone Literature of the Transpacific* and *Open World Empire: Race, Erotics, and the Global Rise of Video Games*; his creative books include *Stamped: an anti-travel novel*, *All Flowers Bloom*, and *Nimrods: a fake-punk self-hurt anti-memoir*.

TAKEO RIVERA (he/him) is assistant professor of English at Boston University and the author of *Model Minority Masochism: Performing the Cultural Politics of*

350 Contributors

Asian American Masculinity (2022). His articles have been published in *AmerAsia Journal*, *Performance Research*, and *asap/Journal*, among others. He is also an award-winning playwright.

YASHENG SHE (they/them and he/him) is a PhD candidate at the Department of Film and Digital Media at the University of California, Santa Cruz. Yasheng is interested in catharsis and trauma narratives in video games, films, and anime. Yasheng has published several articles in peer-reviewed journals and edited collections from the perspectives of postwar Japan, gender, and popular media.

PRABHASH RANJAN TRIPATHY is a PhD candidate at the school of Arts and Aesthetics, Jawaharlal Nehru University, New Delhi, and is currently working on a dissertation titled "Between WorkStation and PlayStation: The Cultural Location of Videogames in India." Interest areas include comic books, anime, video games, sports, and all things popular culture.

GERALD VOORHEES is an associate professor in the Department of Communication Arts at the University of Waterloo. He researches games and new media as sites for the construction and contestation of identity and culture, and he has edited books on masculinities in games, feminism in play, role-playing games, and first-person shooter games.

Index

Page numbers in *italics* refer to figures.

2000 World Cyber Games, 191

AAA game companies, 27, 89, 153, 157, 178, 185, 208, 236, 253–54

Aarseth, Espen, 35

acid communism, 67–69, 77–79, 81. *See also* psychedelic counterculture

addiction, gaming, 5, 73, 144–45. *See also* gamer death; player burnout

adjacency, 6, 69, 71, 75, 78–80; and utopia, 67–68, 76, 82, 83n17

Age of Empires 3: The Asian Dynasties (Ensemble Studios, 2007), 182

aimbotting, 218–20, 223, 226, 228–29

Ainu people, 160, 171, 173

Aksys Games, 251, 259–61; *Fate/EXTRA* (2011), 250, 266n43. See also *Hakuoki*

Albrecht, Monika, 159–60, 162, 167

Alexander, Mitch: *Tusks: The Orc Dating Sim*, 233, 235, 242–47

algorithmic analysis, 13–14, 23n38

Allied Occupation of Japan (1945–1952), 102, 104–5, 119, 159, 161, 163, 170, 172

Analgesic Productions, 275

Anderson-Barkley, Taylor, 296

Andlauer, Leticia, 235

Animal Crossing: New Horizons (*AC*) (Nintendo, 2020), 21, 299–300, 305n6; funerals for Carrie Lam in, 290–*92*, 305n3; networked play and, 293–94, 301–5

animal mayhem games, 237

anime, 33, 153, 240, 258, 261, 266n51, 280, 284; aesthetics of, 20, 52, 95, 97–98, 238, 250; Black fans of, 277–79, 282–83; marketing media mix and, 248n6, 251, 259

Anime Expo 2011, 250, 259

Anime NYC convention (2017), 279, 282–83

Anito: Defend a Land Enraged (Anino Entertainment, 2003), 150, 154

Anodyne series (Kittaka and Han-Tani, 2013–2019), 208, 214, 270

anthropocentrism, 80, 237, 244–45

Anthropy, Anna, 17, 90

anti-Asian sentiment, 7, 105, 122–23, 157, 223–30, 240–41, 273; COVID-19 pandemic and, 10, 15, 18, 54, 56, 63. *See also* racism; white supremacy

anticheat software: BattlEye, 218

anti-Chinese sentiment, 56, 157, 223–30, 240. *See also* racism; white supremacy

anti-Filipino sentiment, 240–41. *See also* racism; white supremacy

anti-Muslim sentiment, 145. *See also* racism; white supremacy

Apex Legends (Respawn and Electronic Arts, 2019), 219–20, 223, 225–27

APM (actions per minute) metric, 195

Appadurai, Arjun, 179–80, 183

arcades, 3, 5, 37, 45, 144, 165; Black gamers and, 278–81, 284–88; Chinatown Fair Arcade (New York City), 280, 284–86, 288; fighting games and, 29–30, 137–38, 146n16,

arcades (continued)
278, 284, 286; masculinity and, 137–38, 279–81, 289; Next Level Arcade (Brooklyn), 280, 286; Playland (New York City), 280, 285

ASEAN (Association of Southeast Asian Nations), 187

Asian American Writers Workshop, 27, 29

Asian hands myth, 133–36, 142, 144–45, 199–202, 212

Asiatic, the, 6, 9, 74, 78, 178, 194, 196; cheating and, 218–19, 224–25, 227–28; definition, 18, 54–56, 64, 186; fetishization and, 7–8, 14, 182, 190, 202; queerness of, 17, 54–63, 68, 234

Assassin's Creed series (Ubisoft, 2007, 2012), 33, 111, 270–71

Association of Asian American Studies (AAAS), 15–16

Atari, 180; *Gauntlet* (1985), 40

authorship, 41, 155

avatars, 40, 70, 103, 109, 122, 237, 311; avatarial capital, 228–30; in *Divinity*, 313–15

Azubu Frost, 197

Azuma, Hiroki, 9, 282

Banerjee, Anando, 178–79

Barthes, Roland, 68, 186

BattlEye (anticheat software), 218

battle royale (BR) shooter games, 219, 224, 228, 230; *Apex Legends*, 219–20, 223, 225–27; *Call of Duty*, 155, 161, 174n6, 182, 185, 227; *PlayerUnknown's Battlegrounds* (*PUBG*), 217–18, 223, 225, 227; procedural racism in, 221–23, 226, 229

Belle, Crystal, 287

Berlant, Lauren, 52

biopolitics, 233, 235–37, 242, 246

BioWare, 91, 96; *Mass Effect* trilogy (2007, 2012, 2020), 84n29, 92–93, 309–11, 313; *Star Wars: Knights of the Old Republic* (2003), 84n29

biraciality, 32, 130; *konketsuji* and *hāfu* identities, 102–12, 113n28; in *Metal Gear Solid* series, 18, 93, 99–100, 102–12, 113n22, 113n28, 113nn30–31, 123, 171–72. *See also* multiracial identities

bishōjo games, 235

Black Lives Matter (BLM) movement, 56, 133, 273, 293–94, 305n6

Black Mirror, 59, 61

Black nerd (Blerd) identity, 17, 20, 277–81; in fighting game community, 283–89, 298n8; as *otaku*, 282–83

Black technophobia, 279

Blizzard Entertainment: *Hearthstone* (2014), 31, 295; *Overwatch* (2016), 57, 296–98, 306n20; *StarCraft* (1998), 30, 179, 191, 193, 195, 208; *World of Warcraft* (2004), 122, 228

Blow, Jonathan: *Braid* (2008), 93

Bluth, Don: *Dragon's Lair* (1983), 37

Bogost, Ian, 15, 102, 221, 291–93, 300

Bolter, Jay David, 196

bootleg games, 90

bootstrap mentality, 140

Borges, Jorge Luis: "The Garden of the Forking Paths," 35–36, 47–49

Bow, Leslie, 7

Bowman, Mitch, 138

Boylorn, Robin, 281

Brack, J. Allen, 295

Braid (Blow, 2008), 93

Braidotti, Rosi, 262

Brock, André, 192, 196

Brood War esports, 198

Buddhist symbolism, 67, 176–77

Burns, Matthew Seiji, 28, 30, 31, 33; *Eliza* (2019), 27, 32–33

Burton, Antoinette, 239–40

bushido philosophy, 139, 255, 258

Butler, Judith, 259

Byrd, Jodi, 23n34

Caillois, Roger, 10–11, 23n30, 143, 163–64

Call of Duty (Activision, 2003–), 155, 161, 174n6, 182, 185, 227

Camera Anima (Gee, 2020), 18, 89, 91

Capcom, 133; *Marvel vs. Capcom 2* (2000), 280–81, 287–88; *Resident Evil 5* (2009), 101, 162, 164; *Street Fighter* series (1987, 1991, 1997, 2016), 29–30, 33, 59, 160, 162–63, 165–66, 180, 278, 283, 285

capitalism, 57, 59, 64, 152, 161, 211, 224, 263; debt-capitalism, 300, 303–4; neoliberal, 55, 77, 222; racial, 9–10, 68, 171, 193–95, 201, 230; realism and, 66–69

Caracciolo, Marco, 237

cárdenas, micha, 10, 13, 24n38

caste, 182, 184

Castronova, Edward, 228

Cen, Henry, 280, 286

Chakrabarti, Siddartha, 182

Chan, Charlie, 5, 75

Chan, Dean, 7, 23n27, 38

Chan, Jeffery Paul, 7

354 Index

Chang, Alenda, 23n36

Chang, Kornel, 224

character tropes, 3, 7–8, 48, 54, 57, 101, 308, 312, 315; in *Choose Your Own Adventure* books, 41–42; in dating games, 234–36, 238, 240–43; in fighting games, 59–60, 162–63, 180–81, 188n14, 189n31, 283; game makers on, 8, 31, 40, 96–97, 155, 195; roboticism and, 123, 228

cheating, 5, 217; aimbotting, 218–20, 223, 226, 228–29; cheat sellers, 226–27; Chineseness and, 20, 122, 194, 218–20, 222–30

Chen, James "jchensor," 133

Chen, Kuan-hsing, 9, 23n26

Chen, Mel Y., 233–34, 238, 240

Cheney-Lippold, John, 57

Cheng, Anne, 54

Chess, Shira, 257

Chin, Frank, 7

China and Chineseness, 19, 64, 161, 163–64, 186–87, 192; Beijing, 149, 272, 274; cheating and, 5, 20, 122, 194, 218–20, 222–30; Chengdu, 97, 208; contagion discourse and, 56, 157, 225, 233, 240; esports and, 136, 199–200, 202; game makers on, 31–32, 43, 90, 97, 150–57, 208–9, 211–12, 214, 269–75; as game setting, 78, 97, 168–71, 175n34, 269, 272, 274; *Genshin Impact* and, 153, 309, 311–12; gold farmers, 122, 194, 228; immigrants and, 5, 105, 123, 157, 223–25, 270, 274–75; "region-lock," 223–25; Shanghai, 149, 269–72, 274; Shenzhen, 208, 212, 214, 227. *See also* People's Republic of China (PRC)

Chinatown Fair Arcade (New York City), 280, 284–86, 288

Chinese Exclusion Act, 105, 157, 224

Cho, Margaret, 68

Choe, Steve, 22n7, 136

Christianity, 162, 165, 174n25, 210, 243, 313; Muscular Christianity movement, 139–40

Chuh, Kandice, 16, 55

Chun, Wendy, 6–7, 54, 192–93, 202

Chung, Ng Wai "Blitzchung," 295–96

Churchill, Winston, 182

cinematic games: *Death Stranding*, 116

Civilization series (MicroProse, 1991–2016), 161, 181–82

Clark, Naomi, 92–93, 95–97, 300; *Consentacle* (2018), 18, 90, 98; *SiSSYFiGHT 2000* (2000), 90

code-based cheats, 220, 223, 225–27. *See also* aimbotting; speed-hacking; wallhacking

Colbert, Stephen, 57

Colebrook, Claire, 188n9

colonialism, 9–10, 14, 45, 55, 67, 144, 310–11, 314; Allied Occupation of Japan (1945–1952), 102, 104–5, 119, 159, 161, 163, 170, 172; Hawai'i, 155–56; Indian subcontinent and, 177, 181–85, 187–88; Japan as colonized, 19, 101–2, 119–20, 125, 159–65, 170–73; Japan as colonizer, 19, 64, 101–2, 118, 125, 153, 159–63, 166–73, 240–41, 275; Philippines and, 153–55, 160, 163, 240–41, 276

colorblindness, 39, 133–34, 137–38, 229. *See also* postracialism

communism, 67–69, 76–79; in *Disco Elysium*, 70, 74, 80–81, 83n17

Consalvo, Mia, 39, 179, 188n11, 220

Consentacle (Clark, 2018), 18, 90, 98

"console cowboy" fantasy, 6, 193, 202

consoles, 38, 184, 279, 284, 286, 302, 312; Amiga, 180; Atari, 180; Microsoft Xbox, 28, 219, 283; Nintendo 3DS, 251, 254, 260; Nintendo 64, 64, 283; Nintendo DS, 254, 259; Nintendo Entertainment System (NES), 5, 180; Nintendo Famicom, 90; Nintendo Gameboy Color, 270; Nintendo GameCube, 283; Nintendo Switch, 153, 251, 293, 299, 301; Sega Dreamcast, 165, 283; Sega Genesis, 83; Sony PlayStation, 28, 33, 156, 165, 219, 251, 254, 260, 283; Super Nintendo, 283

Conway, Steven, 279, 288–89

Cook, Eli, 41

Counter-Strike (Valve, 2009), 18, 27, 29, 96–97, 155, 208, 227

COVID-19 pandemic, 145n1, 193, 202, 214, 272, 291; anti-Asian racism and, 54, 56–57, 64, 157, 224–25, 240; popularity of games during, 156, 299; production of the book during, 10, 15; Wuhan city lockdowns, 275

Crawford, Chris, 95

Crowther, Will: *Colossal Cave Adventure* (1976), 36

Culler, Joey "Mr. Wizard," 132

cultural odor, 6, 9, 23n25, 124–25, 179–80, 187, 188n11, 189n31

cute culture, 178, 195, 253

cutscenes, 37, 48; in *Death Stranding*, 118, 120–22; in *Metal Gear Solid* series, 103, 105, 107

cyberpunk, 151, 153, 192–93, 202

Index **355**

Cyberpunk 2077 (CD Projekt RED, 2020), 92, 156

cyborgs, 120, 122, 124–25

Danico, Mary Yu, 3

dating games, 239, 244–45, 247, 248n20, 259; biopolitics of, 232–37, 242, 246; character tropes in, 234–36, 238, 240–43. *See also* visual novels

deaths, in-game, 40, 64, 108, 118, 236, 257, 265nn26–27

Death Stranding (Kojima Productions, 2019), 115–24, 126–29; cutscenes in, 118, 120–22

de Cuir, Cash, 69

Delany, Samuel, 284–85

Deleuze, Gilles, 188n9

de Peuter, Greig, 60, 65, 161

deracialization, 120, 122, 128, 157

deterritorialization, 20, 179, 183, 187, 188n9

Dhruva Interactive, 178–79

diaspora, 32–33, 94, 184–85; *Disco Elysium* and, 69, 71–73, 76, 78, 82

Dickwolves controversy, 259, 266n41

Disco Elysium (ZA/UM, 2019), 83n14, 83n17, 83n20, 84n30, 84n32; model minority stereotypes and, 68, 70–77, 81–82, 83n13; psychedelic counterculture and, 67–71, 76–80

Dishonored (Bethesda Softworks, 2012, 2016), 84n29

Divinity: Original Sin 2 (Larian Studios, 2017), 313–15

Dobbs v. Jackson Women's Health Organization (2022), 234

Dodo codes, 293, 301

Donald, Dwayne, 159–60, 163

Doom (id Software, 1993), 29, 227

Dosekun, Simidele, 253

Đỗ, Toby, 89, 91, 93, 95–96; *Grass Mud Horse* (2019), 18, 90, 97

Dragon's Lair (Bluth and Dyer, 1983), 37

Du Bois, W. E. B., 83n20, 83n22

Dungeons and Dragons (D&D) (Tactical Studies Rules Inc. 1974; Wizards of the Coast / Hasbro, 1997–), 50, 270; d20, 46–47

Dunning, Eric, 141

Dyer, Richard, 119–20

Dyer, Rick: *Dragon's Lair* (1983), 37

Dyer-Witheford, Nick, 16, 60, 99–100

educational games, 296

"e-girls," 1–2

Eglash, Ron, 281

Electronic Arts (EA), 156; *Apex Legends* (2019), 219–20, 223, 225–27; *The Sims* series (2000–2023), 293–94, 305n6. See also *Mass Effect* trilogy

Elias, Norbert, 141–42

Eliza (Zachtronics, 2019), 27, 32–33

emotional labor, 257–58

ergodic texts, 35

eroticism, 11, 17, 54, 60–61; homoeroticism, 59, 84n24, 119–20, 208; othering through, 8, 63, 212, 237–38, 311–12

Erzberger, Tyler, 201

esports, 38, 136, 138, 231n30; game about, 90, 96; *League of Legends*, 1–2, 57, 191, 193, 196–200, 202–3; professional gamers, 31, 179, 190–92, 195–203, 217; South Korea and, 5, 19, 145, 190–91, 193, 195–203; whiteness and, 1–3, 6, 191–94, 196–99, 202

ethnic studies, 10, 12, 14–16, 73

Eurocentrism, 68, 173; in game theory, 163–64; in postcolonial theory, 159–60

Evans, Adrienne, 262

Everett, Anna, 279, 287, 307

Evolution Championship Series (EVO), 132–35, 145, 285

fan fiction, 84n24, 91, 252, 264

Far Cry 4 (Ubisoft, 2014), 176–77, 182–83, 187, 270

Fate/EXTRA (Aksys Games, 2011), 250, 266n43

feminization, 40, 119, 122, 128, 188n14, 195, 253

Fickle, Tara, 23n30, 44, 73, 162–64, 180, 224, 228–29; on ludo-orientalism, 6, 36, 39, 101, 143, 179, 194, 222; roundtable moderator, 29–30, 34, 97, 152, 210–11, 213

fighting game community (FGC), 3, 19–21, 28–31, 59–60, 201, 278; Black nerd (Blerd) identity and, 282–89, 298n8; commentating in, 280–81, 284, 287–89; Evolution Championship Series (EVO), 132–35, 145, 285; masculinity in, 3, 133–34, 137–40, 280–81, 284, 289; sexual misconduct in, 132–33, 138

Fight the Traitors Together (unknown, 2019), 296–97

Final Fantasy series (Square Enix, 1987–), 91, 160, 169–70, 251, 259, 309; nuclear discourse in, 126, 167–68

Fink, Eugen, 144

first-person shooter (FPS) games, 29–30, 47–48, 91, 99, 185, 219, 221–22, 227, 296.

356 Index

See also battle royale (BR) shooter games; *individual games*

Fisher, Mark, 66–69, 71, 82n8

Fisher, Stephanie, 254

Flower, Sun and Rain (Suda51, 2001), 52

Floyd, George, 305n6

Fnatic, 197

Foglesong, Kira, 296

Fontanez, Victor "Spooky," 284–87. *See also* Team Spooky

forever foreigner trope, 3, 36, 44, 104, 222, 229, 258

Foucault, Michel, 21, 68, 186

F.R.E.E. games, 52

Freeman, Elizabeth, 236

Friedman, Thomas, 179

fujoshi trophy, 252, 260–63, 266n48, 266n51

Fukuyama, Francis, 66, 77

Fu Manchu, 5, 234

Fung, Catherine, 124

Galloway, Alexander, 23n36, 227

Game Awards, The (@thegameawards), 83n15; *Disco Elysium*, 69

Game Developers Conference, 94–95

Game Developers of Color Expo, 28

game industry, 3, 6–8, 12, 21, 62, 67, 138, 197–98, 308, 310; in China, 90, 149–53, 185, 200, 218, 227, 270, 274; Filipina/o identity in, 32, 55, 150, 153–55, 209, 241, 269–71, 274; in Hawai'i, 19, 55, 149–51, 154–56; of Indian subcontinent, 177–79, 183–85, 188n6; in Japan (*see* Japanese game industry); maker roundtable discussions, 5, 15, 27–34, 89–98, 149–57, 207–15, 269–76; neurodivergence in, 209, 214–15; queerness in, 97, 208–15, 233, 243, 269; in South Korea, 8, 153, 173, 185, 190, 200, 202; trans identity in, 209, 214–15; triple-A studios, 27, 89, 153, 157, 178, 185, 208, 236, 253–54; women in, 92, 150, 154–55, 209, 254

game jams, 16, 270

Game Makers club (Cal Arts), 91

gamer death, 136, 144, 179. *See also* addiction, gaming; player burnout

#GamerGate, 11–12, 23n34, 308

Gamers and Gaming Meets Philippines (GnG), 272

gamers, professional, 31, 179, 190–92, 195–203, 217. *See also* esports

game studies, 23n30, 23n34, 35, 99–100, 173, 178, 228, 253, 274, 279; critiquing bias in,

9–17, 21, 24n27, 24n32, 24n36, 159, 161–63, 194, 308–10, 315–17

gamic orientalism, 134. *See also* orientalism; techno-orientalism

gaming houses, 191–92, 198–200

Gandhi, 181–82, 187

Ganzon, Sarah Christina, 235

Gao, Yuxin: *Out for Delivery* (2020), 20, 270, 272–75

Gates, Henry Louis, Jr., 287

Gauntlet (Atari, 1985), 40

Gee, Domini, 92, 94–96; *Camera Anima* (2020), 18, 89, 91

genre, 20, 41, 53, 61, 77, 94–95, 97, 164; dating games and, 233–35, 248n10, 260–61; fighting games and, 137–38, 278; role-playing games and, 311–12; shooter games and, 29–30, 217, 227–28

Genshin Impact (miHoYo, 2020), 153, 311–13

Ghost in the Shell (Mamoru, 1995), 124

Ghost of Tsushima (Sucker Punch, 2020), 92, 94

Gill, Rosalind, 252–53

Glasspool, Lucy, 259

Glissant, Édouard, 314

Glorious Mission (Giant Interactive Group, 2011), 227

Goggin, Joyce, 194

gold farming, 122, 194, 228

Google Earth VR, 164

Goto-Jones, Chris, 134–35, 138, 142, 145n7

Graham, David "Ultradavid," 133

Grand Theft Auto V (*GTA*) (Rockstar Games, 2013), 302

Gray, Kishonna L., 162, 279

Greater East Asia (Dai Tō-A) ideology, 168

Greene, Brendan "PlayerUnknown": *PlayerUnknown's Battlegrounds* and, 217–18, 223, 225, 227

Grieve, Gregory Price, 183

Grusin, Richard, 196

Guattari, Félix, 188n9

Guttmann, Allen, 141

hāfu (biracial foreign subject), 102–10, 112, 113n28

Hakuoki series (Aksys Games, 2014; Idea Factory International, 2017 and 2018), 250–51, 266n43; choice in, 254–58, 263, 265nn23–30; localization and, 252, 258–64, 264n2, 264nn20–21, 265n22, 265n24; sexism in, 252, 254, 257, 260–63

Hamad, Hannah, 253

Index **357**

Han-Tani, Melos, 271–72, 275; *Anodyne* series (2013–2019), 208, 214, 270
Haraway, Donna, 122, 125
Harper, Todd, 7, 134–35, 137, 146n16, 287
Harvey, Alison, 254
Hasegawa, Kazumi, 251, 257
hashtag activism: #LiberateHongKong, 304; #MeiSupportsHongKong, 298; #Stand-WithHK, 304
Hatoful Boyfriend (Moa, 2011), 232–33, 246–47, 248n23, 249n28, 249n33; mechanics of, 241–42; themes of contamination in, 235, 237–40
Hawai'i, 55, 151, 154–56
Hayles, N. Katherine, 231n41
Hearthstone (Blizzard Entertainment, 2014), 31; 2019 Grandmaster Finals for, 295
heteronormativity, 59, 233–34, 254, 281–82; in dating games, 235–36, 238, 242, 245–46; in *Hakuoki*, 251–52, 257, 259, 262–63
high-tech orientalism, 7, 191–93, 195–98, 201. *See also* orientalism; techno-orientalism
Hindpere, Helen, 68–69, 83n14, 83n20
Hinduism, 176, 182, 184, 313
hip-hop, 1–3, 277–78, 280–89
Hjorth, Larissa, 23n27
Hochschild, Arlie, 257
Holland, Patricia, 312
homoeroticism, 59, 84n24, 119–20
homophobia, 39, 133, 138, 243. *See also* #GamerGate
Hong Kong, 29, 31–32, 52, 60, 177, 223, 226, 270; Federation of Students, 294–95; *Liberate Hong Kong*, 295–97; pro-democracy protests in *Overwatch*, 296, *298*; protests emerging from *Animal Crossing*, 21, 290–94, 299–304, 305n3, 305n6, 306n23; Umbrella Movement, 295
Hong Kong Polytech University, 299
HoSaiLei (@hkbhkese), 302–3
Hot Pot for One (Li, 2020), 20, 208–9, 213–14
Huang, Betsy, 5
Huizinga, Johan, 10–11, 23n30, 39, 61, 143, 163–64
Hutchinson, Rachael, 8, 101, 111, 123, 125–26, 179, 188n14
hypervisibility, 7–8, 31, 38, 92, 104, 108, 191

Idea Factory International, 251, 260. See also *Hakuoki*
IFC Yipes, 280–81, 287–88
Igarashi, Yoshikuni, 116, 118–19, 126

imperialism, 33, 133, 159, 174n6, 230, 233, 235, 246–47, 308, 310; animal significance to, 239–40; the Asiatic and, 19, 60, 63–64, 182, 227, 316; British, 21, 159, 172, 239–40; concept of play and, 140, 142, 144; European empire as measure for Asian colonialism, 159; in *Final Fantasy*, 167–68; history in game production and, 3–4, 14; Japan and, 101–2, 152, 154, 161–68, 170, 174n26; in *Metal Gear Solid* series, 99–102, 170–72; Western gaze and, 192, 245
independent games, 53, 68–69, 89, 154, 184–85, 208, 233, 235, 272, 295–97, 305n16; experimentation and, 213, 274, 308; New York City community for, 28. *See also individual games*
Indian subcontinent, 176–77, 180–82, 186–88; game industry of, 178–79, 183–85, 188n6
Indigeneity: game makers and, 15, 41, 150, 153–54, 156–57, 173; in games, 107, 151, 167, 170–71, 311; games as civilizing force, 140–44
internationalism, 104, 134, 137
Intimate, Infinite (Yang, 2014), 47–49
invisibility, 31, 92, 100; of labor, 7–8, 38, 120–25, 128–30, 257, 270–71, 316–17
iSlaves, 64. *See also* labor
itch.io, 91, 97, 236; #StopAsianHateJam Game Jam (2021), 16
Iwabuchi, Koichi, 6, 9, 23n25, 124–25, 179
Iwamura, Jane, 67

Jackson, Sarah, 304
James, C. L. R., 14
Jameson, Fredric, 66, 68
Japan and Japaneseness, 112n11, 188n14, 300; Ainu people, 160, 171, 173; Allied Occupation of (1945–1952), 102, 104–5, 119, 159, 161, 163, 170, 172; anime aesthetics, 20, 52, 95, 97–98, 238, 250; Asian hands myth and, 135, 144, 192, 199, 201–2; Bakamatsu period, 254–55, 264n20; Battle Royale (BR) games and, 217, 223, 225–26; as colonizer, 19, 64, 101–2, 118, 125, 153, 159–63, 166–73, 240–41, 275; cultural odor and, 6, 9, 23n25, 124–25, 179–80, 187, 188n11, 189n31; dating games and, 232, 234–41, 248n10; in *Death Stranding*, 19, 115–16, 118–20, 122–30; in *Disco Elysium*, 72–73, 78; game industry (*see* Japanese game industry); Greater East Asia (Dai Tō-A) ideology, 168; *hāfu* and *konketsuji* identities, 102–12, 113n28; in

358　Index

Hakuoki, 250–52, 254–64, 265n26; intersecting with Black culture, 20–21, 31, 60, 73, 101, 104–5, 111, 227, 277–88, 289n8; in *Metal Gear Solid* series, 18, 99–112, 112n6, 113n17, 113n31, 170–72, 188n11; in *Paradise Killer*, 52–53, 60, 62; postwar discourse and, 118–20, 123–28, 170, 174n25; Shinsengumi in games about, 251, 254–55, 258, *262*, 264n21; Tokugawa period, 160, 164–65, 169, 264n20; US bombing of, 99, 167–68

Japanese game industry, 5–6, 52, 95, 101, 159, 178–79, 185–87, 188n11, 188n14, 278; dating games in, 232, 234–41, 248n10; game makers and, 30–31, 89–90, 92–97, 115, 152–54, 160–62, 232, 275; Japanese role-playing games (JRPGs), 91, 96, 126, 160, 167–70, 251, 259, 309; localization in, 33, 235, 250–52, 254, 258–64, 265n22, 265n24; media mix in, 234, 248n6, 251, 259; *otaku* culture, 21, 135, 251, 260–61, 266n51, 282–89; *otome* games, 235–36, 251, 255, 257–61, 263–64, 264n2, 266n51 (see also *Hakuoki*)

Javier, Paraluman (Luna), 150, 153–54, 156–57

Jiang, Sisi, 90–96; *LIONKILLER* (2020), 89, 91, 96

Joseph, Ralina, 254

Kaizen Game Works, 64n1. See also *Paradise Killer*

Kawai, Yuko, 102

Kijima, Yoshimasa, 278, 282

Kim, Se Young, 22n7, 136

King of Fighters, The (SNK Corporation, 1994–), 165–66

Kirby, 12, 212–13

Kittaka, Marina Ayano, 91, 209–10, 212, 273; *Anodyne* series (2013–2019), 208, 214, 270

Kobo, Abe: *Nawa (The Rope)*, 116

Kojima, Hideo, 93, 99–101, 108, 170, 172, 175n36; *Death Stranding*, 115–24, 126–29. *See also Metal Gear Solid* series

Kojima Productions: *Death Stranding* (2019), 115–24, 126–29

Konami, 153; *Metal Gear Solid* series (1998–2015), 93, 99–112, 112n8, 113n22, 115–16, 126, 130, 160, 163, 170–72, 188n11

Kondo, Dorinne, 4, 13, 61

konketsuji (biracial Japanese subject), 102–12, 113n28

Korean Exodus of 2014, 199–200

Koreanness, 52, 72, 83n22, 92, 135, 173, 188n14, 251; esports and, 5, 19, 145, 190–91, 193, 195–203; Seoul and, 72–73, 75, 78. *See also* South Korea

Kotaku.com, 177

Kurvitz, Robert, 68, 83n14

labor, 3–4, 10, 18, 33, 61, 115, 118, 171, 211, 293; behind streaming, 286–87; as cheapened by Asian stereotypes, 22n7, 22n16, 63–64, 222–25, 228; emotional, 257–58; in esports, 179, 191, 193–201; invisible, 7–8, 38, 120–25, 128–30, 257, 270–71, 316–17; migrant workers, 116, 123, 199, 223–25, 274–75; outsourcing, 5, 155, 178–79, 185, 187, 271–72; of players, 132, 193–94, 199–201, 222, 224, 228, 300–303, 310

Lakshya Digital, 178

Lam, Carrie, 290–*92*, 305n3

Latinx in Gaming, 32

League of Legends (Riot Games, 2009), 1–2, 57, 191, 193, 196–200, 202–3

Lee, Martin, 296

Lefty Paradox Plaza (Facebook Group), 84n31

Le, Minh, 28, 30, 34, 96; *Counter-Strike* (2009), 18, 27, 29, 96–97, 155, 208, 227

Li, Rachel, 207–8, 211; *Hot Pot for One* (2021), 20, 208–9, 213–14

Liberate Hong Kong (Liberate Hong Kong Game Team, 2019), 295–*97*

#LiberateHongKong, 304

Lin, Zhongxuan, 293, 295

Lineage II (NCSOFT, 2003), 228

LIONKILLER (Jiang, 2020), 91, 96

Littler, Jo, 139–40

localization, 9, 55, 150–53; of Japanese games, 33, 235, 250–52, 254, 258–64, 265n22, 265n24

LoL Champions Korea (LCK) league, 197. See also *League of Legends*

Lost Arcade, The (Vincent, 2015), 285–86

Lovecraft, H. P., 59, 63

ludo-orientalism, 6, 36, 39, 42, 163, 191, 194–95, 202, 222, 226. *See also* orientalism

Lye, Colleen, 177–78, 180

Magdalinski, Tara, 140

magic circle of play, 10–11, 39, 61, 163–64

Malkowski, Jennifer, 102, 307

Mamoru, Oshii: *Ghost in the Shell* (1995), 124

Mangiron, Carmen, 252

Martens, Todd, 184

Martin, Paul, 101, 162, 164

Index **359**

Marvel vs. Capcom 2 (Capcom, 2000), 280–81, 287–88

masculinity, 7, 99, 212, 243, 252, 262, 308; at arcades, 137–38, 279–81, 289; biracial, 102, 106; Black, 2–3, 60–61, 279, 281–82, 288–89; "console cowboy" fantasy, 6, 193, 202; in esports, 2, 19, 193–95; in fighting game community, 3, 133–34, 137–40, 280–81, 284, 289; #GamerGate and, 11–12; heteropatriarchal, 59, 80, 191; Japanese, 251, 259–60, 262; remasculinization of Asian men, 254, 260, 263; white, 11, 38–39, 41, 72, 100–101, 118–20; "white man's burden," 119, 182–83

Mass Effect trilogy (BioWare, 2007, 2010, 2012), 84n29, 92–93, 309–11, 313

massively multiplayer online role-playing games (MMORPGs), 122, 228–29, 302. *See also* battle royale (BR) shooter games; role-playing games (RPGs)

Matheson, Calum Lister, 126–27

Mawani, Renisa, 239–40

McGray, Douglas, 277–78

McRobbie, Angela, 252–53

Mehta, Uday Singh, 144

Meier, Sid: *Civilization* series (MicroProse, 1991–2016), 161, 181–82

Melty Blood (Type-Moon, 2002), 280, 284–85

meritocracy, 14, 133–34, 137–43, 145

Metal Gear Solid series (Konami, 1998–2015), 93, 112n6, 113n17, 113n22, 113n31, 160, 163, 170–72, 188n11; antiwar rhetoric in, 99–101, 103, 109–11, 123, 126; *konketsuji* and *hāfu* identities, 102–12, 113n28

Meteor-Strike! (Đỗ, 2018), 90, 96

microaggressions, 72, 155, 273, 316

Microsoft, 29; Geopolitical Review, 31–32; Xbox, 28, 219, 283

Milburn, Colin, 23n36, 61, 64

Miller, Christian Kealoha ("Silver Spook"), 153, 155, 157; *Neofeud* (2017), 149–52, 156

Miller, Patrick, 27–28, 30–31, 33

Milner, Anthony, 186

misogyny, 70, 77, 133, 184, 243; #GamerGate, 11–12, 23n34, 308. *See also* sexism

Missing: Game for a Cause (Flying Robot Studios, 2016), 184

Moa, Hato: *Hatoful Boyfriend* (2011), 232–33, 235, 237–42, 246–47, 248n23, 249n28, 249n33

mobile games, 150, 153, 157, 183, 187, 270, 296, 312; *Yellow Face,* 20, 43–44, 269, 273

modding, 208, 218

model minority stereotypes, 3, 6–7, 18, 22n16, 38, 124, 128, 222; in *Disco Elysium,* 68, 70–77, 81–82, 83n13; in esports, 38, 191; Indian subcontinent and, 179–80, 182

Montgomery, R. A., 41

Moore, Keita, 93, 123, 128–29, 175n36

Morley, David, 192

Morris, Lucy, 251

Morse, Margaret, 224

Moskvina, Olga, 69

Mukherjee, Souvik, 6, 9, 313

mukokuseki, 23n25, 125–26. *See also* odorlessness

multiculturalism, 8, 55, 102, 104, 199, 263, 309–11, 315

multiracial identities, 30, 92, 111, 284, 310; biraciality in *Metal Gear Solid* series, 18, 93, 99–100, 102–12, 113n22, 113n28, 113nn30–31, 123, 171–72; game makers and, 15, 32–33, 55, 209; *konketsuji* and *hāfu,* 102–12, 113n28. *See also* biraciality

Muñoz, José Esteban, 57, 70, 83n17

Murakami, Ryu, 277

Murakami, Takashi, 283

Murray, Janet H., 221

Murray, Soraya, 11, 111–12, 126, 163

Muscular Christianity movement, 139–40

music, 165, 184, 193, 226, 250, 302–3; hip-hop, 278, 281, 283; in *Paradise Killer,* 52–54

Musser, Amber Jamilla, 57

Nakamura, Lisa, 6, 39, 42, 54, 122, 139, 145, 188n14, 221, 228, 307, 311

nationalism, 16–17, 44, 210, 262–63; animacy and, 233, 239–40; Chinese, 220, 227, 298; Japanese, 101, 104, 165, 170, 179, 240, 253, 257–58

Nawa (Kobo), 116

Nehru, Jawaharlal, 181

Neofeud (Silver Spook Games, 2017), 149–52, 156

neoliberalism, 9, 41, 55, 68, 77, 190–92, 199–200, 202, 222; colorblindness and, 229; masculinity and, 195, 254, 262; postfeminism and, 252–54

neurodivergence, 209, 214–15

Next Level Arcade (Brooklyn), 280, 286

Nguyen, Tan Hoang, 8–9

Nintendo, 28, 210; 3DS, 251, 254, 260; *Animal Crossing: New Horizons* (2020),

360 Index

290–94, 299–305; DS, 254, 259; Famicom, 90; Gameboy Color, 270; GameCube, 283; Nintendo 64, 64, 283; Nintendo Entertainment System (NES), 5, 180; Super Nintendo Entertainment System (SNES), 283; Switch, 153, 251, 293, 299, 301

Nishime, LeiLani, 100, 111–12

Niu, Greta A., 5

Nobunaga's Ambition series (Koei, 1983–), 164

Noon, Derek, 99–100

North American *League of Legends* Championship Series (NALCS), 200–201

nuclear discourse, 116, 126–28, 167–68, 181; resistance to, 99–100, 103, 111, 123

Obama, Barack, 283, 287

objectification, 3, 6, 118–20, 122, 161, 212, 252, 257, 311

Ocasio-Cortez, Alexandria, 299

odorlessness, 6, 9, 23n25, 124–25, 179–80, 188n11, 189n31

O'Hagan, Minako, 252

opacity, 314–15

orientalism, 9, 14, 41, 43, 49, 93, 143, 259, 313; Asian hands myth, 133–36, 142, 144–45, 199–202, 212; differentiated from the Asiatic, 54, 57; *Disco Elysium* and, 67–69, 71, 73, 75–78, 81–82; Eurocentrism and, 161–64, 177–78; high-tech orientalism, 7, 191–93, 195–98, 201; Indian subcontinent and, 162–63, 174n15, 177–78, 182–83, 187; ludo-orientalism, 6, 36, 39, 42, 163, 191, 194–95, 202, 222, 226. *See also* techno-orientalism

otaku culture, 21, 135, 251, 260–61, 266n51, 282–89

otome games, 235–36, 251, 255, 257–61, 263–64, 264n2, 266n51. See also *Hakuoki*

Out for Delivery (Gao, 2020), 20, 270, 272–75

outsourcing, 5, 155, 178–79, 185, 187, 271–72

paidia/Ludus distinction, 143

Palumbo-Liu, David, 4, 79

Pande, Rukmini, 264

Pang, Laikwan, 295

Paradise Killer (Kaizen Game Works, 2020), 52–54; Asiatic world-making of, 58–59, 61–64; end-game trial of, 55–58

pathologization of gaming, 4, 144

Patterson, Chris, 38, 162, 164, 167, 174n6, 179–80, 188n11, 222, 235, 309; on the

"Asiatic," 68, 78, 178, 182, 186, 218, 227; roundtable moderator, 32–33, 93–94, 151, 210, 213

Paul, Christopher A., 139

Penix-Tadsen, Phillip, 24n37

People's Republic of China (PRC), 193, 212, 291, 294, 298–99, 300, 303. *See also* China and Chineseness

Philippines, 160, 163, 240–41; game design and, 32, 55, 150, 153–55, 209, 269–72, 274, 276

Phillips, Amanda, 230

playable deniability, 101–3, 111, 130

player burnout, 197–99, *See also* addiction, gaming; gamer death

player choice, 11, 35, 37, 48–49, 58, 84n29, 236; *Choose Your Own Adventure* books and, 40–42; in *Disco Elysium*, 70–74, 77–78, 84n27; in *Hakuoki*, 254–58, 263, 265nn23–30; in *Hatoful Boyfriend*, 241–42; in *Mass Effect*, 310, 313; in *Metal Gear Solid* series, 100, 102–3, 108–11; myth of centrality to game design, 95–96; in *Tusks*, 243–45; in *Yellow Face*, 43–45

player gaze, 116–20, 123, 246

PlayerUnknown's Battlegrounds (PUBG) (Bluehole, 2017), 217–18, 223, 225, 227

Playland (New York City), 280, 285

Play without Apology, 272

Pokémon (Niantic, 1996–), 95, 125, 153, 164, 270, 278, 283

pornography, 97–98, 312

postcolonialism, 125, 159–64, 172–73, 184

postcolonial studies, 17, 159–64, 173

postfeminism, 20, 250–64

postracialism, 10, 100, 252–54, 263. *See also* colorblindness

Prater, Tzarina, 124

prerational play, 133, 141–45

protests, 17, 20, 270, 275–76; in *Animal Crossing*, 21, 290–95, 299–304, 305n3; Black Lives Matter (BLM) movement, 56, 133, 273, 293–*94*; *Liberate Hong Kong* (2019), 295–*97*; #LiberateHongKong, 304; #MeiSupportsHongKong, 298; #StandWithHK, 304; #StopAsianHateJam Game Jam (2021), 16

psychedelic counterculture, 67–71, 76, 80, 183. *See also* acid communism

Punzalan, Pamela, 269–72, 274; *Asian Acceptance* (2020), 20, 275–76

Index   **361**

Qiu, Jack Linchuan, 64

queerness, 18–20, 39, 47–50, 83n17, 84n27, 251, 264, 312, 314; aesthetics and, 53–60, 180; of the Asiatic, 17, 54–63, 68, 234; dating games and, 235–39, 245–47; game makers and, 89, 97, 208–15, 233, 243, 248n10, 269, 272; in game studies, 12, 15, 308; gay characters, 74, 76, 84n27, 208, 210–12, 235, 242; homoeroticism in games, 59, 84n24, 119–20; homophobia and, 39, 133, 138, 243; popularization of, 262–63

Queerness and Games Conference (QGCon), 209

racial capitalism, 9–10, 68, 171, 193–95, 201, 230. *See also* capitalism; labor; racism; white supremacy

racism, 2, 18, 39, 63, 188n11, 212, 243, 258, 309, 316; anti-Chinese, 122–23, 157, 218–20, 225–26, 229, 233; Black nerd identity as challenge to, 279, 282; during COVID-19 pandemic, 54, 56–57, 64, 157, 224–25, 240; in fighting game community, 132–33, 138, 145; game makers and, 31, 92, 151, 156–57, 176–77, 181; #GamerGate, 11–12, 23n34, 308; *Genshin Impact* and, 311–12; procedural, 219–22, 226, 229; racist love, 7; *Yellow Face* critique of, 43–45, 269. *See also* Asian hands myth; orientalism; white supremacy; xenophobia; *individual stereotypes*

Raji: An Ancient Epic (Nodding Heads, 2020), 184

Ramirez, Ryan "FChamp," 133

Rao, Rajesh, 179

real, the, 21–22, 126, 300, 314

realism, 67–69, 77, 81, 126, 180, 227

real-time strategy (RTS) games, 30, 164, 299

Reddit forums, 84n32, 138, 305n6; anti-Chinese discourse in, 218–20, 225, 227; Hong Kong protests and, 296, 298, 304, 306n20, 306n23

Reddy, Chandan, 16

Reedus, Norman, 116–18, 122

remasculinization, 254, 260, 263

Ren'py, 236

Ren Yi, Mike, 270–74; *Yellow Face*, 20, 43–45, 269, 273

Resident Evil 5 (Capcom, 2009), 101, 162, 164

Riley, Sarah, 262

Rivera, Takeo, 6, 83n13, 243

Robins, Kevin, 192

Roh, David S., 5

role-playing games (RPGs), 47, 74, 76, 83n18, 95, 311, 313, 315; computer role-playing games (CRPGs), 71, 96; Japanese (JRPGs), 91, 96, 126, 160, 167–70, 251, 259, 309; massively multiplayer online role-playing games, 122, 228–29, 302; protests in, 296–304, 305n3, 305n6, 306n23; tabletop games, 46, 50, 90, 95, 272, 274. *See also* battle royale (BR) shooter games; first-person shooter (FPS) games; *individual games*

Roof, Judith, 281

Rostov, Aleksander, 70–71, 83n14

Roy, Samya Brata, 182

Ruberg, Bo, 311

Russell, Legacy, 314–15

Russworm, TreaAndrea M., 102, 279, 307–8

SAARC (South Asian Association for Regional Cooperation), 187

Said, Edward, 57, 162, 177

Sakai, Naoki, 134

Salter, Anastasia, 235

Scheiding, Ryan, 164

Sedgwick, Eve Kosofsky, 12, 68, 186

Sega, 278; Dreamcast, 165, 283; Genesis, 83

Seth, Roshan, 180

settler colonialism, 10, 12, 160, 171, 224. *See also* colonialism

sexism, 39, 243, 253; Dickwolves controversy, 259, 266n41; #GamerGate, 11–12, 23n34, 308; in *Hakuoki*, 252, 254, 257, 260–63. *See also* misogyny

sexualization, 3, 6, 9, 118–20, 161, 212, 252, 257, 311

sexual misconduct, 132–33, 138

Shafer, Jon, 181

Shah, Nayan, 56, 225

Shangri-La myth, 183

Shapiro, Michael J., 127

Sharif, Solmaz, 13

Shaw, Adrienne, 8, 13, 23n32, 183, 307–8

Shenmue (Suzuki, 2001), 52

Shibusawa, Naoko, 9–10

Shields, Duncan "Thorin," 197–99

shoryuken.com, 136

Sicart, Miguel, 100, 102

Silver Spook Games: *Neofeud* (2017), 149–52, 156

Sims series, *The* (EA, 2000–2023), 293–94, 305n6

Singh, Julietta, 57

Skolnik, Michael Ryan, 279, 288–89

362 Index

slash fiction, 84n24. *See also* fan fiction

Sobel, Lonnie, 280, 285–86

Sohn, Stephen Hong, 134

Somewhere (Studio Oleomingu, 2015), 184

sonno-jōi, 165, 174n26

Sony Interactive Entertainment and Endeavour (RTS), 132

Sony PlayStation, 28, 33, 156, 165, 219, 251, 254, 260, 283

SoulCalibur series (Bandai Namco Entertainment, 1995–2018), 32, 160, 163–67, 188n14

South Korea, 136, 144, 160, 163, 177, 188n14, 217, 226, 251; capital of esports, 5, 19, 145, 190–91, 193, 195–203; game industry in, 8, 153, 173, 185, 190, 200, 202; Korean Exodus of 2014, 199–200; Seol, 72–73, 75, 78. *See also* Koreanness

Spariosu, Mihai I., 141–42

speed-hacking, 218

Spigel, Lynn, 257–58

Squinkifer, Dietrich (Squinky), 209, 211; *Dominique Pamplemousse* (2013), 207, 213–14

Stand with Hong Kong, 302

Stang, Sarah, 253

Stanley, Eric, 317n21

StarCraft series (Blizzard, 1998), 30, 179, 191, 193, 195, 208

Star Wars: Knights of the Old Republic (BioWare, 2003), 84n29

Steinkuehler, Constance, 218, 228

#StopAsianHateJam Game Jam (2021), 16

Street Fighter series (Capcom, 1987, 1991, 1997, 2016), 33, 59, 160, 162–63, 165–66, 180, 278, 283, 285; Patrick Miller on, 29–31

Striking Vipers game (*Black Mirror*), 59–61

sublime, the, 116, 126–28

Sun-Yat-Sen, 186

tabletop games, 46, 50, 95, 152, 272, 274

Tagore, Rabindranath, 186

Táíwò, Olúfémi O., 312

Taylor, Diana, 247

Taylor, Emily, 235

Team Spooky, 287; Battle by the Gazebo (BBG) tournaments, 280, 284–86

techno-orientalism, 5–6, 8, 22n7, 36, 227, 234; Western gaze and, 23n27, 38, 60, 63, 71, 123, 134, 161, 191–202. *See also* orientalism

Tencent, 153; *Game for Peace* (2019), 227

the-Score eSports, 200

Toma El Paso / Make a Move (Tran, 2014), 152

Tom Clancy's Ghost Recon Predator (Ubisoft, 2010), 182

Tony Hawk's Pro Skater (Activision, 1999), 212

Tosca, Susan, 252

Tran, Lien B., 152, 154–55, 157; *Toma El Paso / Make a Move* (2014), 152

transcreation, 252, 254, 258–63

trans game makers, 15, 207, 209, 214–15

translation, 113n21, 123–24, 140, 151–52, 175n34, 251–52, 260–62, 313, 317n21

trans representation, 15, 20, 210, 322

trauma, 127–28, 160, 184, 276, 316; of war in Japan, 116–18, 120, 125–26

Trinh T. Minh-ha, 186

triple-A (AAA) game companies, 27, 89, 153, 157, 178, 185, 208, 236, 253–54

Trump, Donald, 56, 64, 229–30

Tsing, Anna, 16

Tsuji, Izumi, 282

Tufekci, Zeynep, 299–300, 302

Turay, Abdul, 83n22

Tusks: The Orc Dating Sim (Alexander, 2017), 233, 235, 242–47

Tuulik, Argo, 68

Twitch.tv, 133, 231n30, 280, 284, 286, 288, 296

Ubisoft, 272; *Assassin's Creed* series (2007, 2012), 33, 111, 270–71; *Far Cry 4* (2014), 176–77, 182–83, 187, 270

Ultimate Fighting Gamer 8, 286–87

UltraChenTV, 133

Undertale (Fox, 2015), 84n29

Ung, Emperatriz, 27–29, 32

universalism, 9, 115, 120, 124, 162, 193; in game theory, 12, 143, 161, 314–15

Untitled Goose Game (House, 2019), 237

UStream, 284

utopia, 50, 64, 77, 289, 295; adjacency and, 67–68, 76, 82, 83n17

Vanderhoef, John, 253

Vincent, Kurt: *The Lost Arcade* (2015), 285–86

Virtua Fighter (Sega, 1993), 166, 188n14

Virtual Ninja Code, 134, 139, 144

visual novels, 52–53, 94–96, 233–34, 254, 260, 282. See also *Hakuoki*

Vo, Linda Trinh, 3

wallhacking, 218

wan (idle contemplation), 143

Wark, McKenzie, 23n36, 45

WeChat, 209

Weibo, 209

Weisenfeld, Gennifer, 127

whiteface, 125

whiteness, 34, 38–39, 41, 46, 49, 56, 62, 171, 243; adjacency to, 3, 6, 67–68, 71, 78; arcades and, 279, 288; *Death Stranding* and, 115–25, 128, 130; *Disco Elysium* and, 71–74, 83n20; esports and, 1–3, 6, 191–94, 196–99, 202; game makers and, 32, 92–94, 96, 155–56, 176, 209, 212, 272–76; of game studies, 10–11, 308; labor and, 115–25, 128–30, 224, 228; *Metal Gear Solid* series and, 93, 100–103, 105, 109–10, 130; "white man's burden" myth, 119, 182–83; in *Yellow Face*, 43–45

white supremacy, 8, 31, 68, 120, 192, 240, 310; #GamerGate, 11–12, 23n34, 308

whitewashing, 71, 124

Williams, Dmitri, 186

Williams, R. John, 67–68

women game makers, 92, 150, 154–55, 209, 254

women gamers, 2, 235–36, 251–54, 257–64, 272, 276, 314

Wong, Joshua, 290–92, 295–96

Wong, Mou-Lan, 35–36

world-making, 13, 21, 233, 291, 294, 307, 316–17; distinguished from world-building, 4–5; *Paradise Killer* and, 61–64

wuxia games, 97

xenophobia, 63, 157, 223, 240–41. *See also* racism; white supremacy

Xu, Joe Yizhou, 149–53, 155

Yamamoto, Atsuhisa, 106, 108

yandere character archetype, 236, 241–42

Yang, Bowen, 1–2

Yang, Robert, 207–8, 210, 212–13, 311; *Intimate, Infinite* (2014), 47–49

Yano, Christine Reiko, 9, 125, 253

yaoi games, 248n10, 260

Ye, Josh, 296–*97*

Yee, Nick, 228

Yellow Face (Ren Yi, 2019), 20, 43–45, 269, 273

Yellow Future fantasy, 191, 196–97

yellow peril stereotypes, 3–4, 10, 22n16, 54, 56, 63, 123, 157; Asian gamers and, 191, 196–97, 224; represented in games, 7, 40, 71, 179–80, 182

yogi stereotype, 180

YouTube, 52, 109, 133, 157, 197, 219–20, 223, 226, 280, 287–88, 295

yuri games, 248n10

Yu, Suzuki: *Shenmue* (2001), 52

Zaimont, Mike, 133

ZA/UM, 68, *75*, *79*, *81*, 83n14, See also *Disco Elysium*

Zen, 67

Zuckerberg, Mark, 156

364   Index